# Yakuza Fiancé

## Raise wa Tanin ga Ii

1

STORY & ART BY
Asuka
Konishi

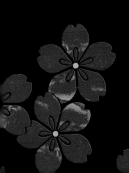

contents

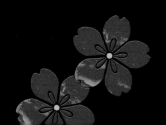

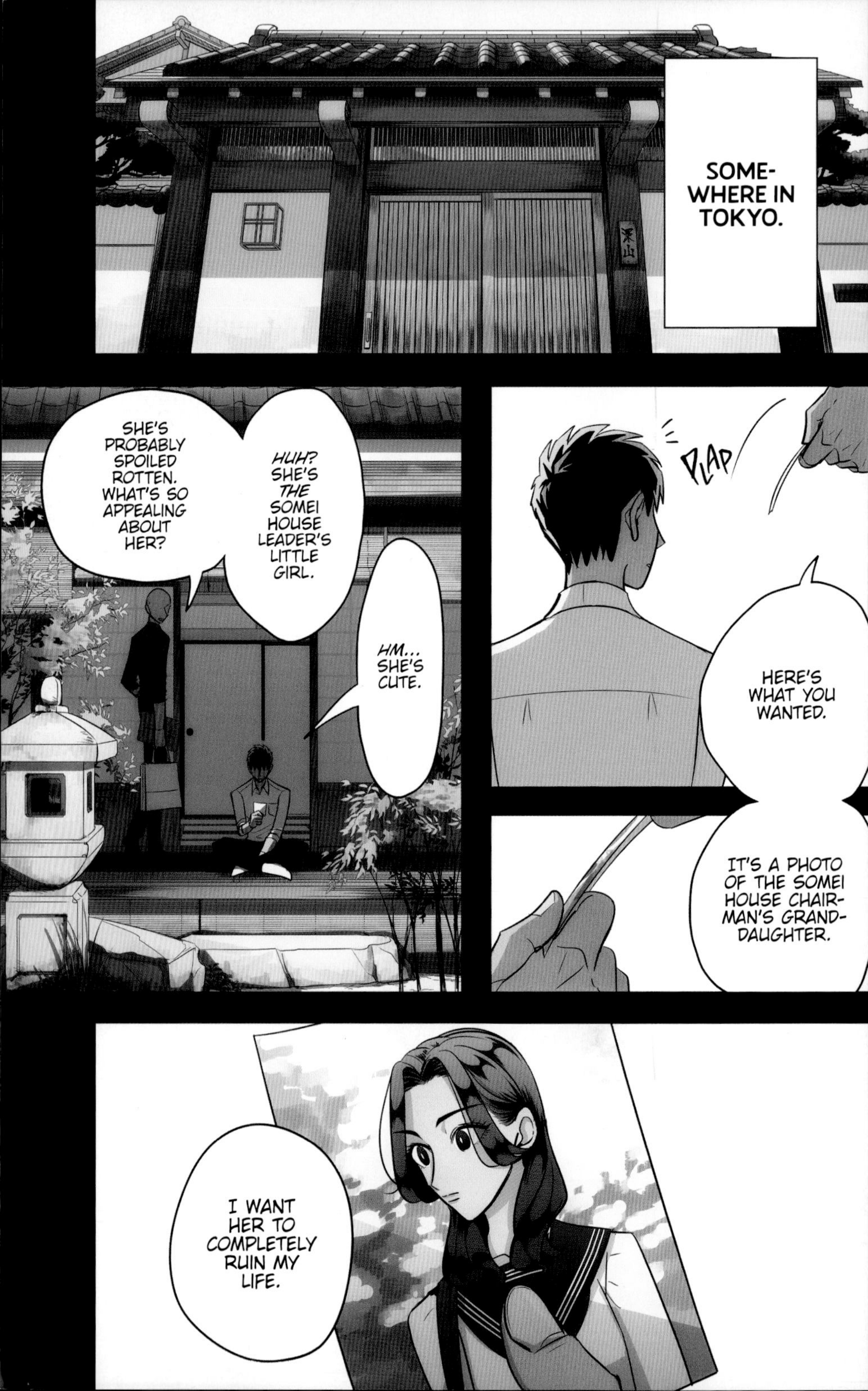
SOME-WHERE IN TOKYO.
PLAP
HERE'S WHAT YOU WANTED.
IT'S A PHOTO OF THE SOMEI HOUSE CHAIR-MAN'S GRAND-DAUGHTER.
HUH? SHE'S *THE* SOMEI HOUSE LEADER'S LITTLE GIRL.
SHE'S PROBABLY SPOILED ROTTEN. WHAT'S SO APPEALING ABOUT HER?
HM... SHE'S CUTE.
I WANT HER TO COMPLETELY RUIN MY LIFE.

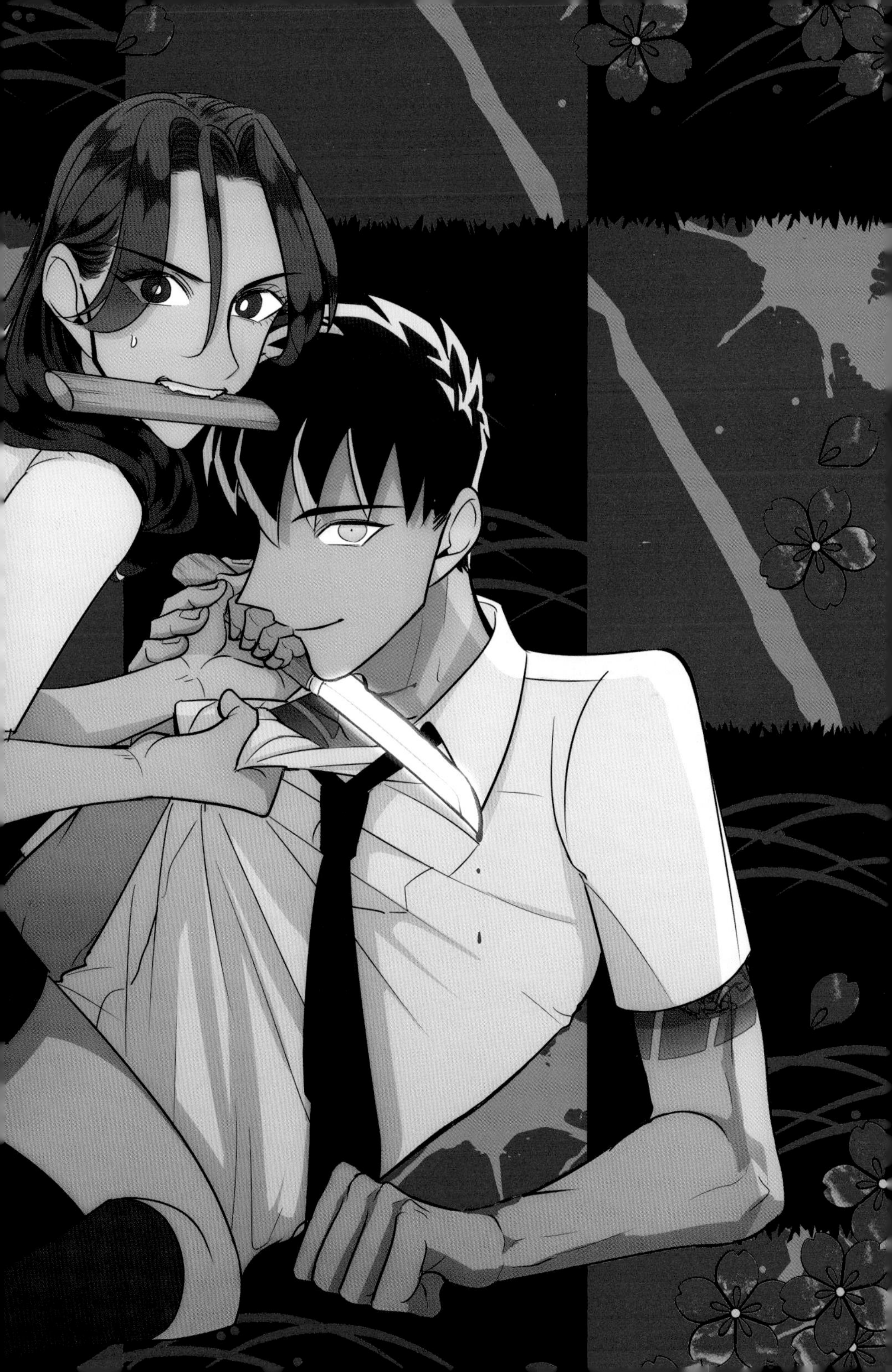

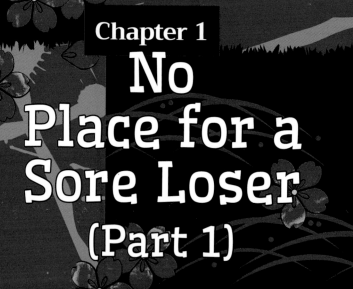

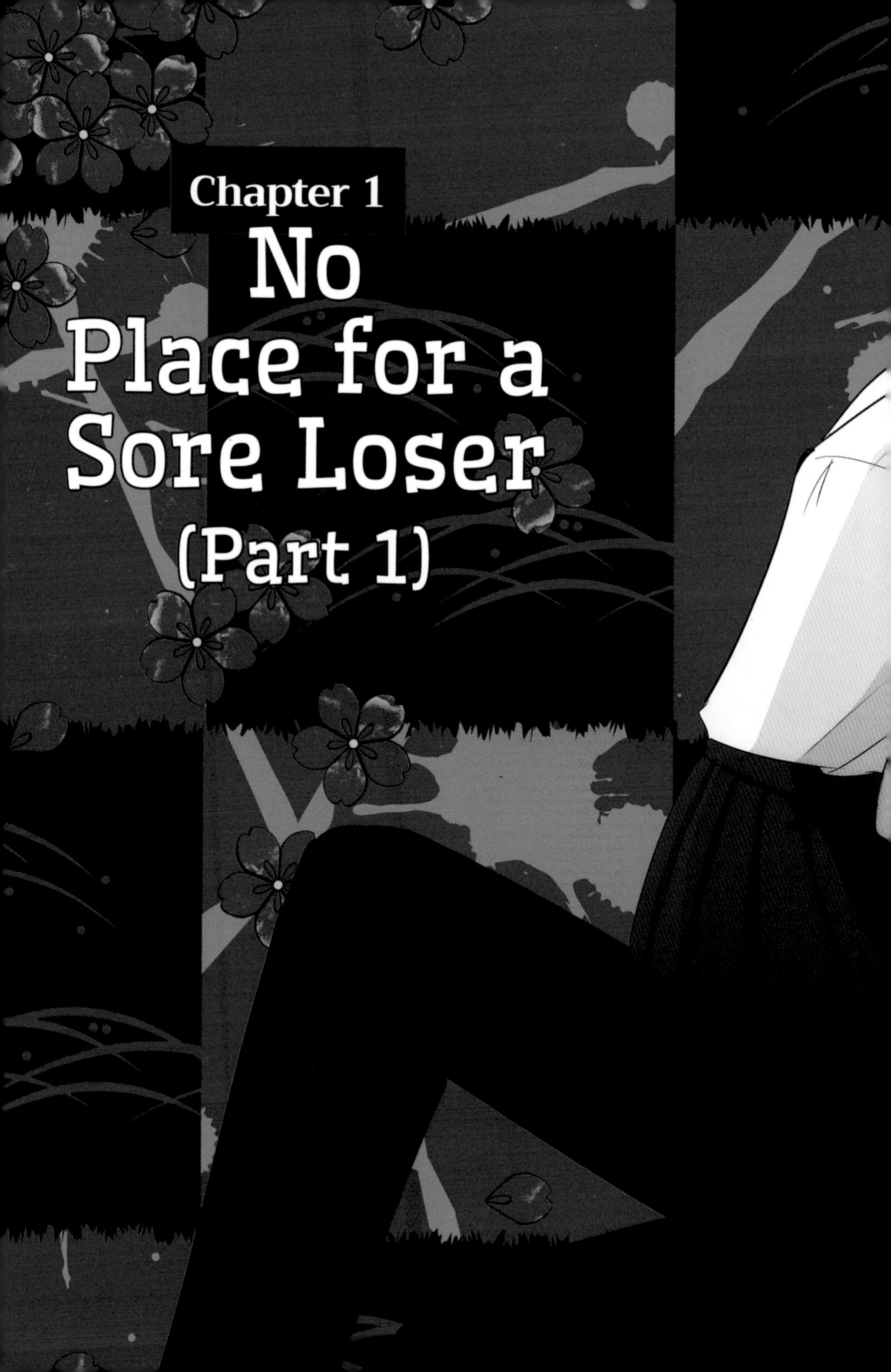

# Chapter 1
# No Place for a Sore Loser
## (Part 1)

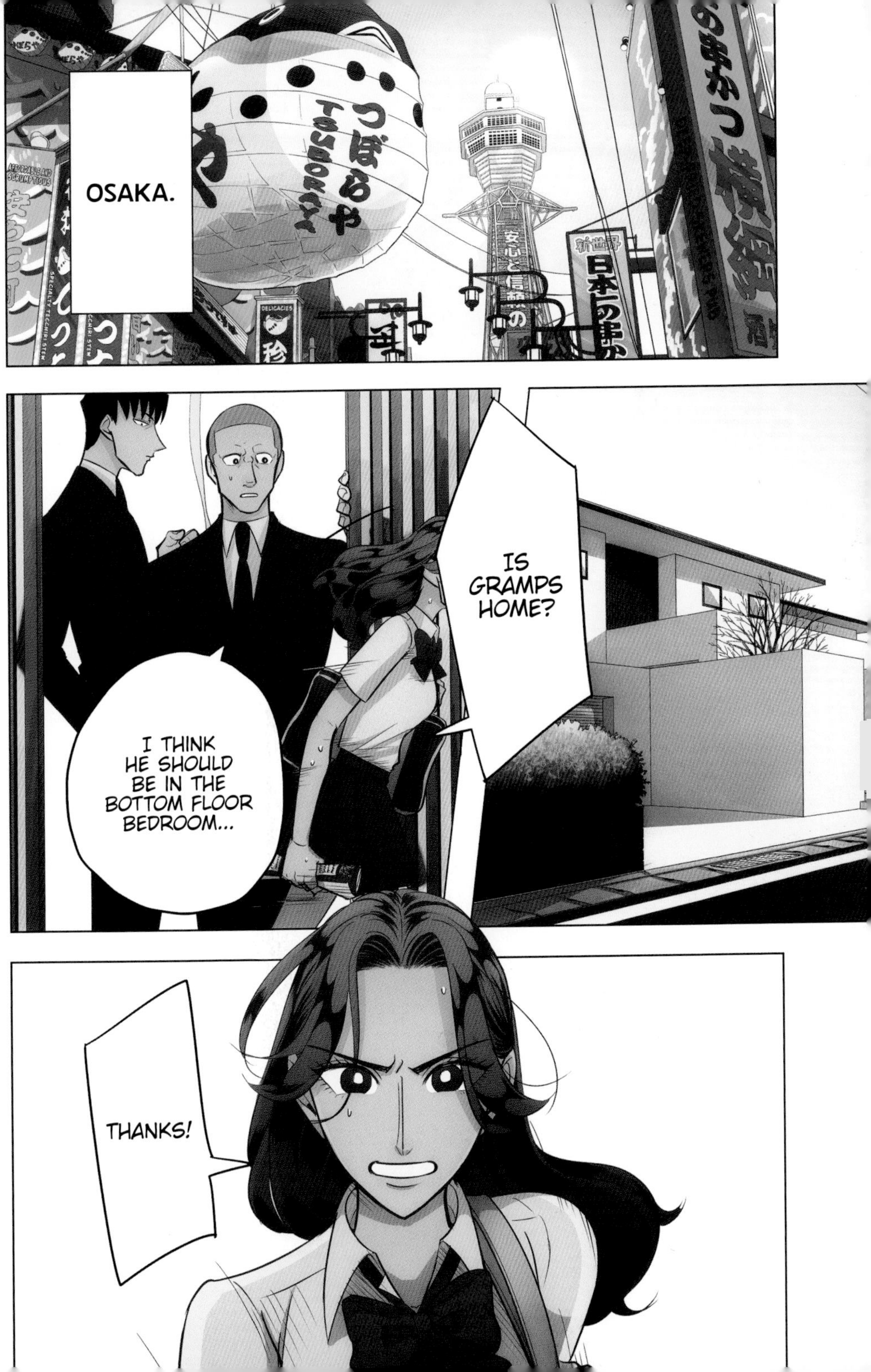
OSAKA.
つぼらや
TSUBORAYA
IS GRAMPS HOME?
I THINK HE SHOULD BE IN THE BOTTOM FLOOR BEDROOM...
THANKS!

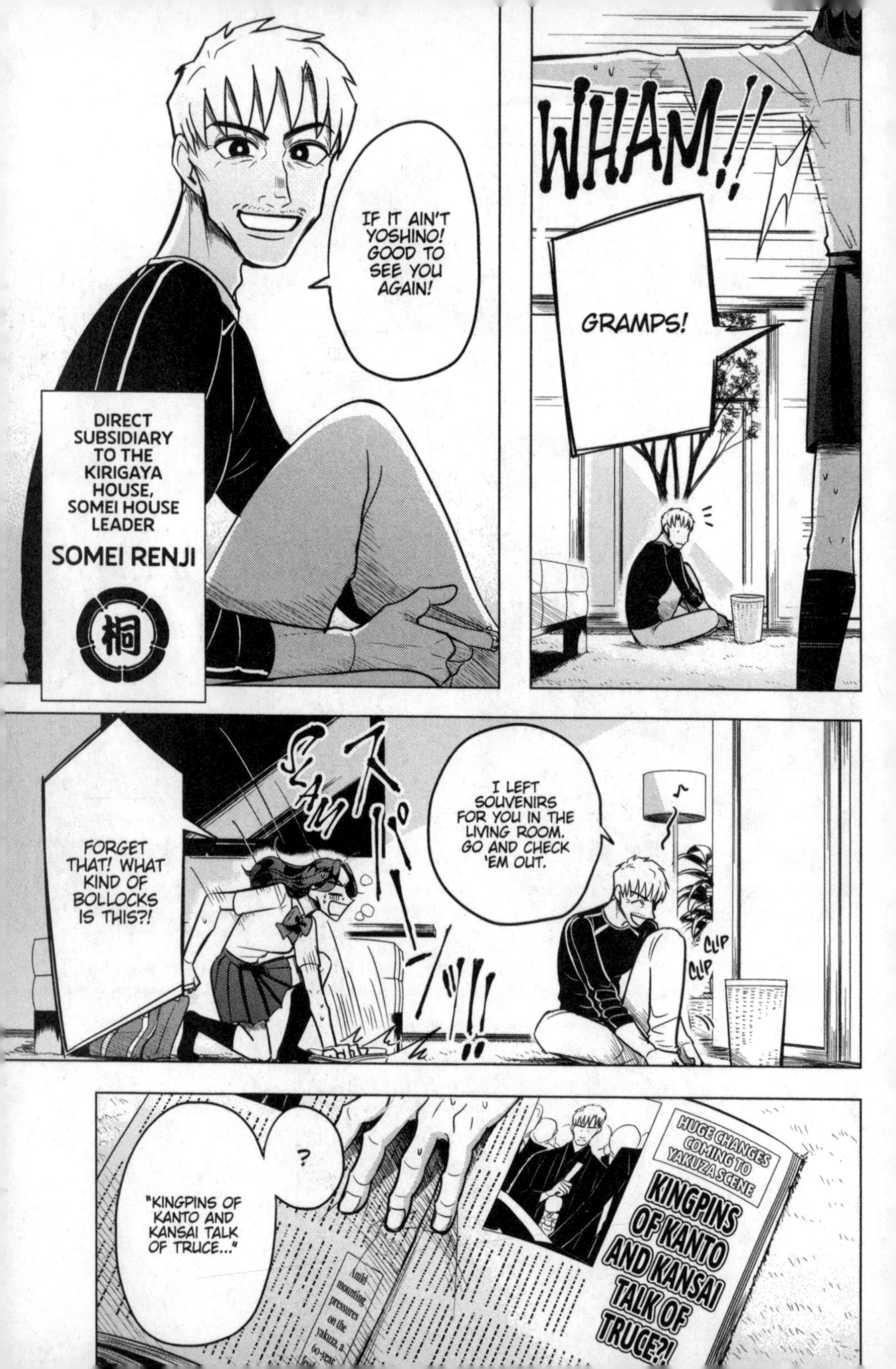
WHAM!!
GRAMPS!
IF IT AIN'T YOSHINO! GOOD TO SEE YOU AGAIN!
DIRECT SUBSIDIARY TO THE KIRIGAYA HOUSE, SOMEI HOUSE LEADER
SOMEI RENJI
桐
I LEFT SOUVENIRS FOR YOU IN THE LIVING ROOM. GO AND CHECK 'EM OUT.
CLIP
CLIP
SLAM
FORGET THAT! WHAT KIND OF BOLLOCKS IS THIS?!
HUGE CHANGES COMING TO YAKUZA SCENE
KINGPINS OF KANTO AND KANSAI TALK OF TRUCE?!
?
"KINGPINS OF KANTO AND KANSAI TALK OF TRUCE..."
Amid mounting pressures on the yakuza, a

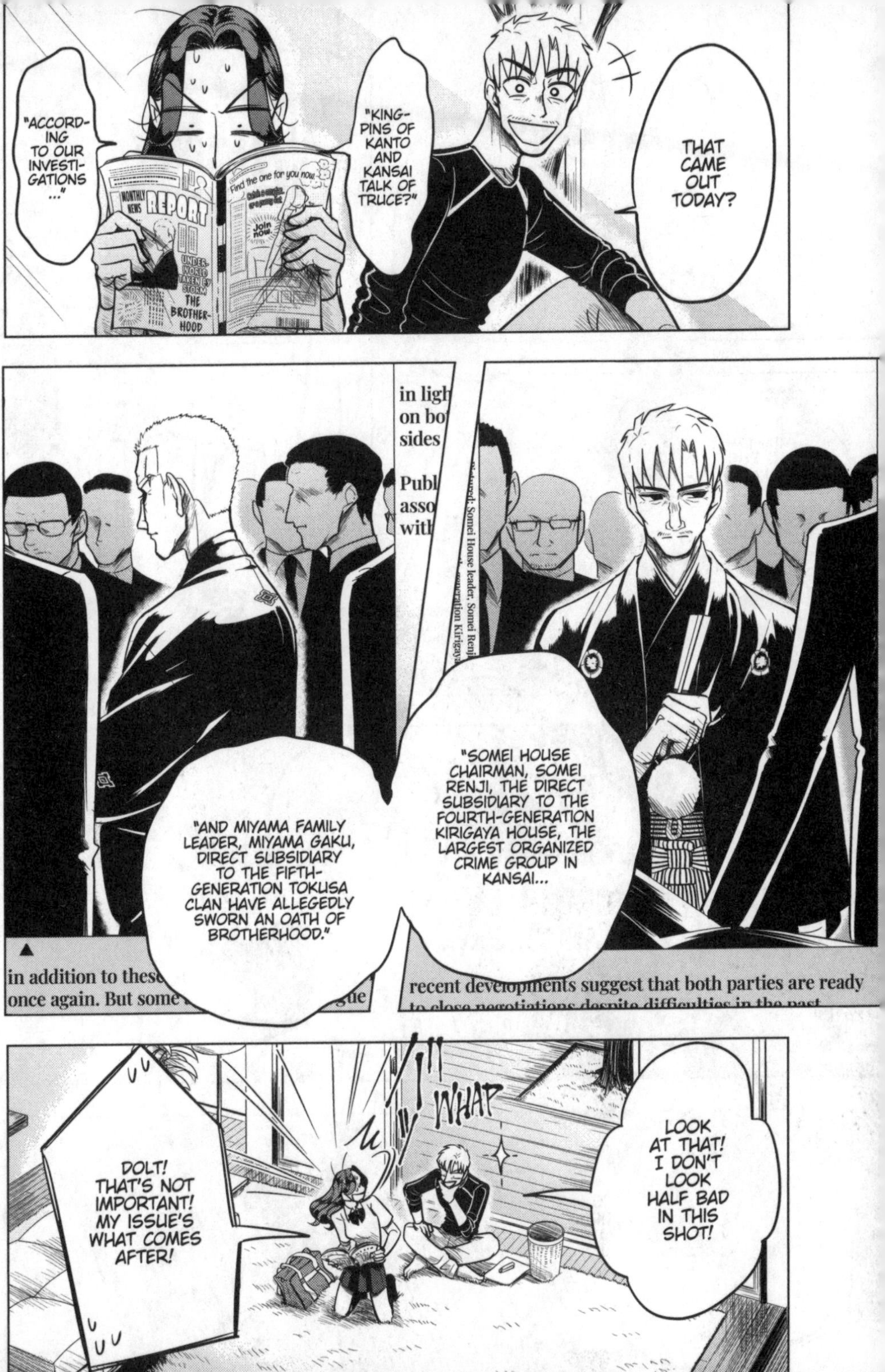
THAT CAME OUT TODAY?
"KING-PINS OF KANTO AND KANSAI TALK OF TRUCE?"
"ACCORDING TO OUR INVESTIGATIONS..."
MONTHLY NEWS REPORT
UNDER-WORLD TAKEN BY STORM
THE BROTHER-HOOD
Find the one for you now.
Join now.
in ligh
on bo
sides
Publ
asso
with
Pictured: Somei House leader, Somei Renji
"SOMEI HOUSE CHAIRMAN, SOMEI RENJI, THE DIRECT SUBSIDIARY TO THE FOURTH-GENERATION KIRIGAYA HOUSE, THE LARGEST ORGANIZED CRIME GROUP IN KANSAI...
"AND MIYAMA FAMILY LEADER, MIYAMA GAKU, DIRECT SUBSIDIARY TO THE FIFTH-GENERATION TOKUSA CLAN HAVE ALLEGEDLY SWORN AN OATH OF BROTHERHOOD."
recent developments suggest that both parties are ready
in addition to these
once again. But some
LOOK AT THAT! I DON'T LOOK HALF BAD IN THIS SHOT!
WHAP
DOLT! THAT'S NOT IMPORTANT! MY ISSUE'S WHAT COMES AFTER!

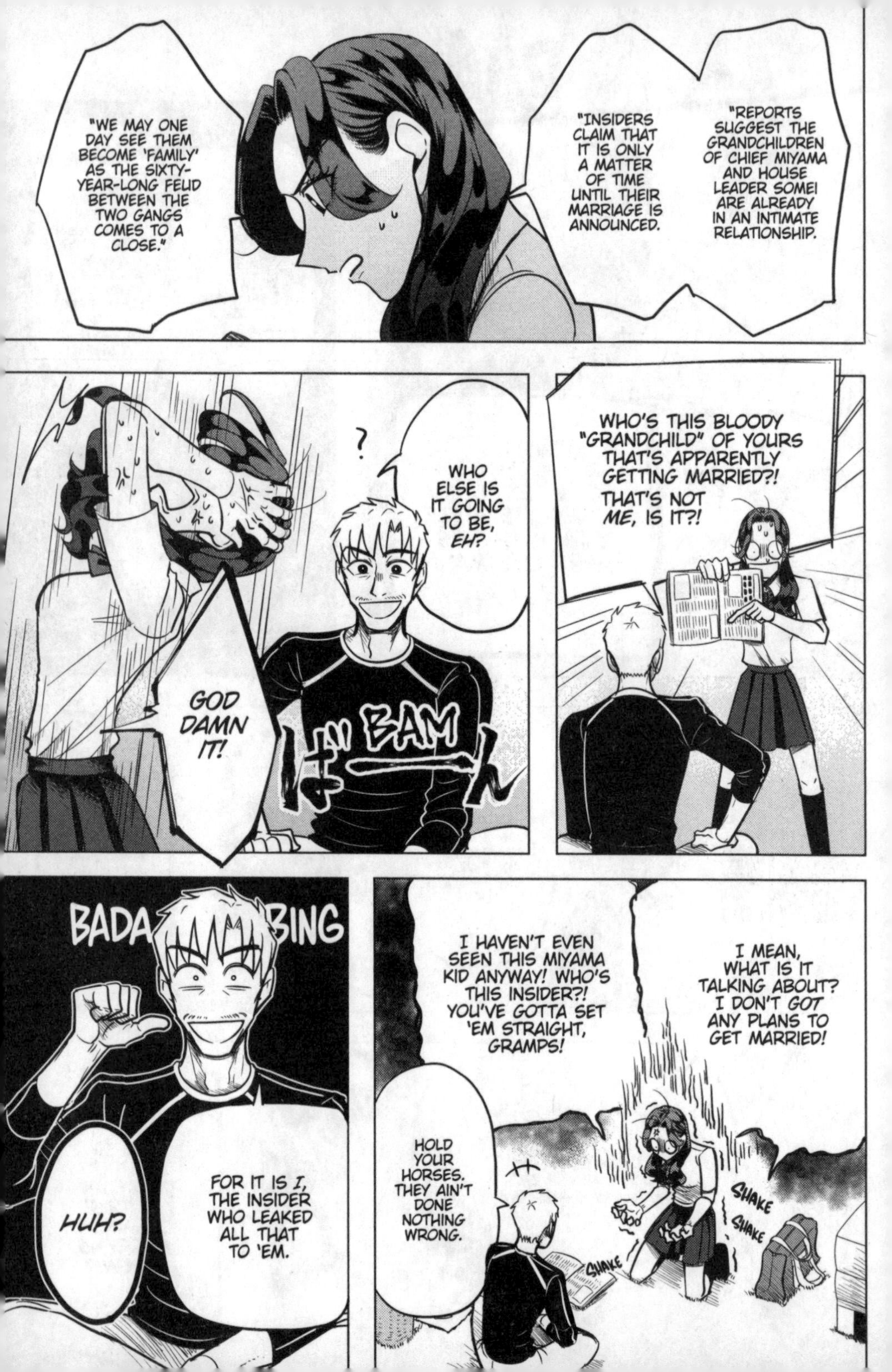
"REPORTS SUGGEST THE GRANDCHILDREN OF CHIEF MIYAMA AND HOUSE LEADER SOMEI ARE ALREADY IN AN INTIMATE RELATIONSHIP.
"INSIDERS CLAIM THAT IT IS ONLY A MATTER OF TIME UNTIL THEIR MARRIAGE IS ANNOUNCED.
"WE MAY ONE DAY SEE THEM BECOME 'FAMILY' AS THE SIXTY-YEAR-LONG FEUD BETWEEN THE TWO GANGS COMES TO A CLOSE."
WHO'S THIS BLOODY "GRANDCHILD" OF YOURS THAT'S APPARENTLY GETTING MARRIED?!
THAT'S NOT *ME*, IS IT?!
?
WHO ELSE IS IT GOING TO BE, *EH*?
GOD DAMN IT!
BAM
I MEAN, WHAT IS IT TALKING ABOUT? I DON'T GOT ANY PLANS TO GET MARRIED!
I HAVEN'T EVEN SEEN THIS MIYAMA KID ANYWAY! WHO'S THIS INSIDER?! YOU'VE GOTTA SET 'EM STRAIGHT, GRAMPS!
HOLD YOUR HORSES. THEY AIN'T DONE NOTHING WRONG.
SHAKE
SHAKE
SHAKE
BADA BING
FOR IT IS *I*, THE INSIDER WHO LEAKED ALL THAT TO 'EM.
HUH?

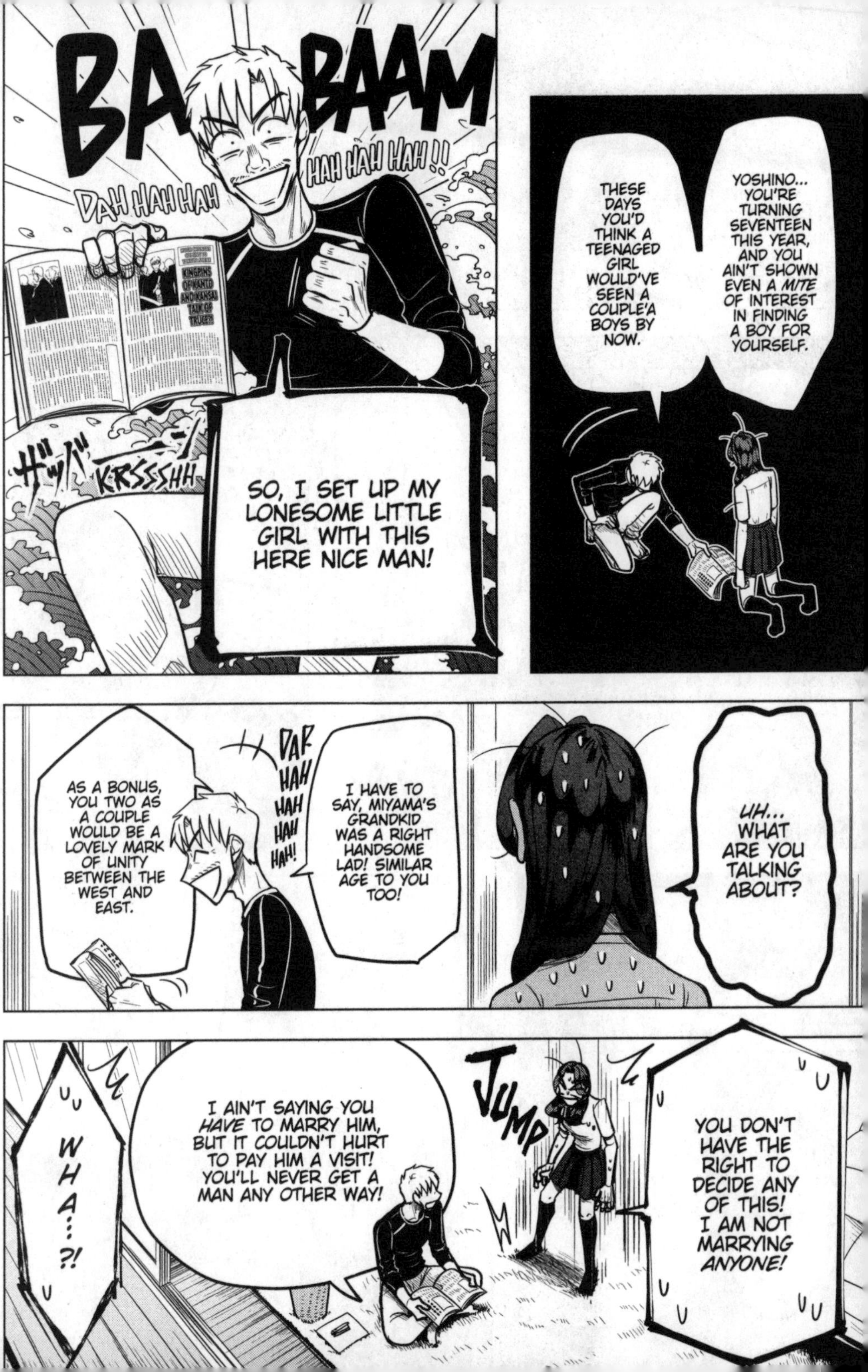
YOSHINO... YOU'RE TURNING SEVENTEEN THIS YEAR, AND YOU AIN'T SHOWN EVEN A *MITE* OF INTEREST IN FINDING A BOY FOR YOURSELF.
THESE DAYS YOU'D THINK A TEENAGED GIRL WOULD'VE SEEN A COUPLE'A BOYS BY NOW.
BA BAAM
HAH HAH HAH!!
DAH HAH HAH
KINGPINS OF KANTO AND KANSAI TALK OF TRUCE?!
SO, I SET UP MY LONESOME LITTLE GIRL WITH THIS HERE NICE MAN!
KRSSSHH
ザッバ
*UH... WHAT ARE YOU TALKING ABOUT?*
I HAVE TO SAY, MIYAMA'S GRANDKID WAS A RIGHT HANDSOME LAD! SIMILAR AGE TO YOU TOO!
DAR HAH HAH HAH HAH!
AS A BONUS, YOU TWO AS A COUPLE WOULD BE A LOVELY MARK OF UNITY BETWEEN THE WEST AND EAST.
YOU DON'T HAVE THE RIGHT TO DECIDE ANY OF THIS! I AM NOT MARRYING *ANYONE!*
JUMP
I AIN'T SAYING YOU *HAVE* TO MARRY HIM, BUT IT COULDN'T HURT TO PAY HIM A VISIT! YOU'LL NEVER GET A MAN ANY OTHER WAY!
WHA...?!

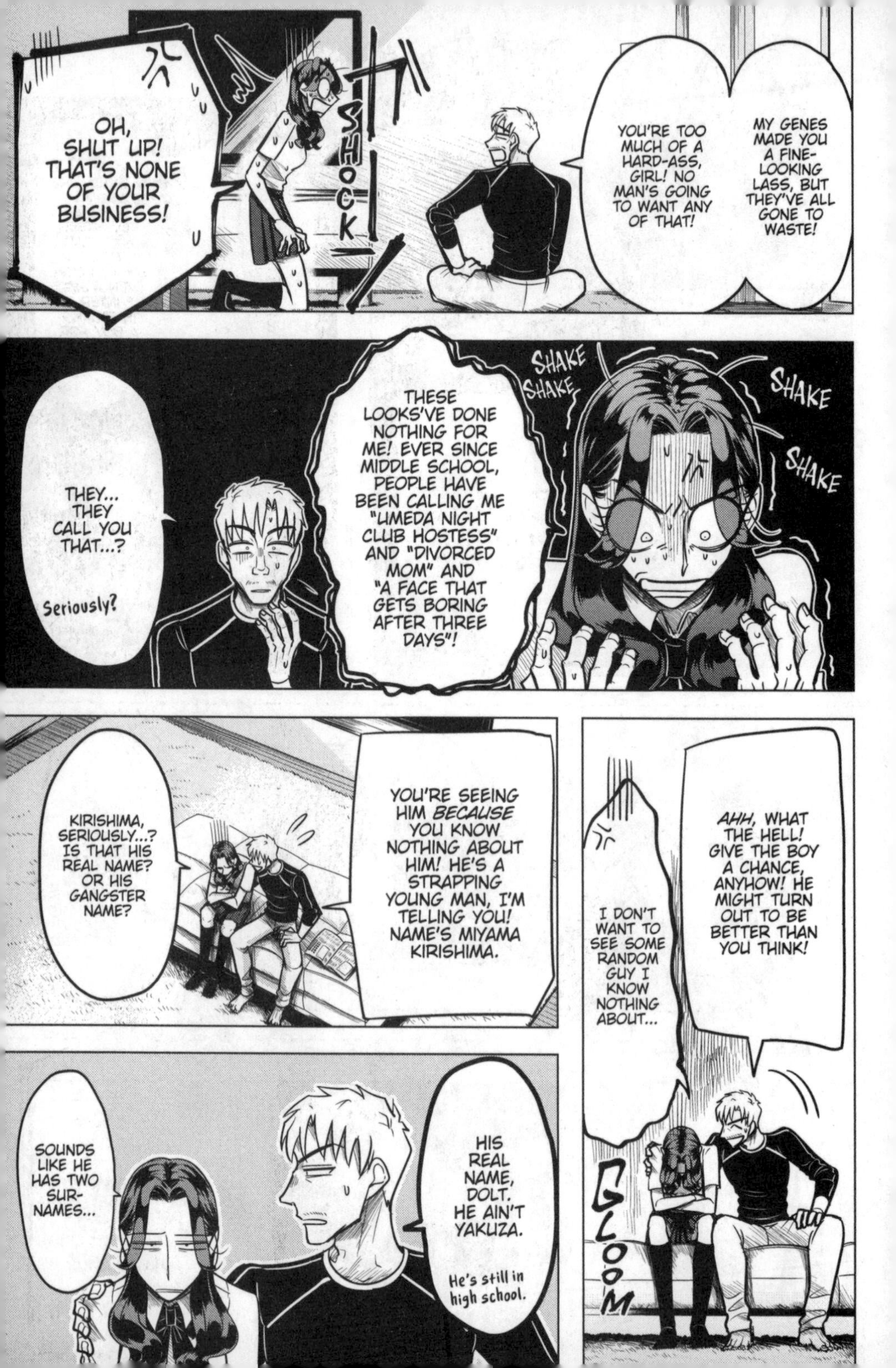
MY GENES MADE YOU A FINE-LOOKING LASS, BUT THEY'VE ALL GONE TO WASTE!
YOU'RE TOO MUCH OF A HARD-ASS, GIRL! NO MAN'S GOING TO WANT ANY OF THAT!
SHOCK
OH, SHUT UP! THAT'S NONE OF YOUR BUSINESS!
SHAKE
SHAKE
SHAKE
SHAKE
THESE LOOKS'VE DONE NOTHING FOR ME! EVER SINCE MIDDLE SCHOOL, PEOPLE HAVE BEEN CALLING ME "UMEDA NIGHT CLUB HOSTESS" AND "DIVORCED MOM" AND "A FACE THAT GETS BORING AFTER THREE DAYS"!
THEY... THEY CALL YOU THAT...?
Seriously?
*AHH*, WHAT THE HELL! GIVE THE BOY A CHANCE, ANYHOW! HE MIGHT TURN OUT TO BE BETTER THAN YOU THINK!
I DON'T WANT TO SEE SOME RANDOM GUY I KNOW NOTHING ABOUT...
GLOOM
YOU'RE SEEING HIM *BECAUSE* YOU KNOW NOTHING ABOUT HIM! HE'S A STRAPPING YOUNG MAN, I'M TELLING YOU! NAME'S MIYAMA KIRISHIMA.
KIRISHIMA, SERIOUSLY...? IS THAT HIS REAL NAME? OR HIS GANGSTER NAME?
HIS REAL NAME, DOLT. HE AIN'T YAKUZA.
He's still in high school.
SOUNDS LIKE HE HAS TWO SUR-NAMES...

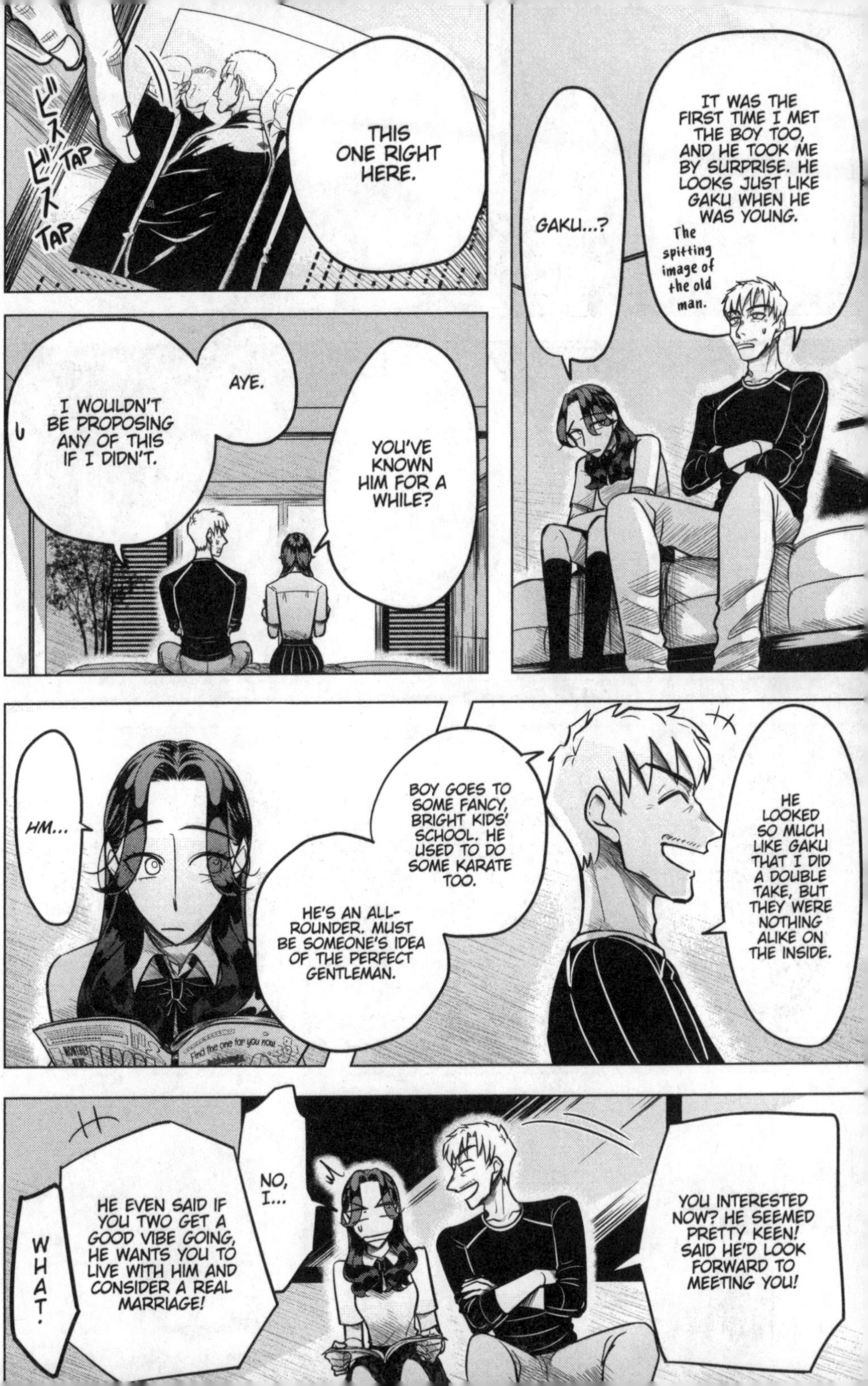
IT WAS THE FIRST TIME I MET THE BOY TOO, AND HE TOOK ME BY SURPRISE. HE LOOKS JUST LIKE GAKU WHEN HE WAS YOUNG.
The spitting image of the old man.
GAKU...?
ビス ビス
TAP TAP
THIS ONE RIGHT HERE.
YOU'VE KNOWN HIM FOR A WHILE?
AYE.
I WOULDN'T BE PROPOSING ANY OF THIS IF I DIDN'T.
HE LOOKED SO MUCH LIKE GAKU THAT I DID A DOUBLE TAKE, BUT THEY WERE NOTHING ALIKE ON THE INSIDE.
BOY GOES TO SOME FANCY, BRIGHT KIDS' SCHOOL. HE USED TO DO SOME KARATE TOO.
HE'S AN ALL-ROUNDER. MUST BE SOMEONE'S IDEA OF THE PERFECT GENTLEMAN.
HM...
Find the one for you now
YOU INTERESTED NOW? HE SEEMED PRETTY KEEN! SAID HE'D LOOK FORWARD TO MEETING YOU!
NO, I...
HE EVEN SAID IF YOU TWO GET A GOOD VIBE GOING, HE WANTS YOU TO LIVE WITH HIM AND CONSIDER A REAL MARRIAGE!
WHAT.

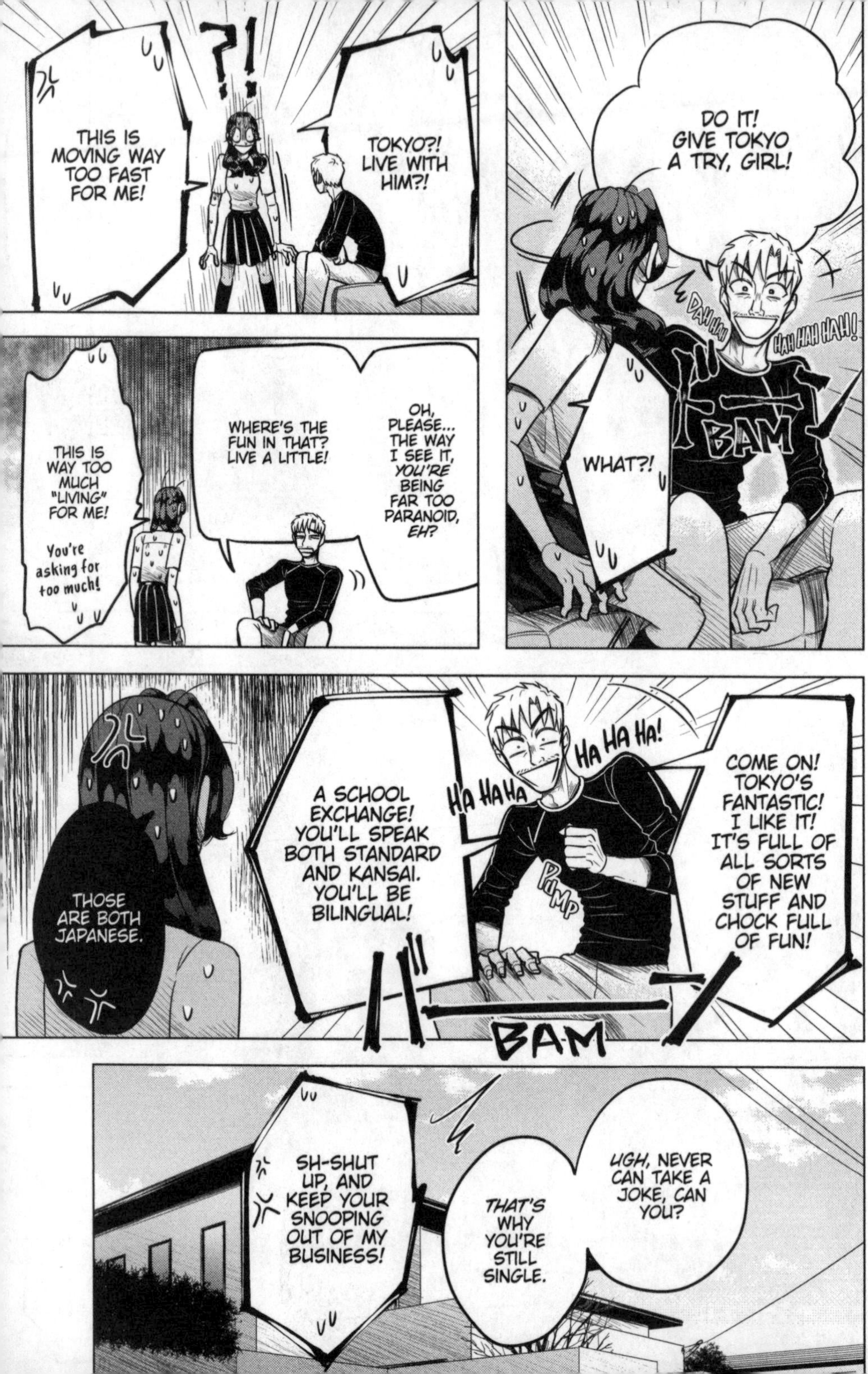
DO IT! GIVE TOKYO A TRY, GIRL!
DAH HAH
HAH HAH HAH!
BAM
WHAT?!
TOKYO?! LIVE WITH HIM?!
?!
THIS IS MOVING WAY TOO FAST FOR ME!
OH, PLEASE... THE WAY I SEE IT, *YOU'RE* BEING FAR TOO PARANOID, *EH?*
WHERE'S THE FUN IN THAT? LIVE A LITTLE!
THIS IS WAY TOO MUCH "LIVING" FOR ME!
You're asking for too much!
COME ON! TOKYO'S FANTASTIC! I LIKE IT! IT'S FULL OF ALL SORTS OF NEW STUFF AND CHOCK FULL OF FUN!
HA HA HA!
HA HA HA
PAMP
A SCHOOL EXCHANGE! YOU'LL SPEAK BOTH STANDARD AND KANSAI. YOU'LL BE BILINGUAL!
BAM
THOSE ARE BOTH JAPANESE.
UGH, NEVER CAN TAKE A JOKE, CAN YOU?
*THAT'S* WHY YOU'RE STILL SINGLE.
SH-SHUT UP, AND KEEP YOUR SNOOPING OUT OF MY BUSINESS!

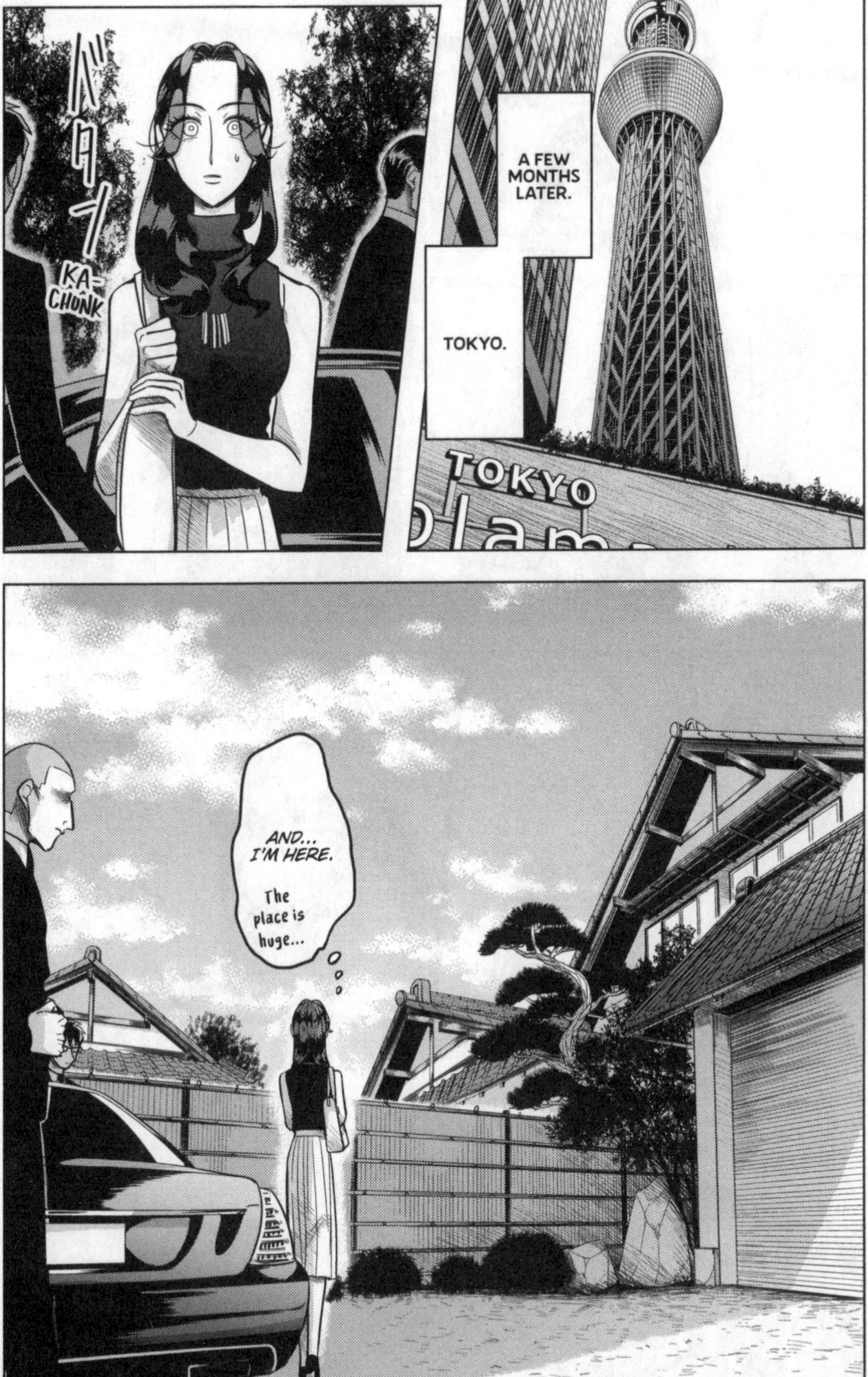
A FEW MONTHS LATER.
TOKYO.
TOKYO
KA-CHUNK
AND... I'M HERE.
The place is huge...

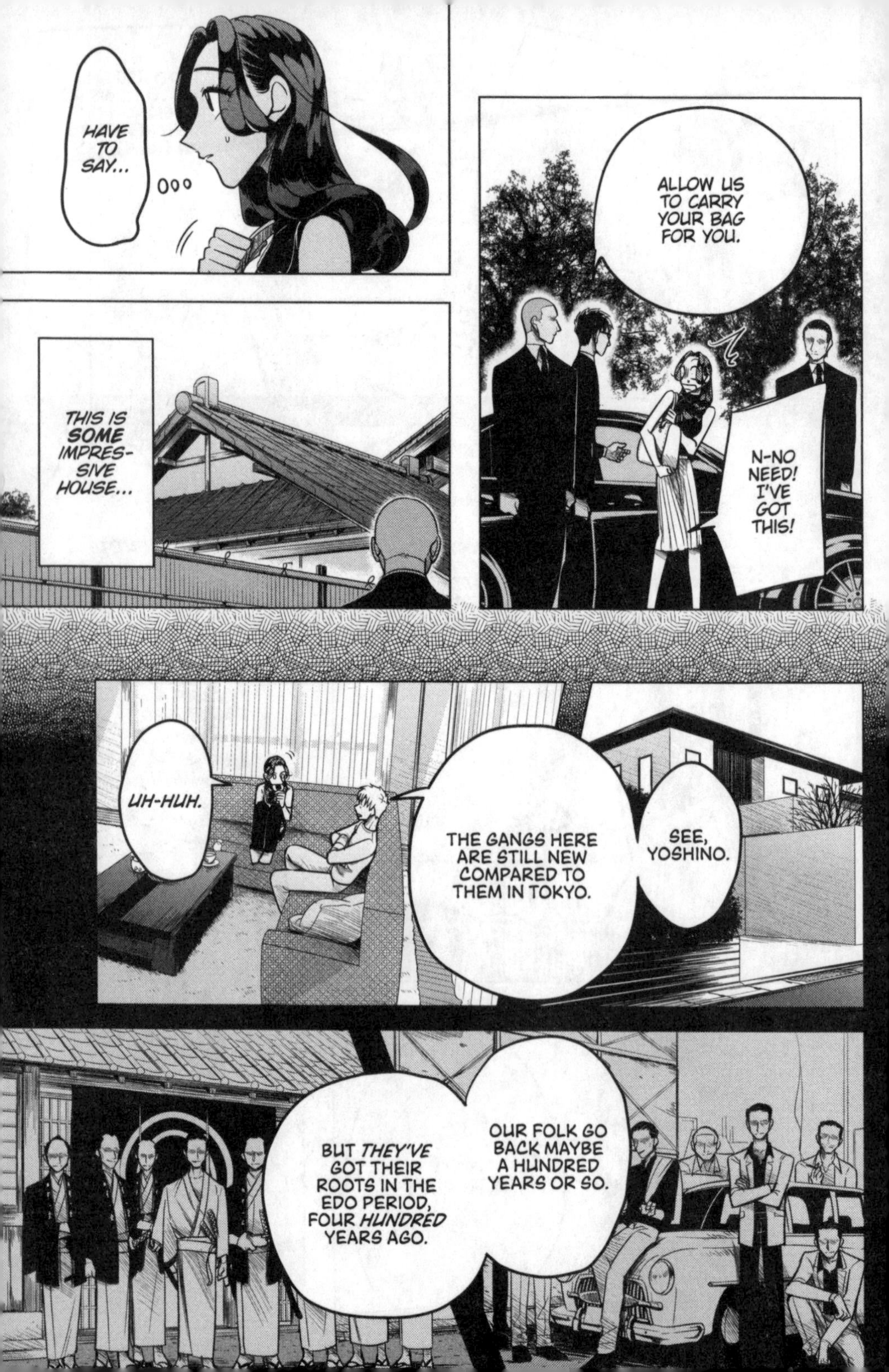
ALLOW US TO CARRY YOUR BAG FOR YOU.
N-NO NEED! I'VE GOT THIS!
HAVE TO SAY...
THIS IS SOME IMPRESSIVE HOUSE...
SEE, YOSHINO.
THE GANGS HERE ARE STILL NEW COMPARED TO THEM IN TOKYO.
UH-HUH.
OUR FOLK GO BACK MAYBE A HUNDRED YEARS OR SO.
BUT *THEY'VE* GOT THEIR ROOTS IN THE EDO PERIOD, FOUR *HUNDRED* YEARS AGO.

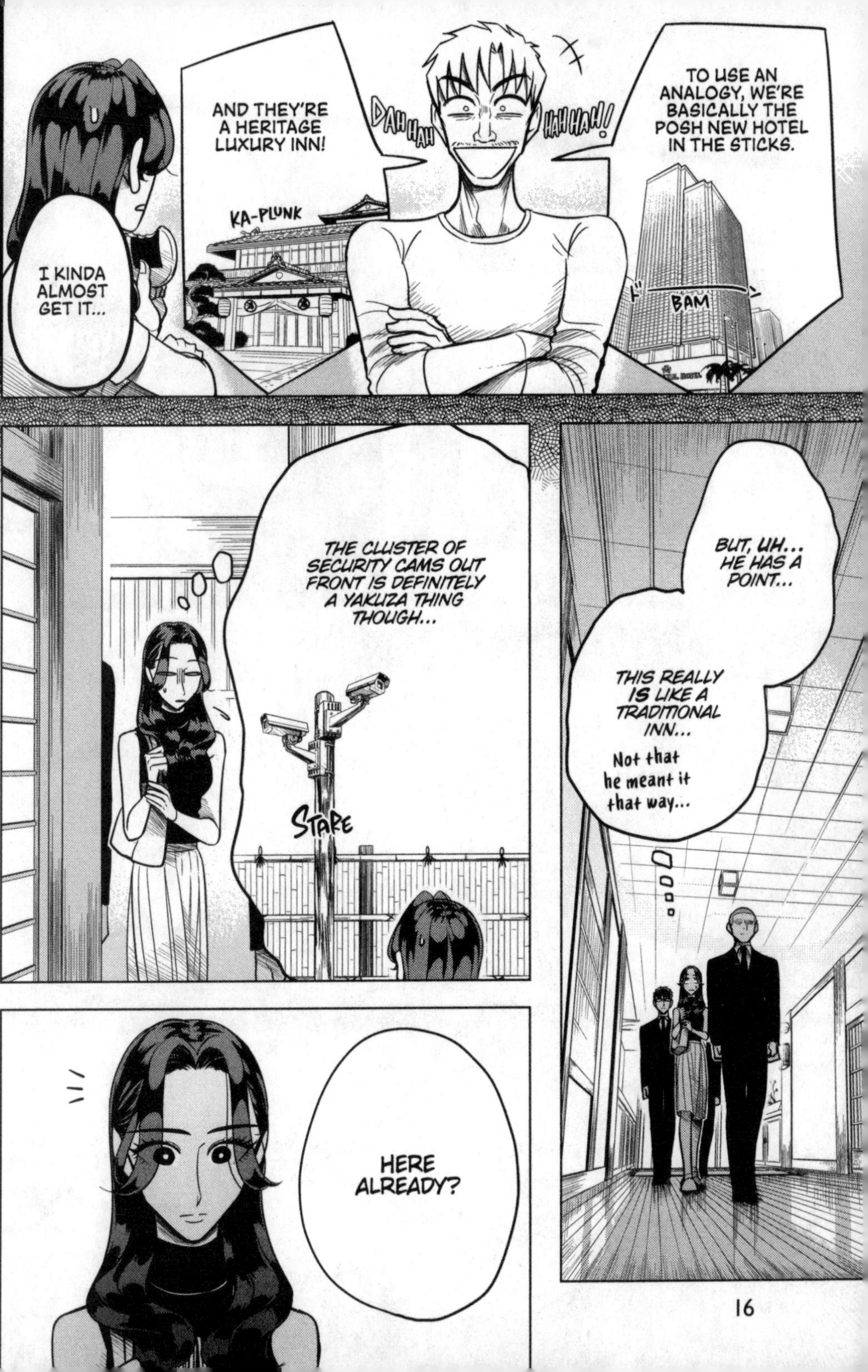
TO USE AN ANALOGY, WE'RE BASICALLY THE POSH NEW HOTEL IN THE STICKS.
HAH HAH!
DAH HAH
AND THEY'RE A HERITAGE LUXURY INN!
BAM
KA-PLUNK
I KINDA ALMOST GET IT...
BUT, UH... HE HAS A POINT...
THIS REALLY IS LIKE A TRADITIONAL INN...
Not that he meant it that way...
THE CLUSTER OF SECURITY CAMS OUT FRONT IS DEFINITELY A YAKUZA THING THOUGH...
STARE
HERE ALREADY?

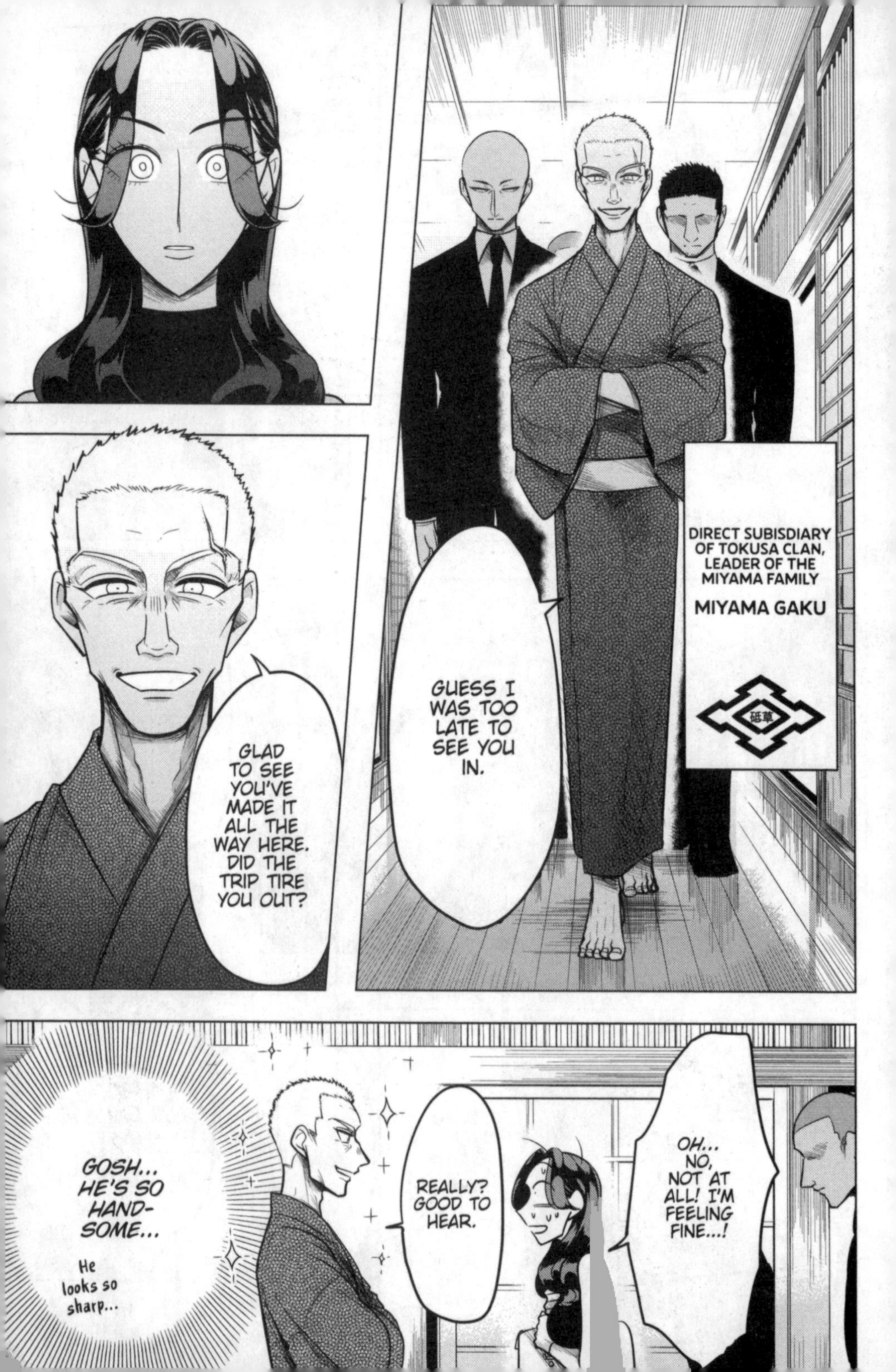
DIRECT SUBISDIARY OF TOKUSA CLAN, LEADER OF THE MIYAMA FAMILY
MIYAMA GAKU
砥草
GUESS I WAS TOO LATE TO SEE YOU IN.
GLAD TO SEE YOU'VE MADE IT ALL THE WAY HERE. DID THE TRIP TIRE YOU OUT?
OH... NO, NOT AT ALL! I'M FEELING FINE...!
REALLY? GOOD TO HEAR.
GOSH... HE'S SO HAND-SOME...
He looks so sharp...

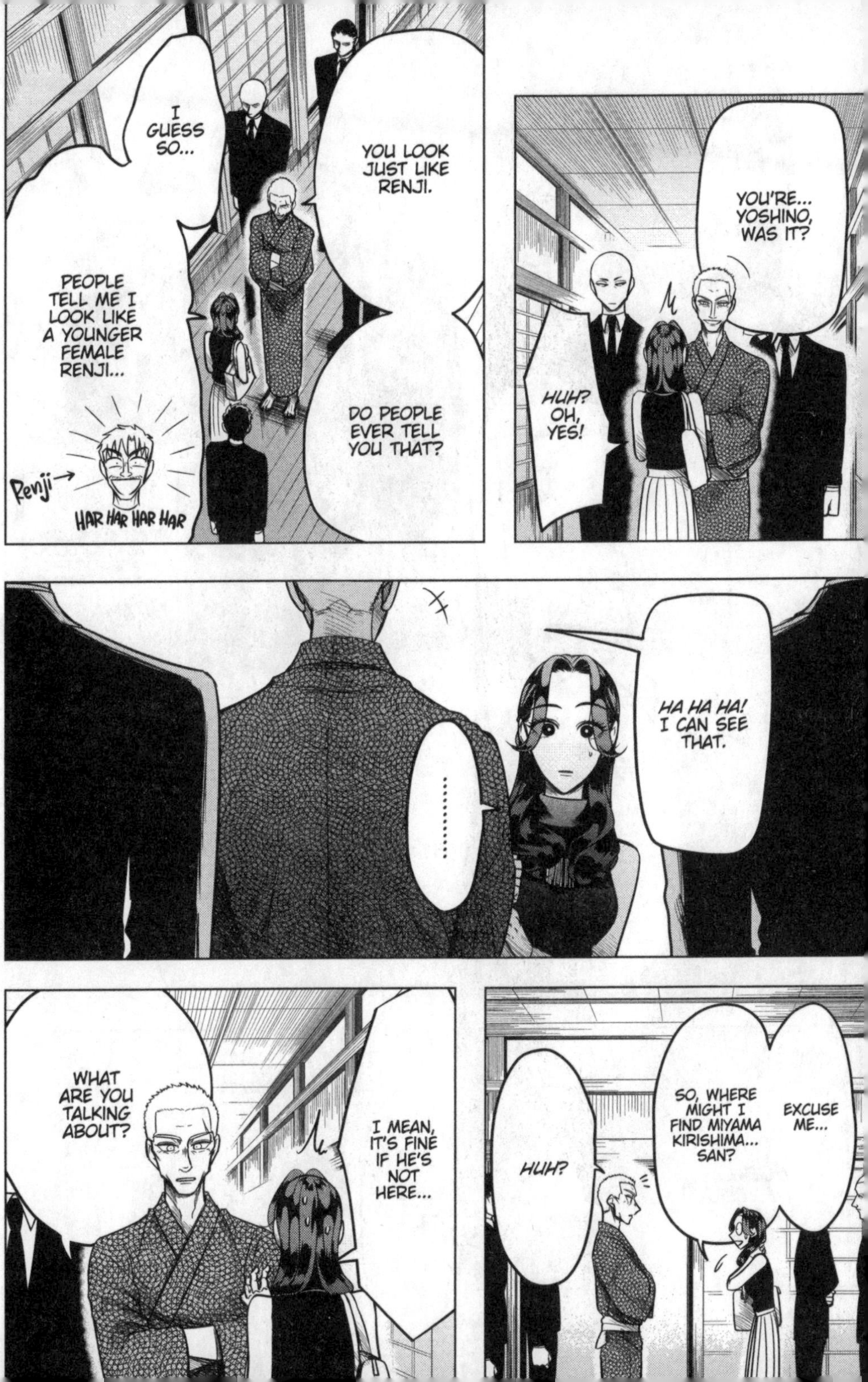
YOU'RE... YOSHINO, WAS IT?
HUH? OH, YES!
YOU LOOK JUST LIKE RENJI.
DO PEOPLE EVER TELL YOU THAT?
I GUESS SO...
PEOPLE TELL ME I LOOK LIKE A YOUNGER FEMALE RENJI...
Renji
HAR HAR HAR HAR
HA HA HA! I CAN SEE THAT.
......
EXCUSE ME...
SO, WHERE MIGHT I FIND MIYAMA KIRISHIMA... SAN?
HUH?
I MEAN, IT'S FINE IF HE'S NOT HERE...
WHAT ARE YOU TALKING ABOUT?

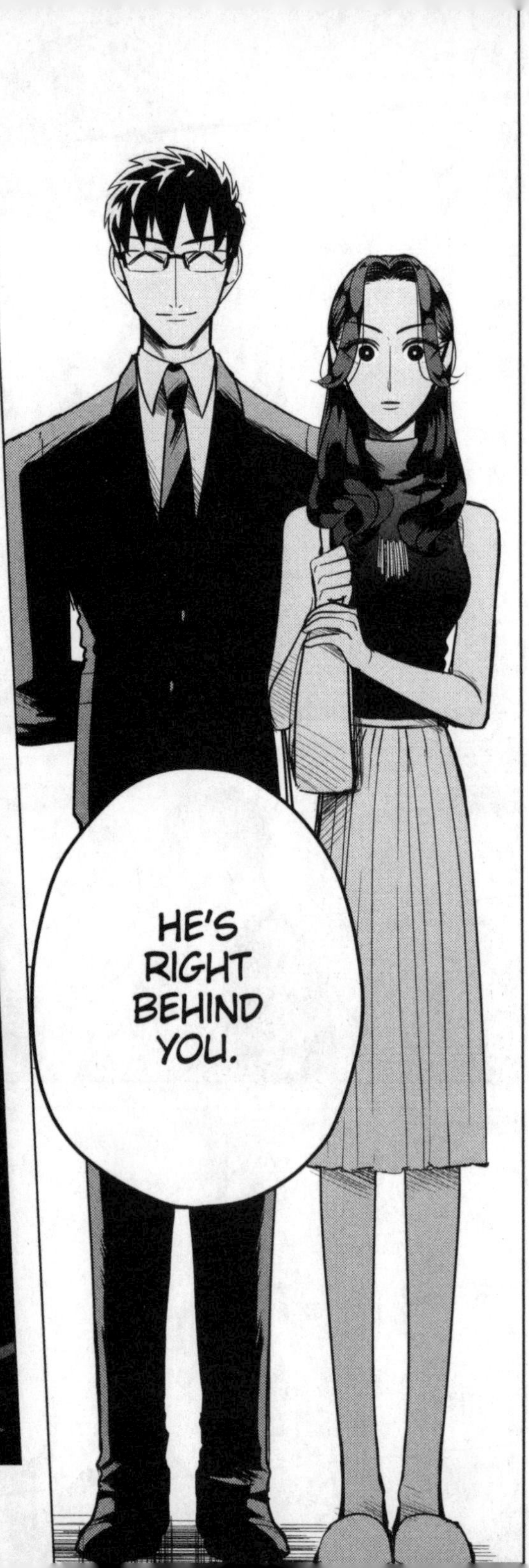
HE'S RIGHT BEHIND YOU.

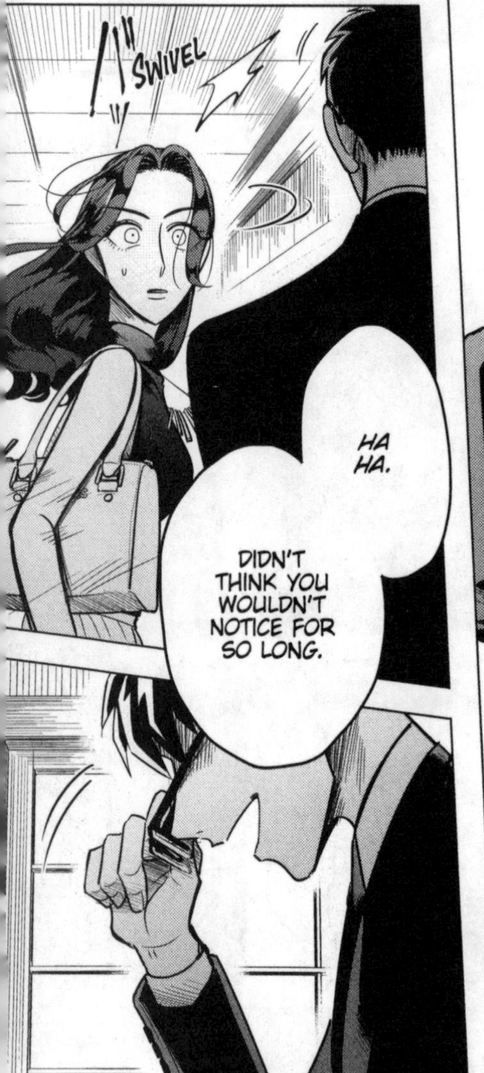
SWIVEL
HA HA.
DIDN'T THINK YOU WOULDN'T NOTICE FOR SO LONG.

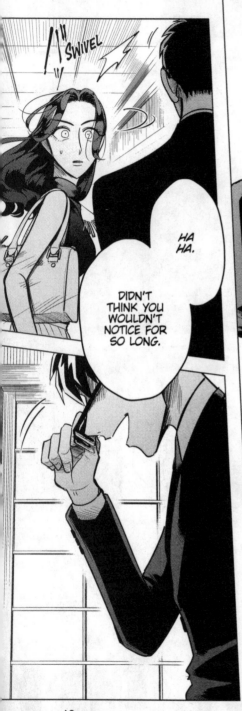

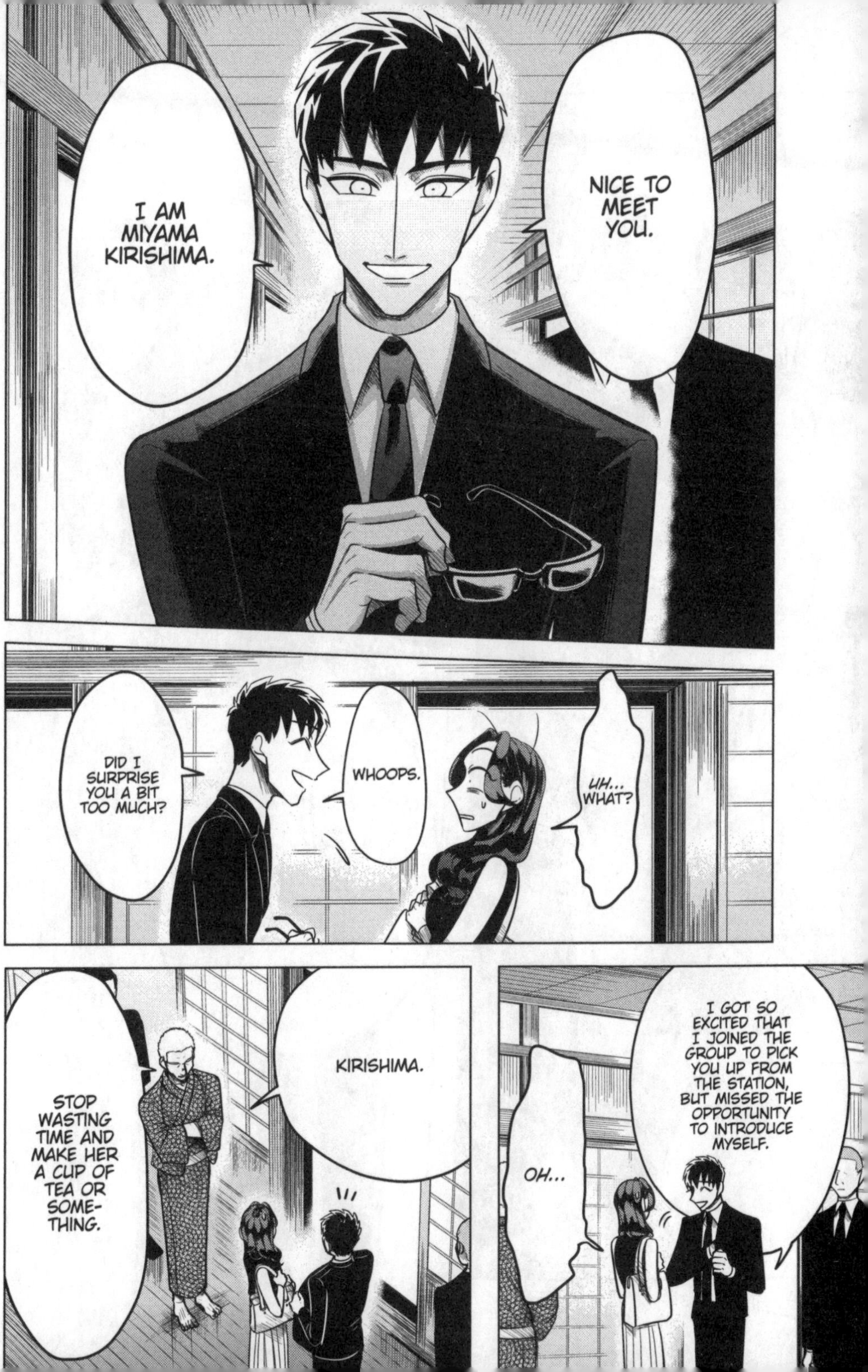
NICE TO MEET YOU.
I AM MIYAMA KIRISHIMA.
UH... WHAT?
WHOOPS.
DID I SURPRISE YOU A BIT TOO MUCH?
I GOT SO EXCITED THAT I JOINED THE GROUP TO PICK YOU UP FROM THE STATION, BUT MISSED THE OPPORTUNITY TO INTRODUCE MYSELF.
OH...
KIRISHIMA.
STOP WASTING TIME AND MAKE HER A CUP OF TEA OR SOME-THING.

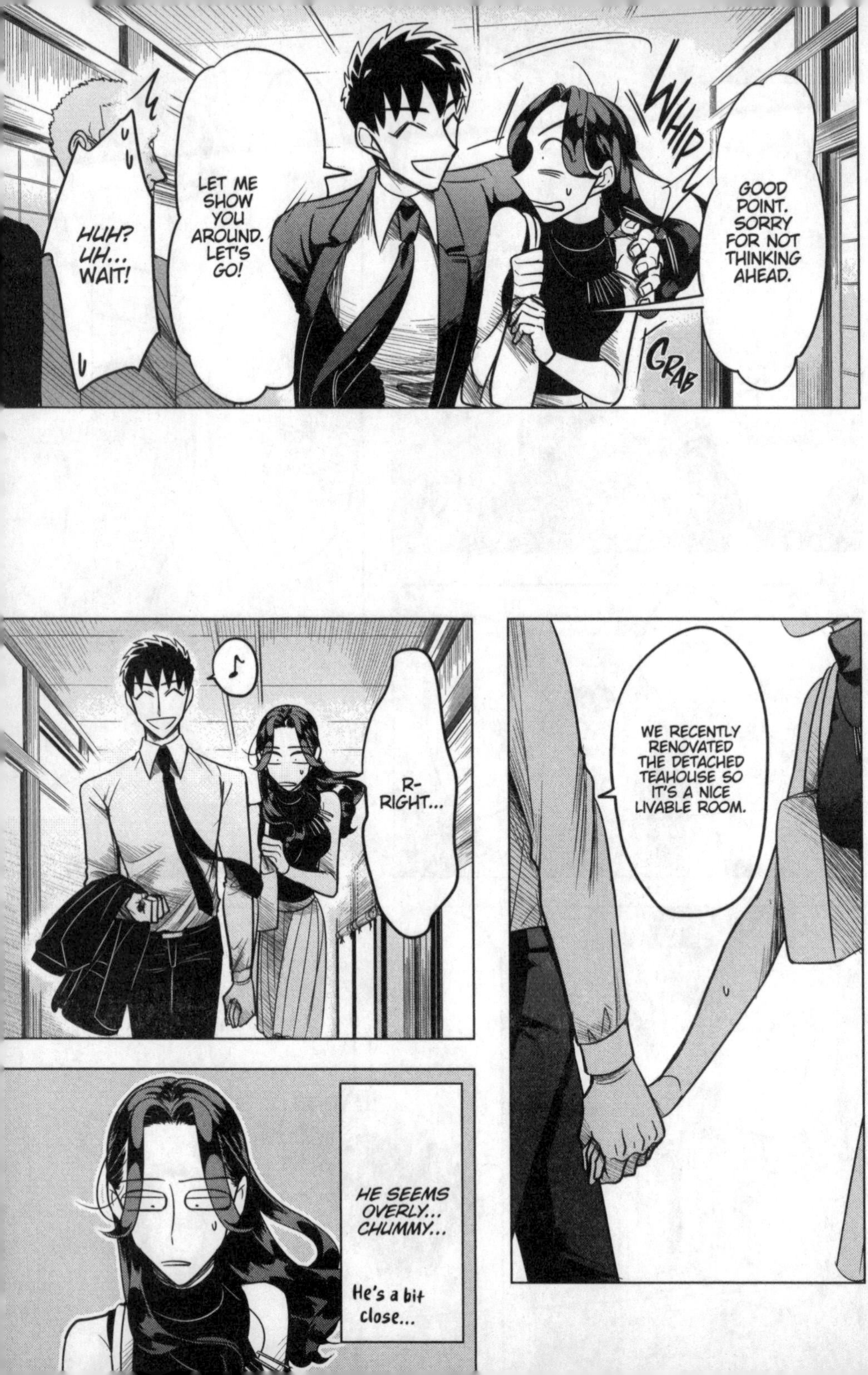
GOOD POINT. SORRY FOR NOT THINKING AHEAD.
WHIP
GRAB
LET ME SHOW YOU AROUND. LET'S GO!
HUH? UH... WAIT!
WE RECENTLY RENOVATED THE DETACHED TEAHOUSE SO IT'S A NICE LIVABLE ROOM.
R-RIGHT...
♪
HE SEEMS OVERLY... CHUMMY...
He's a bit close...

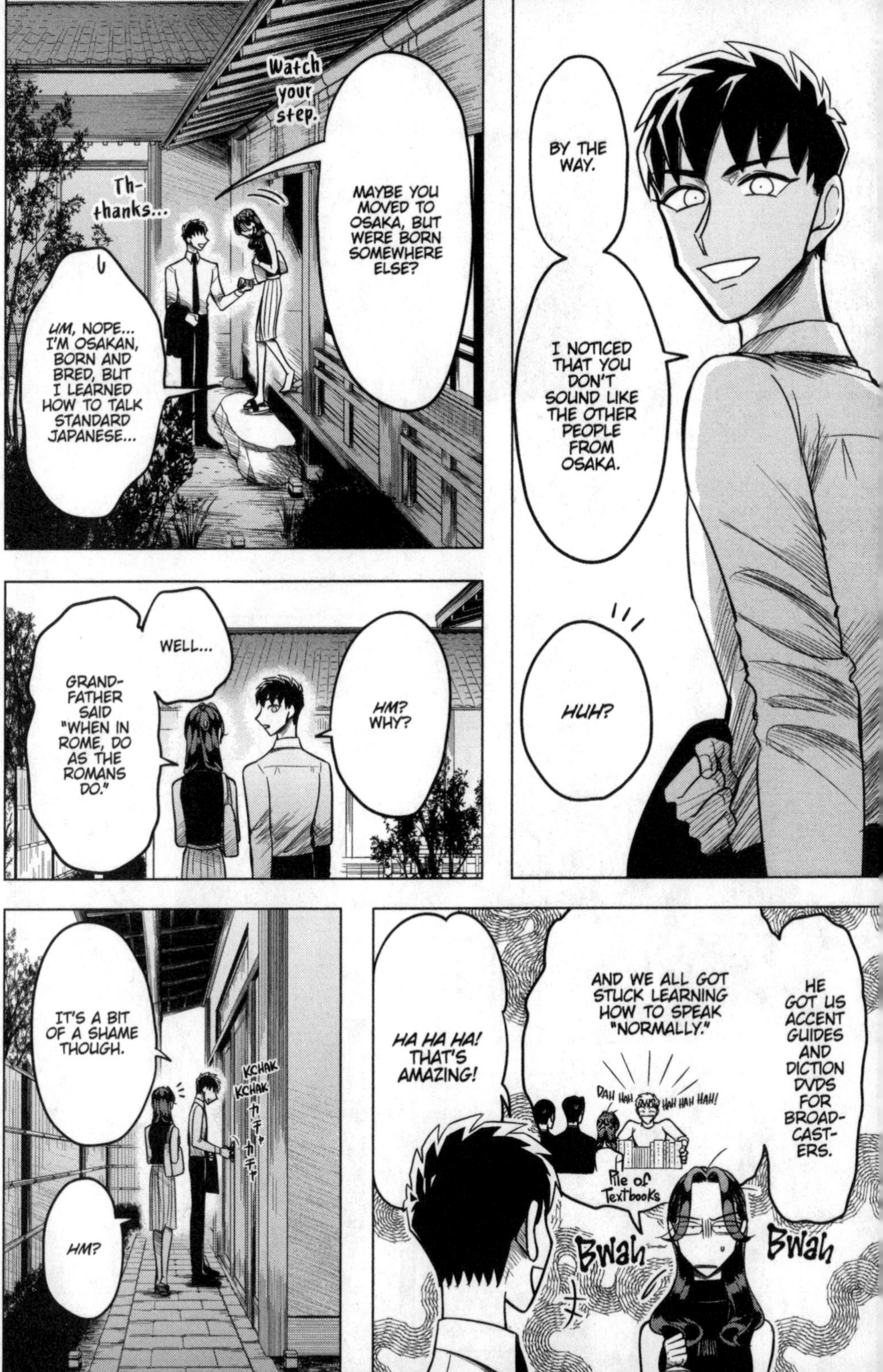

BY THE WAY.
I NOTICED THAT YOU DON'T SOUND LIKE THE OTHER PEOPLE FROM OSAKA.
HUH?
Watch your step.
MAYBE YOU MOVED TO OSAKA, BUT WERE BORN SOMEWHERE ELSE?
Th-thanks...
UM, NOPE... I'M OSAKAN, BORN AND BRED, BUT I LEARNED HOW TO TALK STANDARD JAPANESE...
HM? WHY?
WELL...
GRANDFATHER SAID "WHEN IN ROME, DO AS THE ROMANS DO."
HE GOT US ACCENT GUIDES AND DICTION DVDS FOR BROADCASTERS.
AND WE ALL GOT STUCK LEARNING HOW TO SPEAK "NORMALLY."
DAH HAH HAH HAH HAH!
Pile of Textbooks
Bwah
Bwah
HA HA HA! THAT'S AMAZING!
IT'S A BIT OF A SHAME THOUGH.
KCHAK KCHAK
HM?

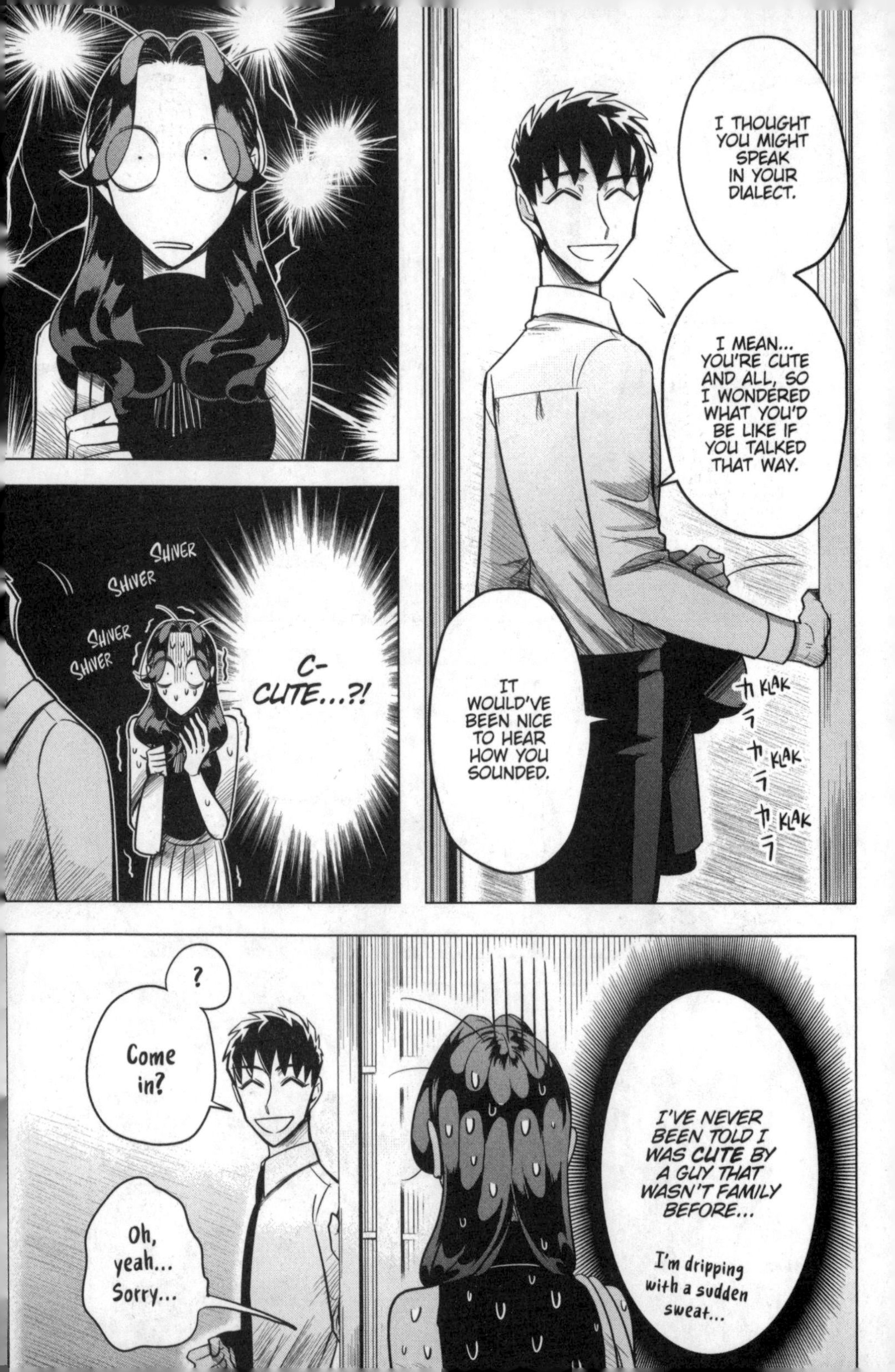
I THOUGHT YOU MIGHT SPEAK IN YOUR DIALECT.
I MEAN... YOU'RE CUTE AND ALL, SO I WONDERED WHAT YOU'D BE LIKE IF YOU TALKED THAT WAY.
IT WOULD'VE BEEN NICE TO HEAR HOW YOU SOUNDED.
KLAK
KLAK
KLAK
SHIVER
SHIVER
SHIVER
SHIVER
C-CUTE...?!
I'VE NEVER BEEN TOLD I WAS CUTE BY A GUY THAT WASN'T FAMILY BEFORE...
I'm dripping with a sudden sweat...
?
Come in?
Oh, yeah... Sorry...

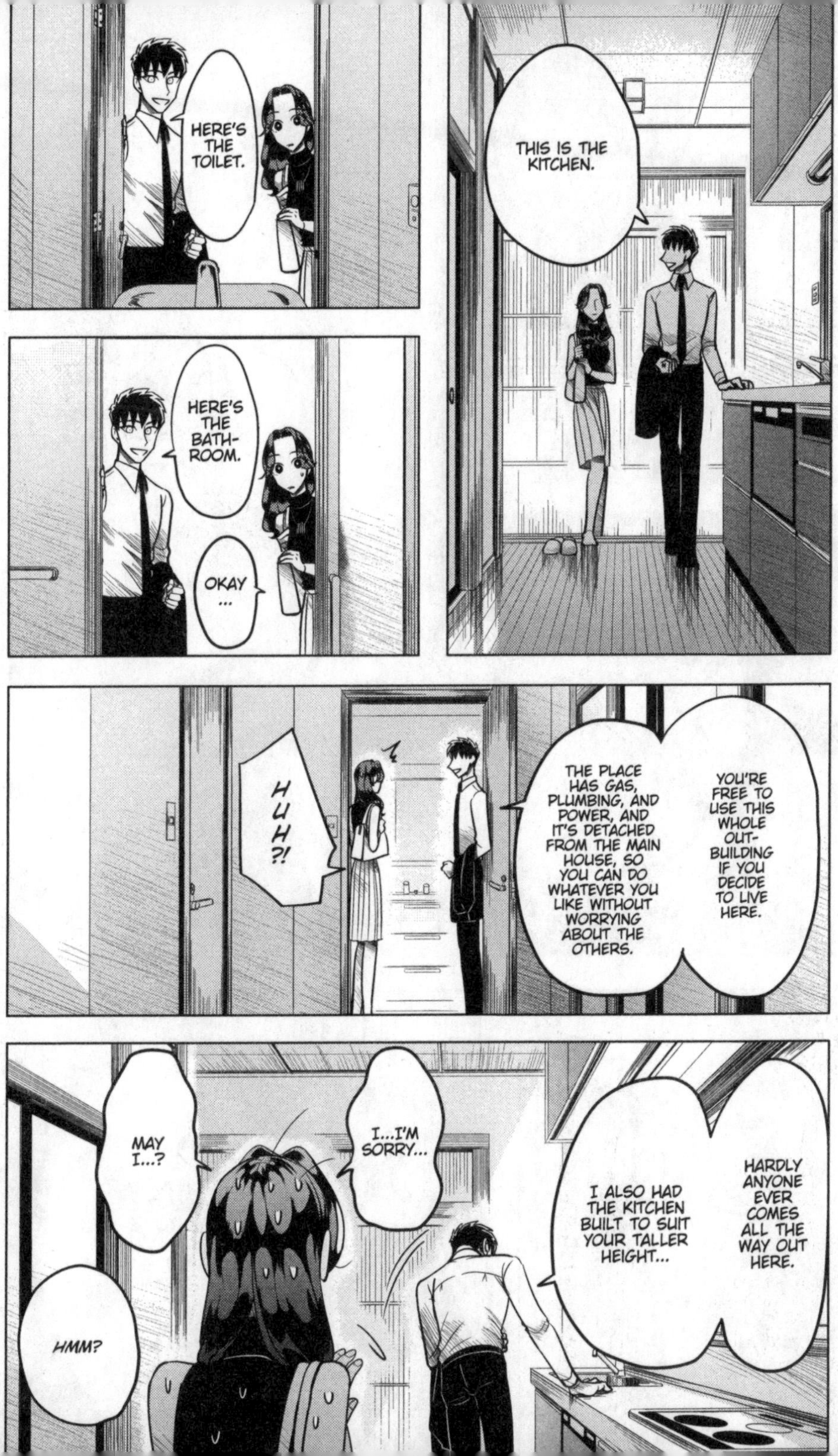
THIS IS THE KITCHEN.
HERE'S THE TOILET.
HERE'S THE BATH-ROOM.
OKAY...
YOU'RE FREE TO USE THIS WHOLE OUT-BUILDING IF YOU DECIDE TO LIVE HERE.
THE PLACE HAS GAS, PLUMBING, AND POWER, AND IT'S DETACHED FROM THE MAIN HOUSE, SO YOU CAN DO WHATEVER YOU LIKE WITHOUT WORRYING ABOUT THE OTHERS.
HUH?!
HARDLY ANYONE EVER COMES ALL THE WAY OUT HERE.
I ALSO HAD THE KITCHEN BUILT TO SUIT YOUR TALLER HEIGHT...
I...I'M SORRY...
MAY I...?
HMM?

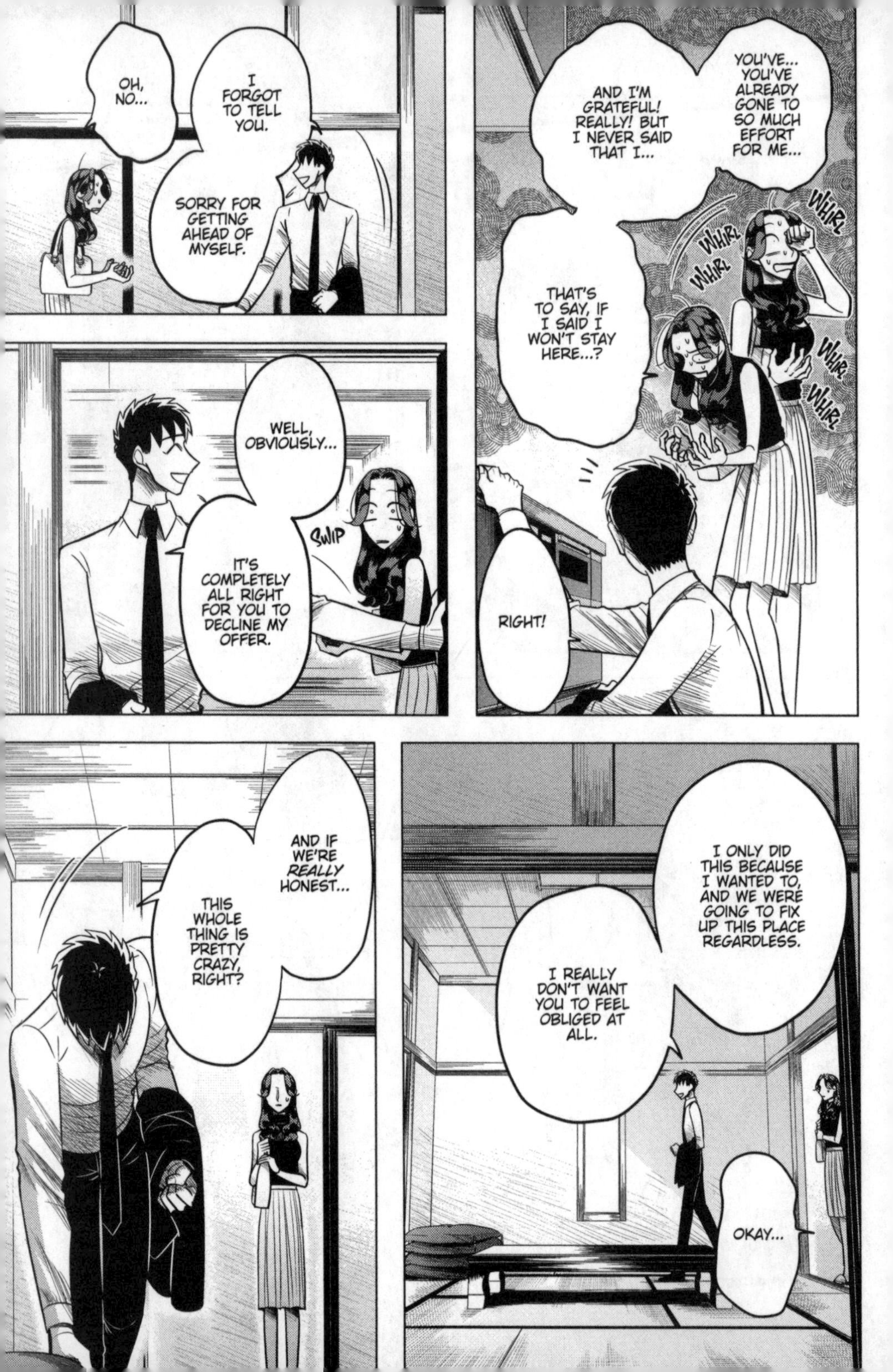
YOU'VE... YOU'VE ALREADY GONE TO SO MUCH EFFORT FOR ME...
AND I'M GRATEFUL! REALLY! BUT I NEVER SAID THAT I...
WHIRL
WHIRL
WHIRL
THAT'S TO SAY, IF I SAID I WON'T STAY HERE...?
WHIRL
WHIRL
RIGHT!
I FORGOT TO TELL YOU.
OH, NO...
SORRY FOR GETTING AHEAD OF MYSELF.
WELL, OBVIOUSLY...
SWIP
IT'S COMPLETELY ALL RIGHT FOR YOU TO DECLINE MY OFFER.
I ONLY DID THIS BECAUSE I WANTED TO, AND WE WERE GOING TO FIX UP THIS PLACE REGARDLESS.
I REALLY DON'T WANT YOU TO FEEL OBLIGED AT ALL.
OKAY...
AND IF WE'RE *REALLY* HONEST...
THIS WHOLE THING IS PRETTY CRAZY, RIGHT?

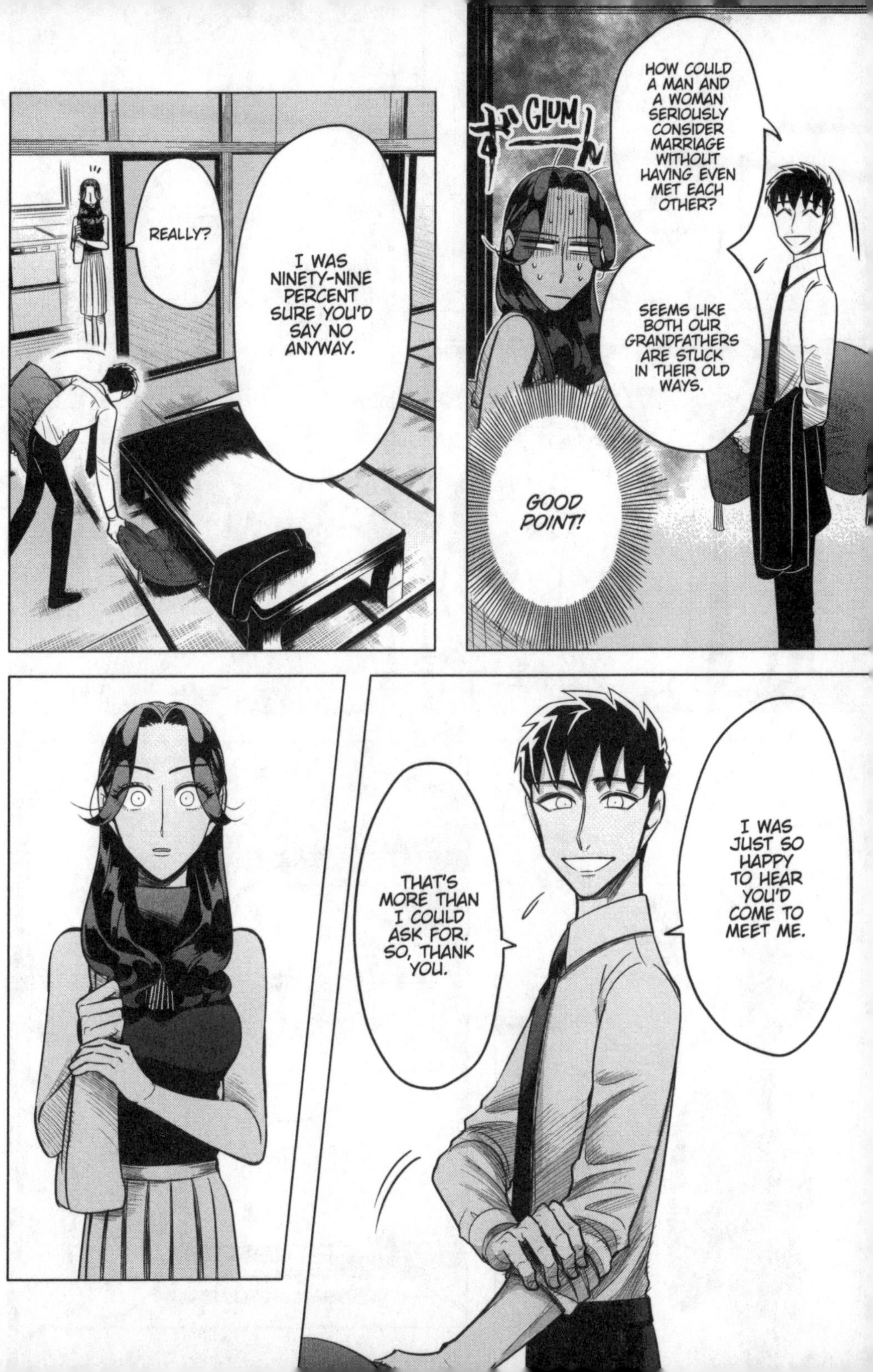
HOW COULD A MAN AND A WOMAN SERIOUSLY CONSIDER MARRIAGE WITHOUT HAVING EVEN MET EACH OTHER?
GLUM
SEEMS LIKE BOTH OUR GRANDFATHERS ARE STUCK IN THEIR OLD WAYS.
GOOD POINT!
I WAS NINETY-NINE PERCENT SURE YOU'D SAY NO ANYWAY.
REALLY?
I WAS JUST SO HAPPY TO HEAR YOU'D COME TO MEET ME.
THAT'S MORE THAN I COULD ASK FOR. SO, THANK YOU.

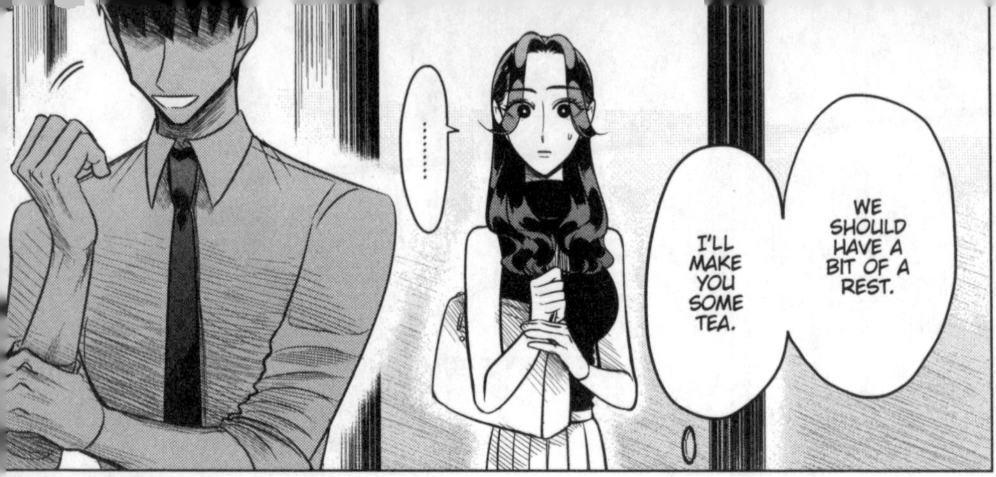
WE SHOULD HAVE A BIT OF A REST.
I'LL MAKE YOU SOME TEA.
......

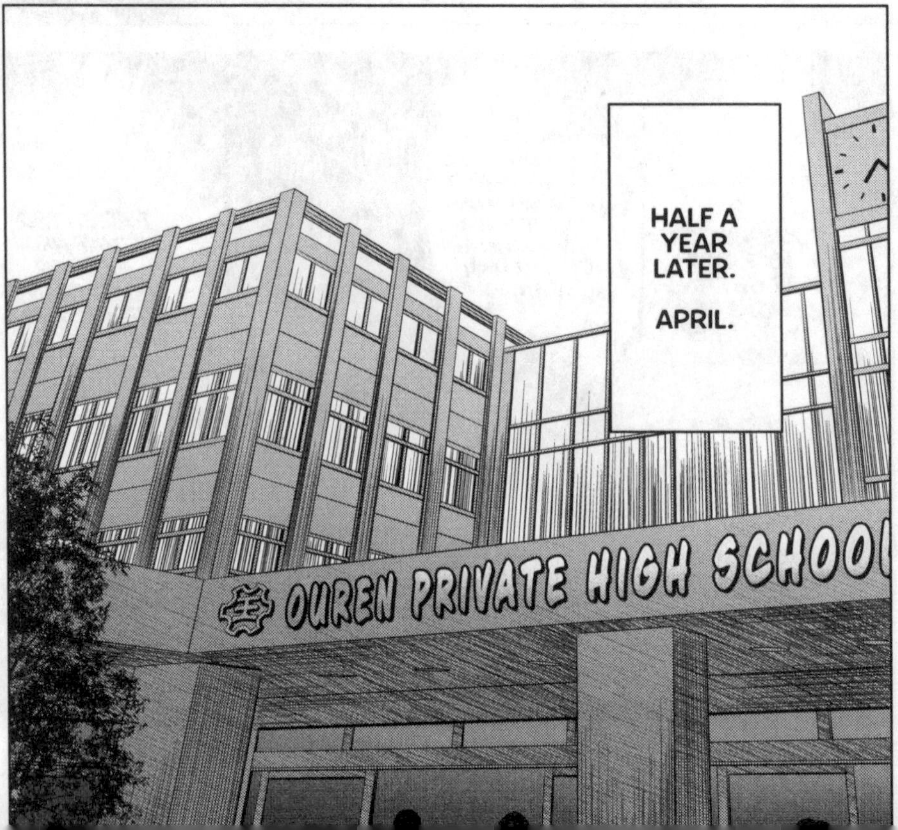
HALF A YEAR LATER.
APRIL.
OUREN PRIVATE HIGH SCHOO

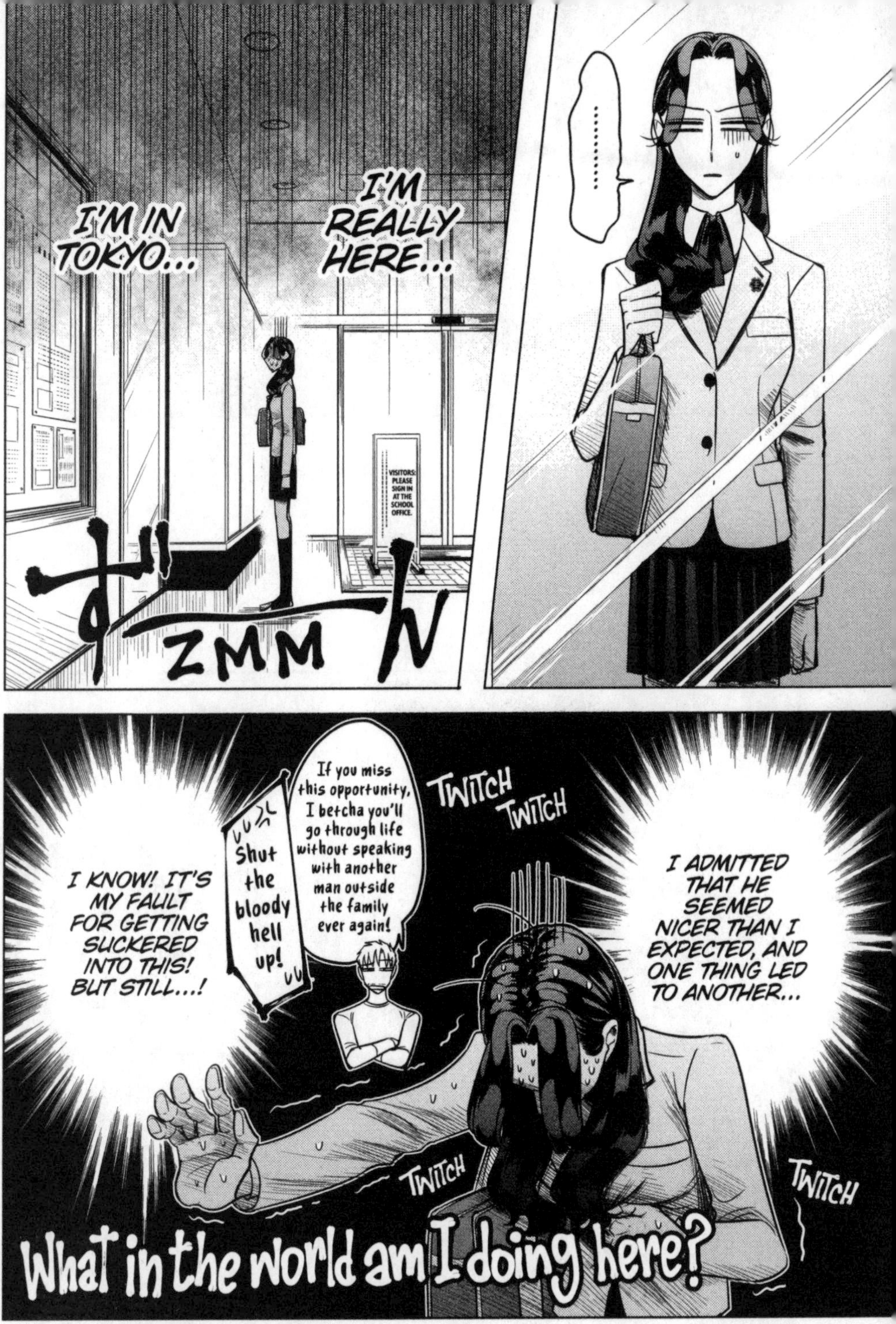
......
I'M REALLY HERE...
I'M IN TOKYO...
VISITORS: PLEASE SIGN IN AT THE SCHOOL OFFICE.
ZMM
I ADMITTED THAT HE SEEMED NICER THAN I EXPECTED, AND ONE THING LED TO ANOTHER...
TWITCH TWITCH
If you miss this opportunity, I betcha you'll go through life without speaking with another man outside the family ever again!
Shut the bloody hell up!
I KNOW! IT'S MY FAULT FOR GETTING SUCKERED INTO THIS! BUT STILL...!
TWITCH
TWITCH
What in the world am I doing here?

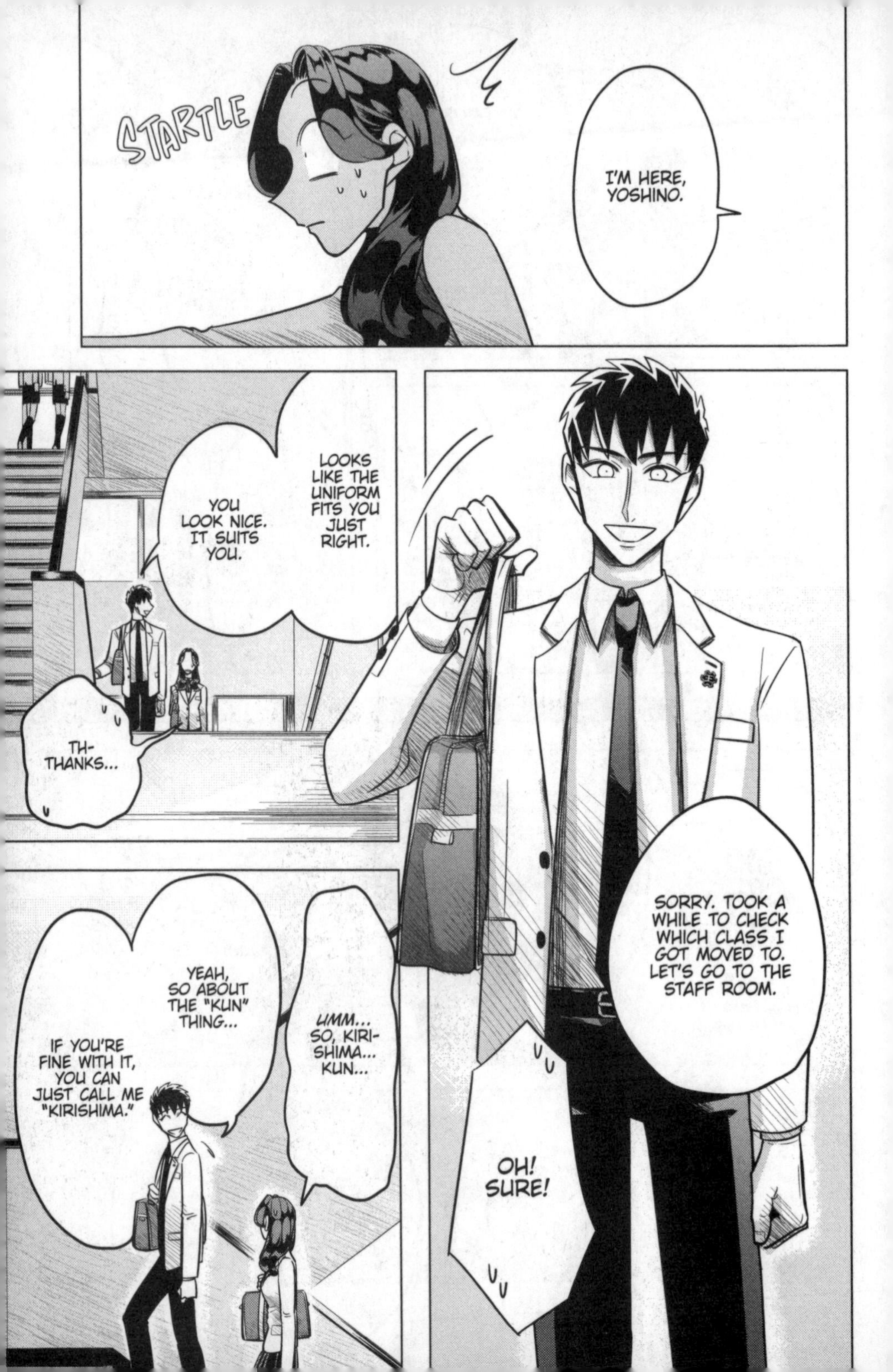
I'M HERE, YOSHINO.
STARTLE
SORRY. TOOK A WHILE TO CHECK WHICH CLASS I GOT MOVED TO. LET'S GO TO THE STAFF ROOM.
OH! SURE!
LOOKS LIKE THE UNIFORM FITS YOU JUST RIGHT.
YOU LOOK NICE. IT SUITS YOU.
TH- THANKS...
UMM... SO, KIRI- SHIMA... KUN...
YEAH, SO ABOUT THE "KUN" THING...
IF YOU'RE FINE WITH IT, YOU CAN JUST CALL ME "KIRISHIMA."

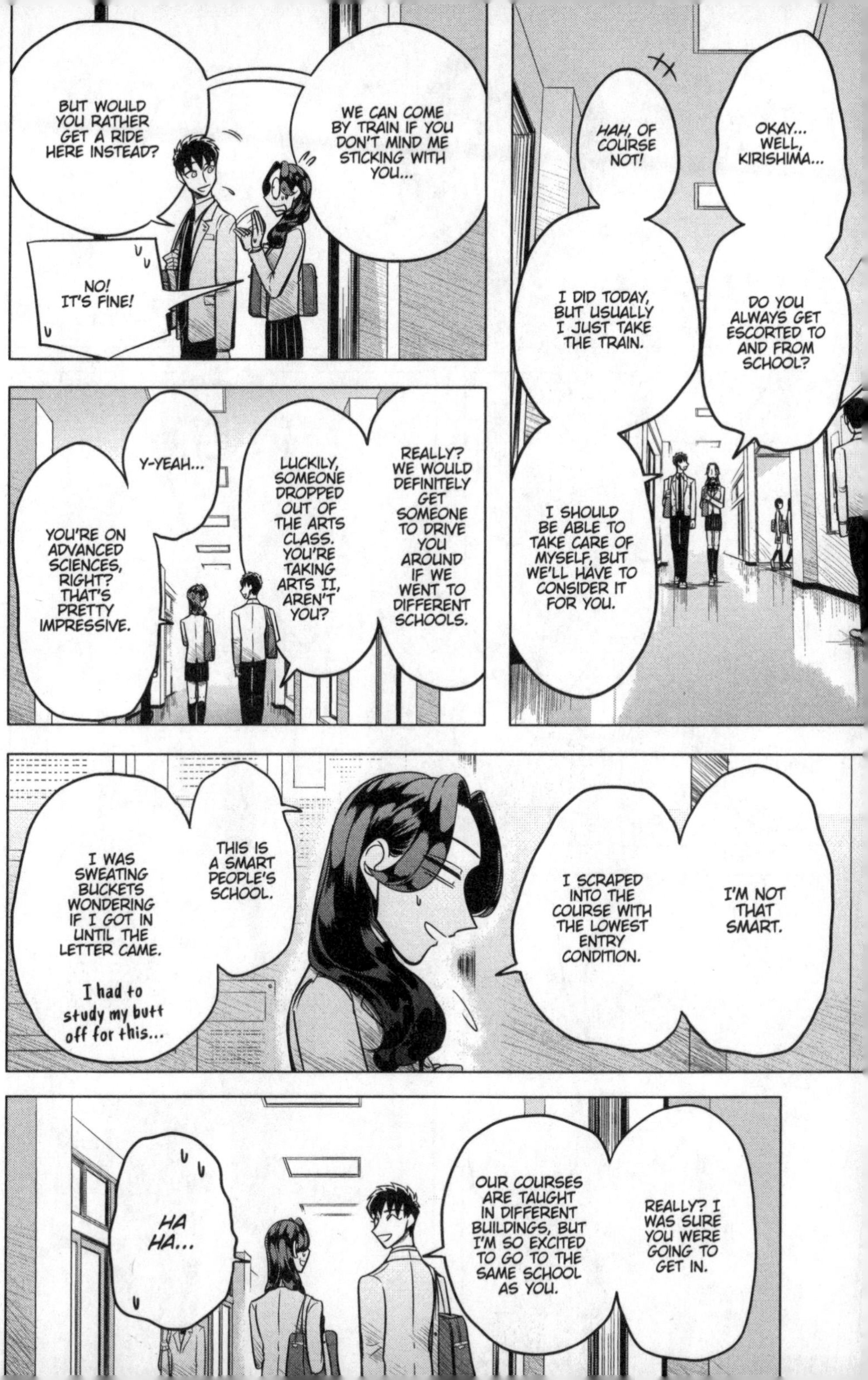
OKAY... WELL, KIRISHIMA...
HAH, OF COURSE NOT!
DO YOU ALWAYS GET ESCORTED TO AND FROM SCHOOL?
I DID TODAY, BUT USUALLY I JUST TAKE THE TRAIN.
I SHOULD BE ABLE TO TAKE CARE OF MYSELF, BUT WE'LL HAVE TO CONSIDER IT FOR YOU.
WE CAN COME BY TRAIN IF YOU DON'T MIND ME STICKING WITH YOU...
BUT WOULD YOU RATHER GET A RIDE HERE INSTEAD?
NO! IT'S FINE!
REALLY? WE WOULD DEFINITELY GET SOMEONE TO DRIVE YOU AROUND IF WE WENT TO DIFFERENT SCHOOLS.
LUCKILY, SOMEONE DROPPED OUT OF THE ARTS CLASS. YOU'RE TAKING ARTS II, AREN'T YOU?
Y-YEAH...
YOU'RE ON ADVANCED SCIENCES, RIGHT? THAT'S PRETTY IMPRESSIVE.
I'M NOT THAT SMART.
I SCRAPED INTO THE COURSE WITH THE LOWEST ENTRY CONDITION.
THIS IS A SMART PEOPLE'S SCHOOL.
I WAS SWEATING BUCKETS WONDERING IF I GOT IN UNTIL THE LETTER CAME.
I had to study my butt off for this...
REALLY? I WAS SURE YOU WERE GOING TO GET IN.
OUR COURSES ARE TAUGHT IN DIFFERENT BUILDINGS, BUT I'M SO EXCITED TO GO TO THE SAME SCHOOL AS YOU.
HA HA...

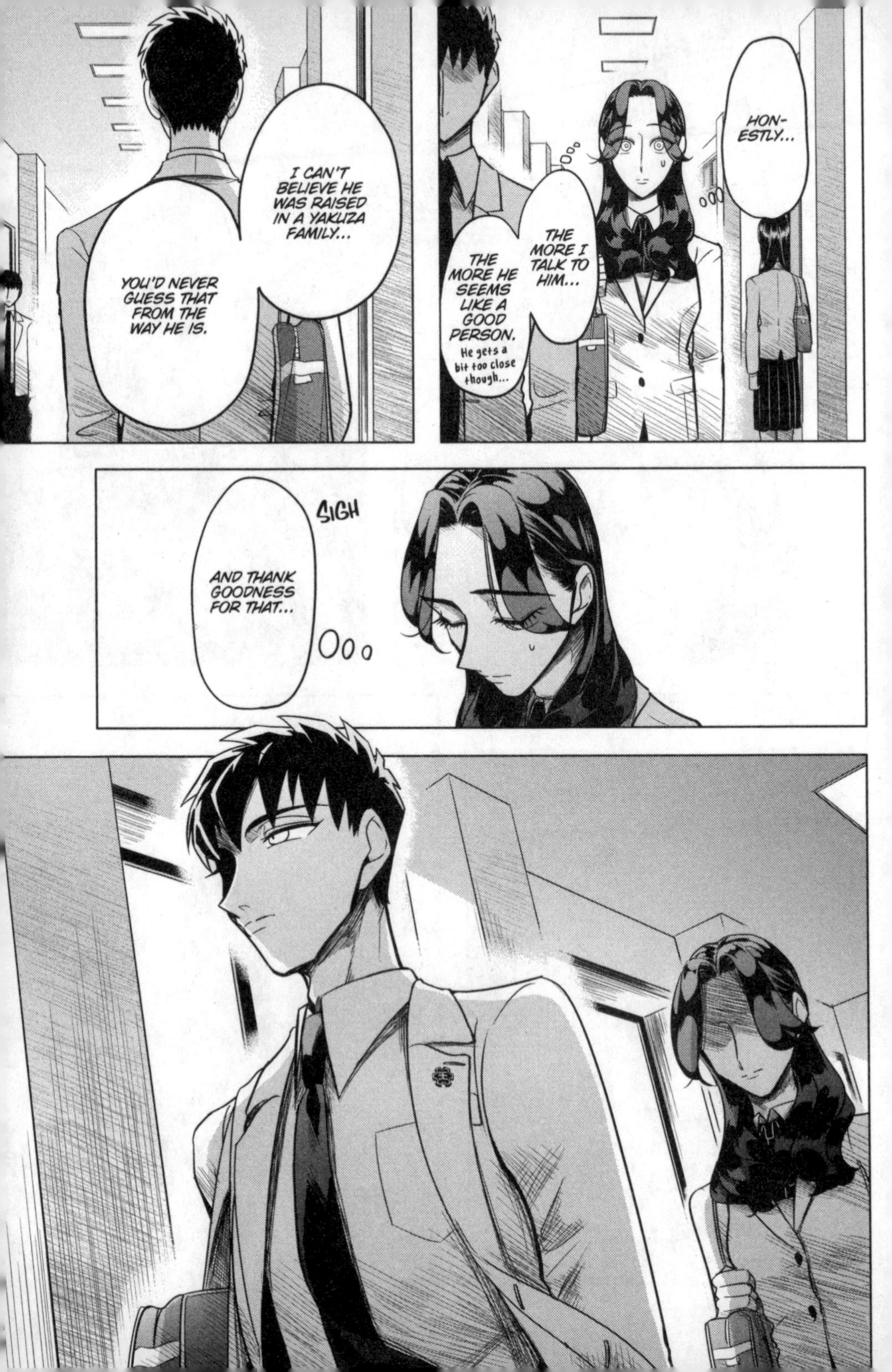
HON-ESTLY...
THE MORE I TALK TO HIM...
THE MORE HE SEEMS LIKE A GOOD PERSON.
He gets a bit too close though...
I CAN'T BELIEVE HE WAS RAISED IN A YAKUZA FAMILY...
YOU'D NEVER GUESS THAT FROM THE WAY HE IS.
SIGH
AND THANK GOODNESS FOR THAT...

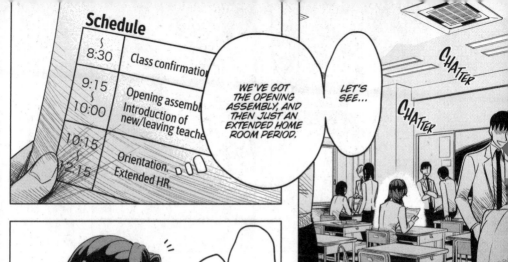

## Schedule

| | |
|---|---|
| ~8:30 | Class confirmation |
| 9:15~10:00 | Opening assembly Introduction of new/leaving teachers |
| 10:15~12:15 | Orientation. Extended HR. |

WE'VE GOT THE OPENING ASSEMBLY, AND THEN JUST AN EXTENDED HOME ROOM PERIOD.

LET'S SEE...

CHATTER

CHATTER

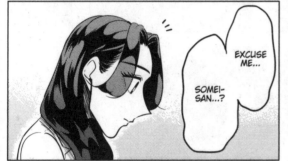

EXCUSE ME...

SOMEI-SAN...?

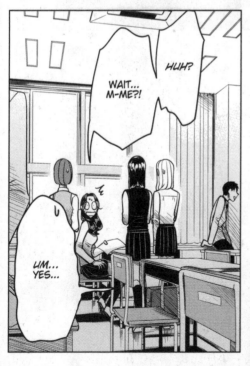

WAIT... M-ME?!

HUH?

UM... YES...

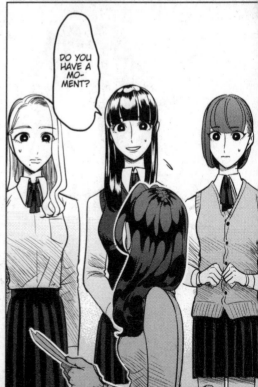

DO YOU HAVE A MOMENT?

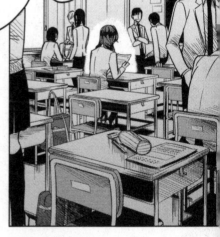

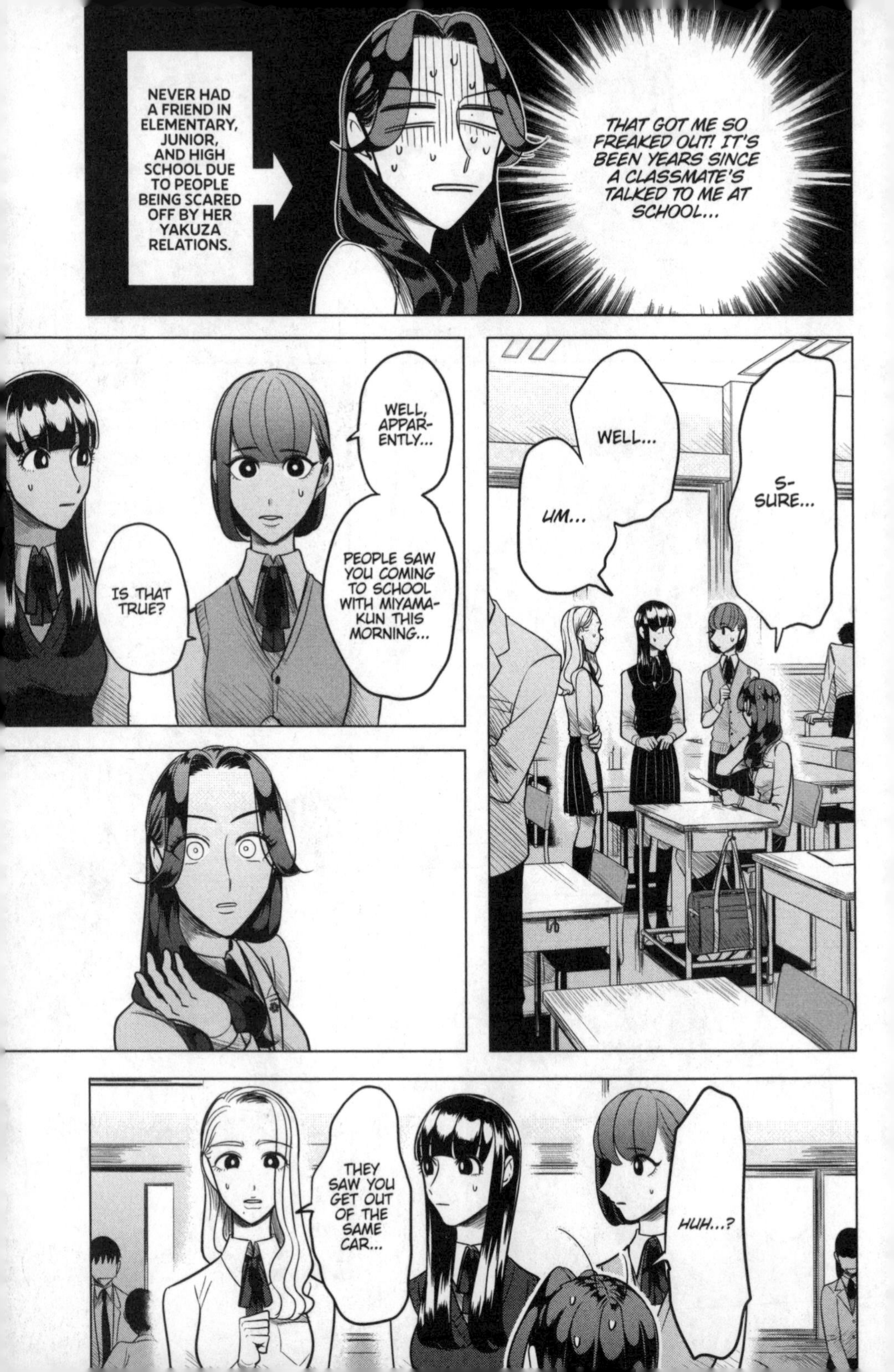
THAT GOT ME SO FREAKED OUT! IT'S BEEN YEARS SINCE A CLASSMATE'S TALKED TO ME AT SCHOOL...
NEVER HAD A FRIEND IN ELEMENTARY, JUNIOR, AND HIGH SCHOOL DUE TO PEOPLE BEING SCARED OFF BY HER YAKUZA RELATIONS.
S-SURE...
WELL...
UM...
WELL, APPARENTLY...
PEOPLE SAW YOU COMING TO SCHOOL WITH MIYAMA-KUN THIS MORNING...
IS THAT TRUE?
HUH...?
THEY SAW YOU GET OUT OF THE SAME CAR...

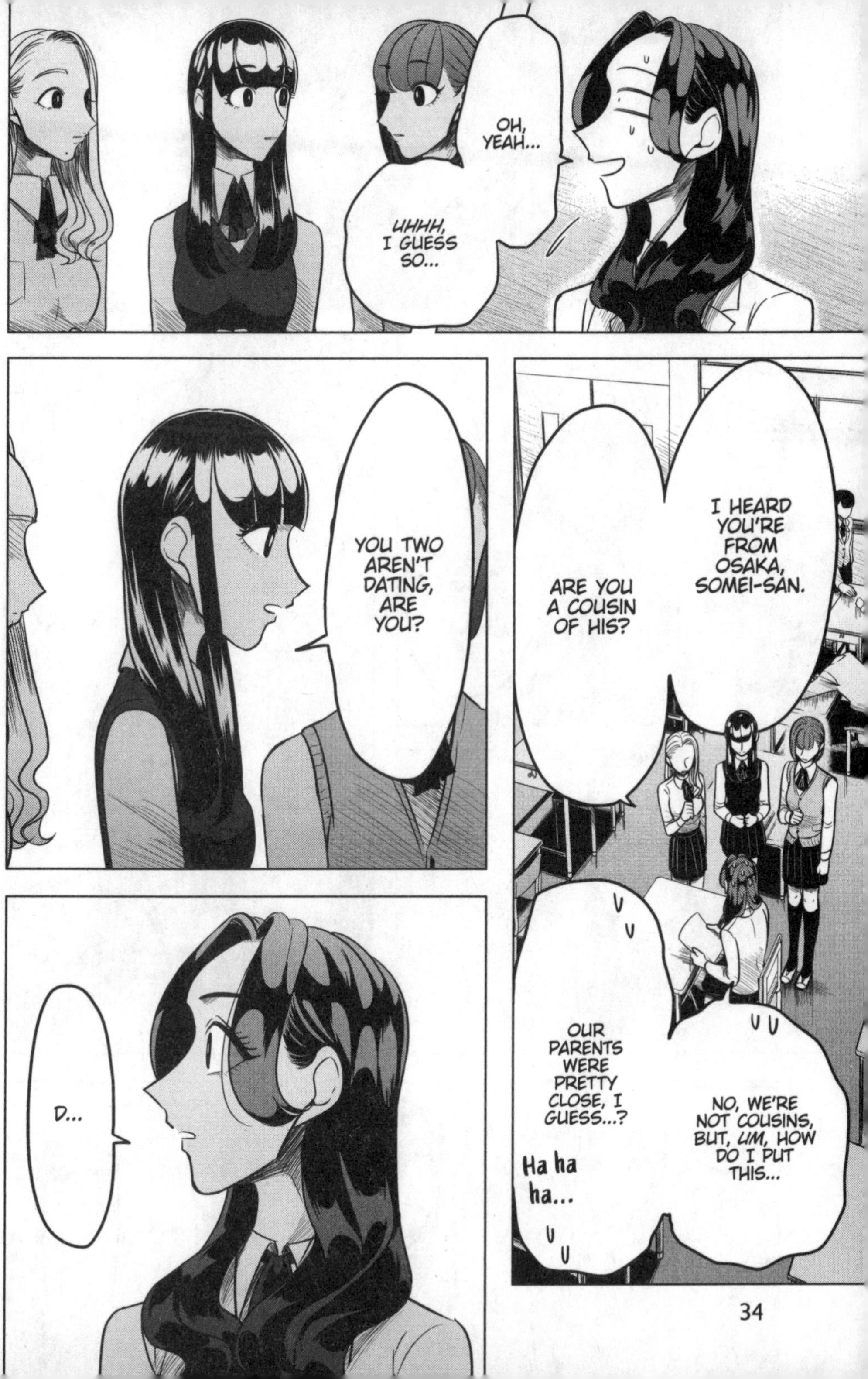
OH, YEAH...
UHHH, I GUESS SO...
I HEARD YOU'RE FROM OSAKA, SOMEI-SAN.
ARE YOU A COUSIN OF HIS?
NO, WE'RE NOT COUSINS, BUT, UM, HOW DO I PUT THIS...
OUR PARENTS WERE PRETTY CLOSE, I GUESS...?
Ha ha ha...
YOU TWO AREN'T DATING, ARE YOU?
D...

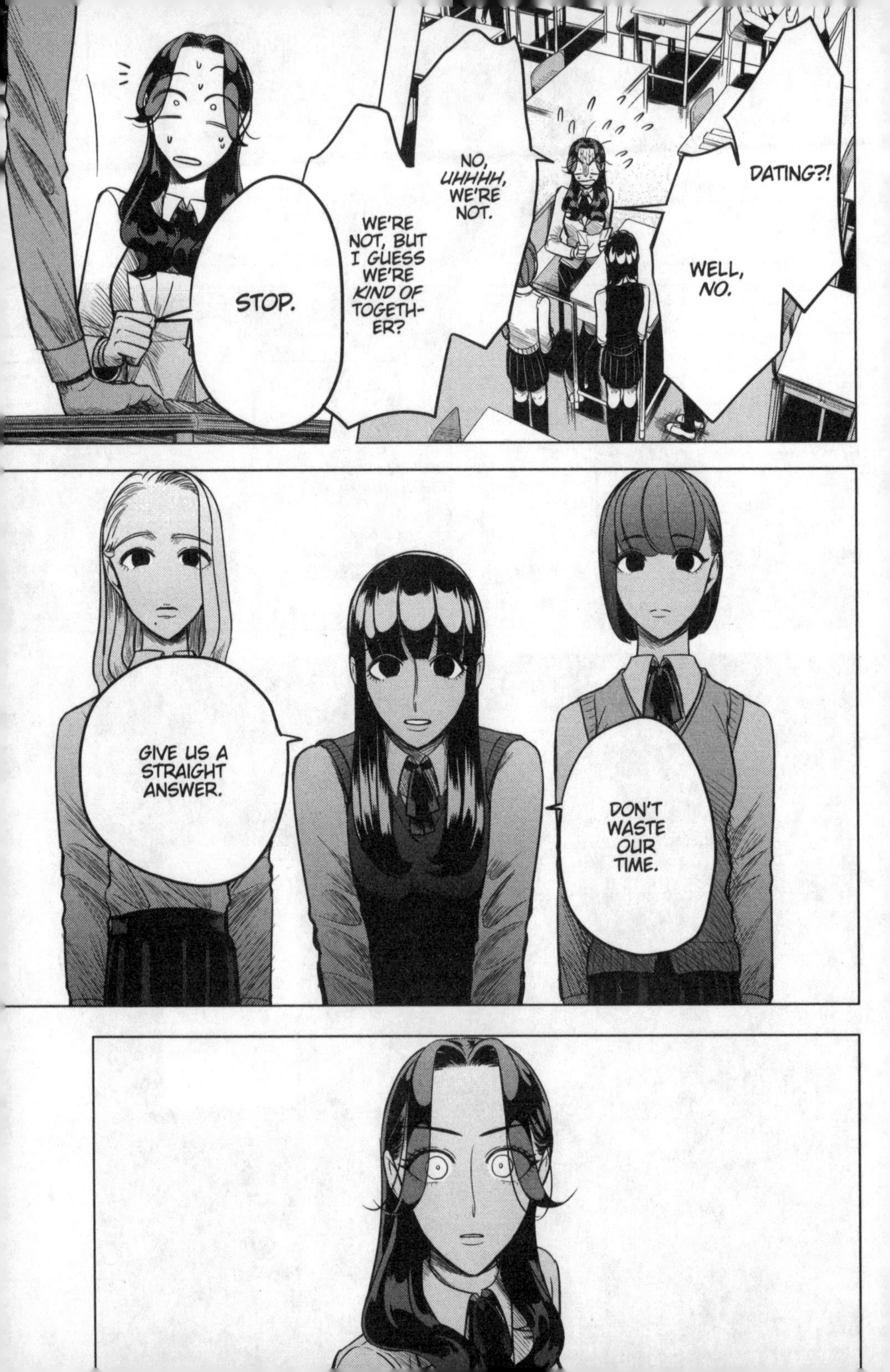
DATING?!
WELL, NO.
NO, UHHHH, WE'RE NOT.
WE'RE NOT, BUT I GUESS WE'RE KIND OF TOGETH-ER?
STOP.
DON'T WASTE OUR TIME.
GIVE US A STRAIGHT ANSWER.

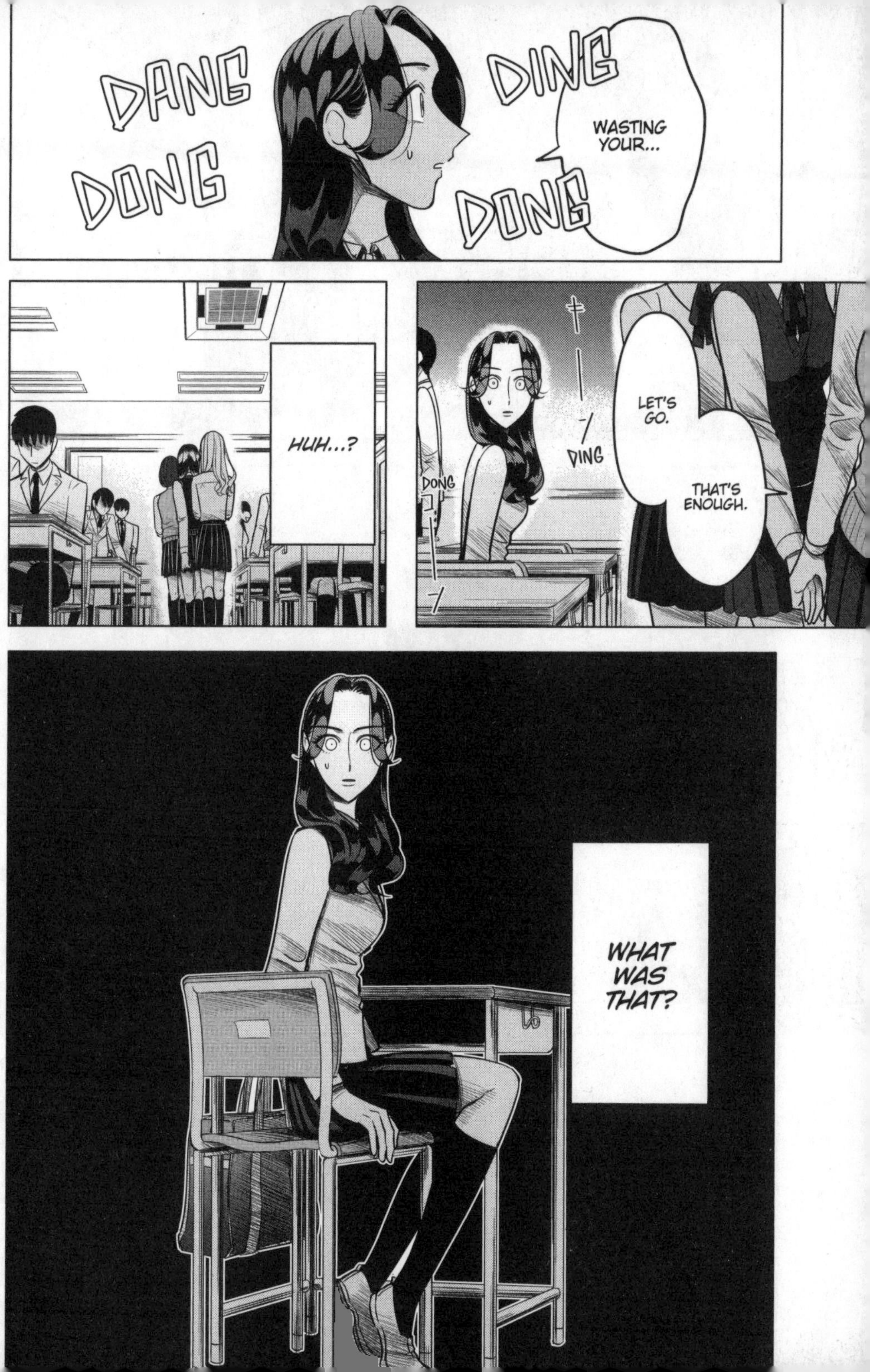
DING
WASTING YOUR...
DANG
DONG
DONG
LET'S GO.
THAT'S ENOUGH.
DING
DONG
HUH...?
WHAT WAS THAT?

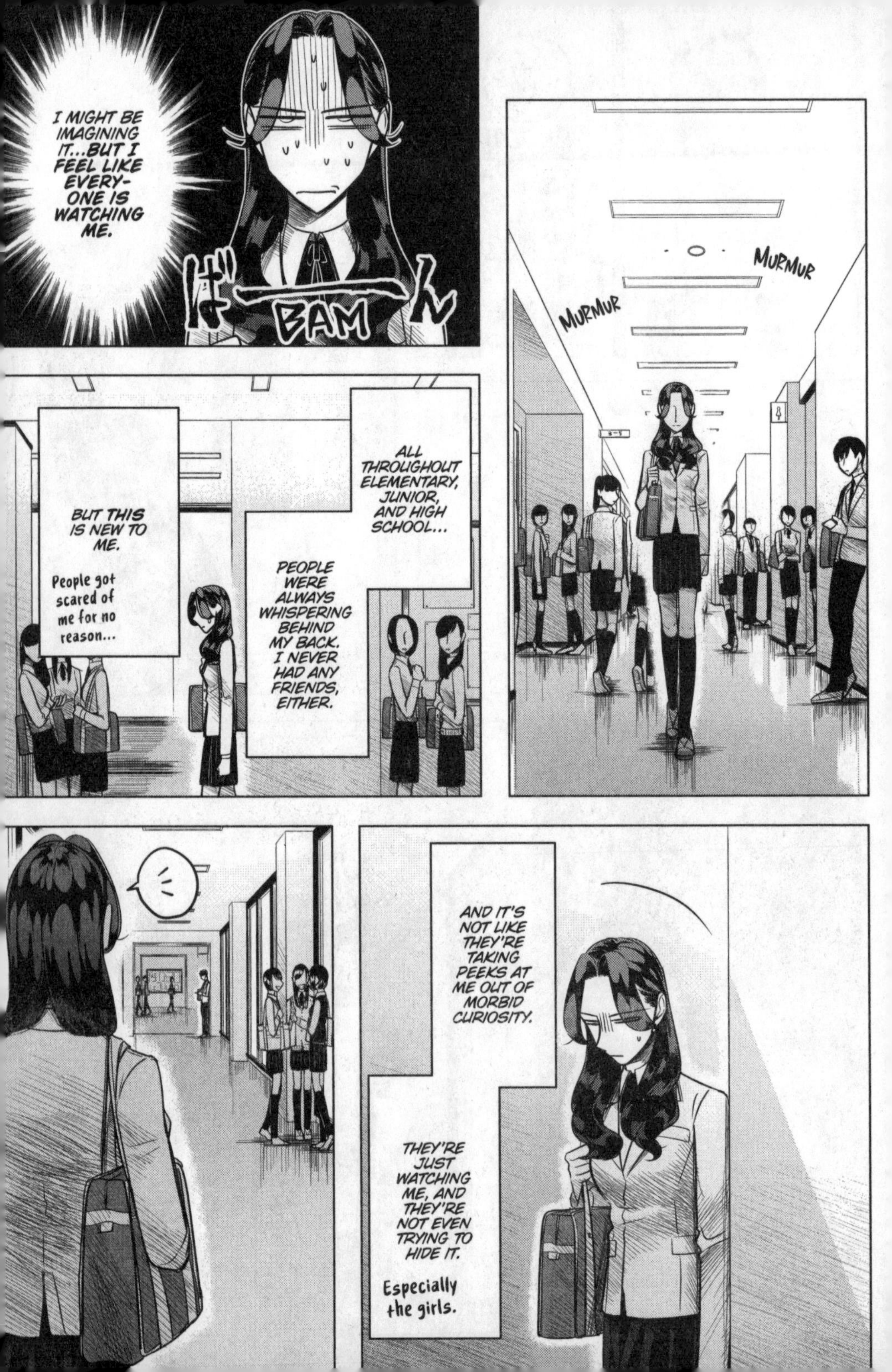

MURMUR
MURMUR
I MIGHT BE IMAGINING IT...BUT I FEEL LIKE EVERY-ONE IS WATCHING ME.
ば一ん
BAM
ALL THROUGHOUT ELEMENTARY, JUNIOR, AND HIGH SCHOOL...
PEOPLE WERE ALWAYS WHISPERING BEHIND MY BACK. I NEVER HAD ANY FRIENDS, EITHER.
BUT THIS IS NEW TO ME.
People got scared of me for no reason...
AND IT'S NOT LIKE THEY'RE TAKING PEEKS AT ME OUT OF MORBID CURIOSITY.
THEY'RE JUST WATCHING ME, AND THEY'RE NOT EVEN TRYING TO HIDE IT.
Especially the girls.

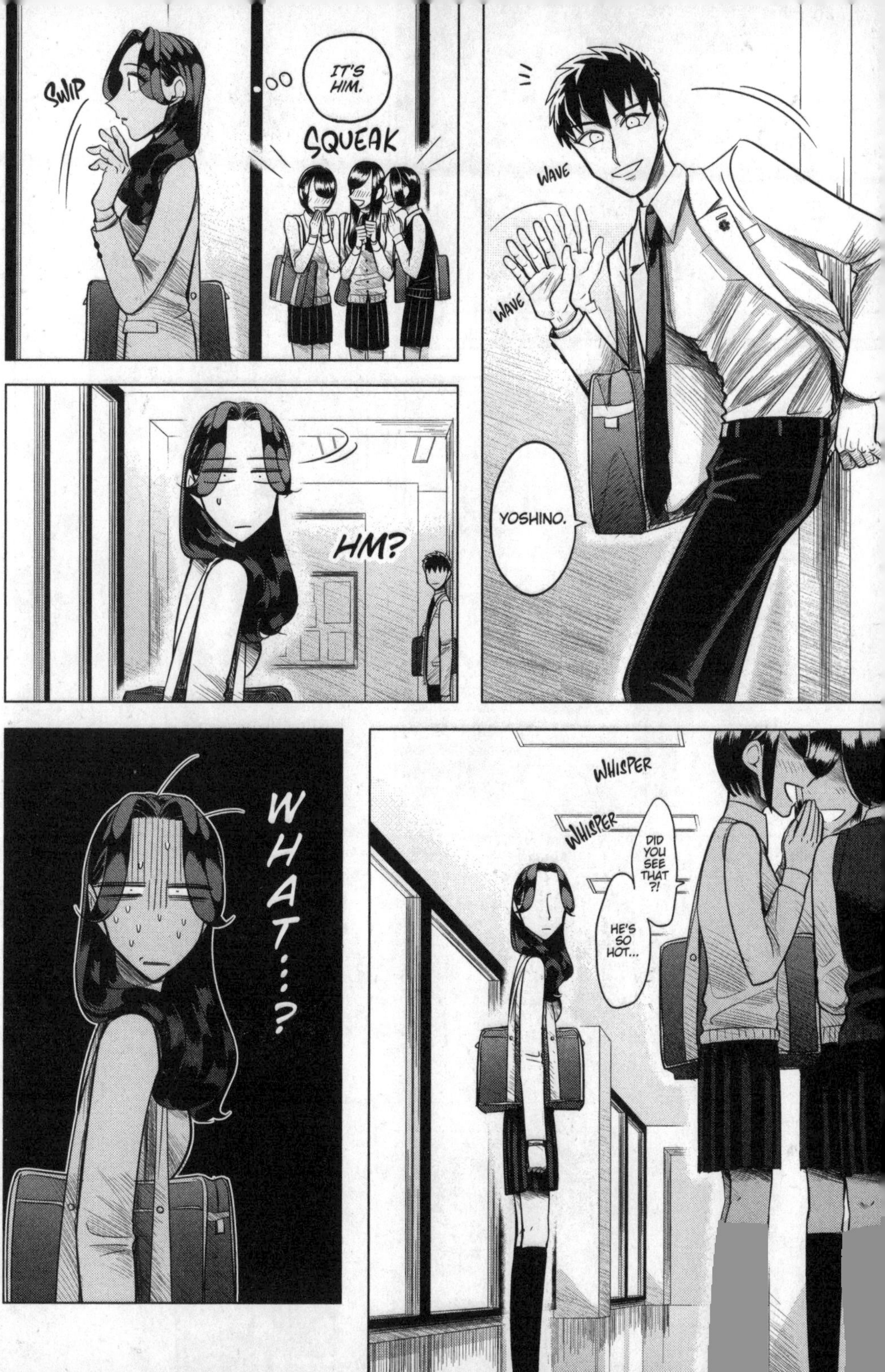

WAVE
WAVE
YOSHINO.
IT'S HIM.
SQUEAK
SWIP
HM?
WHISPER
WHISPER
DID YOU SEE THAT?!
HE'S SO HOT...
WHAT...?

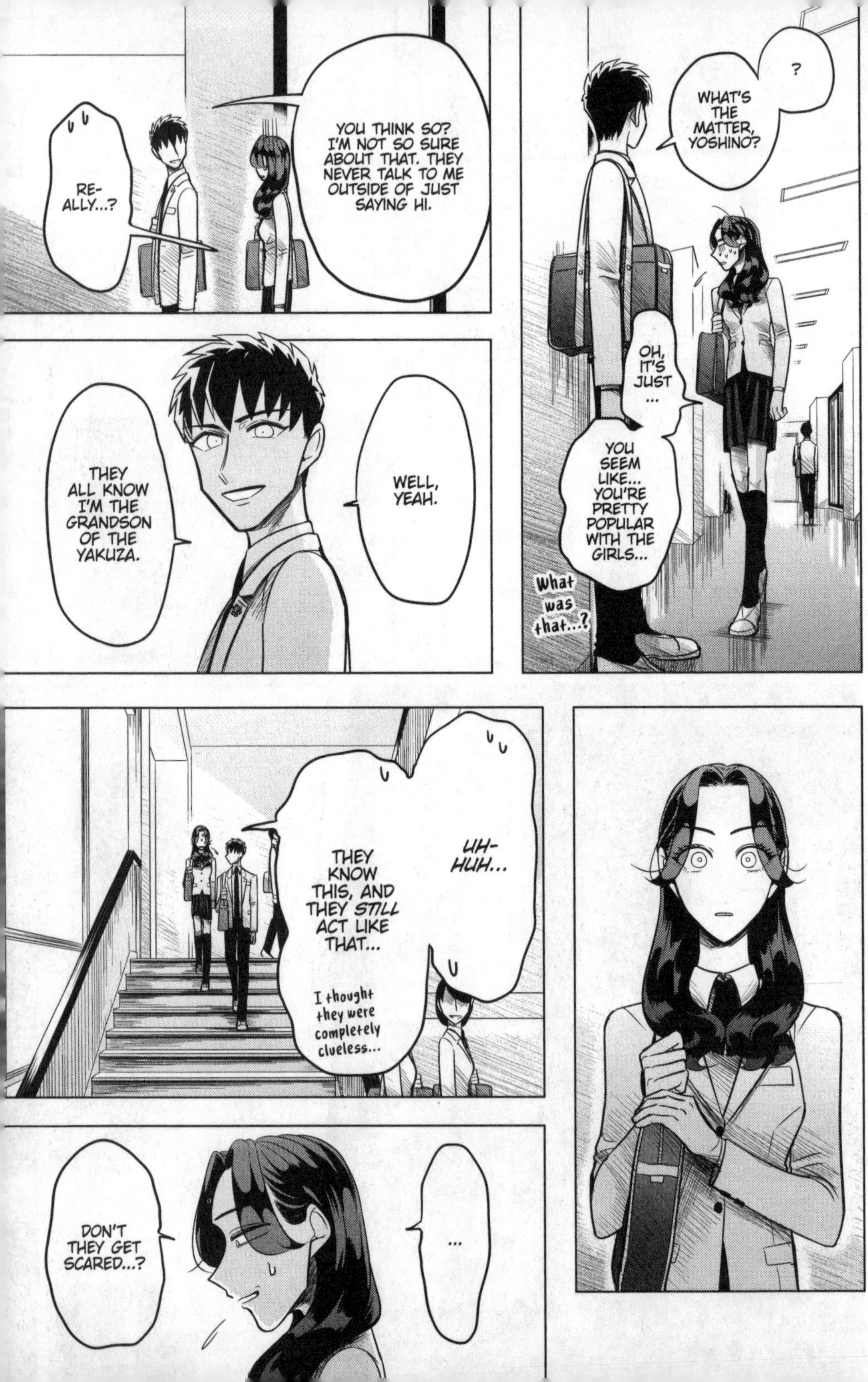
?
WHAT'S THE MATTER, YOSHINO?
OH, IT'S JUST ...
YOU SEEM LIKE... YOU'RE PRETTY POPULAR WITH THE GIRLS...
What was that...?
YOU THINK SO? I'M NOT SO SURE ABOUT THAT. THEY NEVER TALK TO ME OUTSIDE OF JUST SAYING HI.
RE-ALLY...?
WELL, YEAH.
THEY ALL KNOW I'M THE GRANDSON OF THE YAKUZA.
UH-HUH...
THEY KNOW THIS, AND THEY *STILL* ACT LIKE THAT...
I thought they were completely clueless...
...
DON'T THEY GET SCARED...?

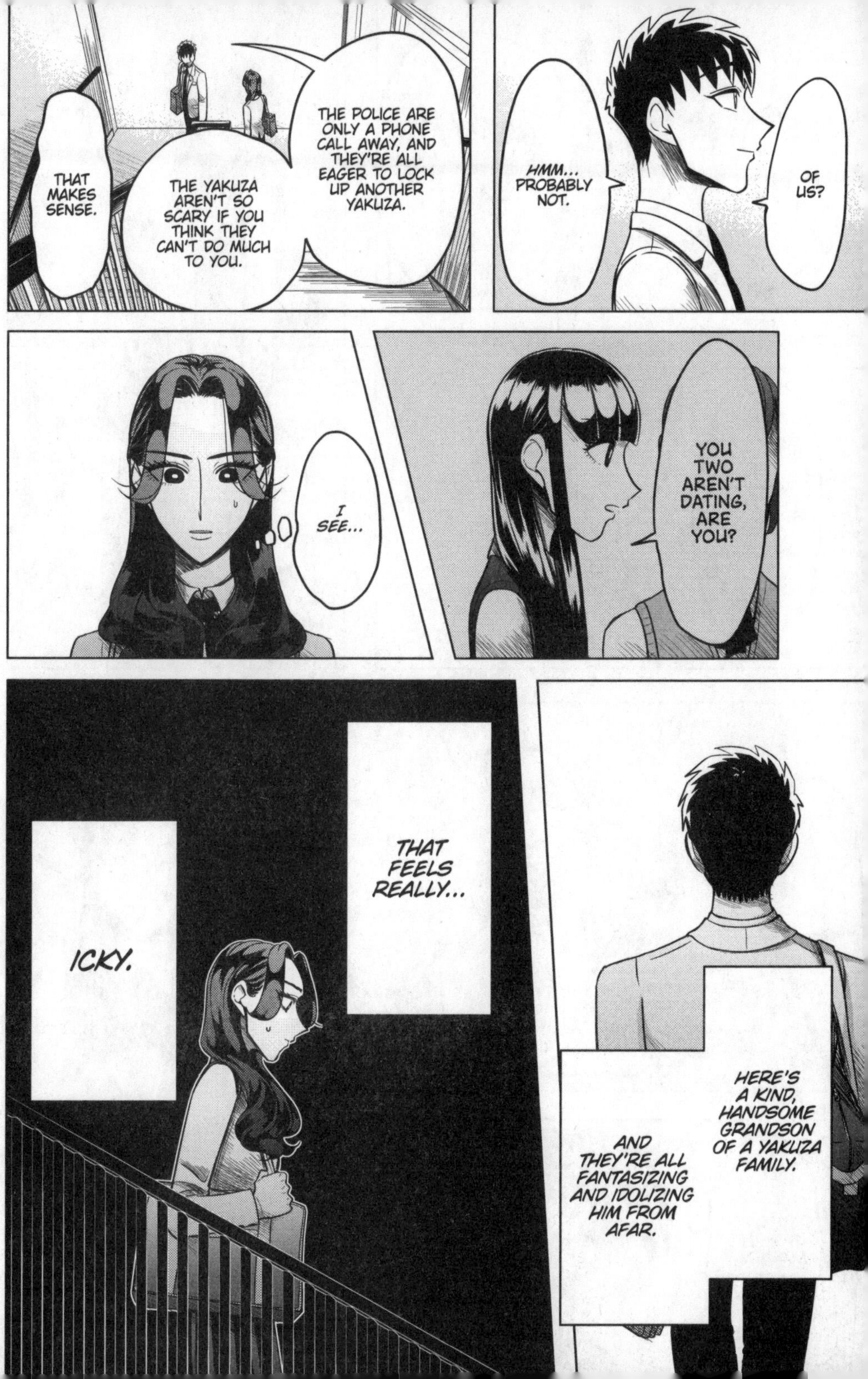
OF US?
HMM... PROBABLY NOT.
THE POLICE ARE ONLY A PHONE CALL AWAY, AND THEY'RE ALL EAGER TO LOCK UP ANOTHER YAKUZA.
THE YAKUZA AREN'T SO SCARY IF YOU THINK THEY CAN'T DO MUCH TO YOU.
THAT MAKES SENSE.
YOU TWO AREN'T DATING, ARE YOU?
I SEE...
HERE'S A KIND, HANDSOME GRANDSON OF A YAKUZA FAMILY.
AND THEY'RE ALL FANTASIZING AND IDOLIZING HIM FROM AFAR.
THAT FEELS REALLY...
ICKY.

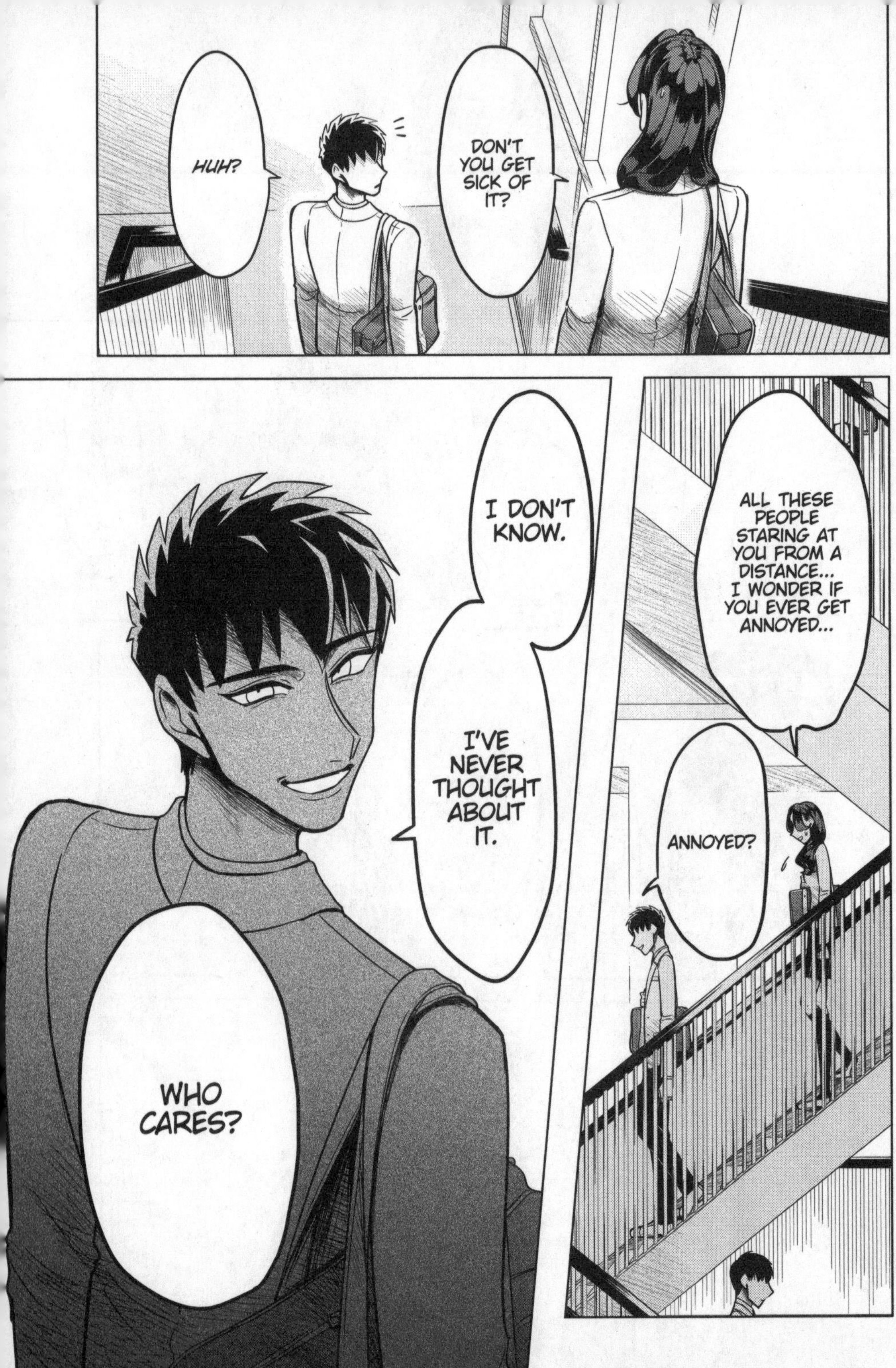
DON'T YOU GET SICK OF IT?
HUH?
ALL THESE PEOPLE STARING AT YOU FROM A DISTANCE... I WONDER IF YOU EVER GET ANNOYED...
ANNOYED?
I DON'T KNOW.
I'VE NEVER THOUGHT ABOUT IT.
WHO CARES?

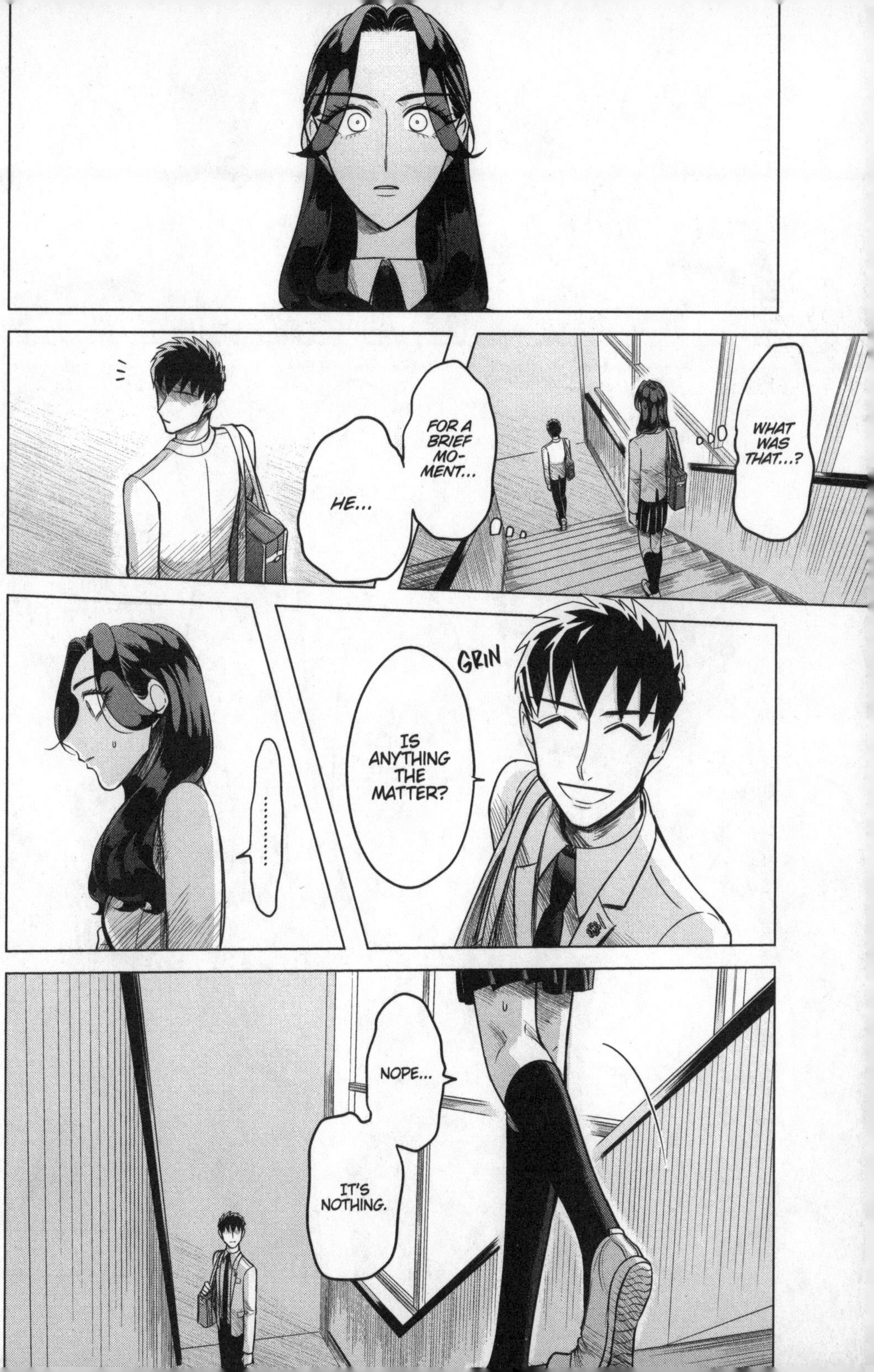
WHAT WAS THAT...?
FOR A BRIEF MO-MENT...
HE...
GRIN
IS ANYTHING THE MATTER?
......
NOPE...
IT'S NOTHING.

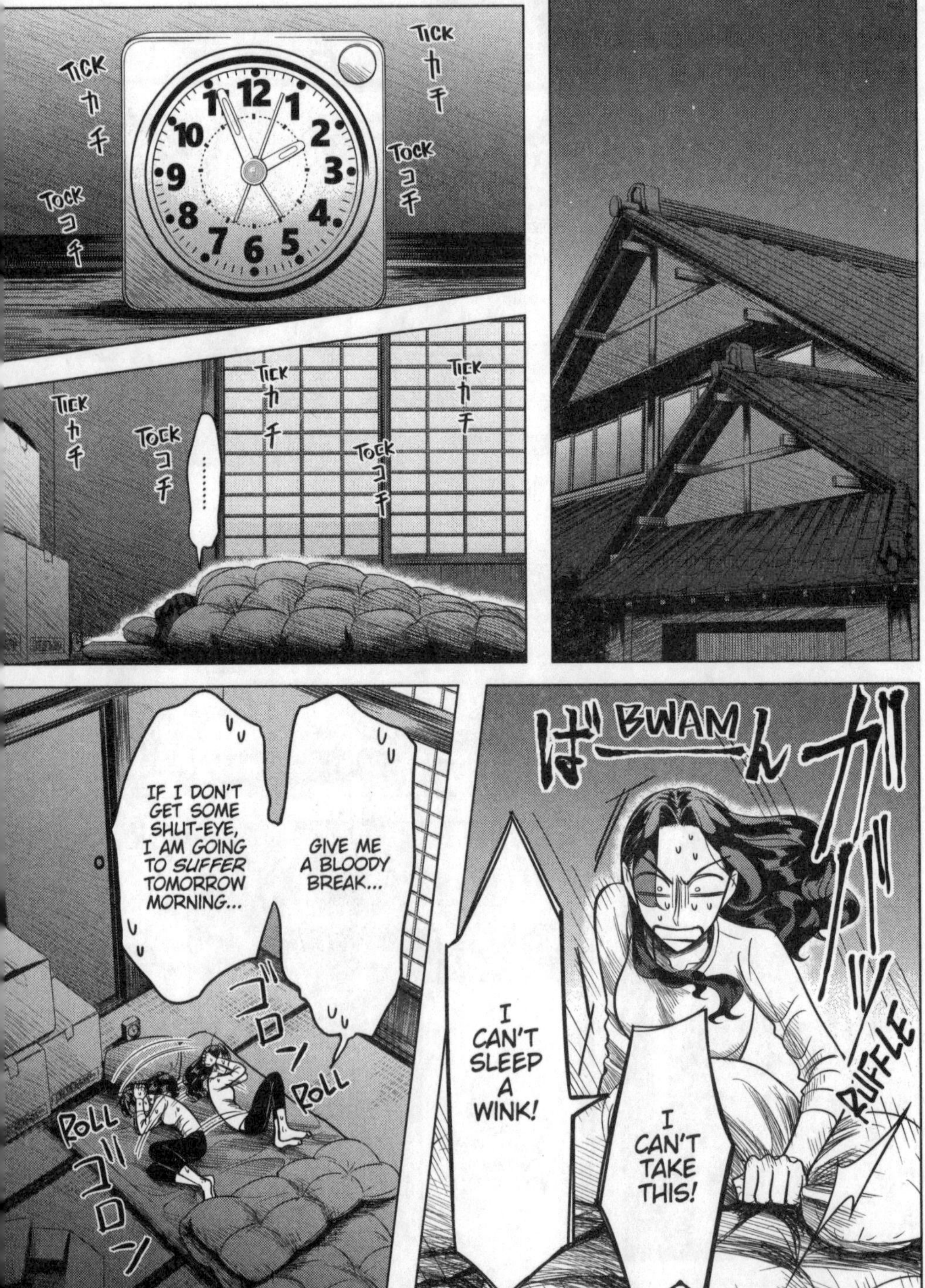
TICK
カチ
TOCK
コチ
TICK
カチ
TOCK
コチ
TICK
カチ
TOCK
コチ
TICK
カチ
......
TOCK
コチ
TICK
カチ
ば一ーん BWAM
ガバ
RUFFLE
I CAN'T TAKE THIS!
I CAN'T SLEEP A WINK!
GIVE ME A BLOODY BREAK...
IF I DON'T GET SOME SHUT-EYE, I AM GOING TO SUFFER TOMORROW MORNING...
ゴローン ROLL
ROLL ゴロン

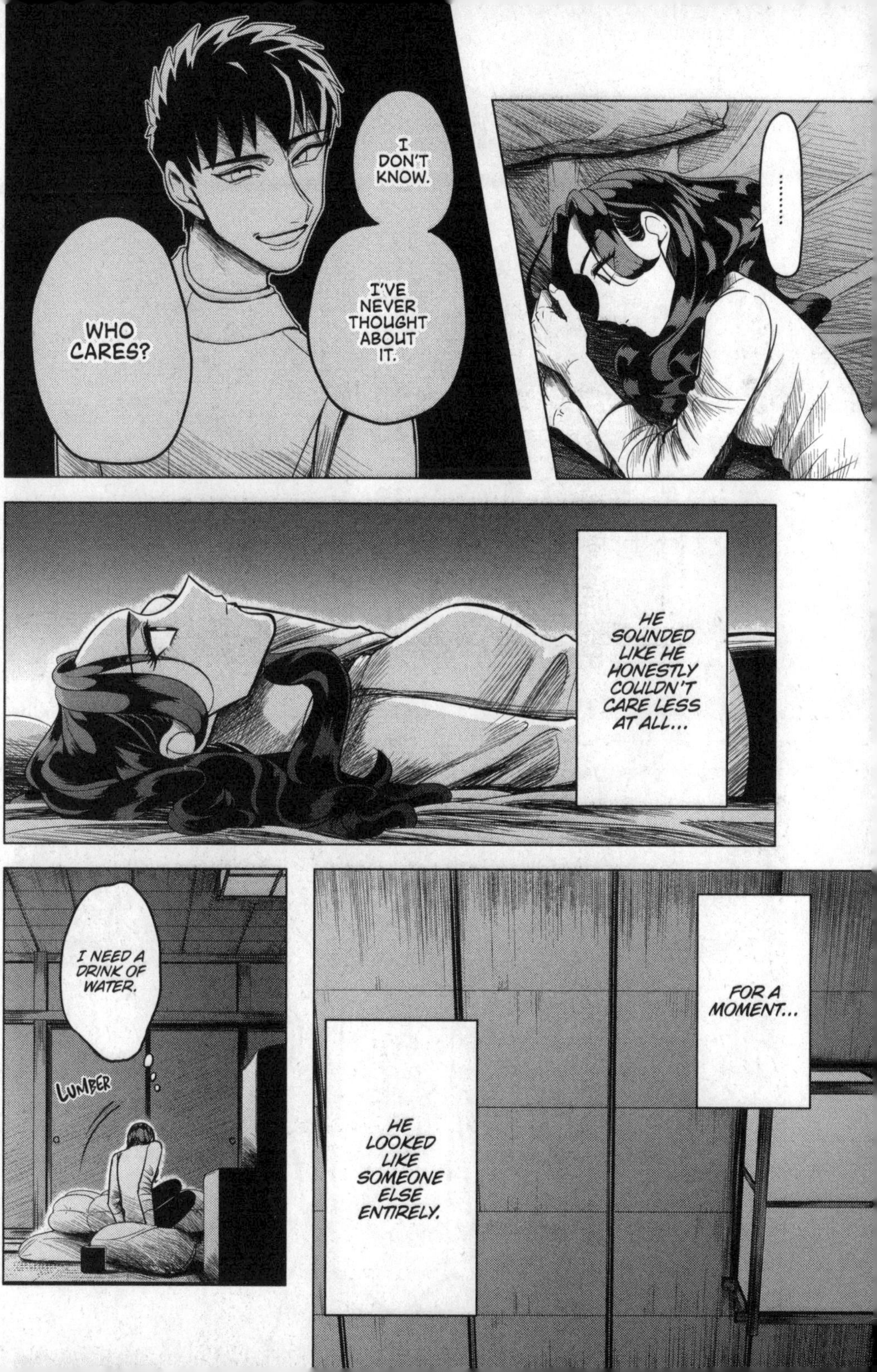
……
I DON'T KNOW.
I'VE NEVER THOUGHT ABOUT IT.
WHO CARES?
HE SOUNDED LIKE HE HONESTLY COULDN'T CARE LESS AT ALL…
FOR A MOMENT…
HE LOOKED LIKE SOMEONE ELSE ENTIRELY.
I NEED A DRINK OF WATER.
LUMBER

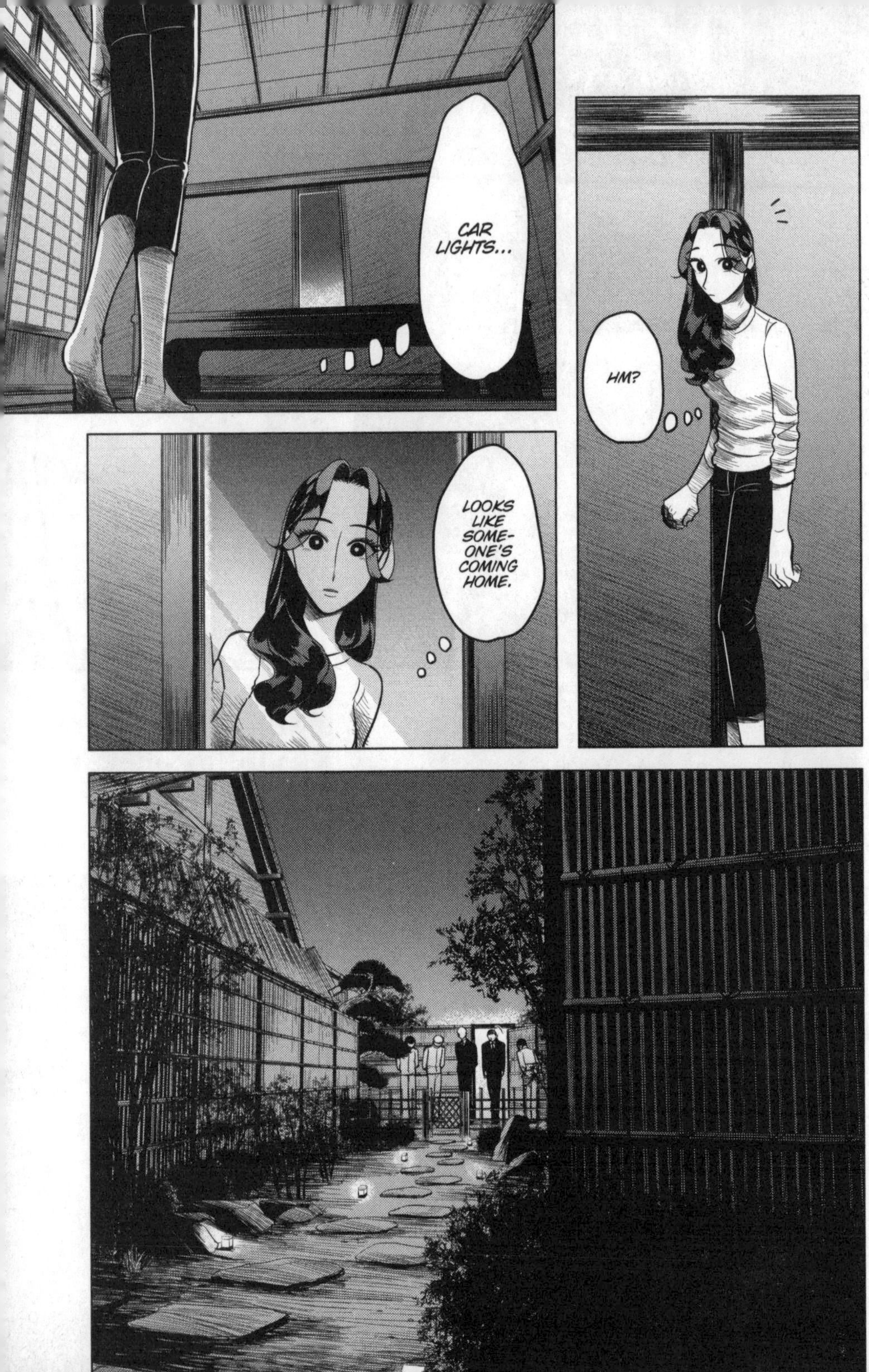
HM?
CAR LIGHTS...
LOOKS LIKE SOME-ONE'S COMING HOME.

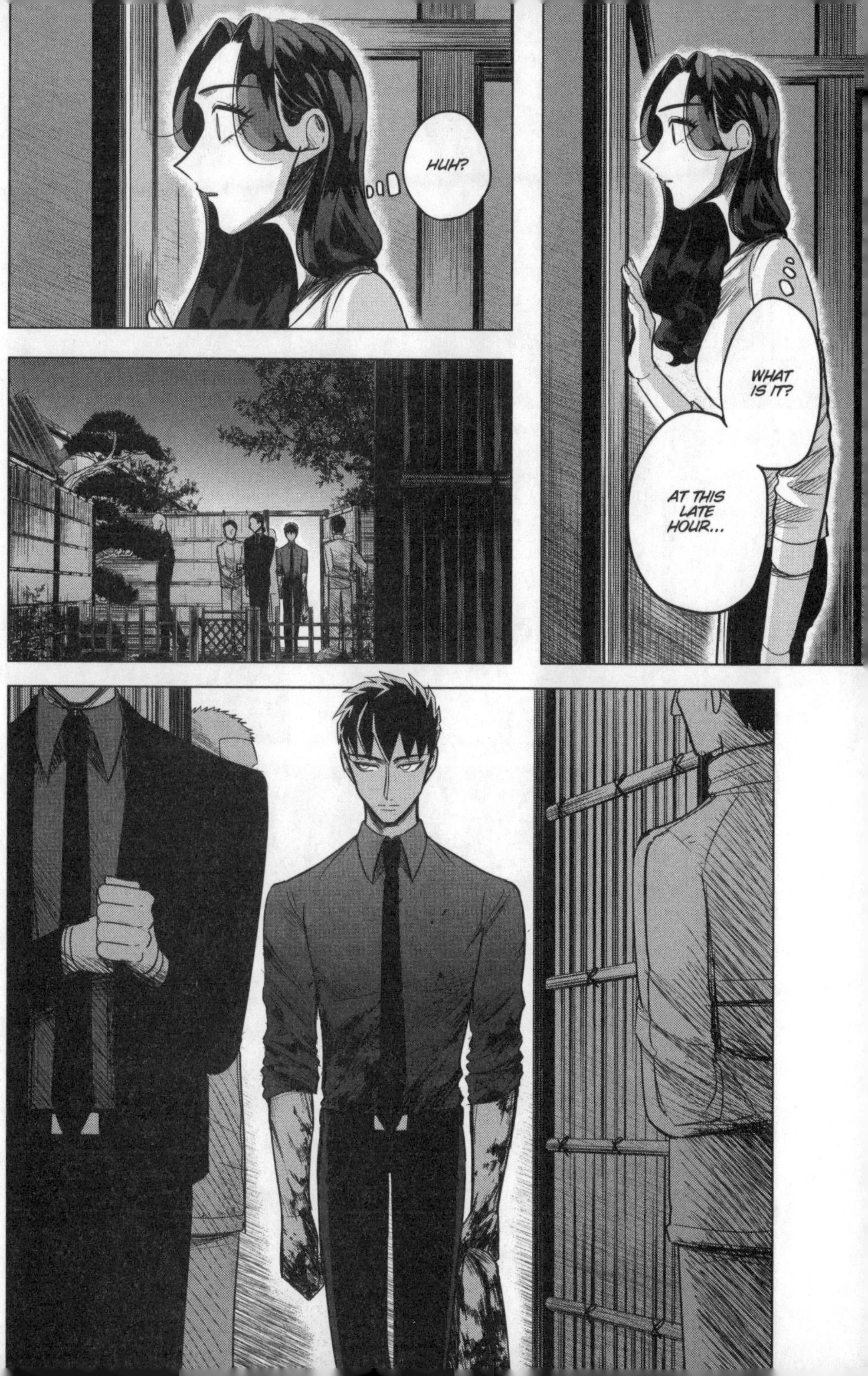
WHAT IS IT?
AT THIS LATE HOUR...
HUH?

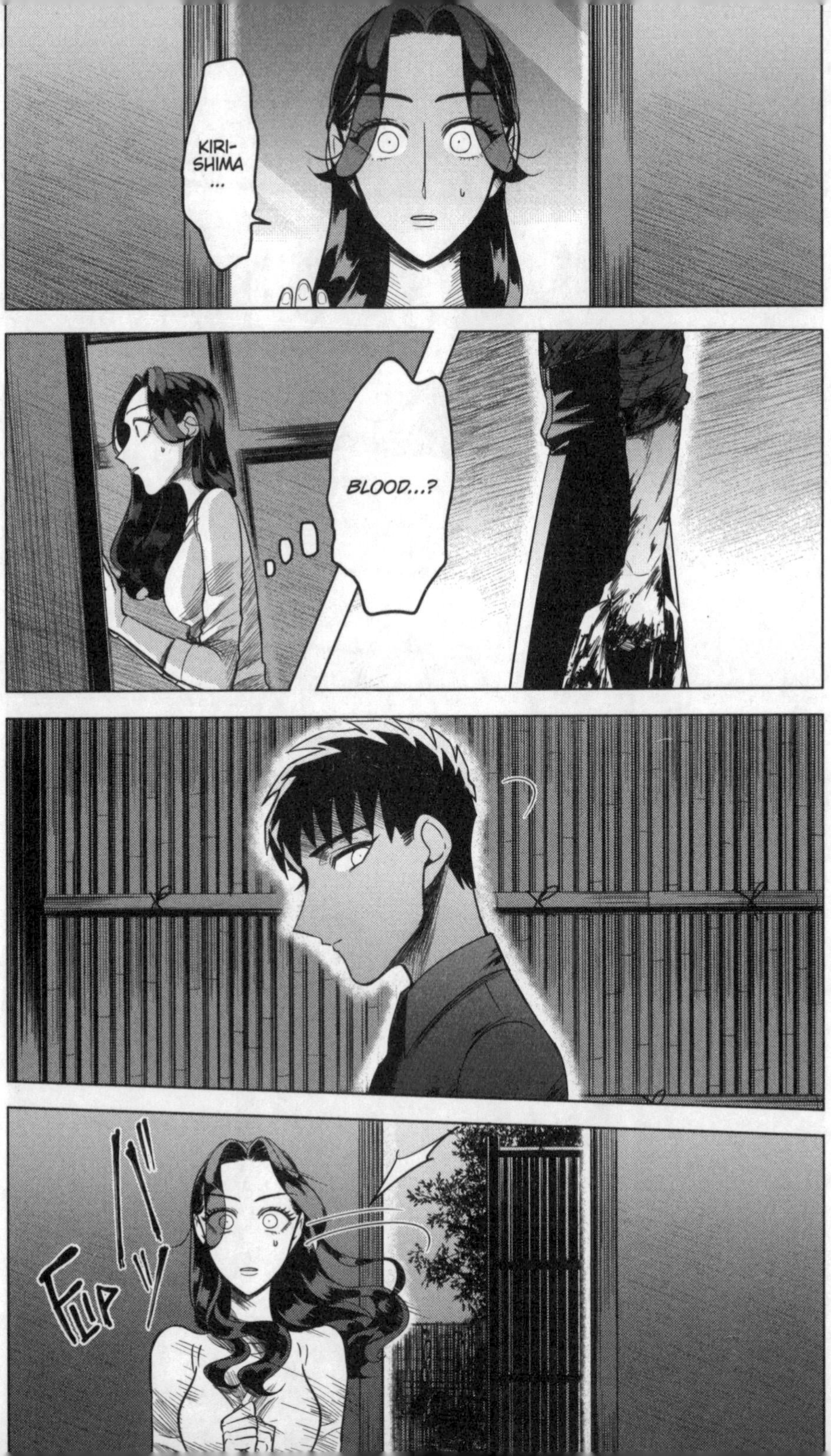
KIRI-SHIMA ...
BLOOD...?
バッ
FLIP

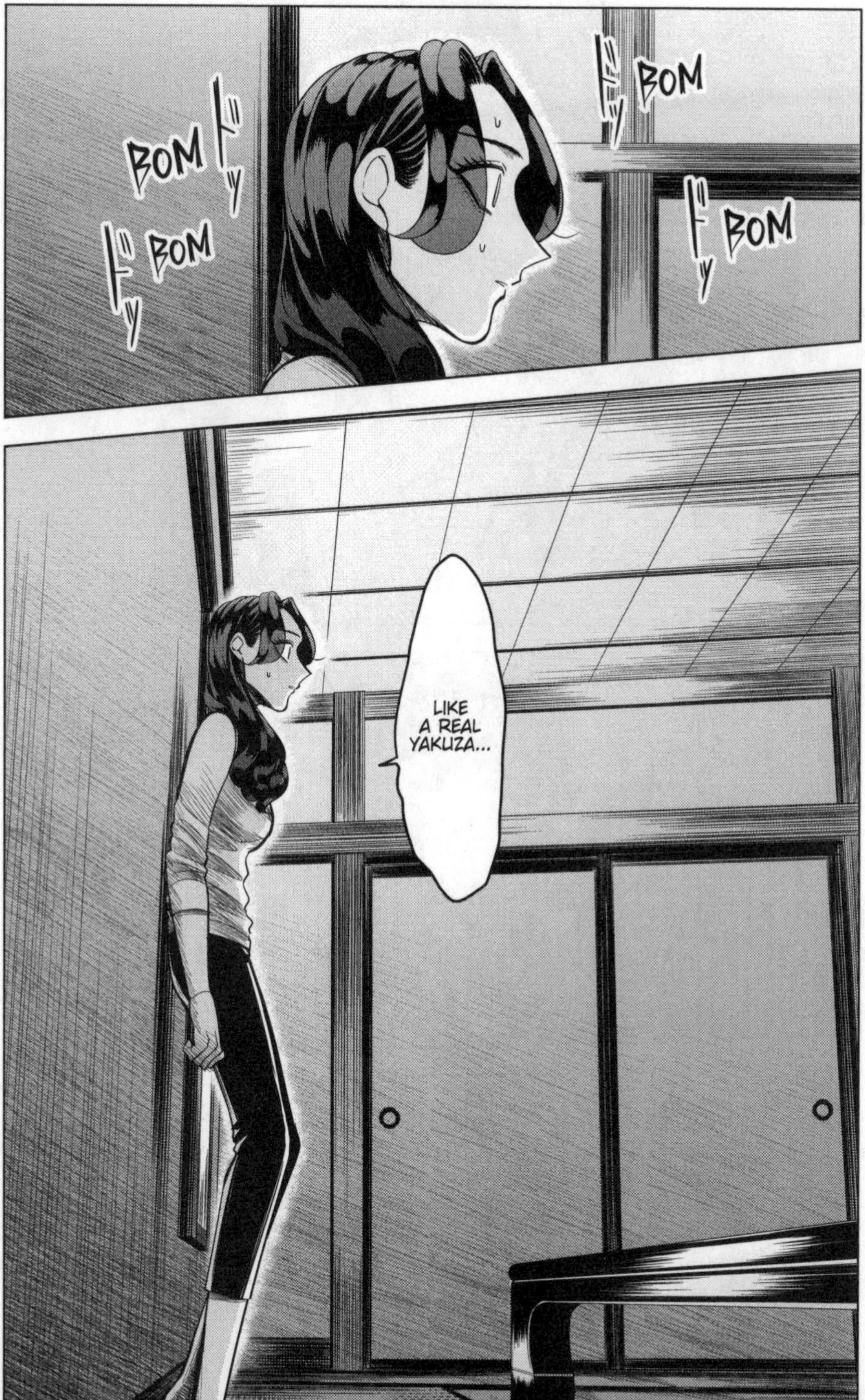
ドッ BOM
ドッ BOM
BOM ドッ
ドッ BOM
LIKE A REAL YAKUZA...

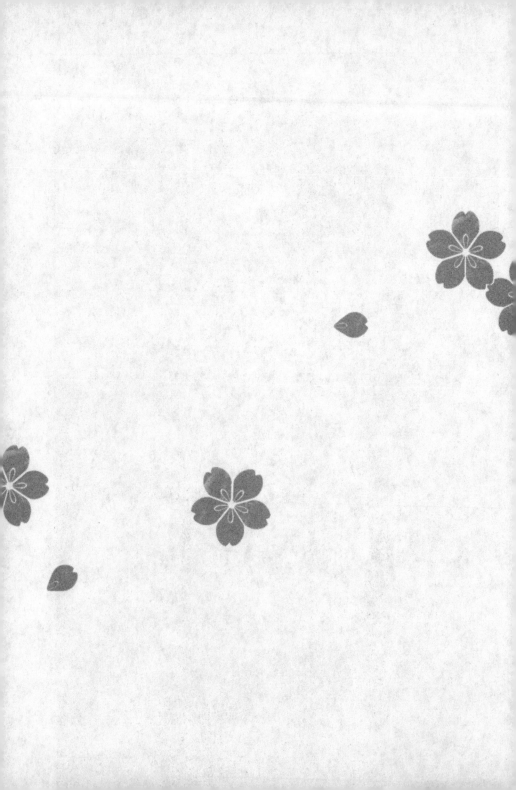

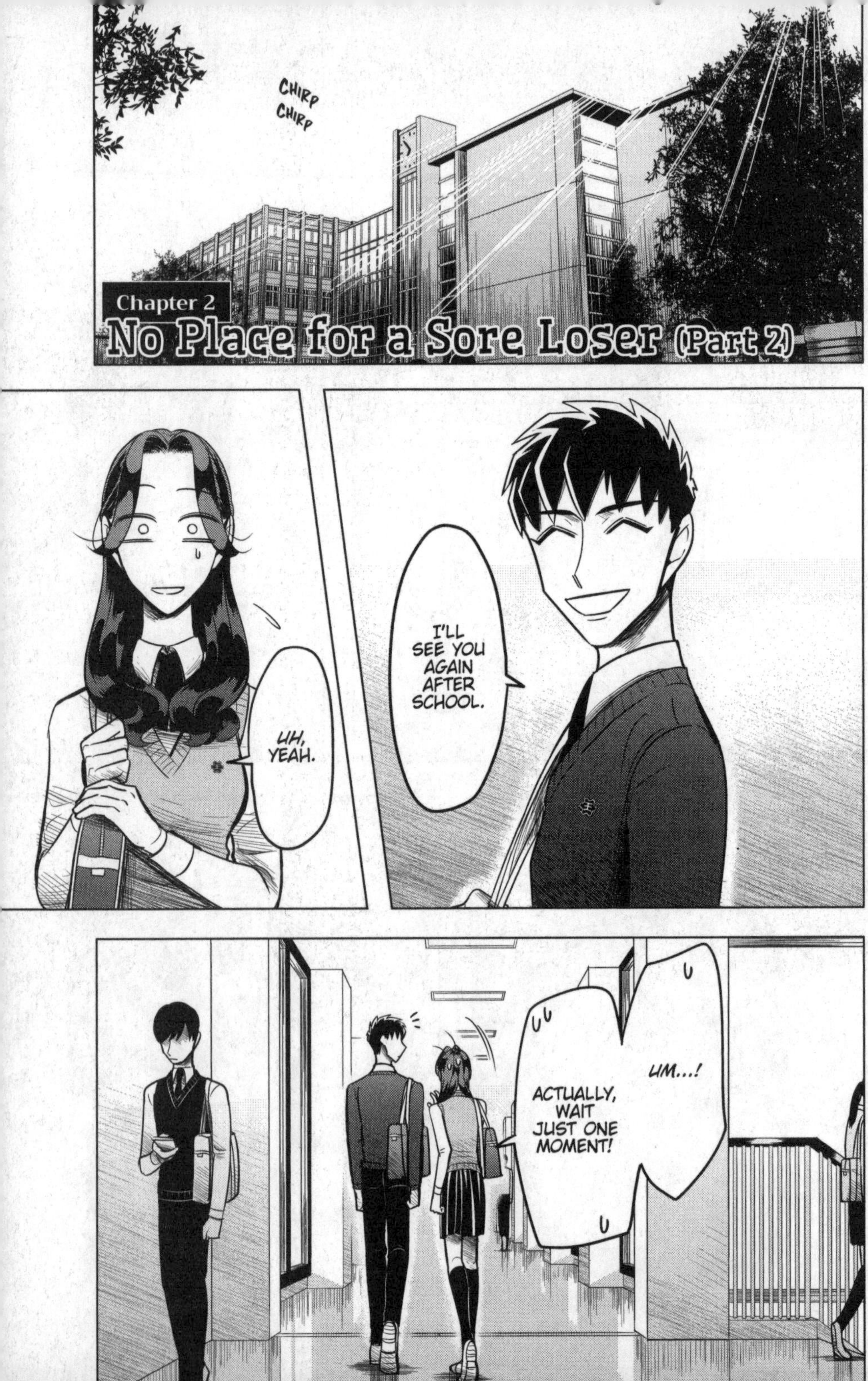
CHIRP
CHIRP
Chapter 2
No Place for a Sore Loser (Part 2)
I'LL SEE YOU AGAIN AFTER SCHOOL.
UH, YEAH.
UM...!
ACTUALLY, WAIT JUST ONE MOMENT!

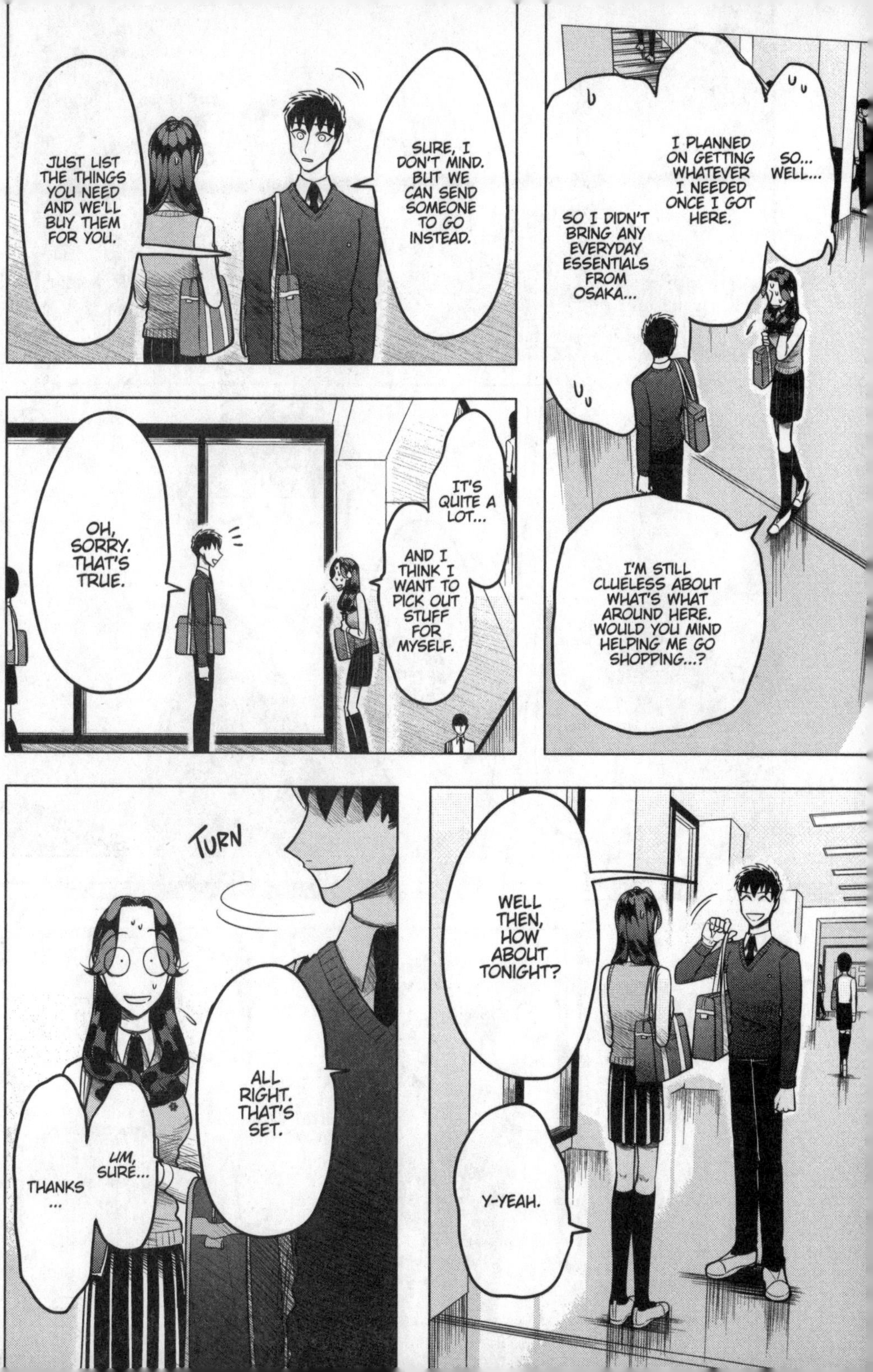
SO... WELL...
I PLANNED ON GETTING WHATEVER I NEEDED ONCE I GOT HERE.
SO I DIDN'T BRING ANY EVERYDAY ESSENTIALS FROM OSAKA...
I'M STILL CLUELESS ABOUT WHAT'S WHAT AROUND HERE. WOULD YOU MIND HELPING ME GO SHOPPING...?
SURE, I DON'T MIND. BUT WE CAN SEND SOMEONE TO GO INSTEAD.
JUST LIST THE THINGS YOU NEED AND WE'LL BUY THEM FOR YOU.
IT'S QUITE A LOT...
AND I THINK I WANT TO PICK OUT STUFF FOR MYSELF.
OH, SORRY. THAT'S TRUE.
WELL THEN, HOW ABOUT TONIGHT?
Y-YEAH.
TURN
ALL RIGHT. THAT'S SET.
UM, SURE...
THANKS ...

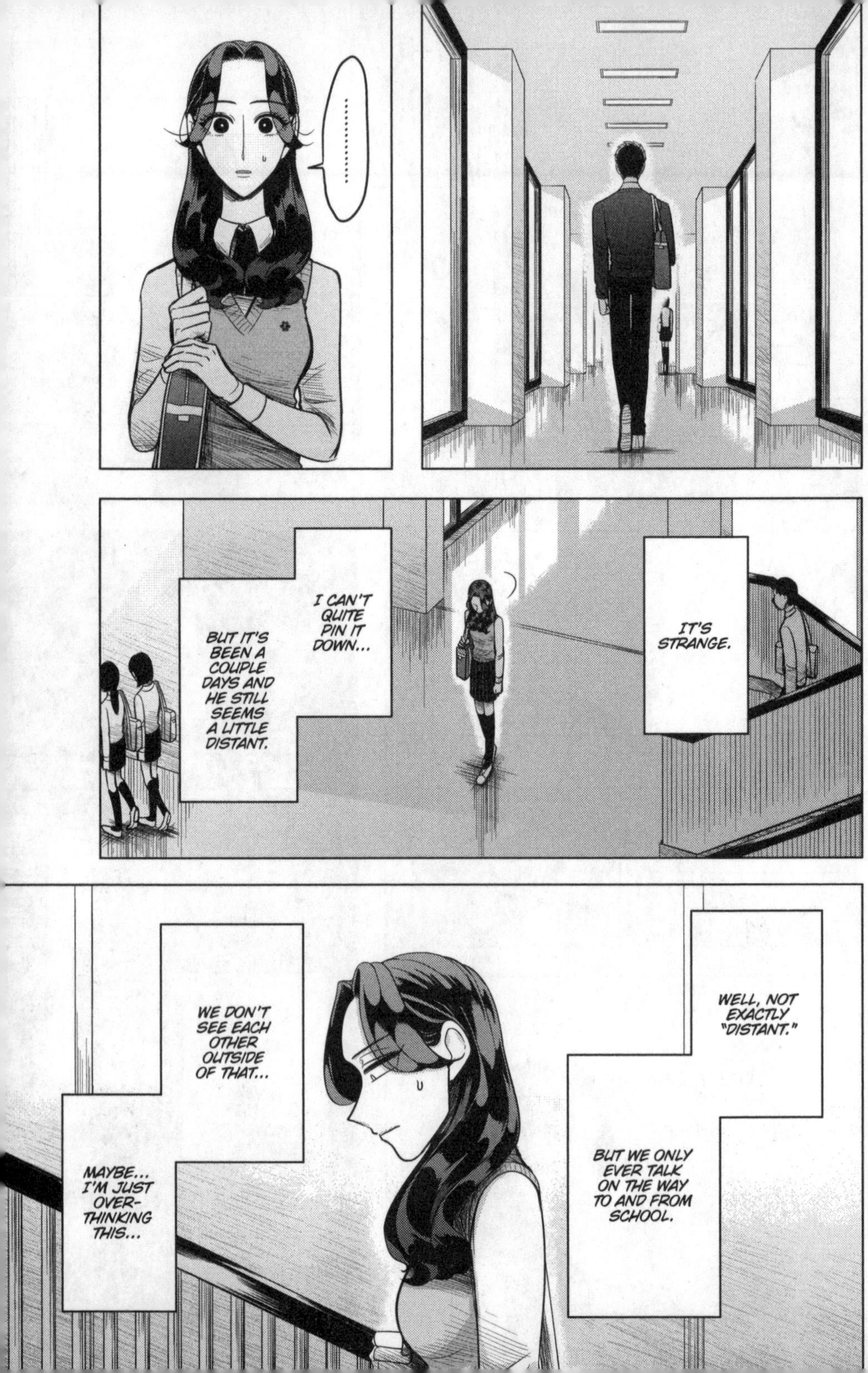
......
IT'S STRANGE.
I CAN'T QUITE PIN IT DOWN...
BUT IT'S BEEN A COUPLE DAYS AND HE STILL SEEMS A LITTLE DISTANT.
WELL, NOT EXACTLY "DISTANT."
BUT WE ONLY EVER TALK ON THE WAY TO AND FROM SCHOOL.
WE DON'T SEE EACH OTHER OUTSIDE OF THAT...
MAYBE... I'M JUST OVER-THINKING THIS...

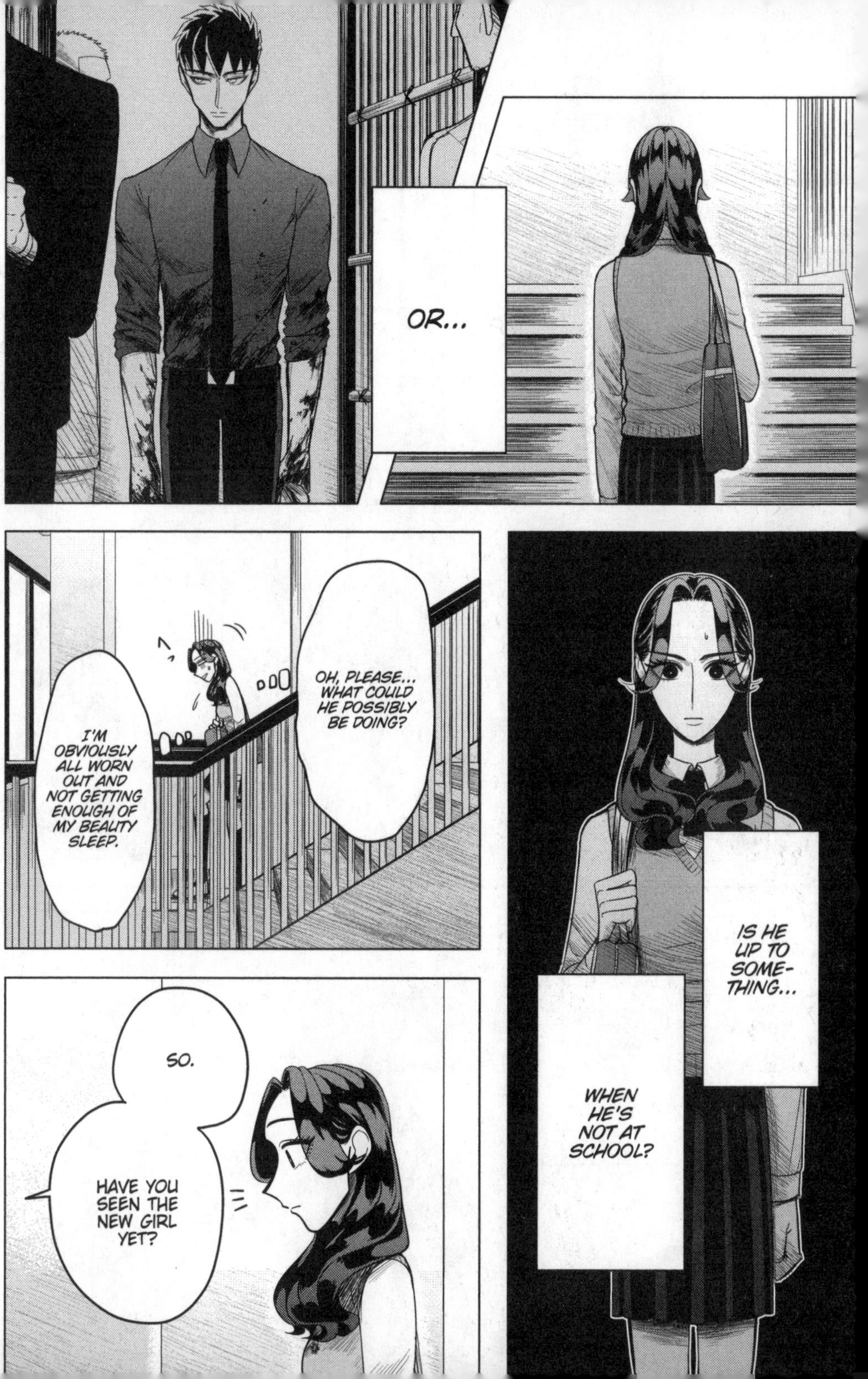
OR...
IS HE UP TO SOMETHING...
WHEN HE'S NOT AT SCHOOL?
OH, PLEASE... WHAT COULD HE POSSIBLY BE DOING?
I'M OBVIOUSLY ALL WORN OUT AND NOT GETTING ENOUGH OF MY BEAUTY SLEEP.
SO.
HAVE YOU SEEN THE NEW GIRL YET?

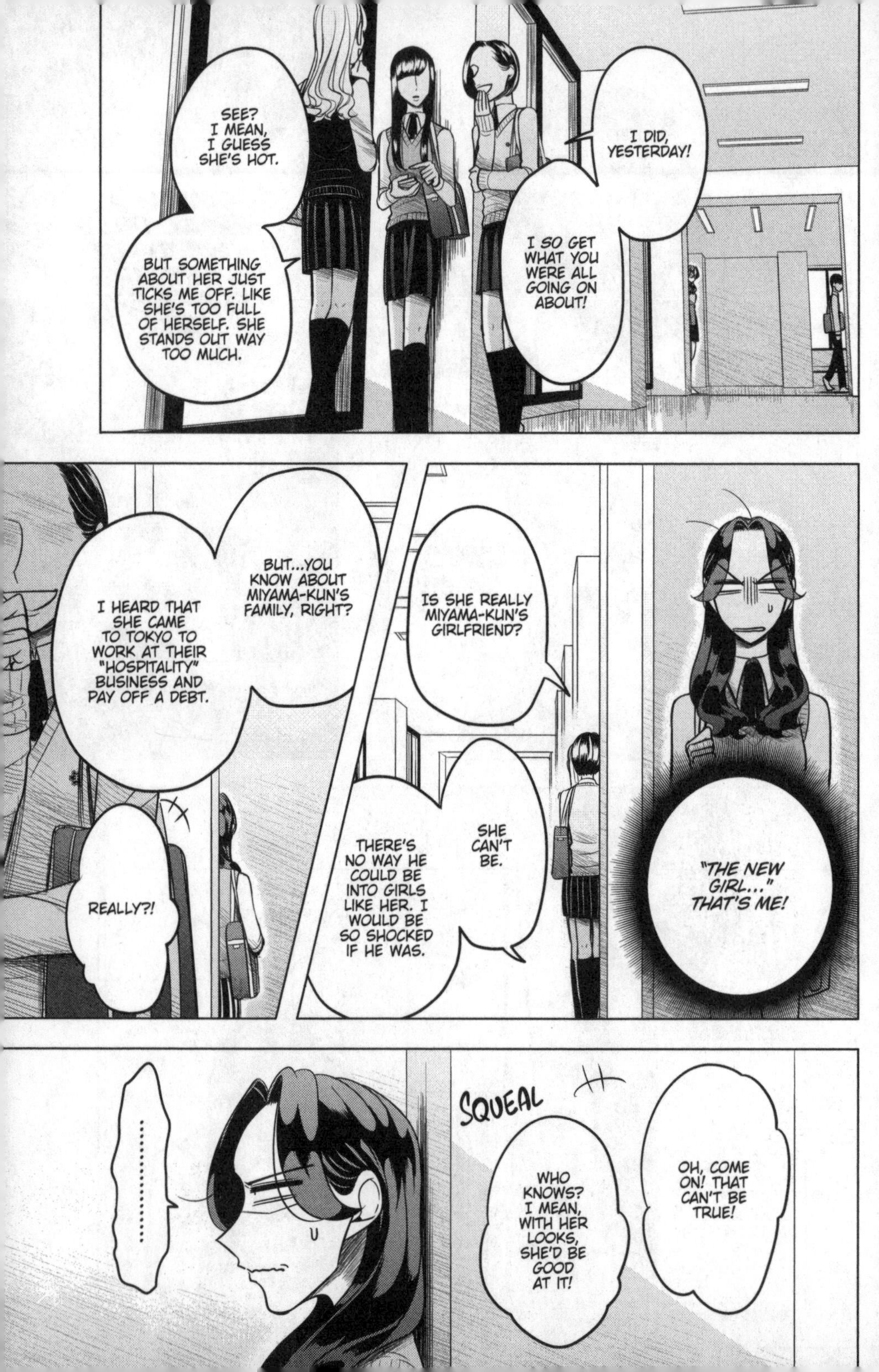
I DID, YESTERDAY!
I SO GET WHAT YOU WERE ALL GOING ON ABOUT!
SEE? I MEAN, I GUESS SHE'S HOT.
BUT SOMETHING ABOUT HER JUST TICKS ME OFF. LIKE SHE'S TOO FULL OF HERSELF. SHE STANDS OUT WAY TOO MUCH.
"THE NEW GIRL..." THAT'S ME!
IS SHE REALLY MIYAMA-KUN'S GIRLFRIEND?
SHE CAN'T BE.
THERE'S NO WAY HE COULD BE INTO GIRLS LIKE HER. I WOULD BE SO SHOCKED IF HE WAS.
BUT...YOU KNOW ABOUT MIYAMA-KUN'S FAMILY, RIGHT?
I HEARD THAT SHE CAME TO TOKYO TO WORK AT THEIR "HOSPITALITY" BUSINESS AND PAY OFF A DEBT.
REALLY?!
OH, COME ON! THAT CAN'T BE TRUE!
SQUEAL
WHO KNOWS? I MEAN, WITH HER LOOKS, SHE'D BE GOOD AT IT!
......

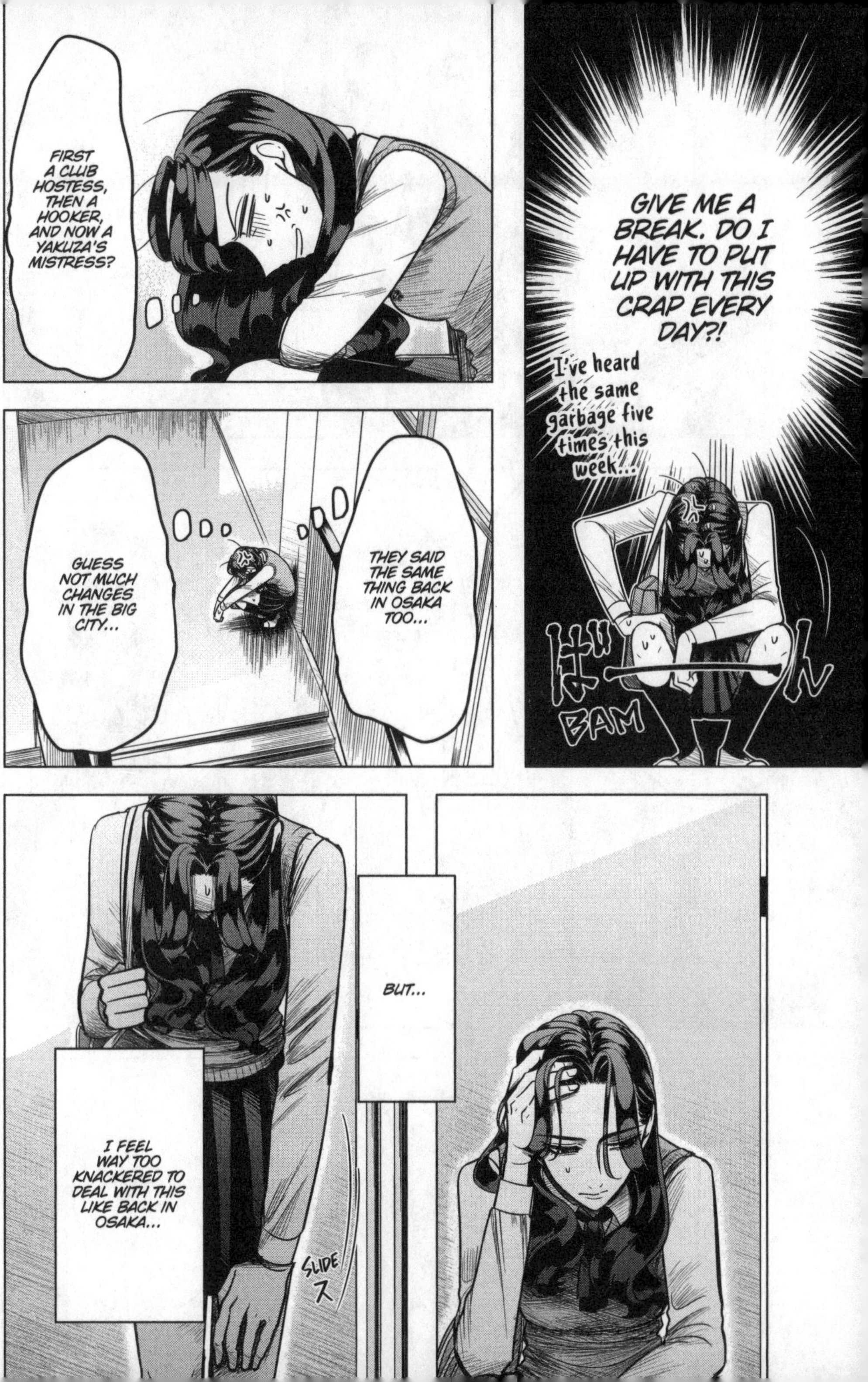
GIVE ME A BREAK. DO I HAVE TO PUT UP WITH THIS CRAP EVERY DAY?!
I've heard the same garbage five times this week...
BAM
FIRST A CLUB HOSTESS, THEN A HOOKER, AND NOW A YAKUZA'S MISTRESS?
THEY SAID THE SAME THING BACK IN OSAKA TOO...
GUESS NOT MUCH CHANGES IN THE BIG CITY...
BUT...
I FEEL WAY TOO KNACKERED TO DEAL WITH THIS LIKE BACK IN OSAKA...
SLIDE
ス

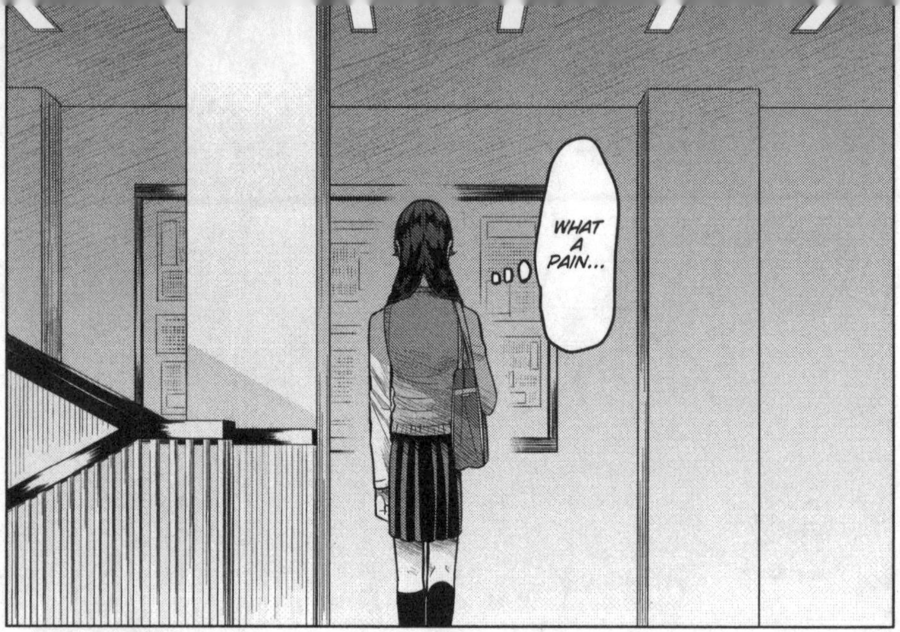
WHAT A PAIN...

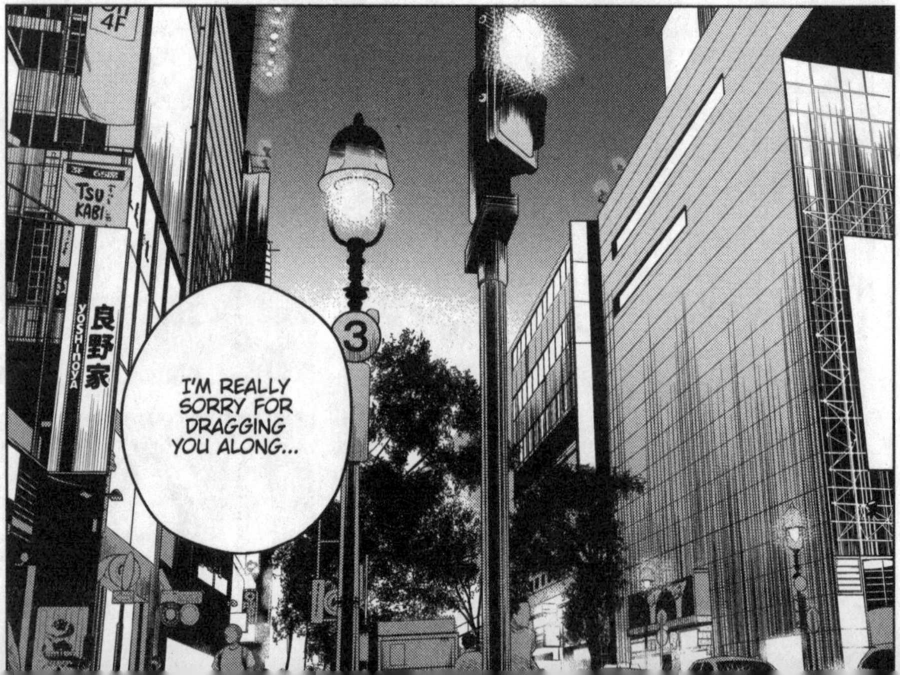
I'M REALLY SORRY FOR DRAGGING YOU ALONG...
4F
TSU KABI
良野家
YOSHINOYA
3

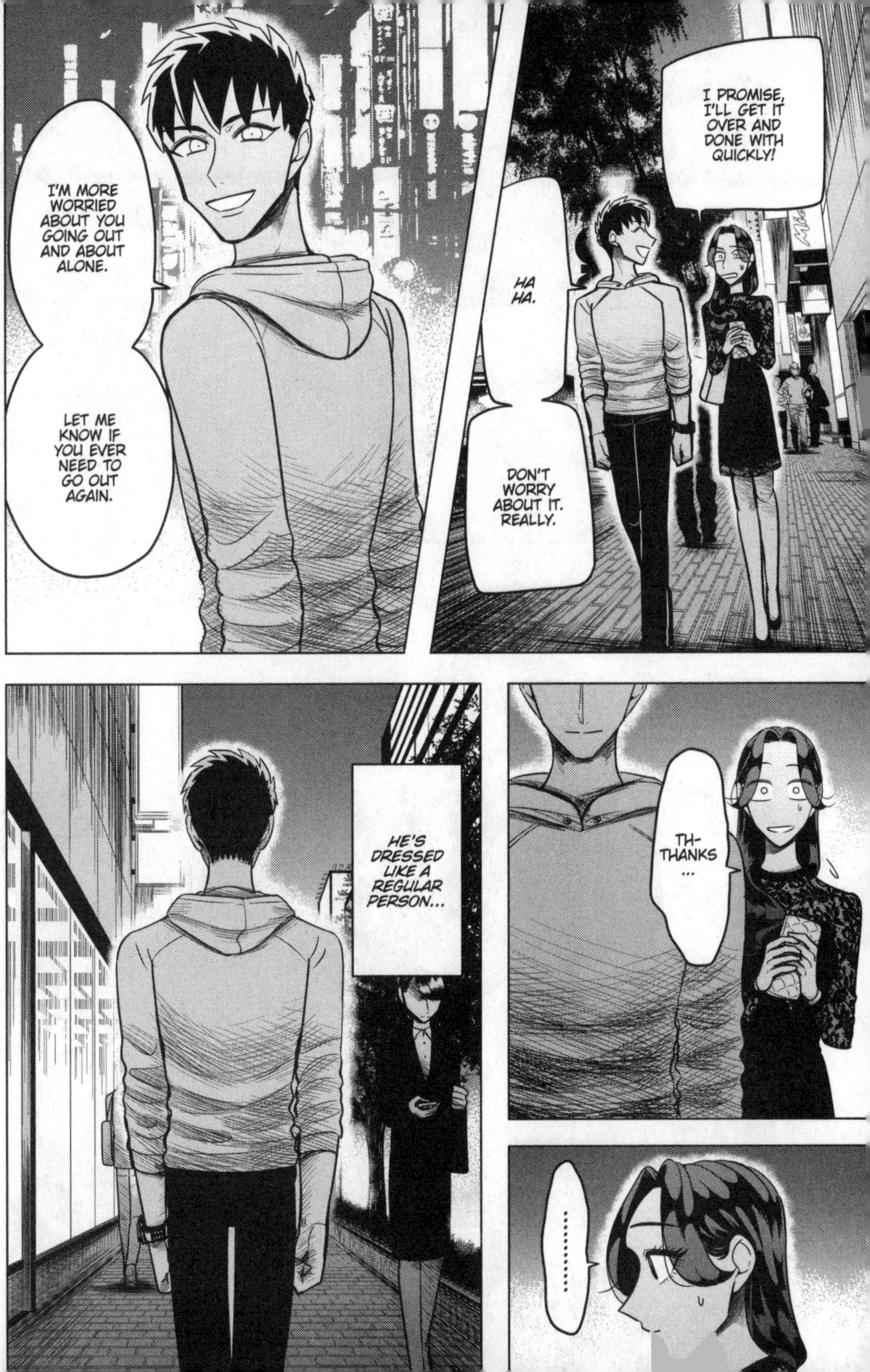
I PROMISE, I'LL GET IT OVER AND DONE WITH QUICKLY!
HA HA.
DON'T WORRY ABOUT IT. REALLY.
I'M MORE WORRIED ABOUT YOU GOING OUT AND ABOUT ALONE.
LET ME KNOW IF YOU EVER NEED TO GO OUT AGAIN.
TH-THANKS...
......
HE'S DRESSED LIKE A REGULAR PERSON...

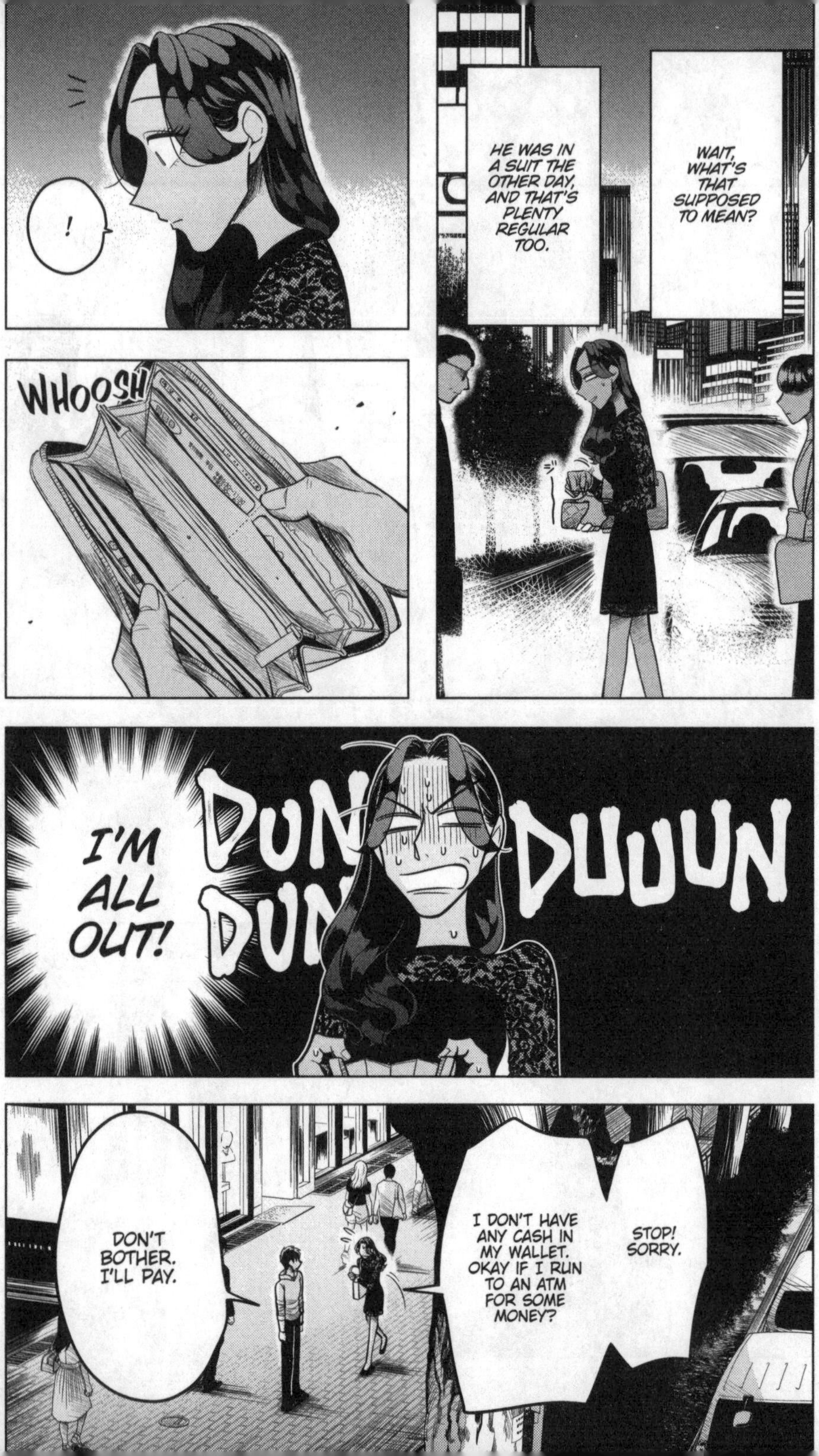
WAIT, WHAT'S THAT SUPPOSED TO MEAN?
HE WAS IN A SUIT THE OTHER DAY, AND THAT'S PLENTY REGULAR TOO.
!
WHOOSH
DUN DUN DUUUN
I'M ALL OUT!
STOP! SORRY.
I DON'T HAVE ANY CASH IN MY WALLET. OKAY IF I RUN TO AN ATM FOR SOME MONEY?
DON'T BOTHER. I'LL PAY.

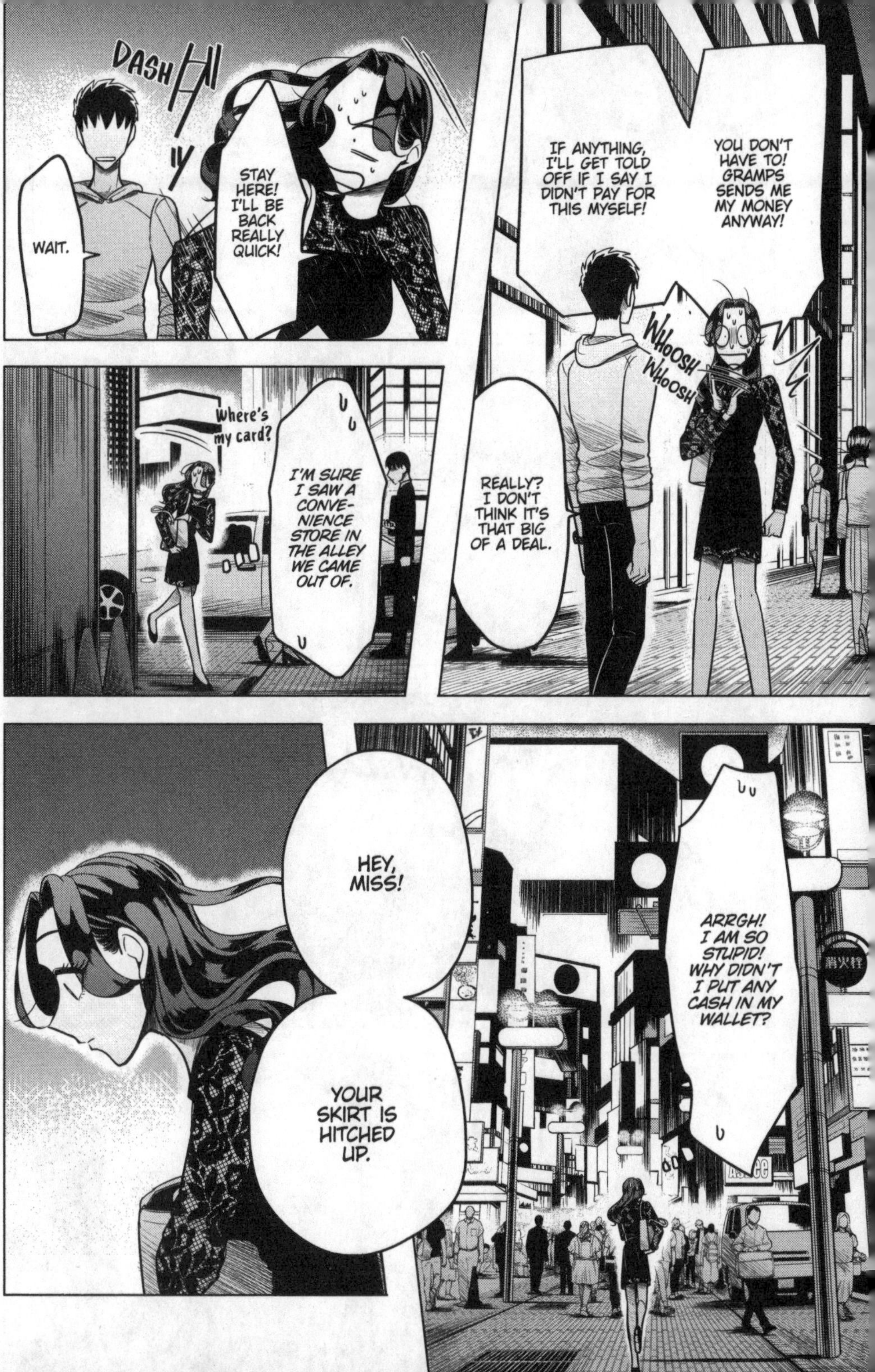
YOU DON'T HAVE TO! GRAMPS SENDS ME MY MONEY ANYWAY!
IF ANYTHING, I'LL GET TOLD OFF IF I SAY I DIDN'T PAY FOR THIS MYSELF!
WHOOSH WHOOSH
REALLY? I DON'T THINK IT'S THAT BIG OF A DEAL.
DASH
STAY HERE! I'LL BE BACK REALLY QUICK!
WAIT.
I'M SURE I SAW A CONVE-NIENCE STORE IN THE ALLEY WE CAME OUT OF.
Where's my card?
ARRGH! I AM SO STUPID! WHY DIDN'T I PUT ANY CASH IN MY WALLET?
HEY, MISS!
YOUR SKIRT IS HITCHED UP.

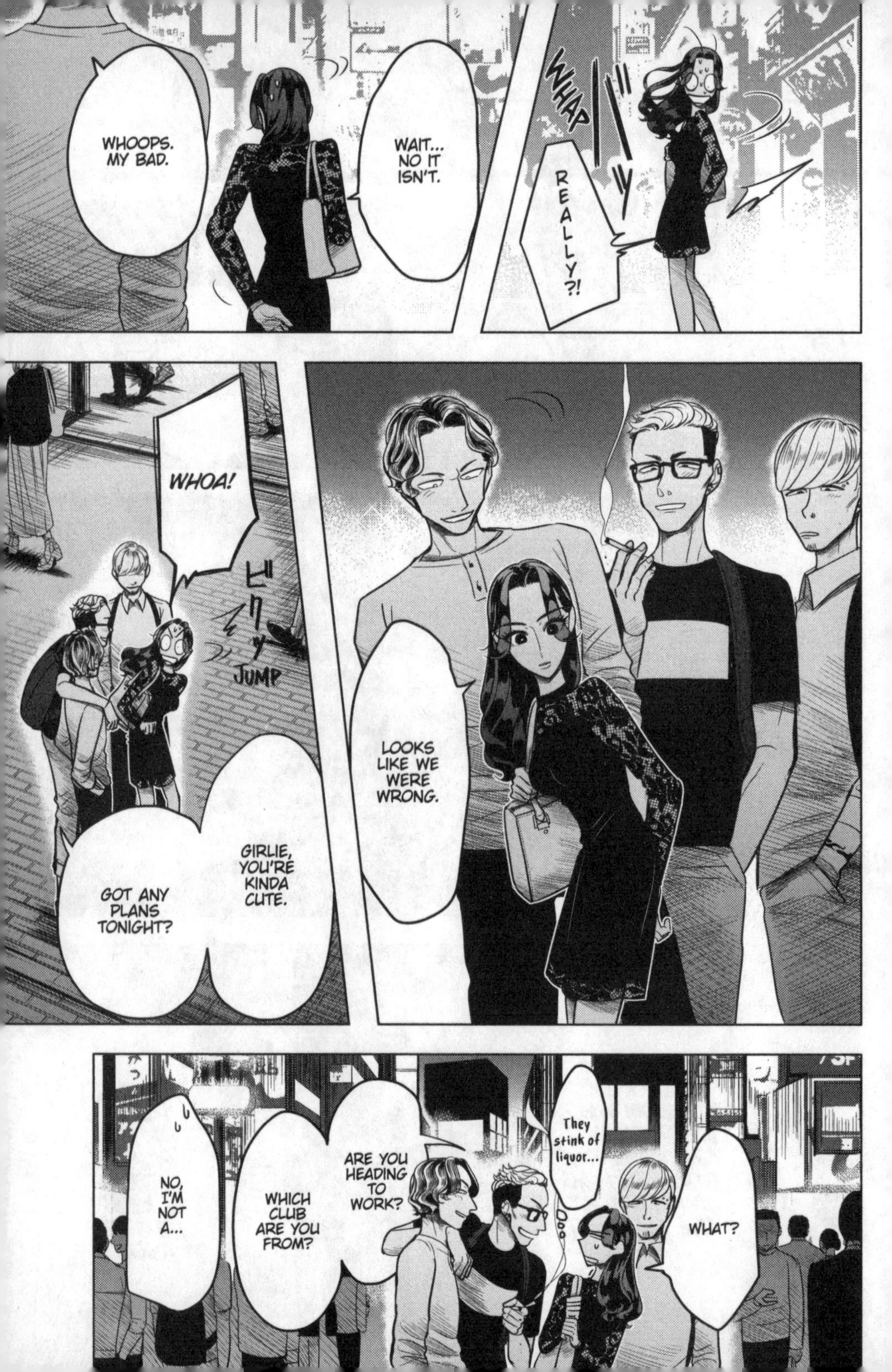
WHAP
REALLY?!
WAIT... NO IT ISN'T.
WHOOPS. MY BAD.
LOOKS LIKE WE WERE WRONG.
WHOA!
ビクッ
JUMP
GIRLIE, YOU'RE KINDA CUTE.
GOT ANY PLANS TONIGHT?
WHAT?
They stink of liquor...
ARE YOU HEADING TO WORK?
WHICH CLUB ARE YOU FROM?
NO, I'M NOT A...

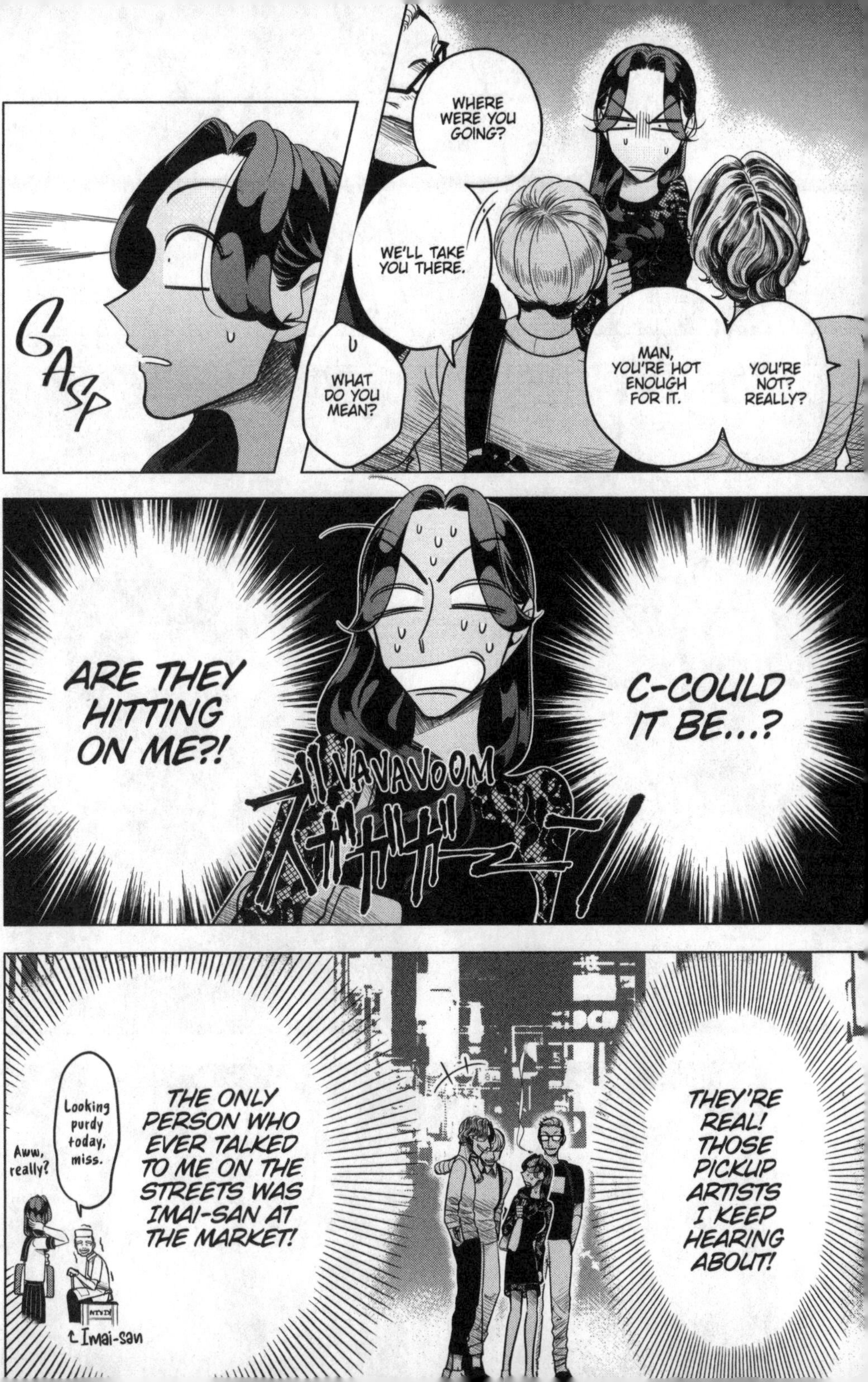
WHERE WERE YOU GOING?
WE'LL TAKE YOU THERE.
WHAT DO YOU MEAN?
YOU'RE NOT? REALLY?
MAN, YOU'RE HOT ENOUGH FOR IT.
GASP
C-COULD IT BE...?
ARE THEY HITTING ON ME?!
VAVAVOOM
THEY'RE REAL! THOSE PICKUP ARTISTS I KEEP HEARING ABOUT!
THE ONLY PERSON WHO EVER TALKED TO ME ON THE STREETS WAS IMAI-SAN AT THE MARKET!
Looking purdy today, miss.
Aww, really?
Imai-san

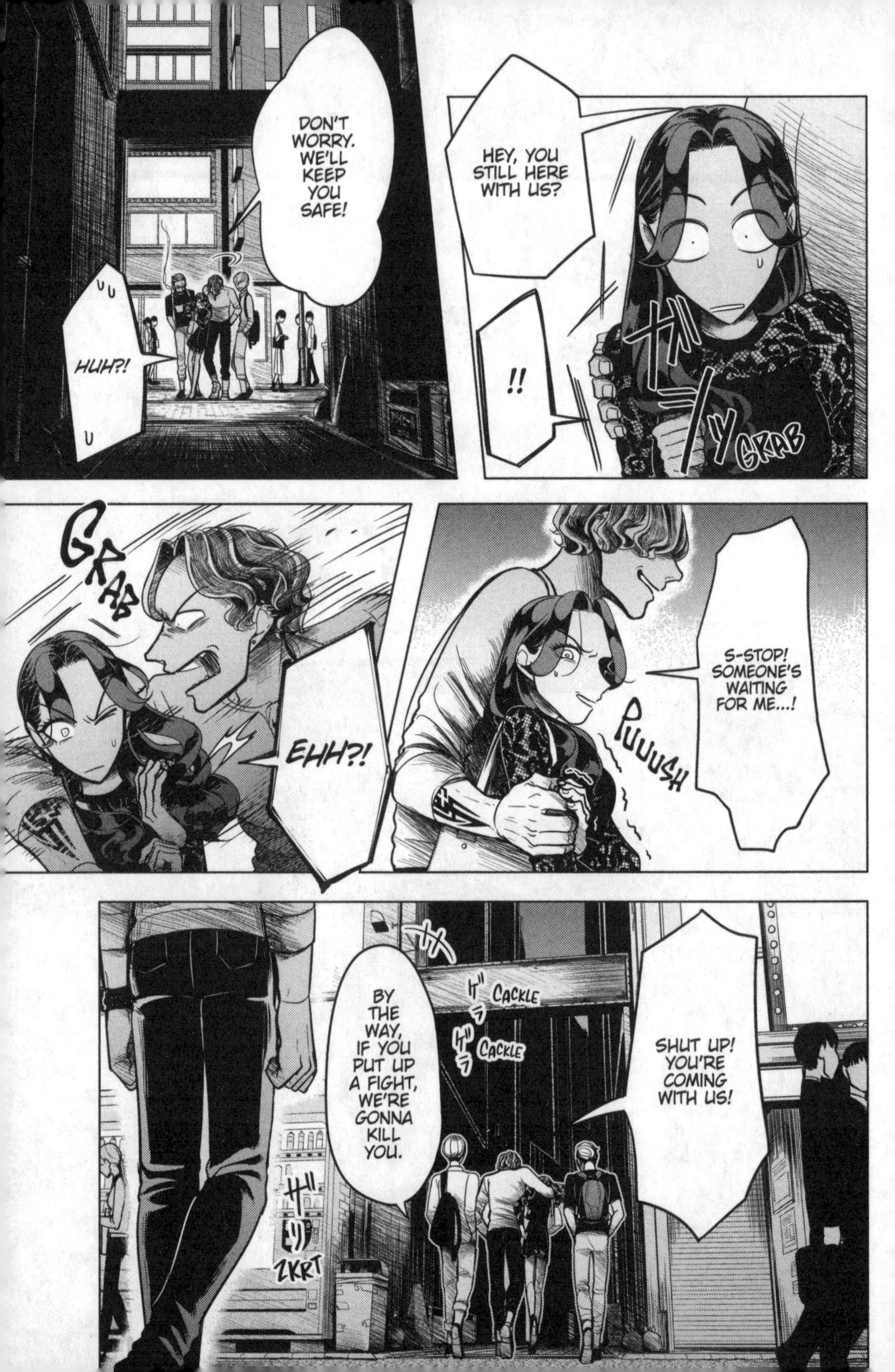
HEY, YOU STILL HERE WITH US?
!!
GRAB
DON'T WORRY. WE'LL KEEP YOU SAFE!
HUH?!
S-STOP! SOMEONE'S WAITING FOR ME...!
PUUUSH
GRAB
EHH?!
SHUT UP! YOU'RE COMING WITH US!
CACKLE
CACKLE
BY THE WAY, IF YOU PUT UP A FIGHT, WE'RE GONNA KILL YOU.
ZKRT

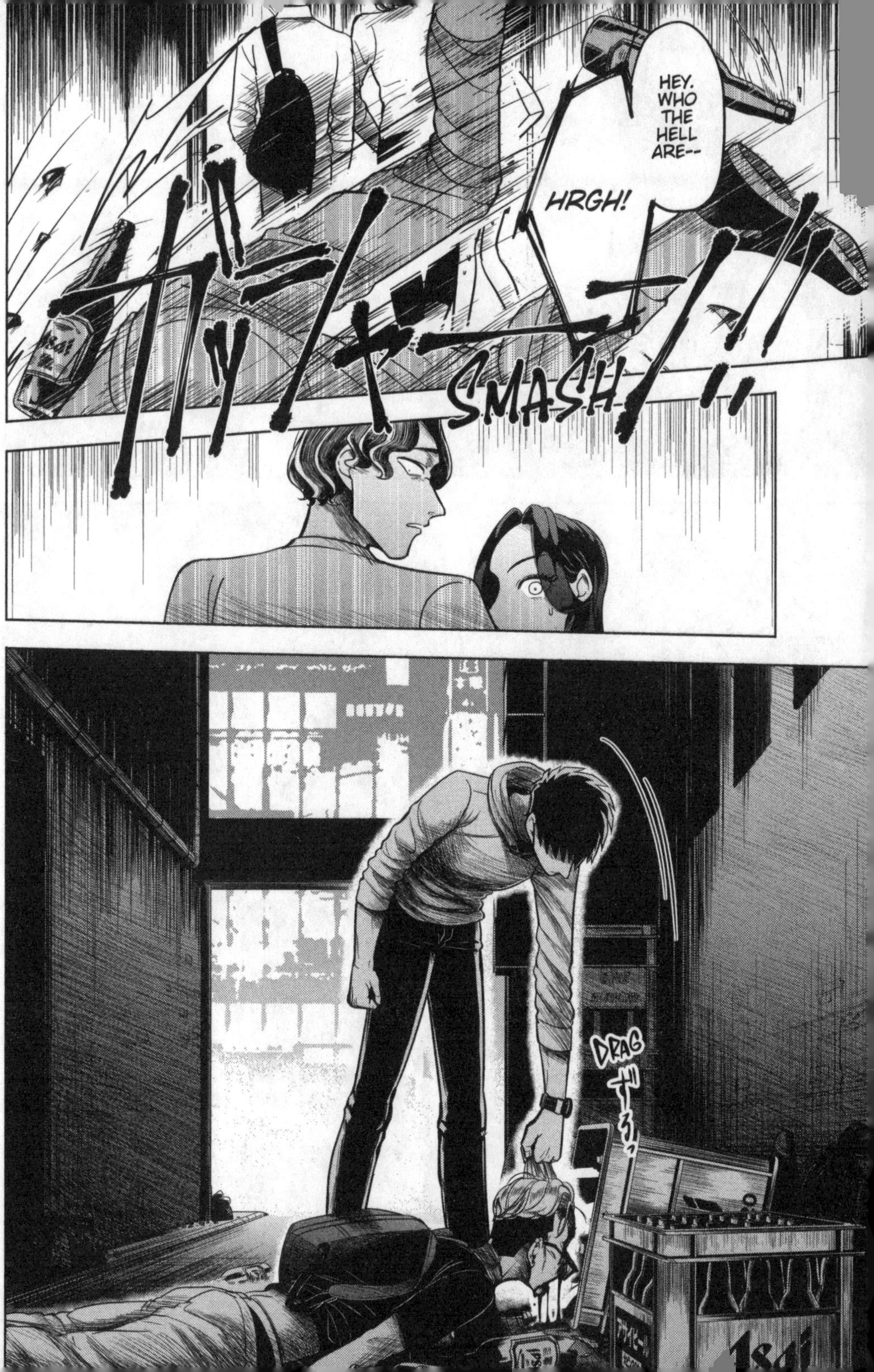
HEY. WHO THE HELL ARE--
HRGH!
SMASH
DRAG

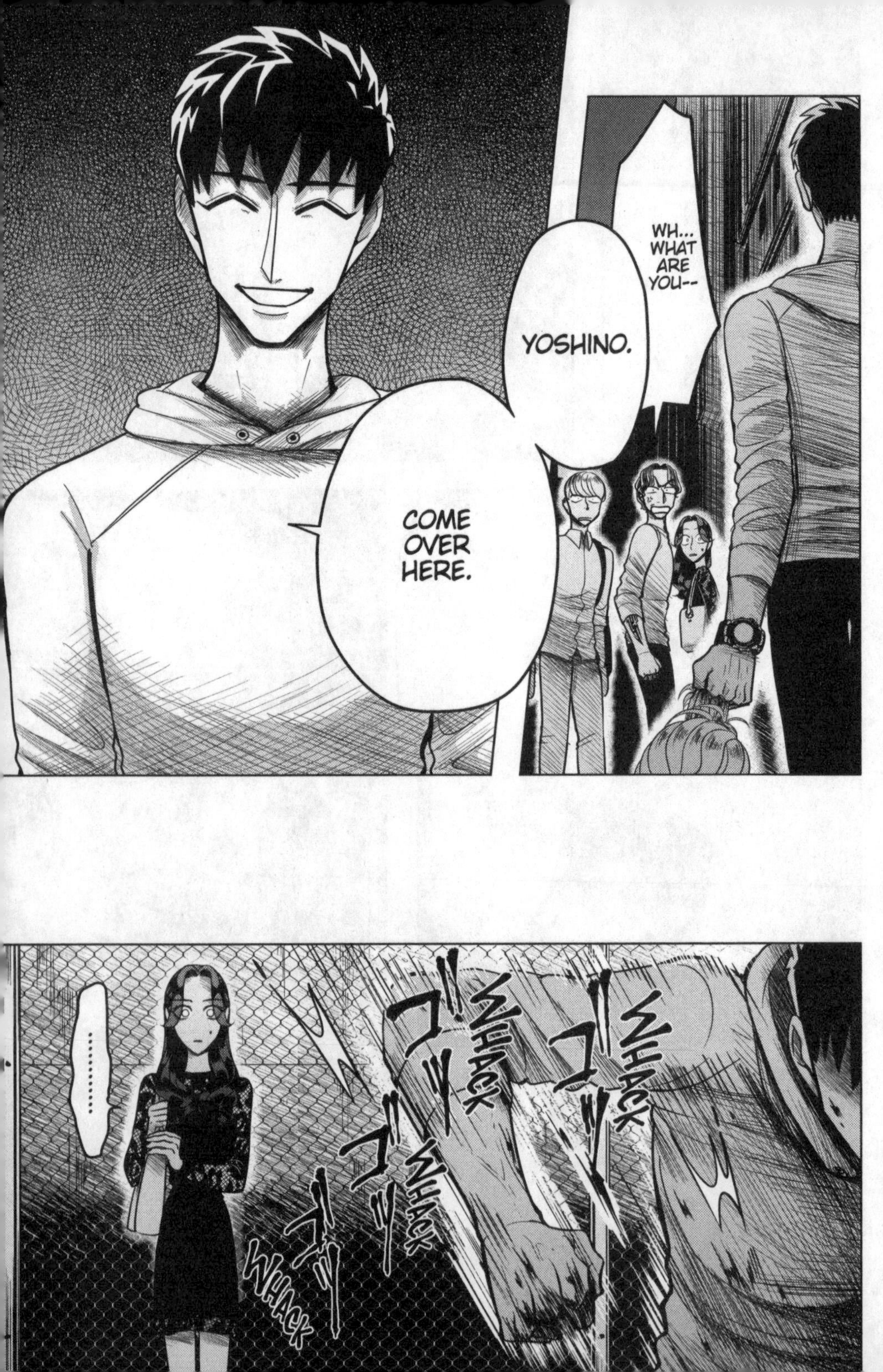
WH... WHAT ARE YOU--
YOSHINO.
COME OVER HERE.
WHACK
ゴッ
WHACK
ゴッ
WHACK
ゴッ
WHACK
ゴッ
......

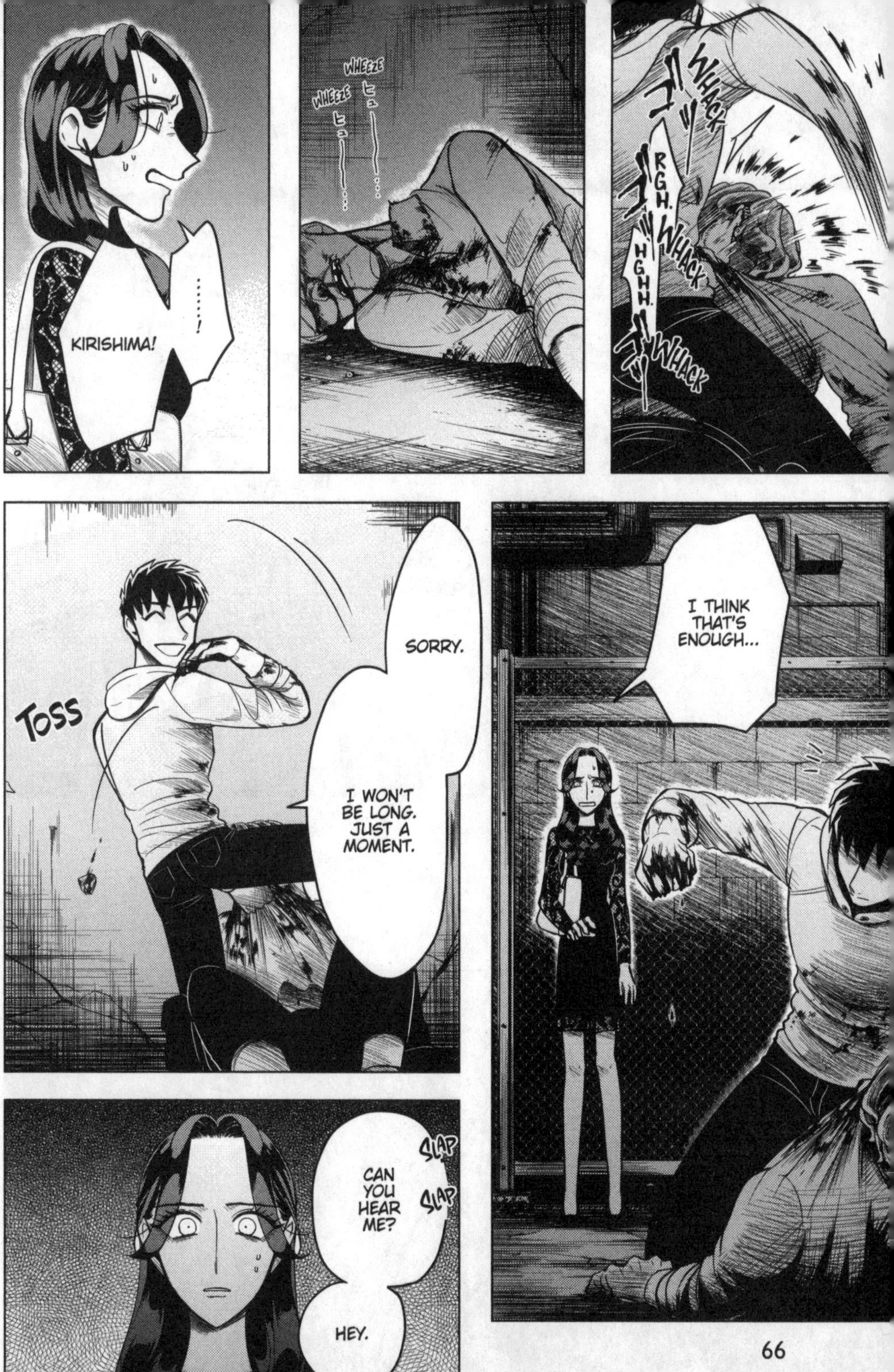
WHACK
RGH. HGHH.
WHACK
WHACK
WHEEZE
WHEEZE
......!
KIRISHIMA!
I THINK THAT'S ENOUGH...
SORRY.
I WON'T BE LONG. JUST A MOMENT.
TOSS
SLAP
SLAP
CAN YOU HEAR ME?
HEY.

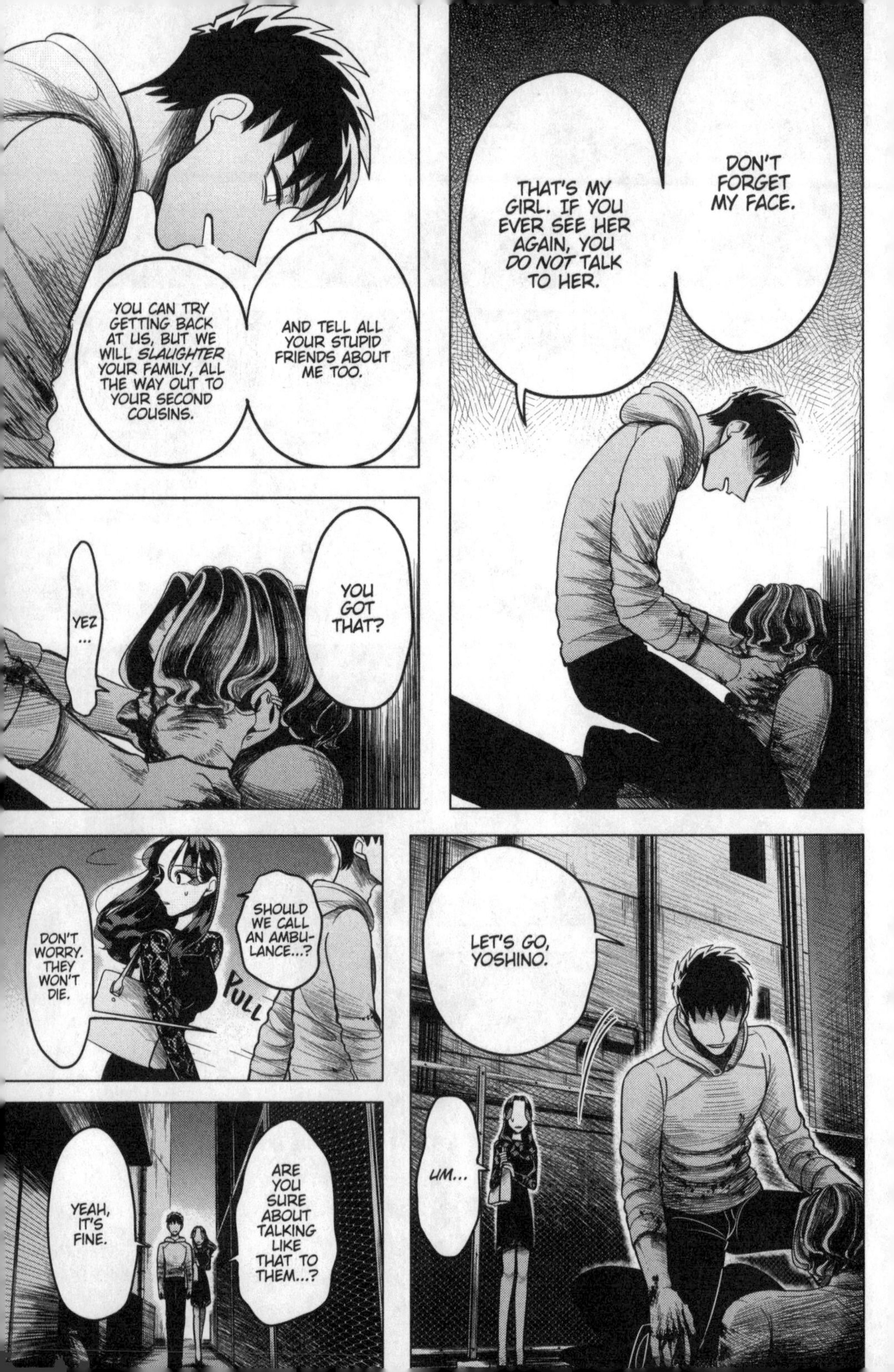
DON'T FORGET MY FACE.
THAT'S MY GIRL. IF YOU EVER SEE HER AGAIN, YOU *DO NOT* TALK TO HER.
AND TELL ALL YOUR STUPID FRIENDS ABOUT ME TOO.
YOU CAN TRY GETTING BACK AT US, BUT WE WILL *SLAUGHTER* YOUR FAMILY, ALL THE WAY OUT TO YOUR SECOND COUSINS.
YOU GOT THAT?
YEZ ...
LET'S GO, YOSHINO.
UM...
SHOULD WE CALL AN AMBULANCE...?
PULL
DON'T WORRY. THEY WON'T DIE.
ARE YOU SURE ABOUT TALKING LIKE THAT TO THEM...?
YEAH, IT'S FINE.

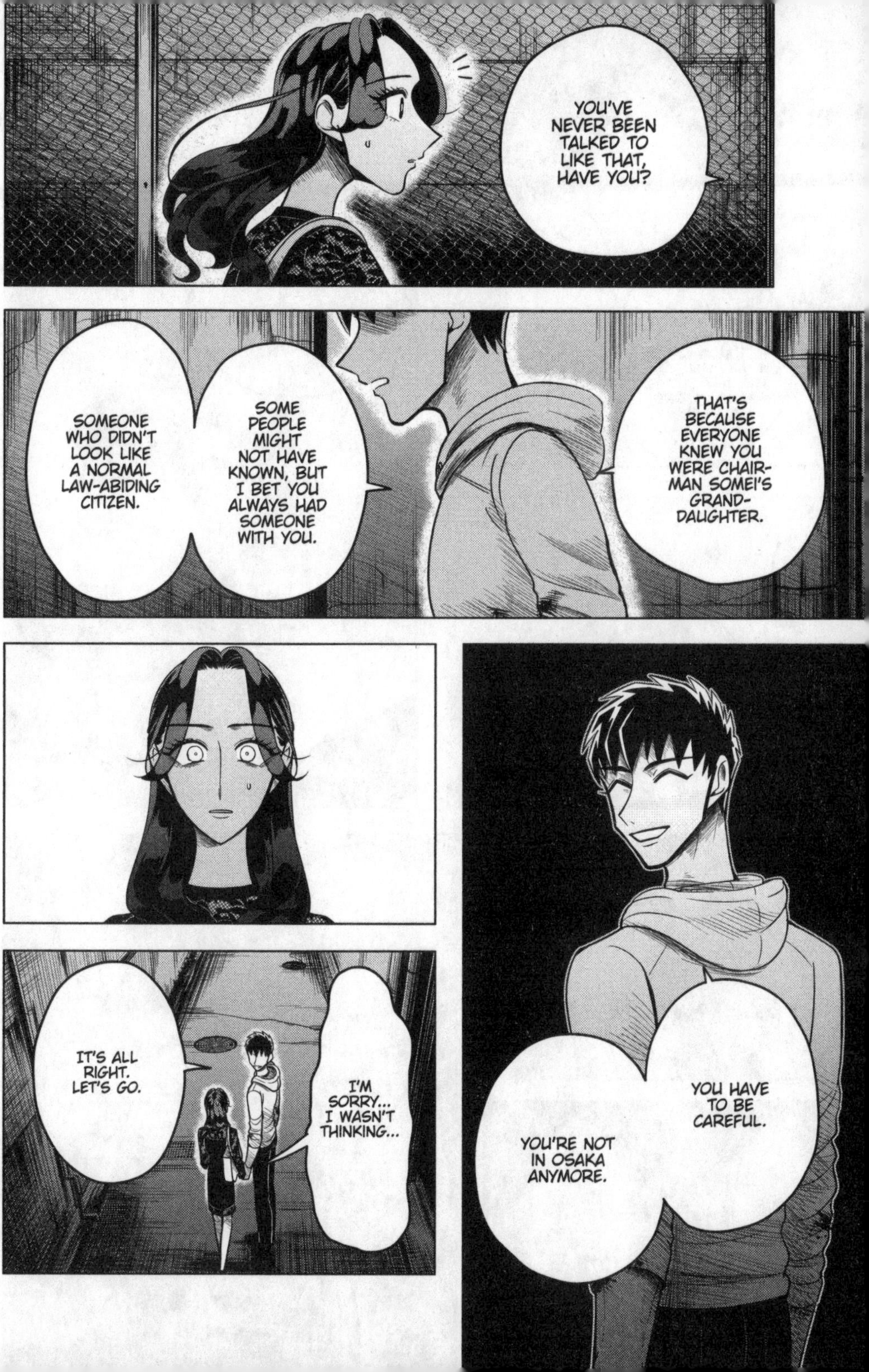
YOU'VE NEVER BEEN TALKED TO LIKE THAT, HAVE YOU?
THAT'S BECAUSE EVERYONE KNEW YOU WERE CHAIRMAN SOMEI'S GRANDDAUGHTER.
SOME PEOPLE MIGHT NOT HAVE KNOWN, BUT I BET YOU ALWAYS HAD SOMEONE WITH YOU.
SOMEONE WHO DIDN'T LOOK LIKE A NORMAL LAW-ABIDING CITIZEN.
YOU HAVE TO BE CAREFUL.
YOU'RE NOT IN OSAKA ANYMORE.
I'M SORRY... I WASN'T THINKING...
IT'S ALL RIGHT. LET'S GO.

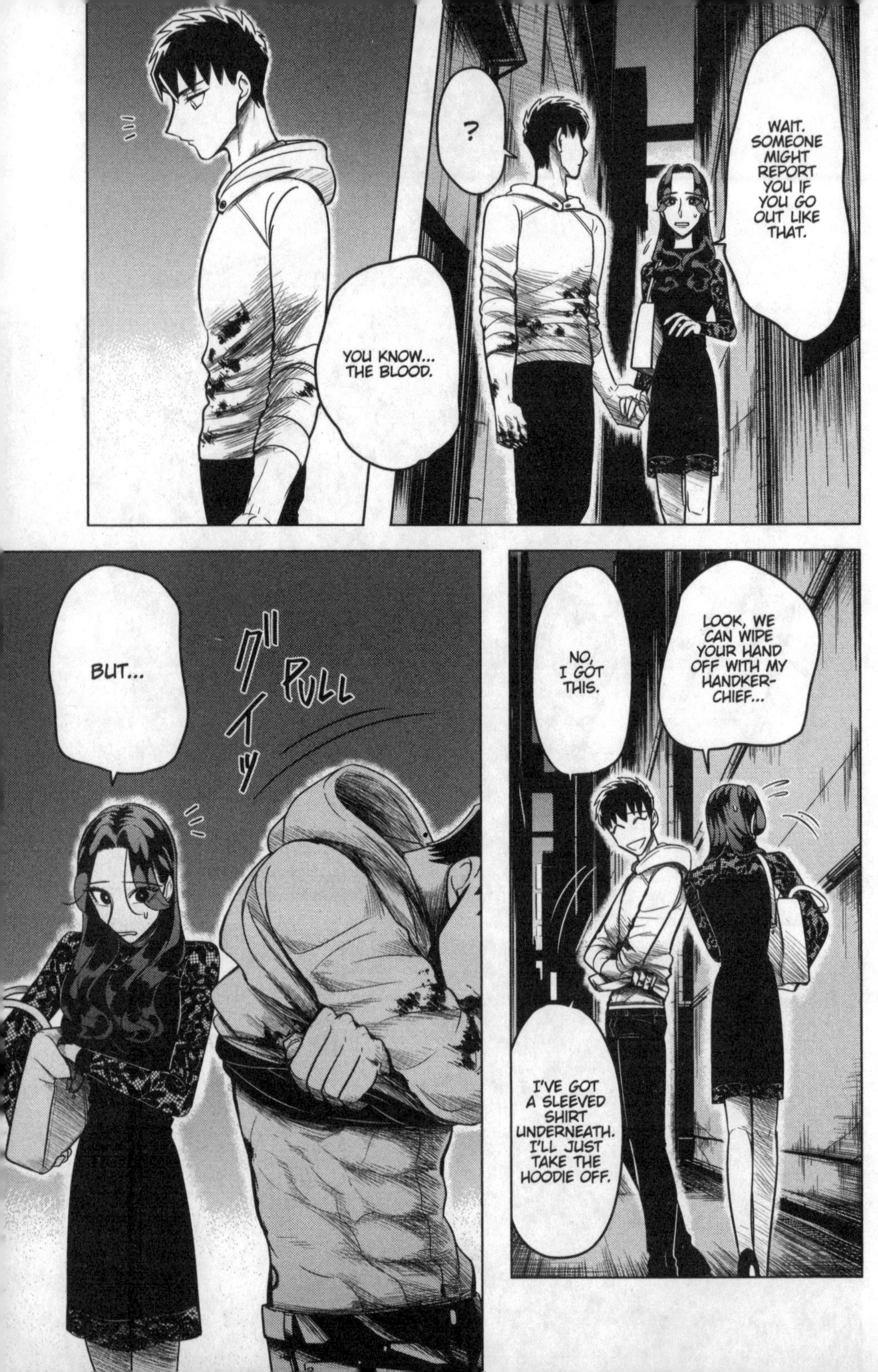
WAIT. SOMEONE MIGHT REPORT YOU IF YOU GO OUT LIKE THAT.
?
YOU KNOW... THE BLOOD.
LOOK, WE CAN WIPE YOUR HAND OFF WITH MY HANDKER-CHIEF...
NO, I GOT THIS.
I'VE GOT A SLEEVED SHIRT UNDERNEATH. I'LL JUST TAKE THE HOODIE OFF.
BUT...
グイッ
PULL

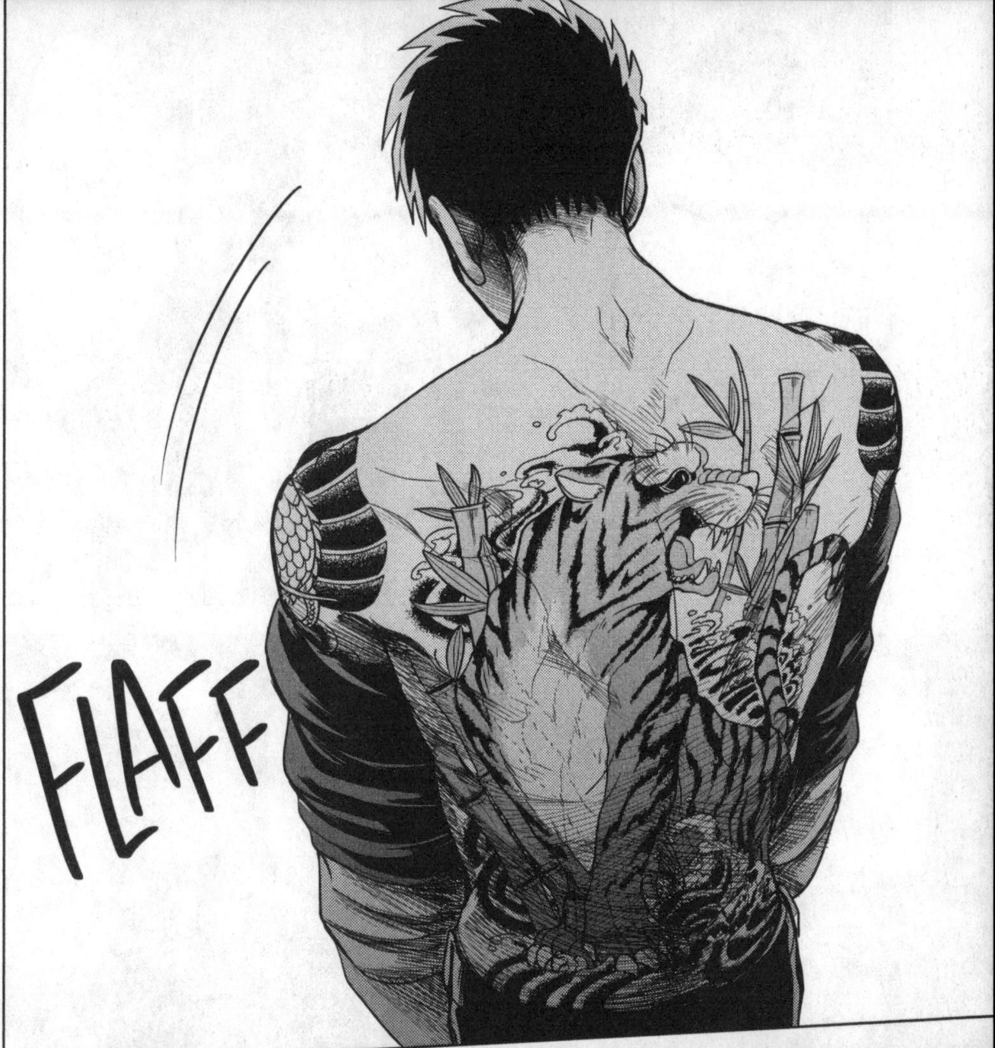
FLAFF
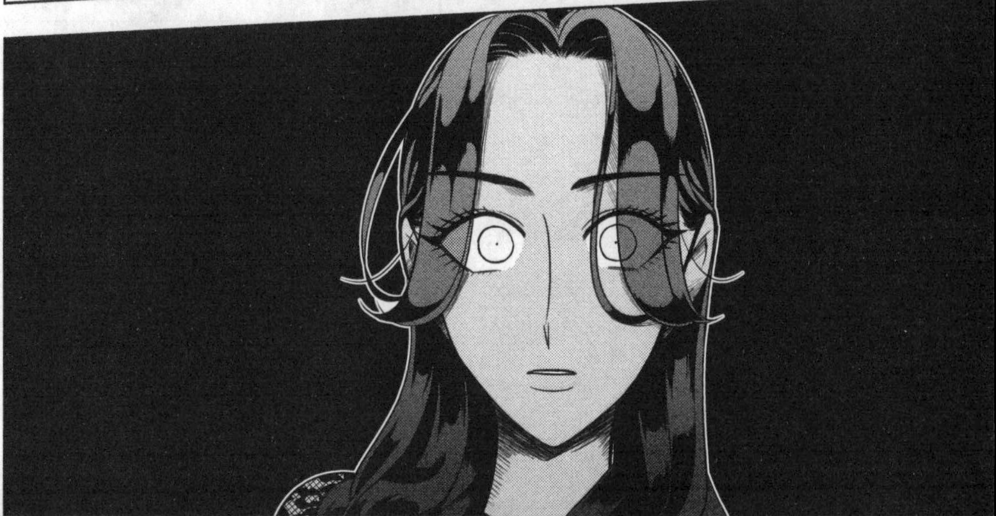

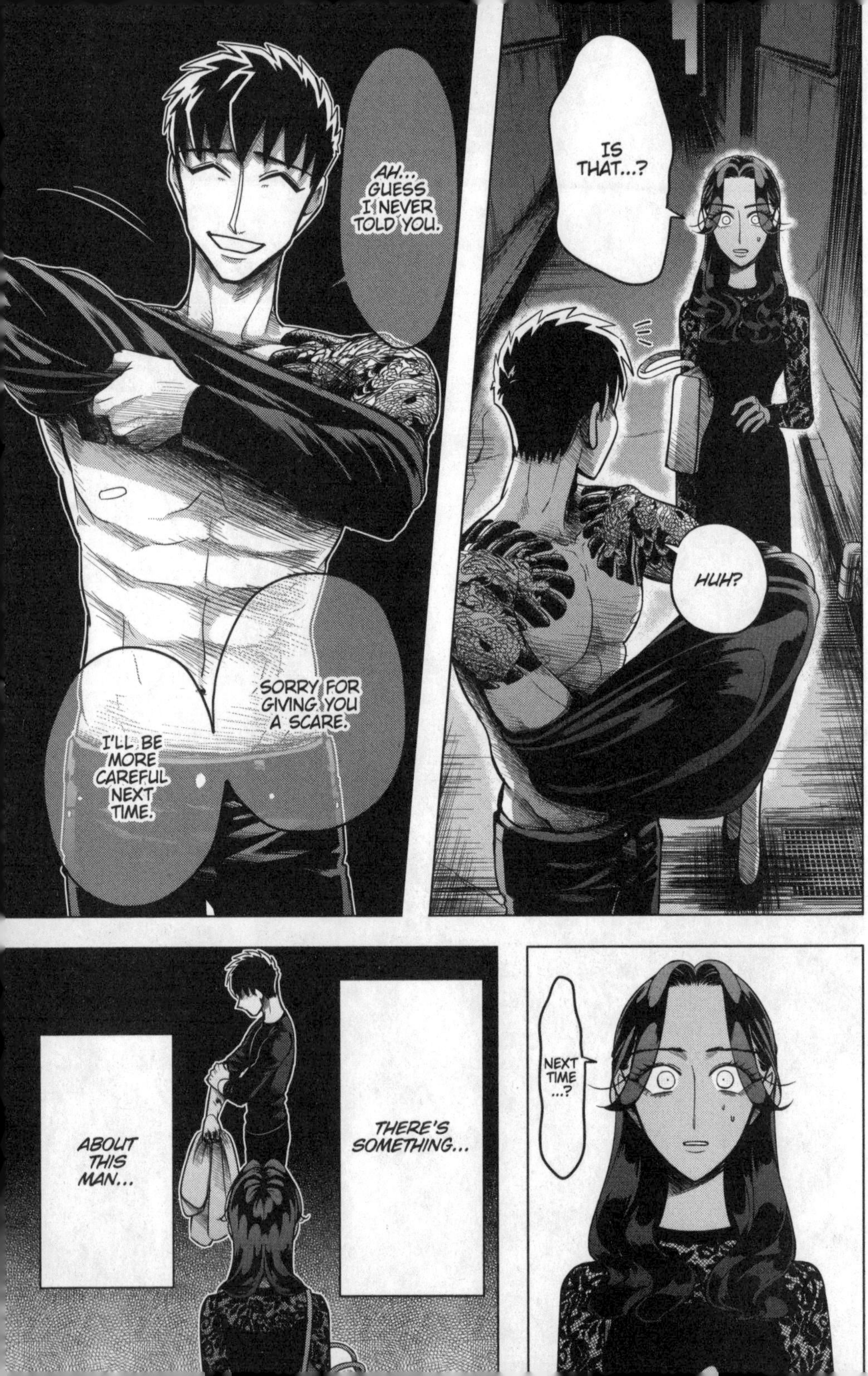
IS THAT...?
HUH?
AH... GUESS I NEVER TOLD YOU.
SORRY FOR GIVING YOU A SCARE.
I'LL BE MORE CAREFUL NEXT TIME.
NEXT TIME ...?
THERE'S SOMETHING...
ABOUT THIS MAN...

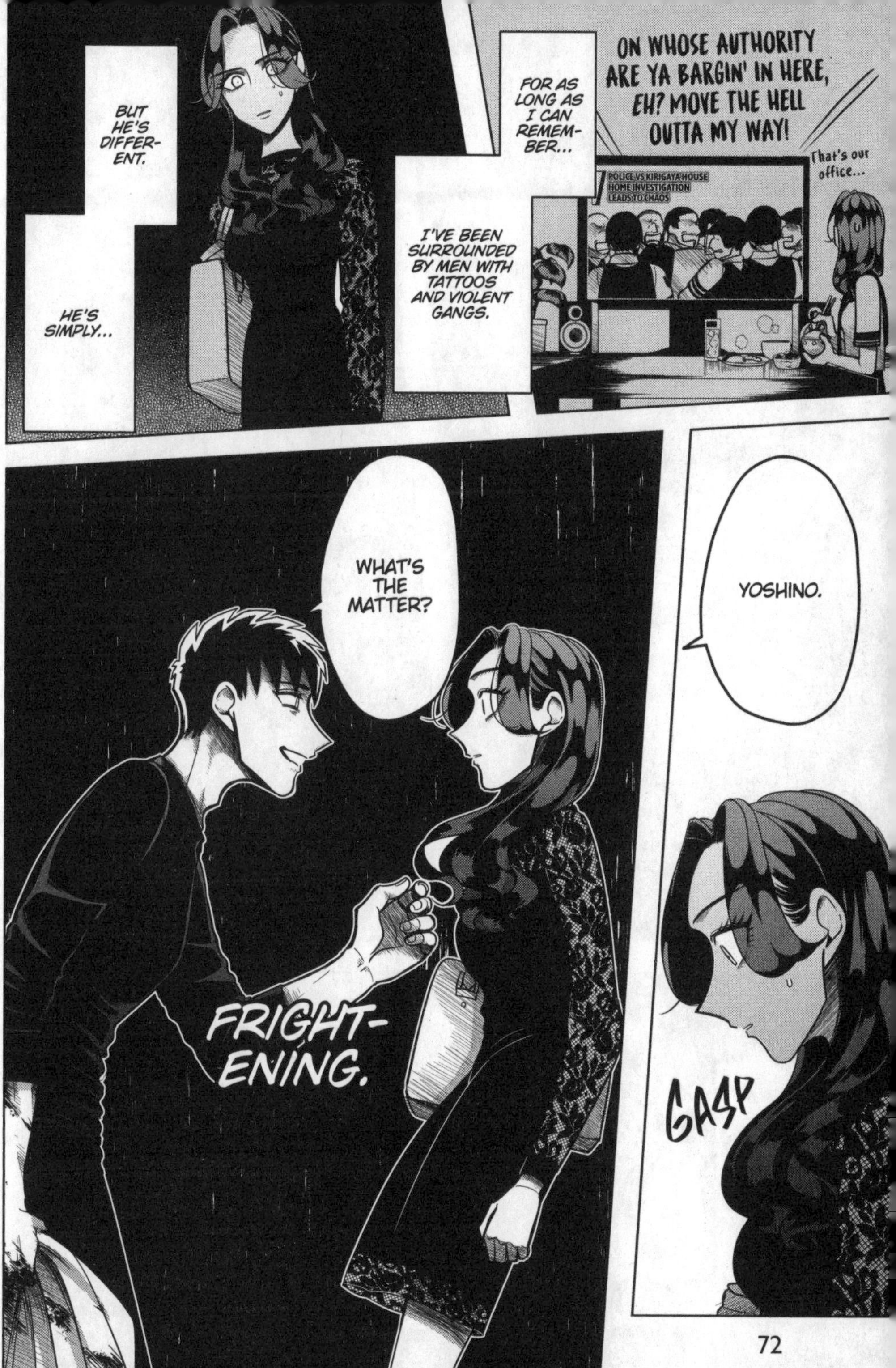
ON WHOSE AUTHORITY ARE YA BARGIN' IN HERE, EH? MOVE THE HELL OUTTA MY WAY!
That's our office...
POLICE VS KIRIGAYA HOUSE HOME INVESTIGATION LEADS TO CHAOS
FOR AS LONG AS I CAN REMEMBER...
I'VE BEEN SURROUNDED BY MEN WITH TATTOOS AND VIOLENT GANGS.
BUT HE'S DIFFERENT.
HE'S SIMPLY...
YOSHINO.
GASP
WHAT'S THE MATTER?
FRIGHTENING.

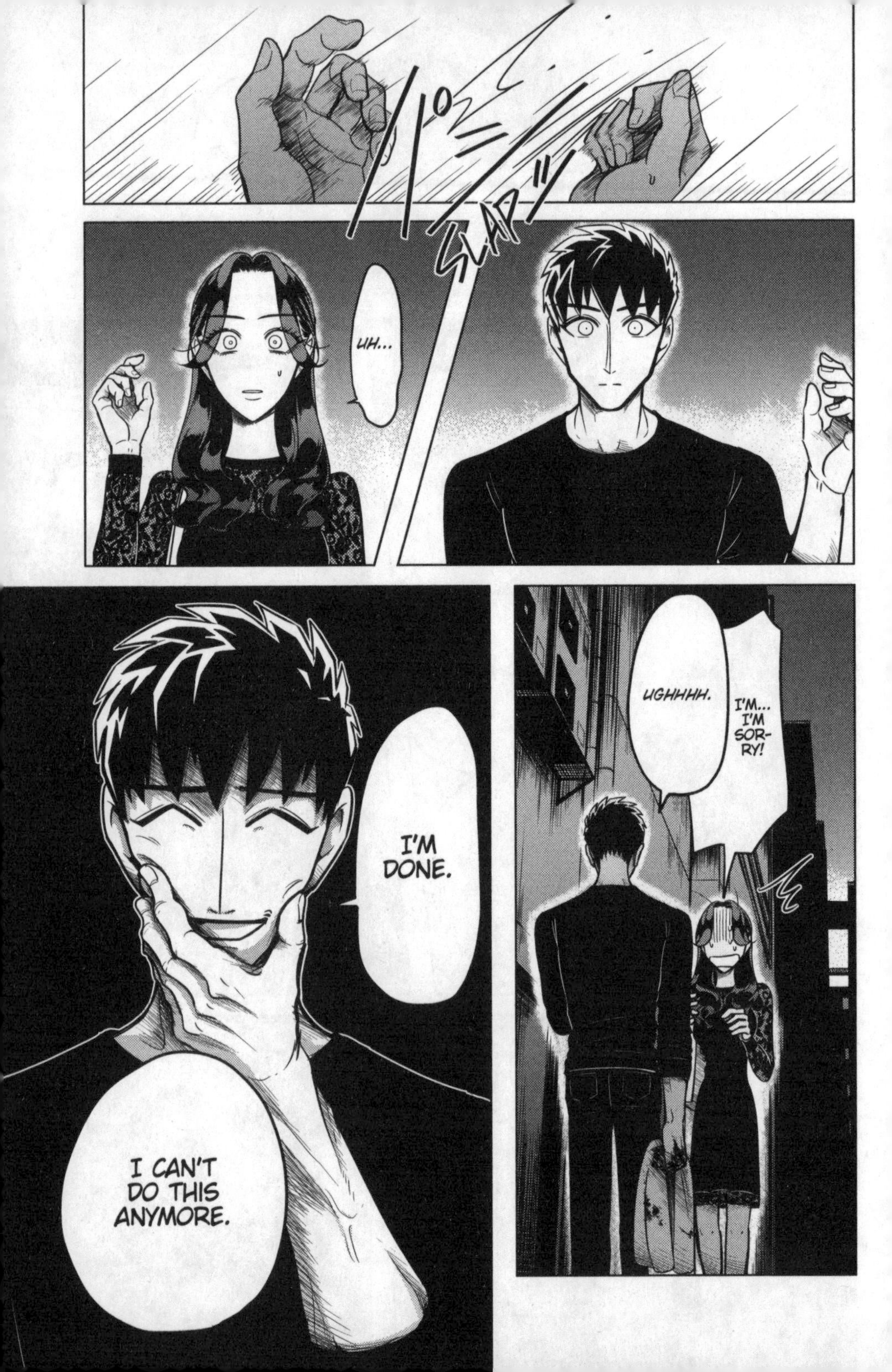

パン
SLAP
UH...
I'M... I'M SOR-RY!
UGHHHH.
I'M DONE.
I CAN'T DO THIS ANYMORE.

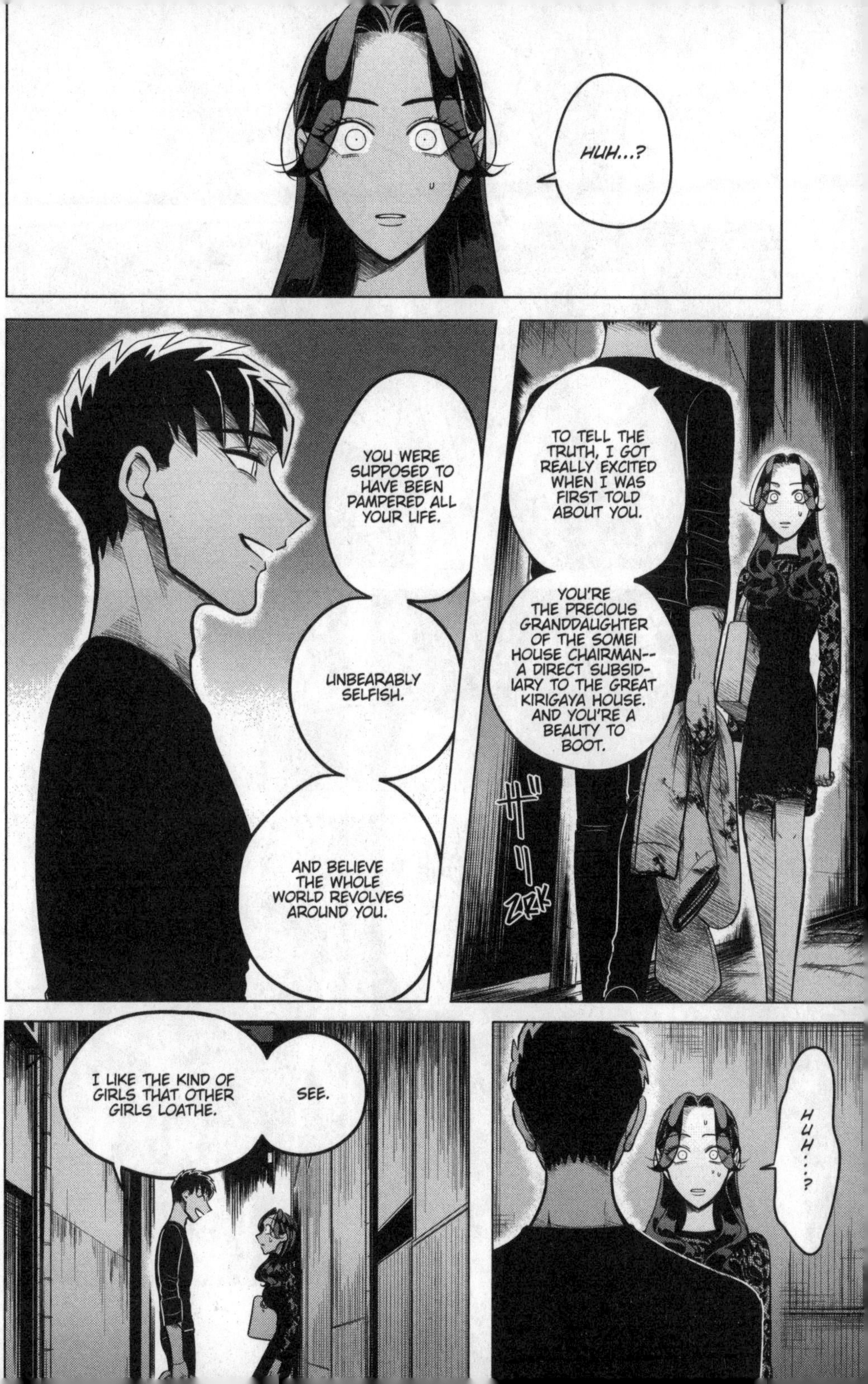
HUH...?
TO TELL THE TRUTH, I GOT REALLY EXCITED WHEN I WAS FIRST TOLD ABOUT YOU.
YOU'RE THE PRECIOUS GRANDDAUGHTER OF THE SOMEI HOUSE CHAIRMAN-- A DIRECT SUBSIDIARY TO THE GREAT KIRIGAYA HOUSE. AND YOU'RE A BEAUTY TO BOOT.
ZRK
YOU WERE SUPPOSED TO HAVE BEEN PAMPERED ALL YOUR LIFE.
UNBEARABLY SELFISH.
AND BELIEVE THE WHOLE WORLD REVOLVES AROUND YOU.
HUH...?
SEE.
I LIKE THE KIND OF GIRLS THAT OTHER GIRLS LOATHE.

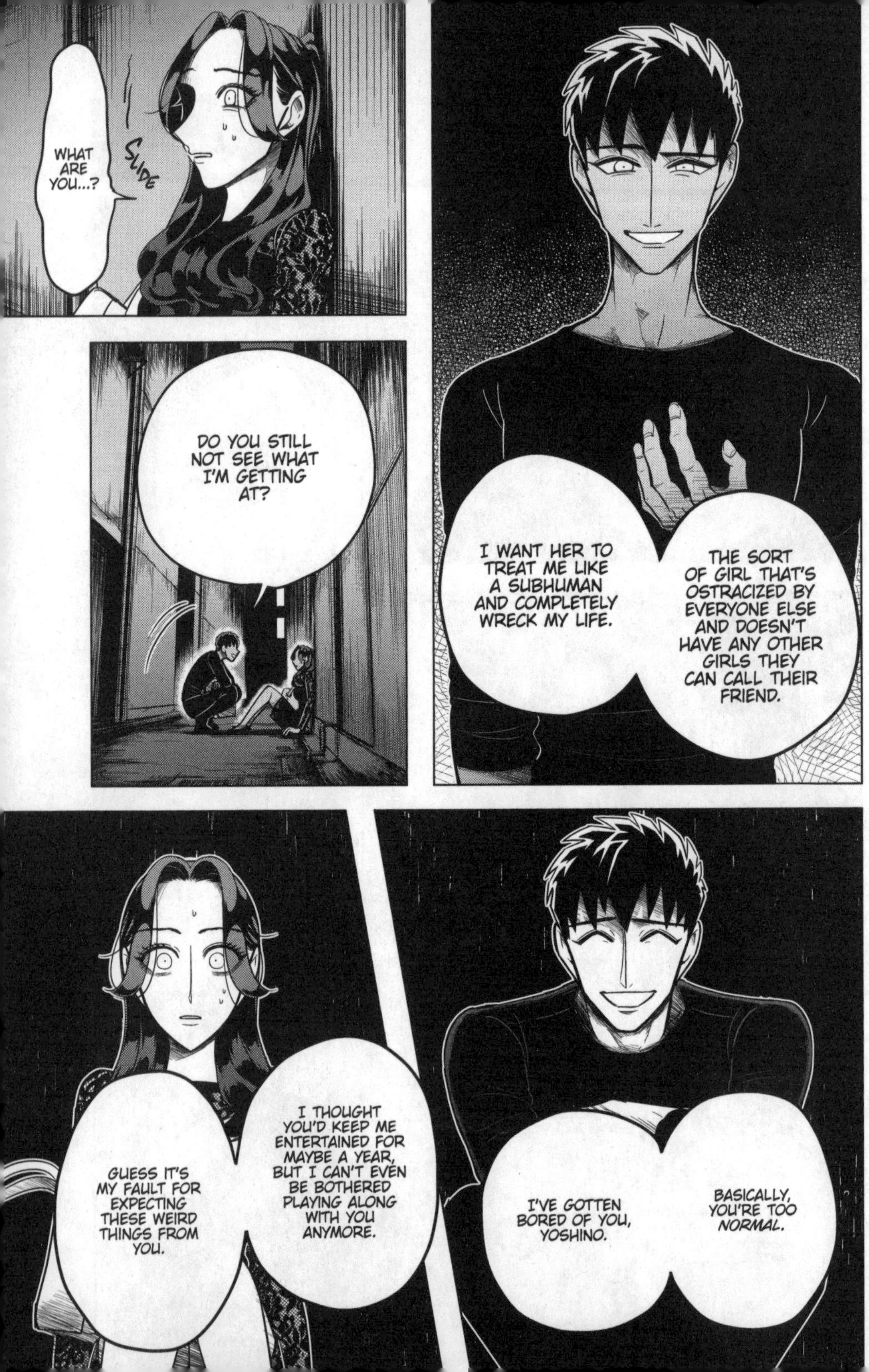
THE SORT OF GIRL THAT'S OSTRACIZED BY EVERYONE ELSE AND DOESN'T HAVE ANY OTHER GIRLS THEY CAN CALL THEIR FRIEND.
I WANT HER TO TREAT ME LIKE A SUBHUMAN AND COMPLETELY WRECK MY LIFE.
SLIDE
WHAT ARE YOU...?
DO YOU STILL NOT SEE WHAT I'M GETTING AT?
BASICALLY, YOU'RE TOO *NORMAL*.
I'VE GOTTEN BORED OF YOU, YOSHINO.
I THOUGHT YOU'D KEEP ME ENTERTAINED FOR MAYBE A YEAR, BUT I CAN'T EVEN BE BOTHERED PLAYING ALONG WITH YOU ANYMORE.
GUESS IT'S MY FAULT FOR EXPECTING THESE WEIRD THINGS FROM YOU.

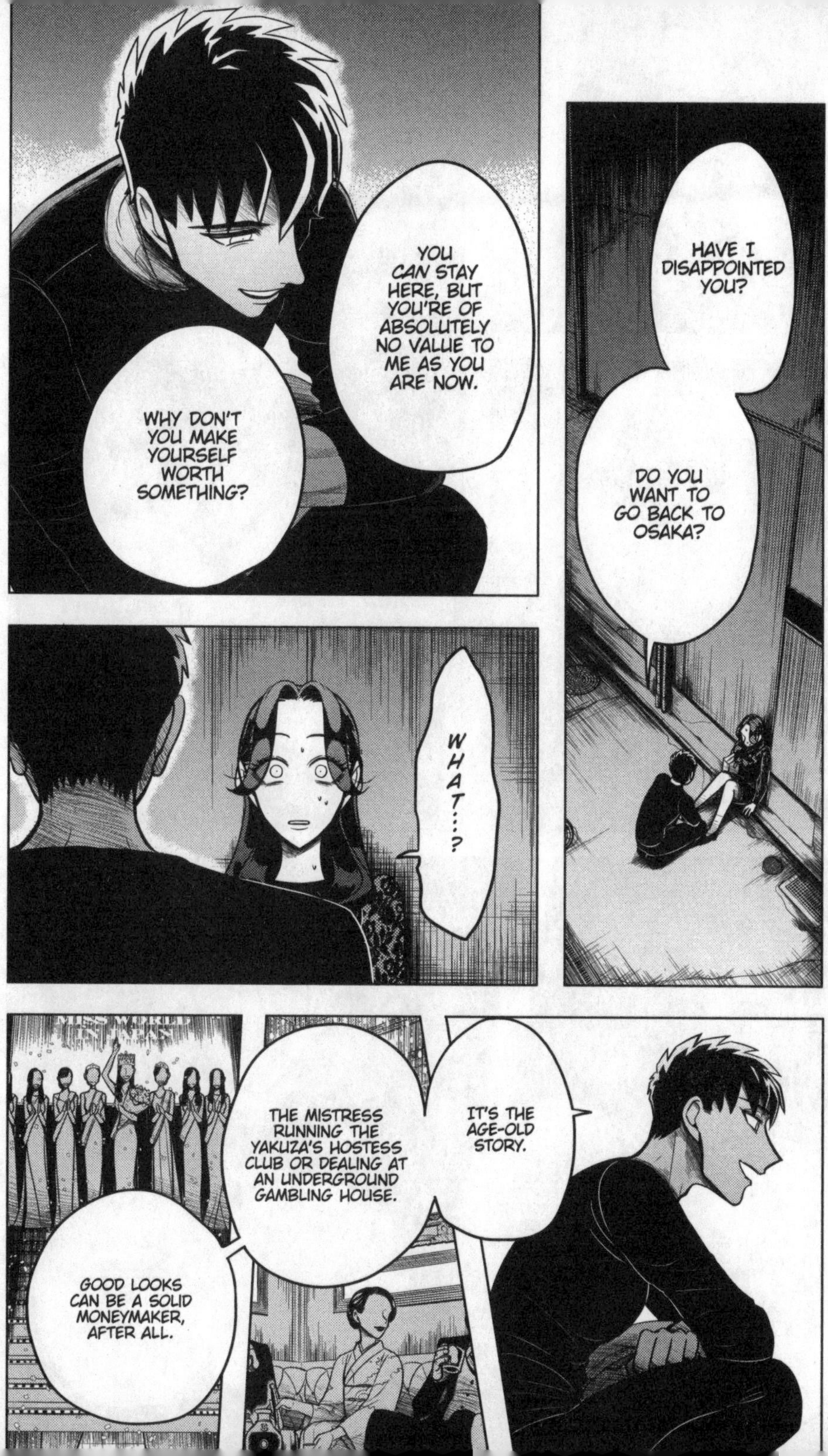
HAVE I DISAPPOINTED YOU?
DO YOU WANT TO GO BACK TO OSAKA?
YOU CAN STAY HERE, BUT YOU'RE OF ABSOLUTELY NO VALUE TO ME AS YOU ARE NOW.
WHY DON'T YOU MAKE YOURSELF WORTH SOMETHING?
WHAT...?
IT'S THE AGE-OLD STORY.
THE MISTRESS RUNNING THE YAKUZA'S HOSTESS CLUB OR DEALING AT AN UNDERGROUND GAMBLING HOUSE.
GOOD LOOKS CAN BE A SOLID MONEYMAKER, AFTER ALL.

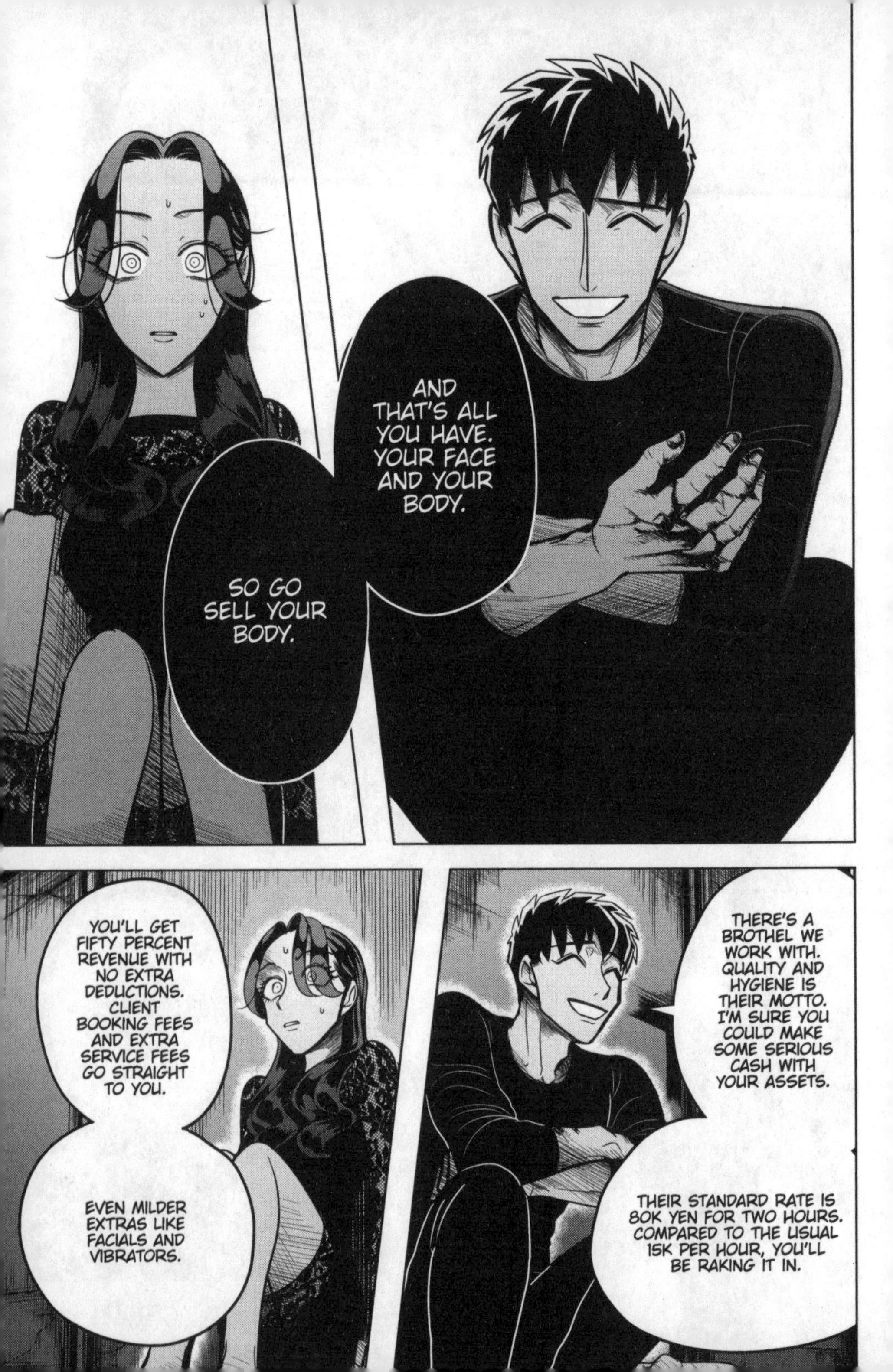
AND THAT'S ALL YOU HAVE. YOUR FACE AND YOUR BODY.
SO GO SELL YOUR BODY.
THERE'S A BROTHEL WE WORK WITH. QUALITY AND HYGIENE IS THEIR MOTTO. I'M SURE YOU COULD MAKE SOME SERIOUS CASH WITH YOUR ASSETS.
THEIR STANDARD RATE IS 80K YEN FOR TWO HOURS. COMPARED TO THE USUAL 15K PER HOUR, YOU'LL BE RAKING IT IN.
YOU'LL GET FIFTY PERCENT REVENUE WITH NO EXTRA DEDUCTIONS. CLIENT BOOKING FEES AND EXTRA SERVICE FEES GO STRAIGHT TO YOU.
EVEN MILDER EXTRAS LIKE FACIALS AND VIBRATORS.

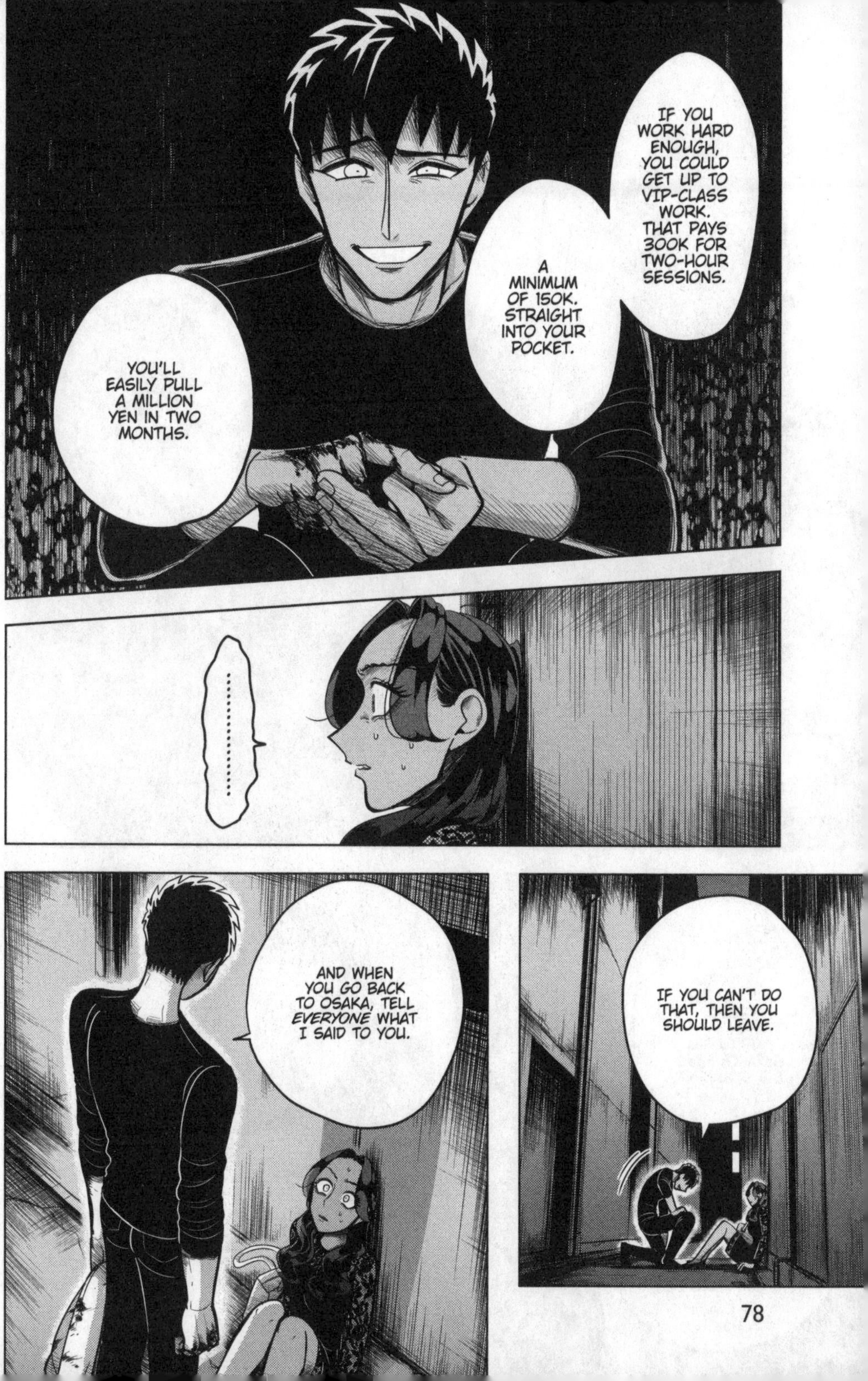
IF YOU WORK HARD ENOUGH, YOU COULD GET UP TO VIP-CLASS WORK. THAT PAYS 300K FOR TWO-HOUR SESSIONS.
A MINIMUM OF 150K. STRAIGHT INTO YOUR POCKET.
YOU'LL EASILY PULL A MILLION YEN IN TWO MONTHS.
......
IF YOU CAN'T DO THAT, THEN YOU SHOULD LEAVE.
AND WHEN YOU GO BACK TO OSAKA, TELL *EVERYONE* WHAT I SAID TO YOU.

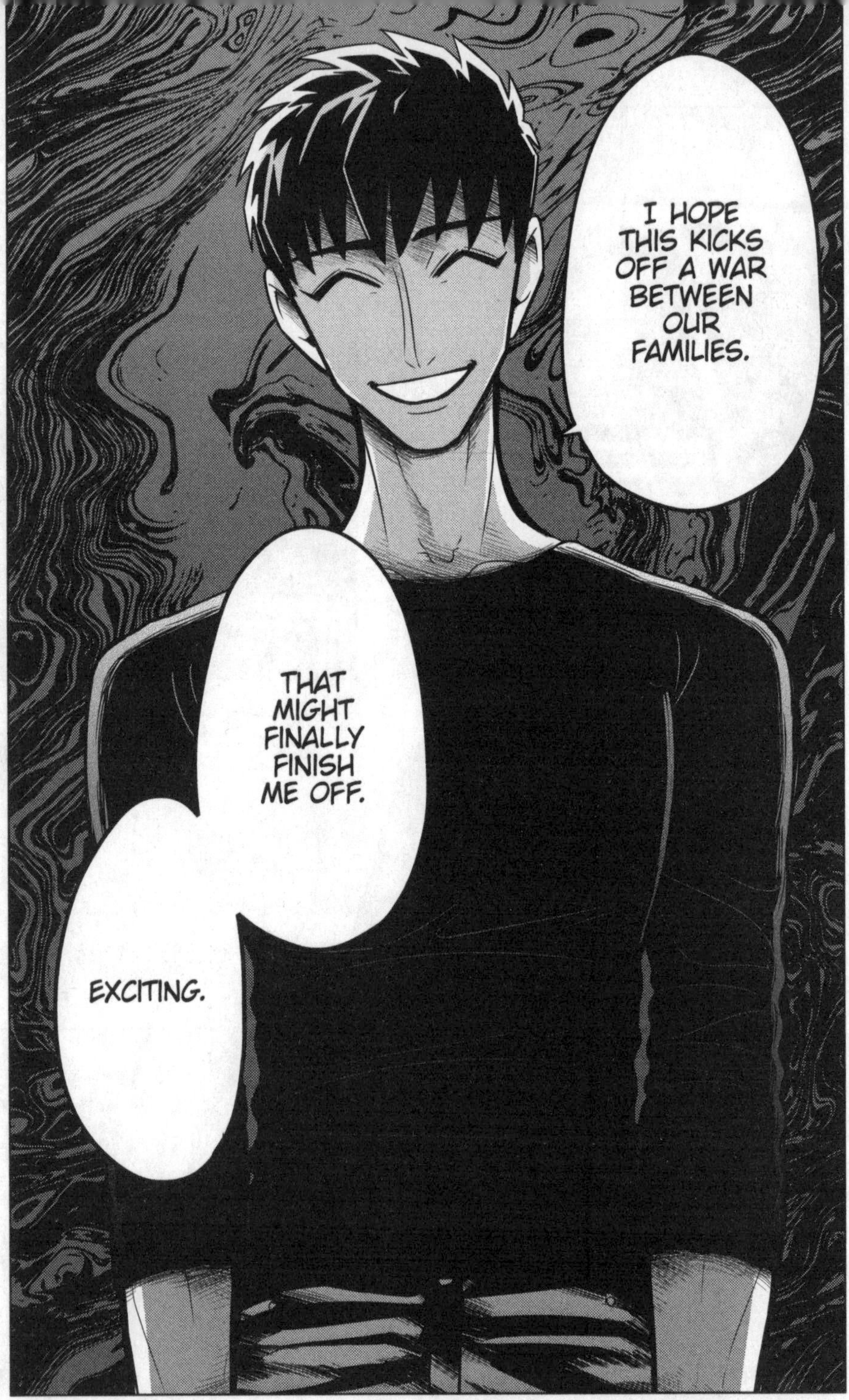
I HOPE THIS KICKS OFF A WAR BETWEEN OUR FAMILIES.
THAT MIGHT FINALLY FINISH ME OFF.
EXCITING.

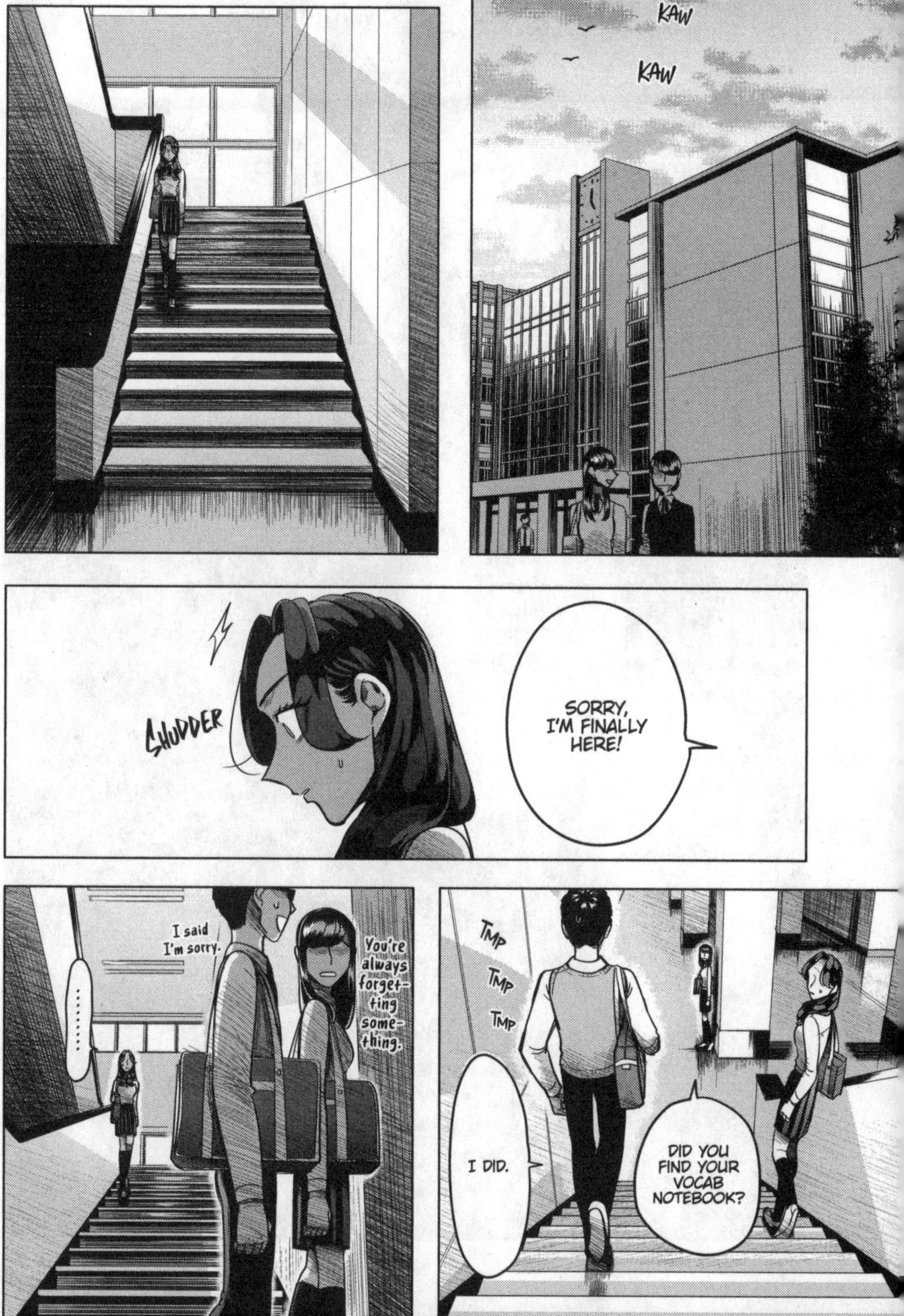
KAW
KAW
SORRY, I'M FINALLY HERE!
SHUDDER
TMP
TMP
TMP
DID YOU FIND YOUR VOCAB NOTEBOOK?
I DID.
You're always forget-ting some-thing.
I said I'm sorry.
......

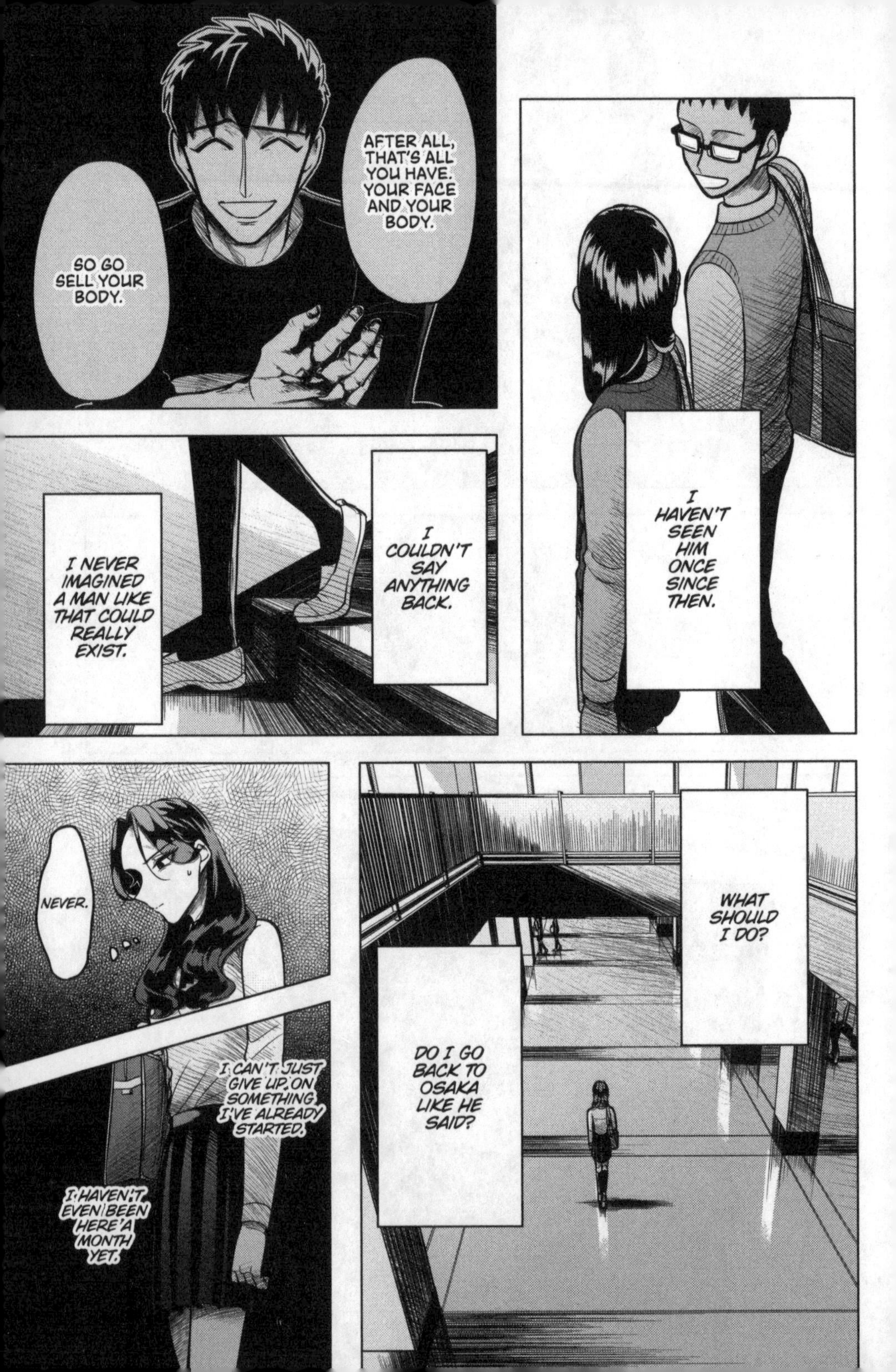
AFTER ALL, THAT'S ALL YOU HAVE. YOUR FACE AND YOUR BODY.
SO GO SELL YOUR BODY.
I COULDN'T SAY ANYTHING BACK.
I NEVER IMAGINED A MAN LIKE THAT COULD REALLY EXIST.
I HAVEN'T SEEN HIM ONCE SINCE THEN.
WHAT SHOULD I DO?
DO I GO BACK TO OSAKA LIKE HE SAID?
NEVER.
I CAN'T JUST GIVE UP ON SOMETHING I'VE ALREADY STARTED.
I HAVEN'T EVEN BEEN HERE A MONTH YET.

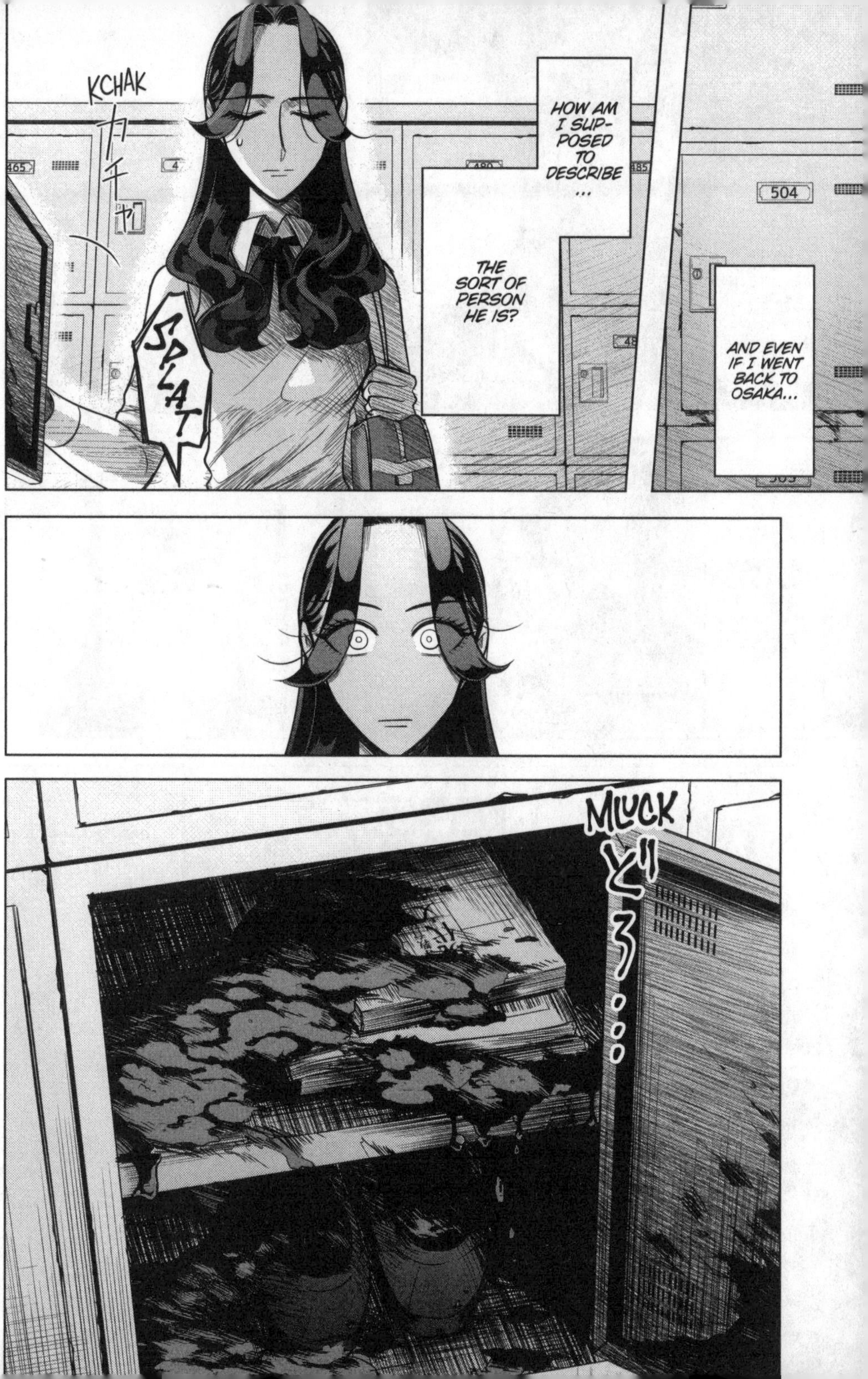
HOW AM I SUP-POSED TO DESCRIBE ...
THE SORT OF PERSON HE IS?
AND EVEN IF I WENT BACK TO OSAKA...
KCHAK
カチャ
SPLAT
MUCK
どろ…

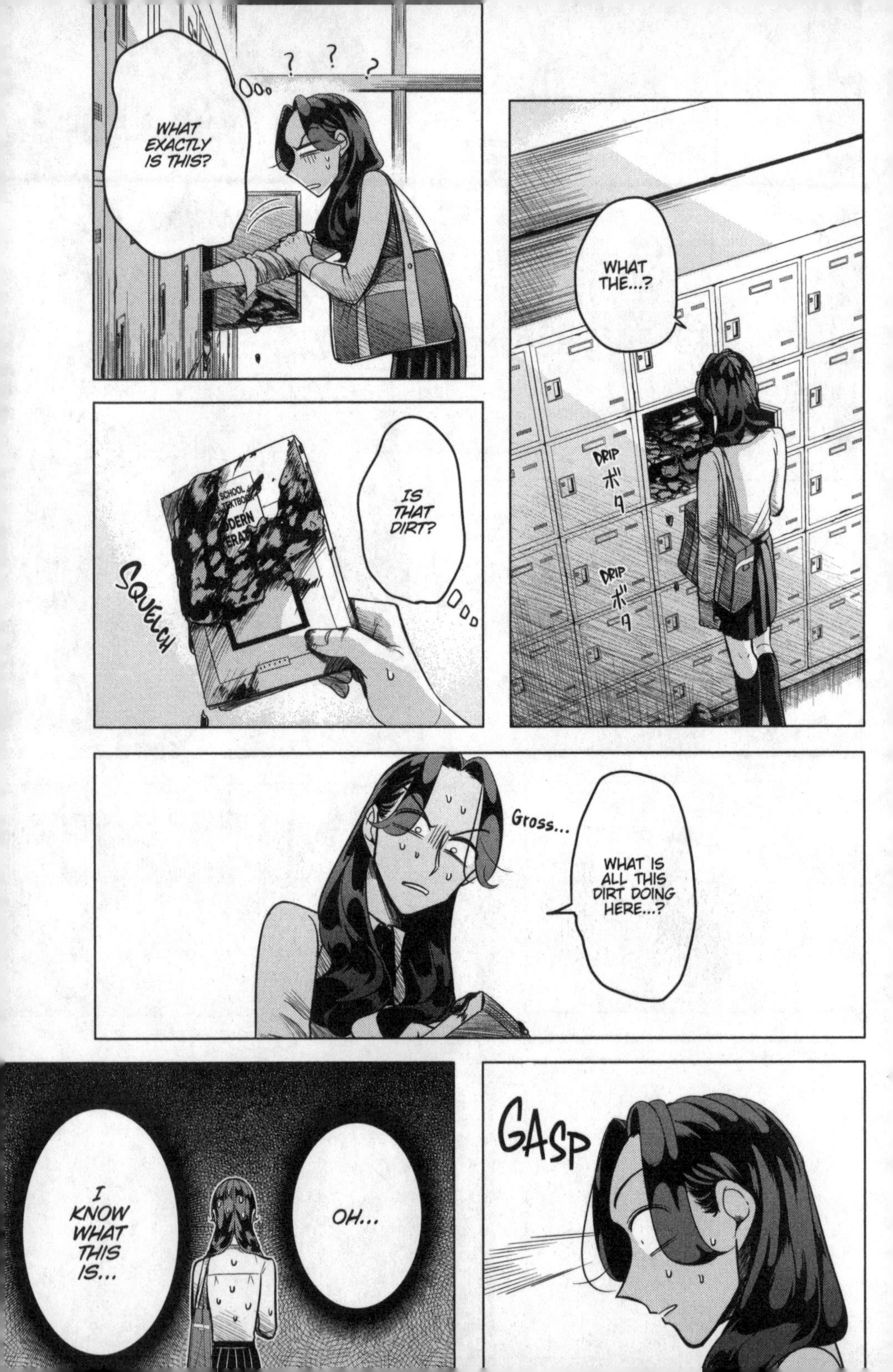
WHAT THE...?
DRIP ボタ
DRIP ボタ
WHAT EXACTLY IS THIS?
IS THAT DIRT?
SQUELCH
Gross...
WHAT IS ALL THIS DIRT DOING HERE...?
GASP
OH...
I KNOW WHAT THIS IS...

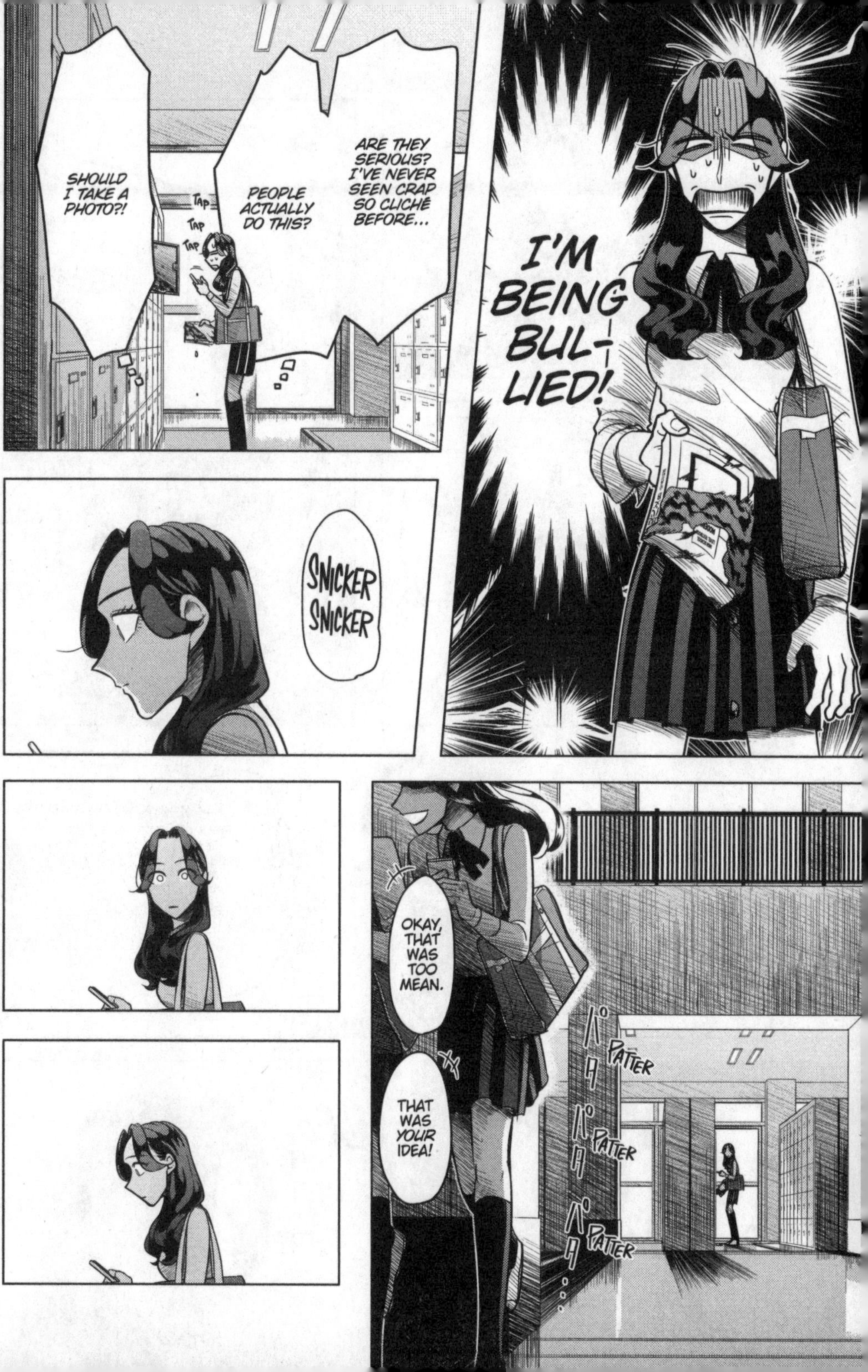
I'M BEING BUL-LIED!
ARE THEY SERIOUS? I'VE NEVER SEEN CRAP SO CLICHÉ BEFORE…
PEOPLE ACTUALLY DO THIS?
SHOULD I TAKE A PHOTO?!
TAP
TAP
TAP
SNICKER SNICKER
OKAY, THAT WAS TOO MEAN.
THAT WAS YOUR IDEA!
PATTER
PATTER
PATTER

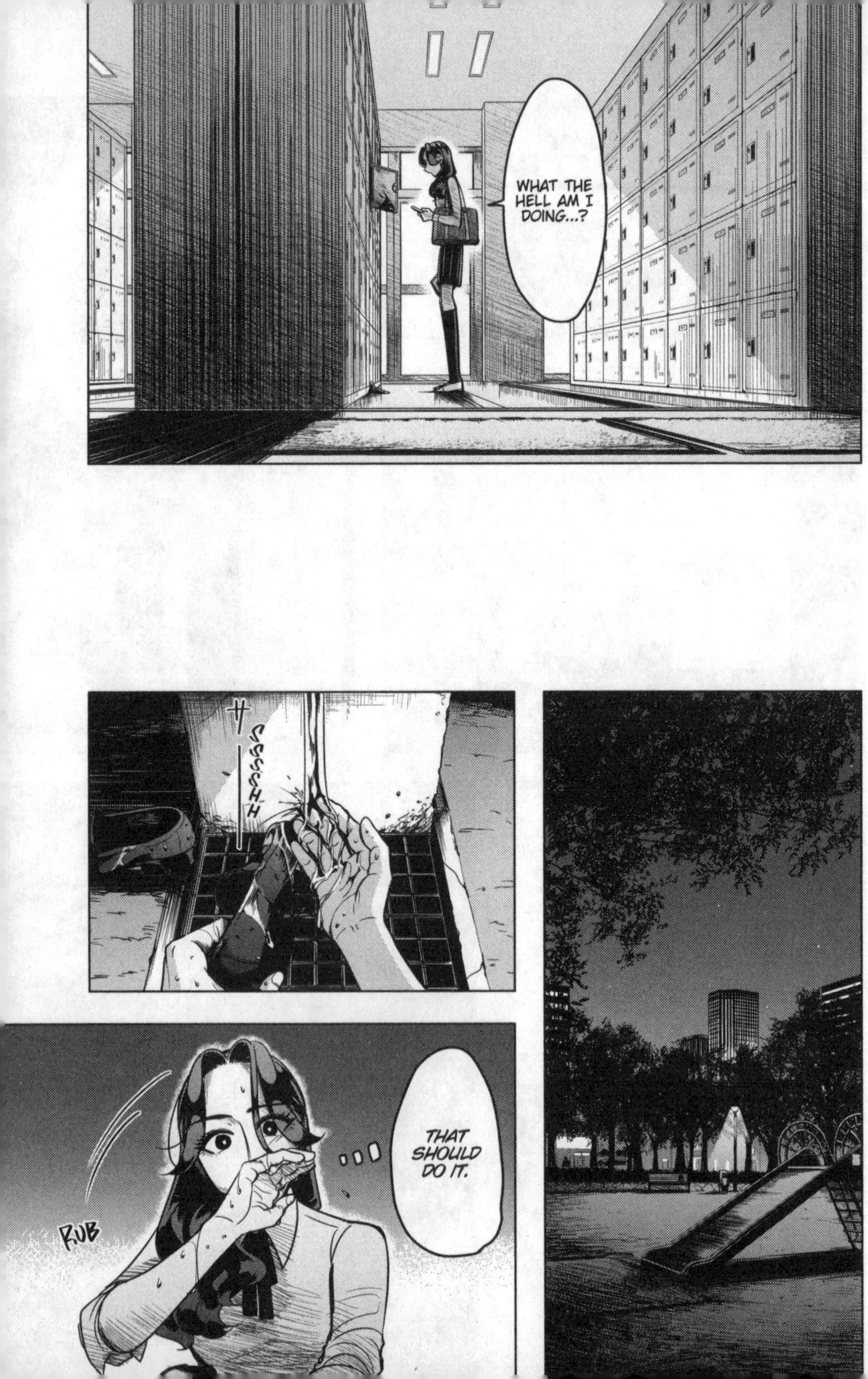
WHAT THE HELL AM I DOING...?
SSSSHH
...
THAT SHOULD DO IT.
RUB

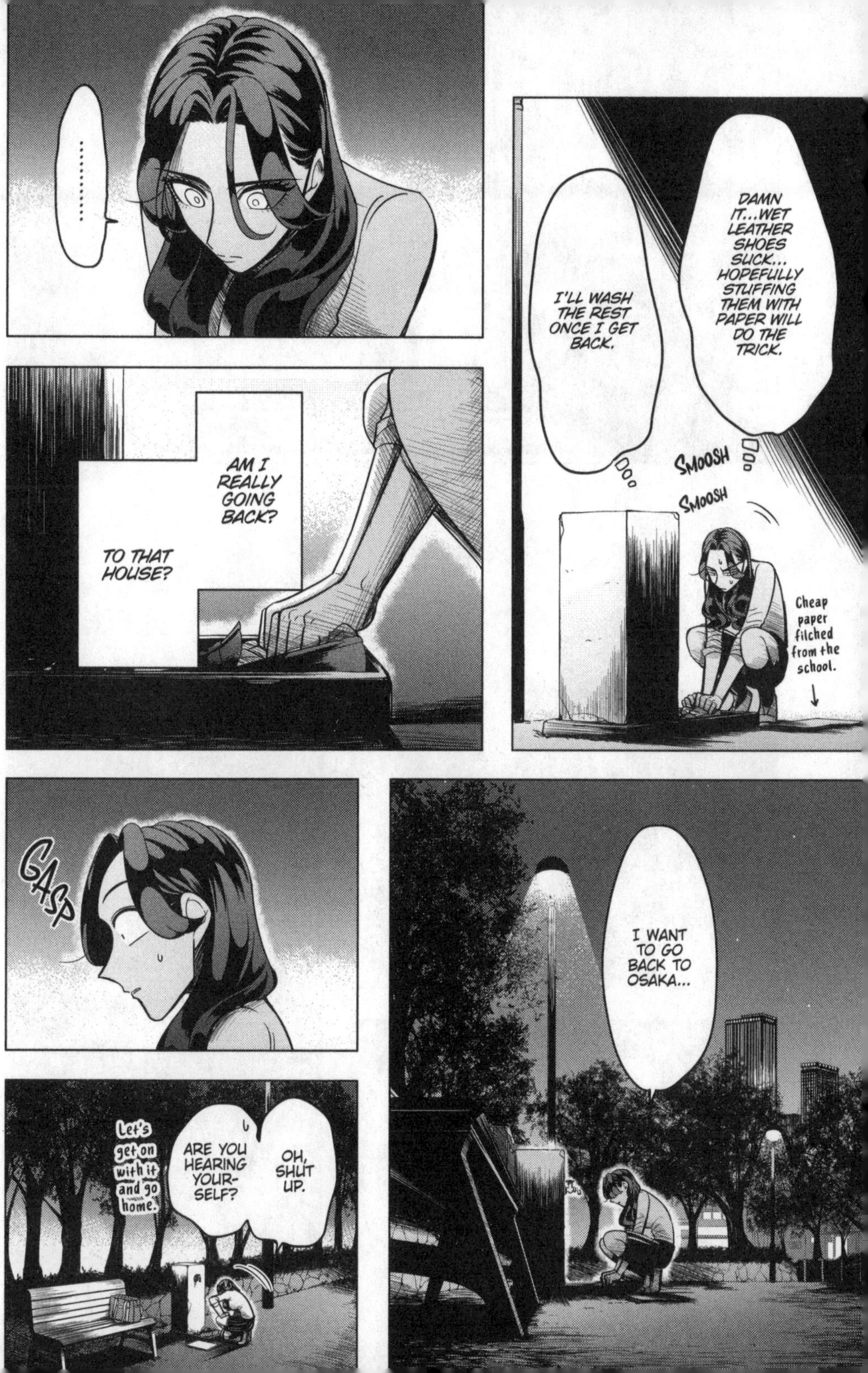
DAMN IT...WET LEATHER SHOES SUCK... HOPEFULLY STUFFING THEM WITH PAPER WILL DO THE TRICK.
I'LL WASH THE REST ONCE I GET BACK.
SMOOSH
SMOOSH
Cheap paper filched from the school.
......
AM I REALLY GOING BACK?
TO THAT HOUSE?
I WANT TO GO BACK TO OSAKA...
GASP
OH, SHUT UP.
ARE YOU HEARING YOURSELF?
Let's get on with it and go home.

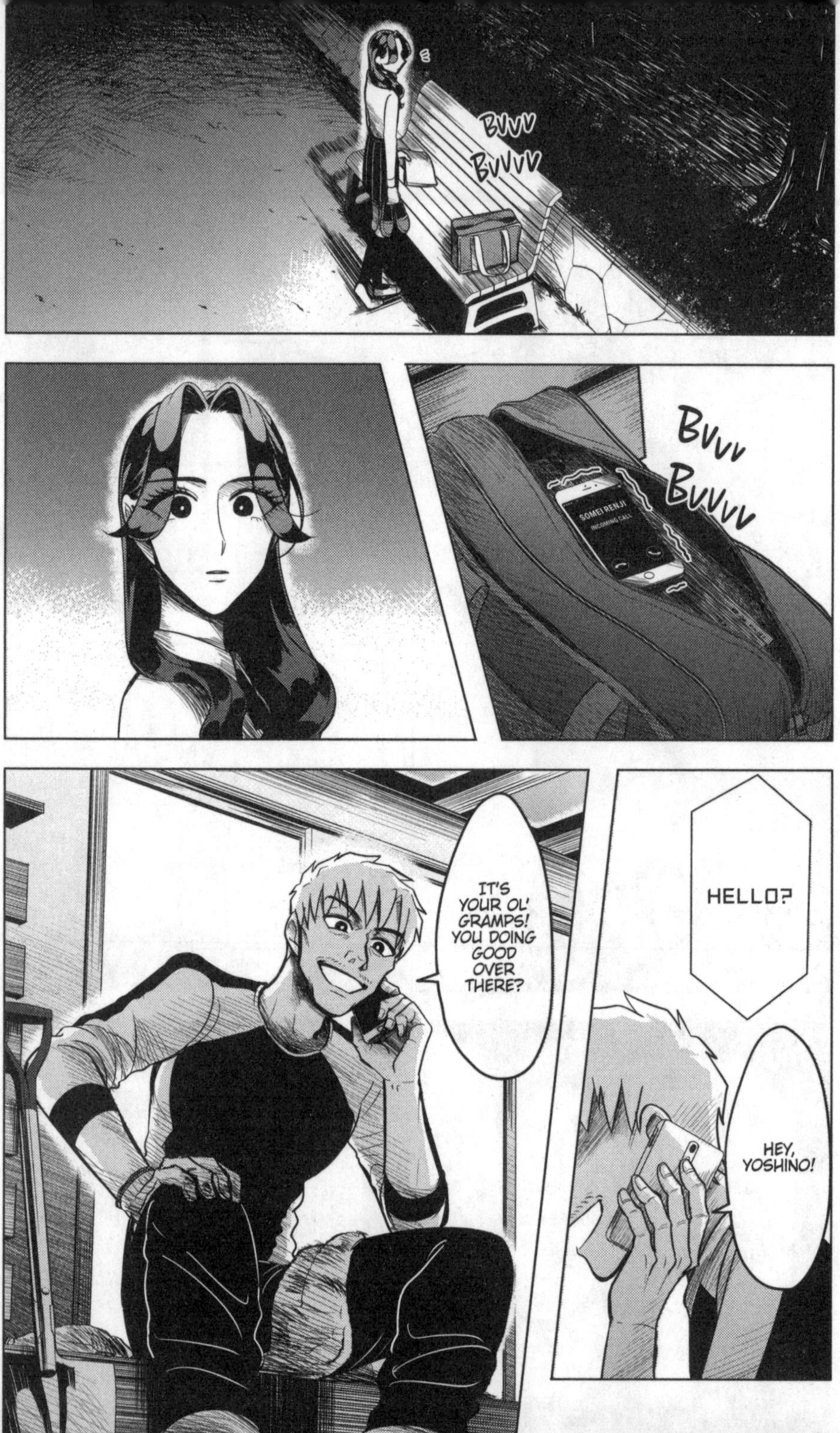
BVVV
BVVVV
SOMEI RENJI
INCOMING CALL
BVVV
BVVVV
HELLO?
HEY, YOSHINO!
IT'S YOUR OL' GRAMPS! YOU DOING GOOD OVER THERE?

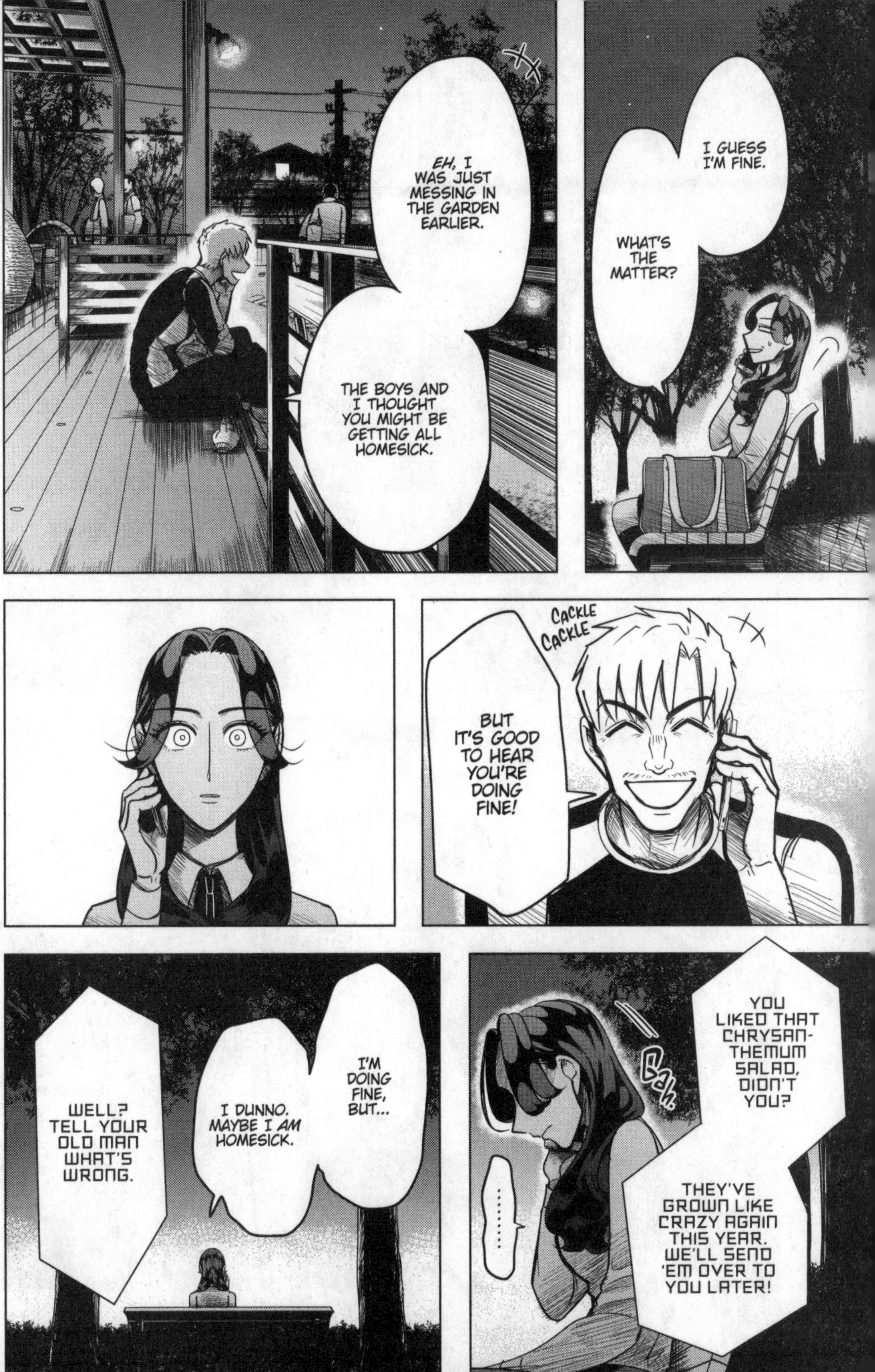
I GUESS I'M FINE.
WHAT'S THE MATTER?
EH, I WAS JUST MESSING IN THE GARDEN EARLIER.
THE BOYS AND I THOUGHT YOU MIGHT BE GETTING ALL HOMESICK.
CACKLE CACKLE
BUT IT'S GOOD TO HEAR YOU'RE DOING FINE!
YOU LIKED THAT CHRYSANTHEMUM SALAD, DIDN'T YOU?
THEY'VE GROWN LIKE CRAZY AGAIN THIS YEAR. WE'LL SEND 'EM OVER TO YOU LATER!
......
I'M DOING FINE, BUT...
I DUNNO. MAYBE I AM HOMESICK.
WELL? TELL YOUR OLD MAN WHAT'S WRONG.

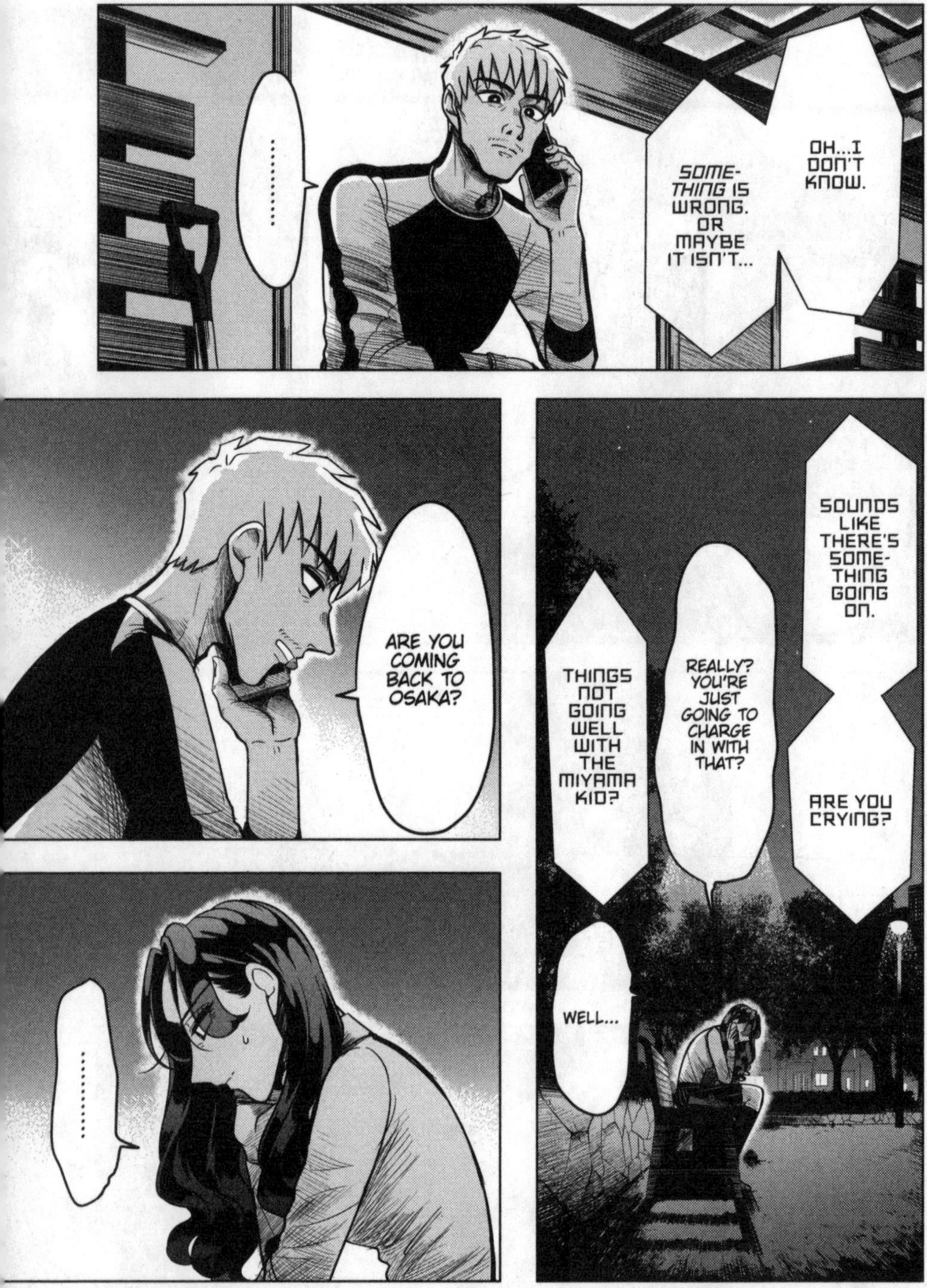
OH...I DON'T KNOW.
*SOMETHING* IS WRONG. OR MAYBE IT ISN'T...
......
SOUNDS LIKE THERE'S SOMETHING GOING ON.
ARE YOU CRYING?
REALLY? YOU'RE JUST GOING TO CHARGE IN WITH THAT?
THINGS NOT GOING WELL WITH THE MIYAMA KID?
WELL...
ARE YOU COMING BACK TO OSAKA?
......

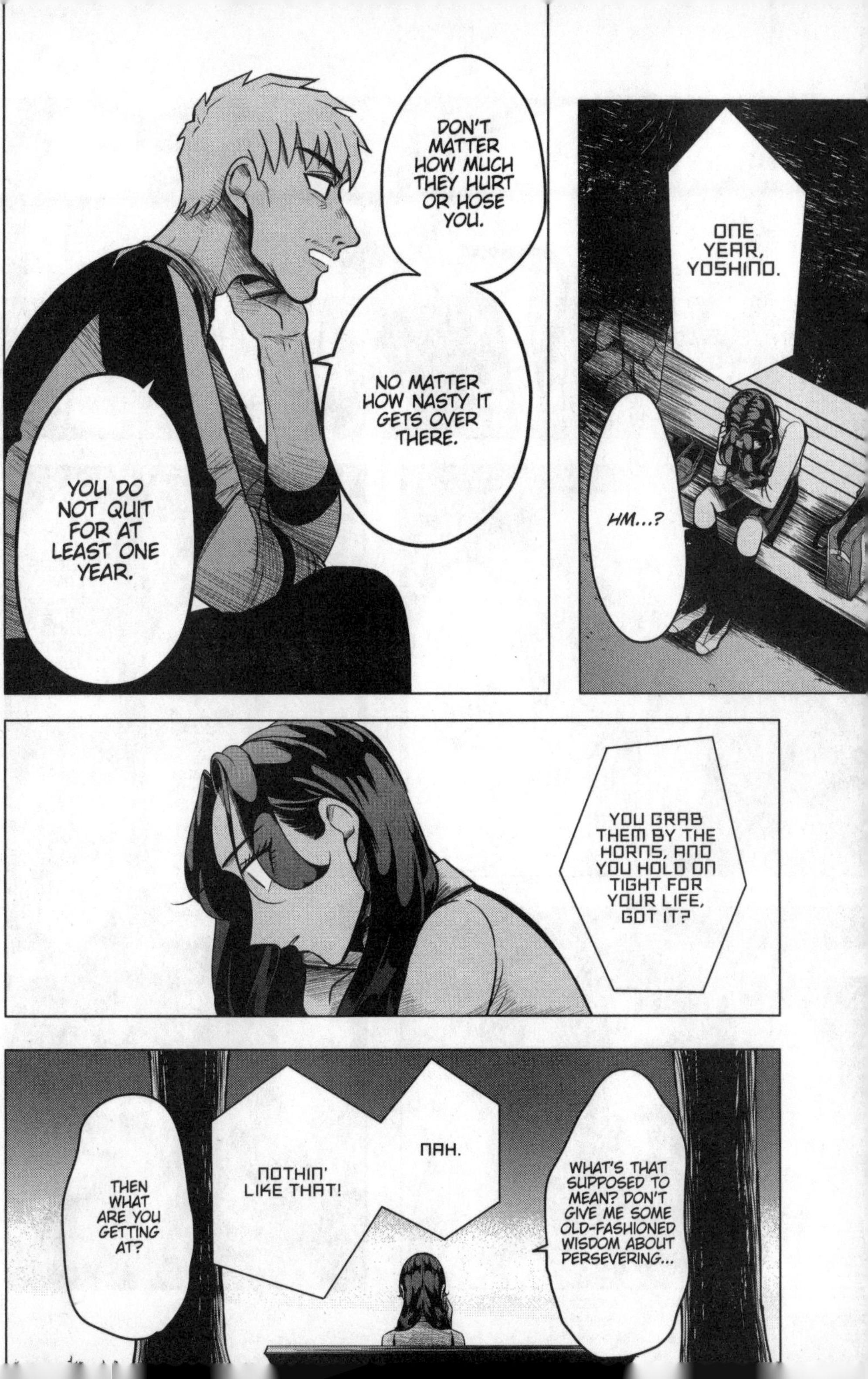
ONE YEAR, YOSHINO.
HM...?
DON'T MATTER HOW MUCH THEY HURT OR HOSE YOU.
NO MATTER HOW NASTY IT GETS OVER THERE.
YOU DO NOT QUIT FOR AT LEAST ONE YEAR.
YOU GRAB THEM BY THE HORNS, AND YOU HOLD ON TIGHT FOR YOUR LIFE, GOT IT?
WHAT'S THAT SUPPOSED TO MEAN? DON'T GIVE ME SOME OLD-FASHIONED WISDOM ABOUT PERSEVERING...
NAH.
NOTHIN' LIKE THAT!
THEN WHAT ARE YOU GETTING AT?

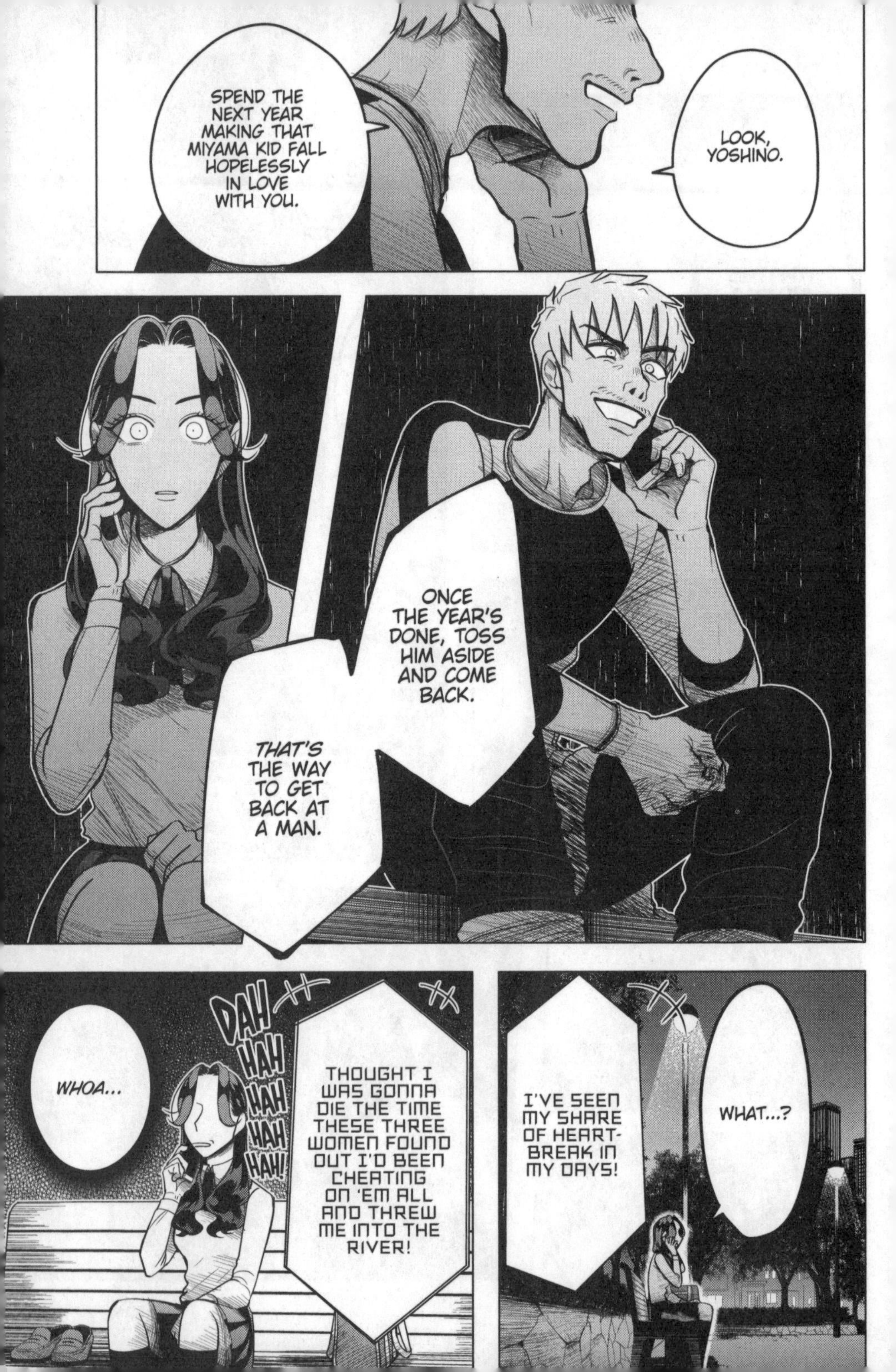
LOOK, YOSHINO.
SPEND THE NEXT YEAR MAKING THAT MIYAMA KID FALL HOPELESSLY IN LOVE WITH YOU.
ONCE THE YEAR'S DONE, TOSS HIM ASIDE AND COME BACK.
*THAT'S* THE WAY TO GET BACK AT A MAN.
WHAT...?
I'VE SEEN MY SHARE OF HEART-BREAK IN MY DAYS!
THOUGHT I WAS GONNA DIE THE TIME THESE THREE WOMEN FOUND OUT I'D BEEN CHEATING ON 'EM ALL AND THREW ME INTO THE RIVER!
DAH HAH HAH HAH HAH!
WHOA...

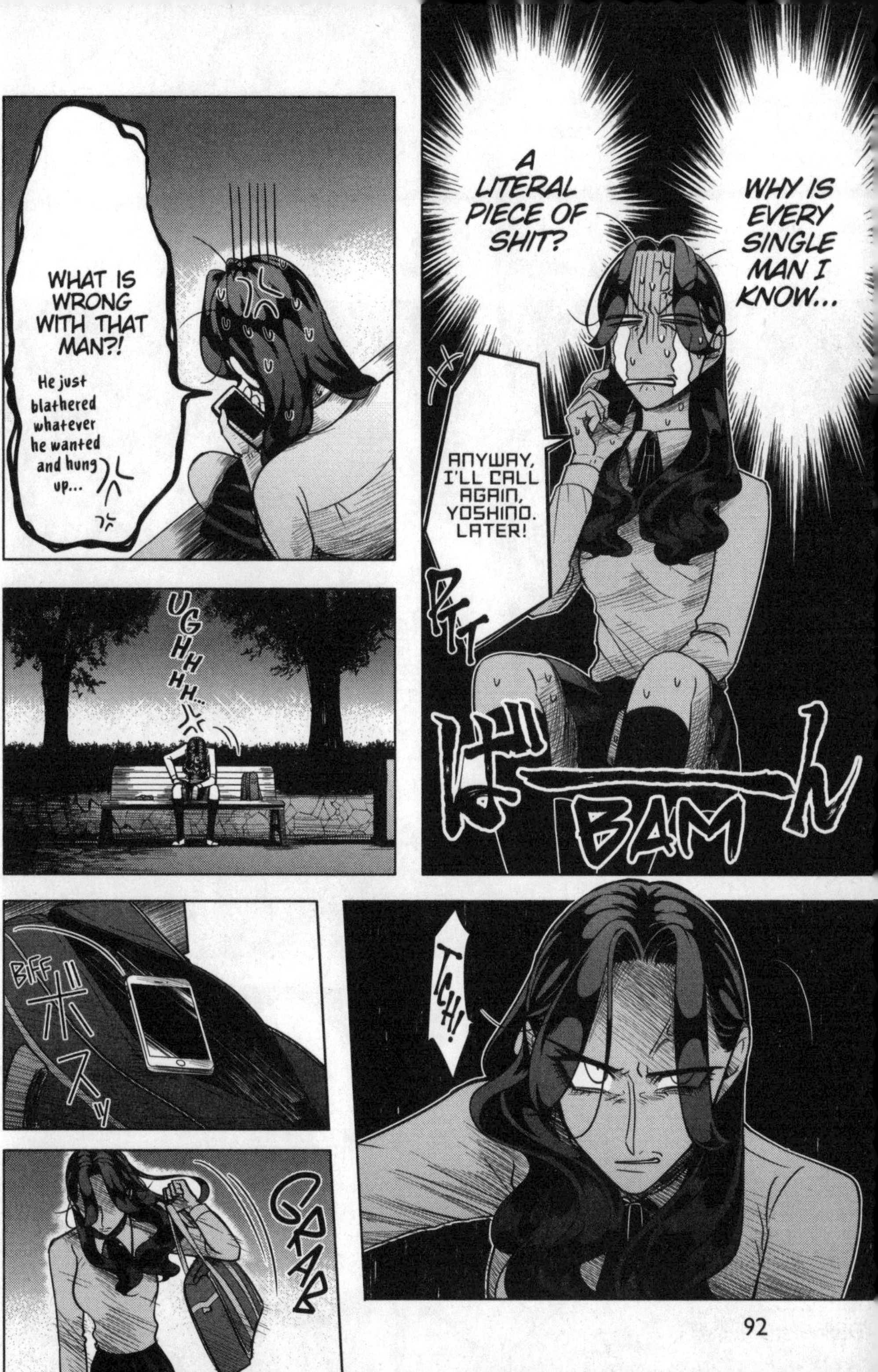
WHY IS EVERY SINGLE MAN I KNOW...
A LITERAL PIECE OF SHIT?
ANYWAY, I'LL CALL AGAIN, YOSHINO. LATER!
PTT
BAM
WHAT IS WRONG WITH THAT MAN?!
He just blathered whatever he wanted and hung up...
UGHHHH...
TCH!
BIFF
GRAB

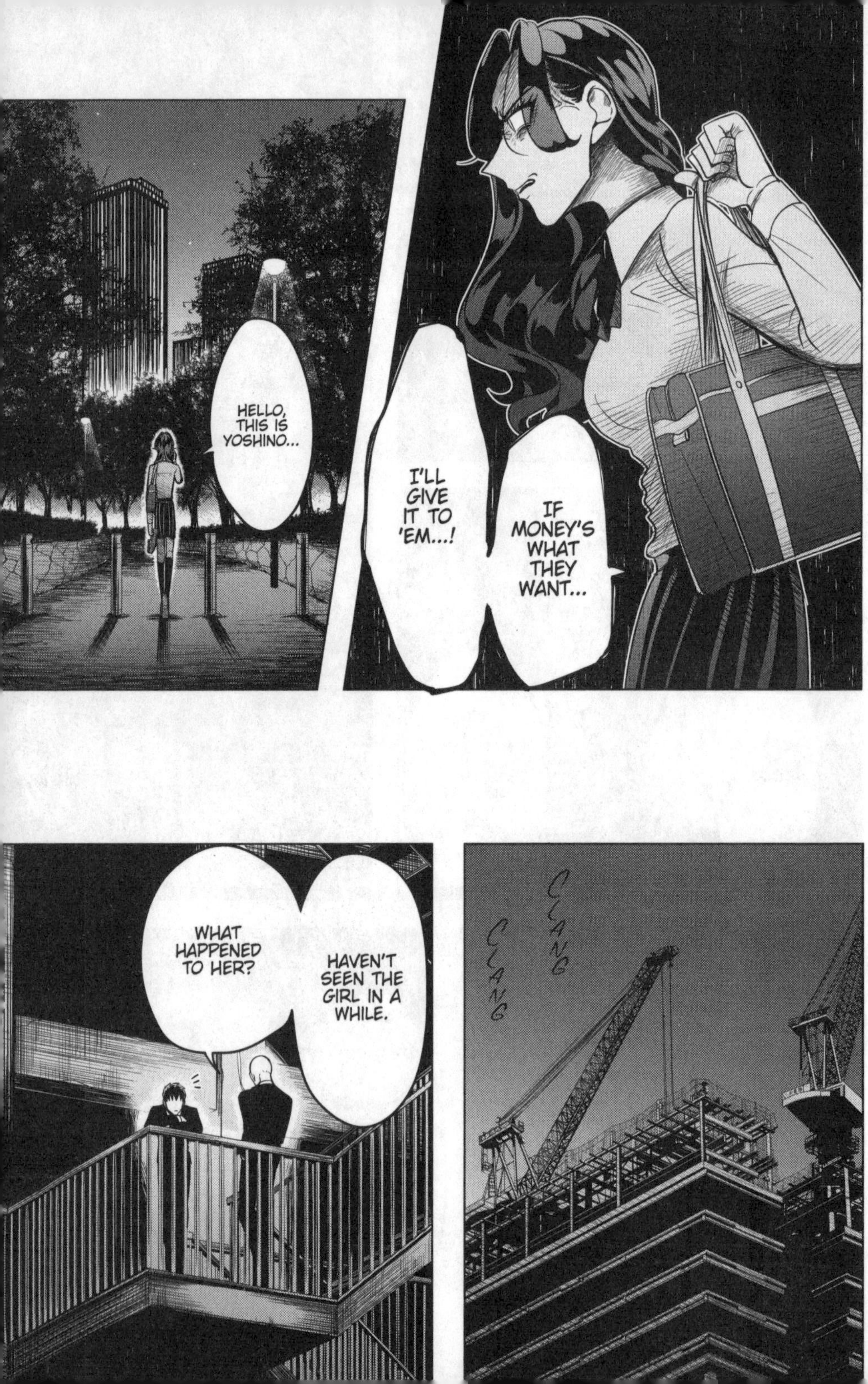
IF MONEY'S WHAT THEY WANT...
I'LL GIVE IT TO 'EM...!
HELLO, THIS IS YOSHINO...
CLANG
CLANG
HAVEN'T SEEN THE GIRL IN A WHILE.
WHAT HAPPENED TO HER?

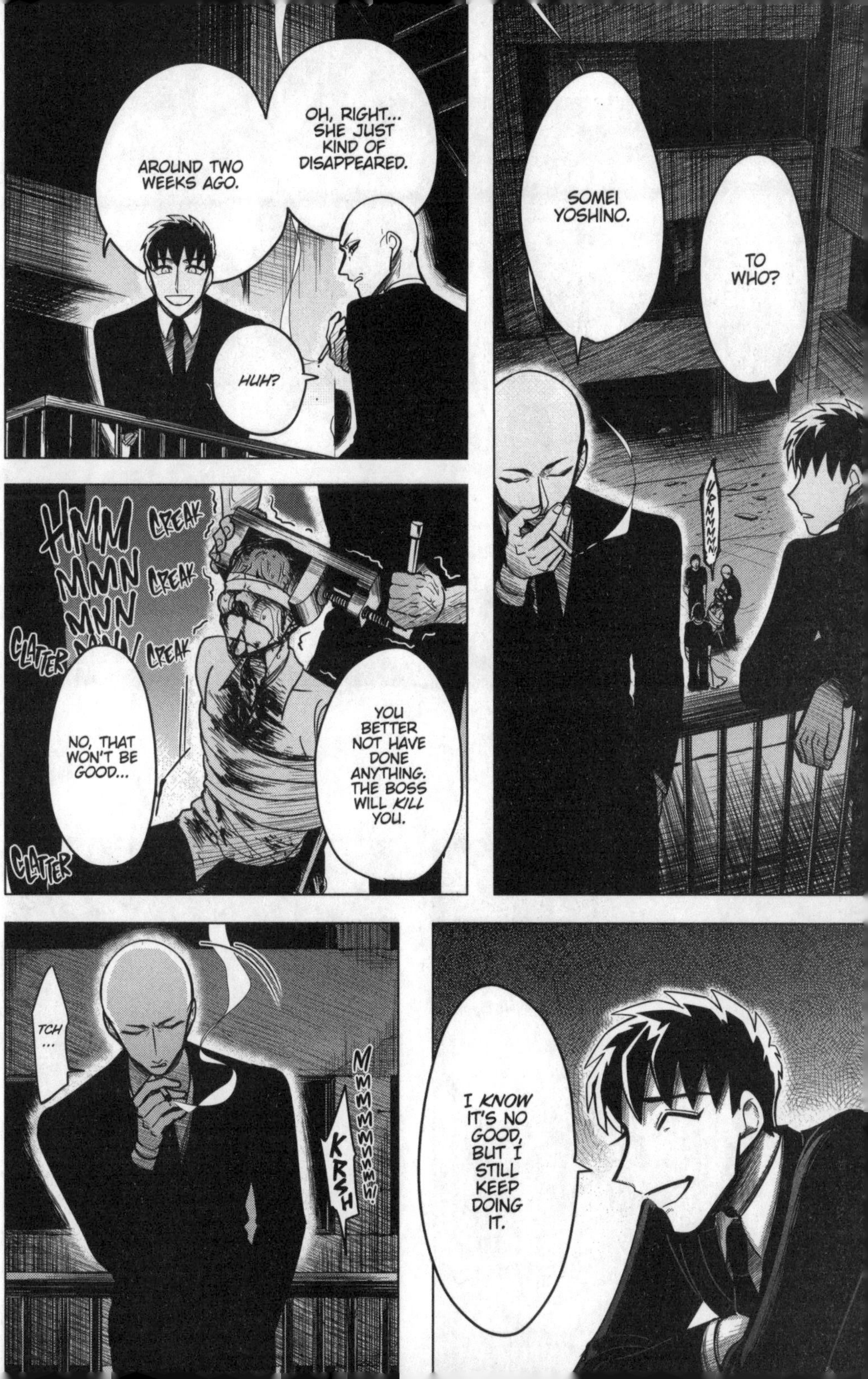
TO WHO?
SOMEI YOSHINO.
HRMMMMN!
OH, RIGHT... SHE JUST KIND OF DISAPPEARED.
AROUND TWO WEEKS AGO.
HUH?
HMM MMN MNN
CREAK
CREAK
CREAK
CLATTER
YOU BETTER NOT HAVE DONE ANYTHING. THE BOSS WILL *KILL* YOU.
NO, THAT WON'T BE GOOD...
CLATTER
I *KNOW* IT'S NO GOOD, BUT I STILL KEEP DOING IT.
MMMMMMMM!
KRSH
TCH ...

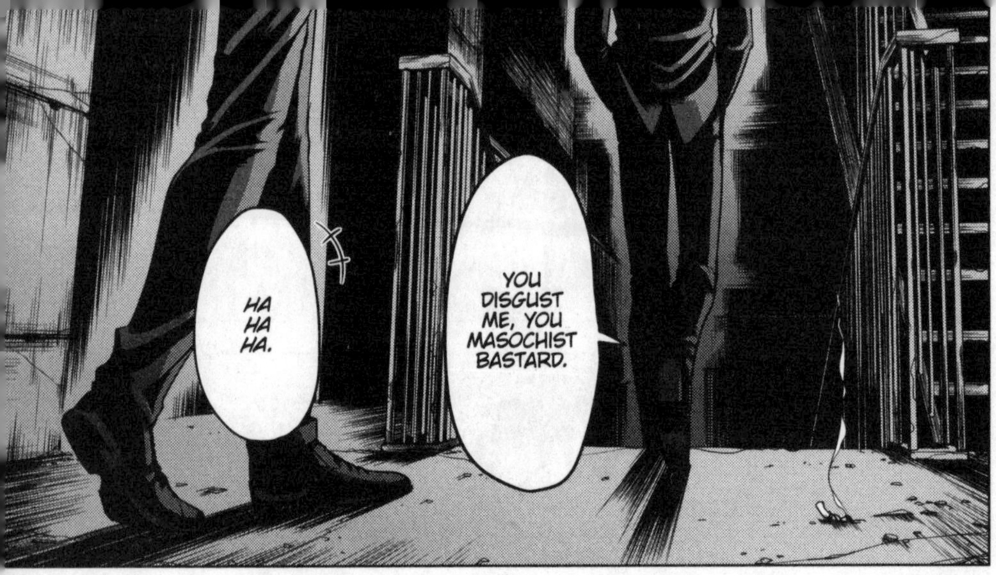
YOU DISGUST ME, YOU MASOCHIST BASTARD.
HA HA HA.

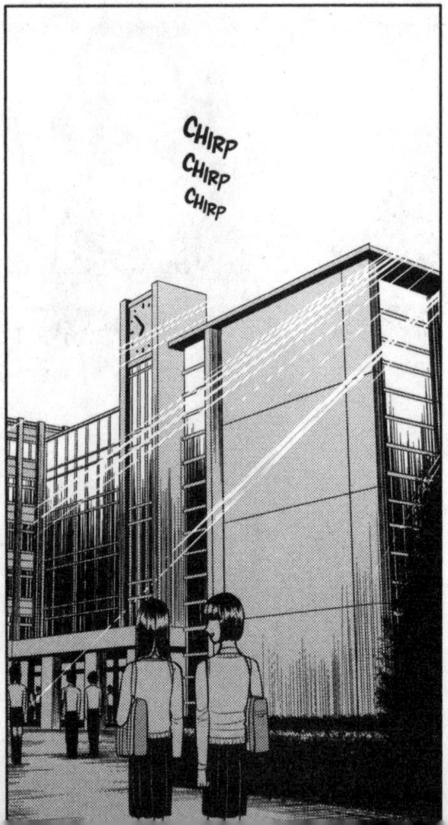
CHIRP
CHIRP
CHIRP

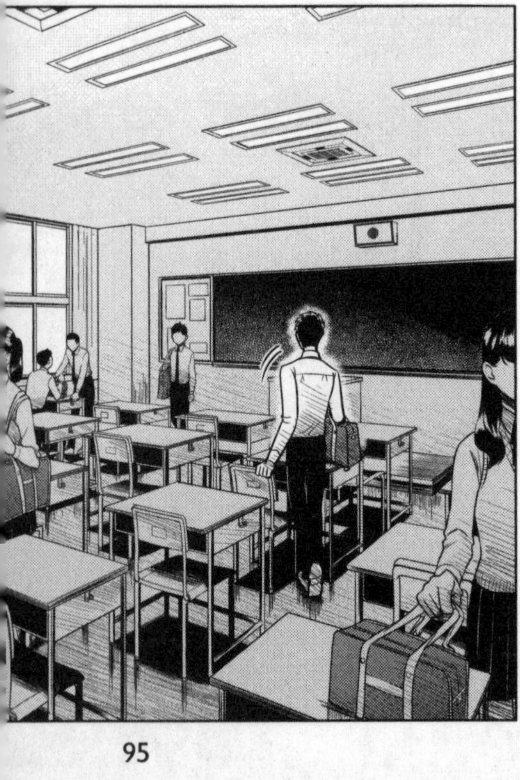

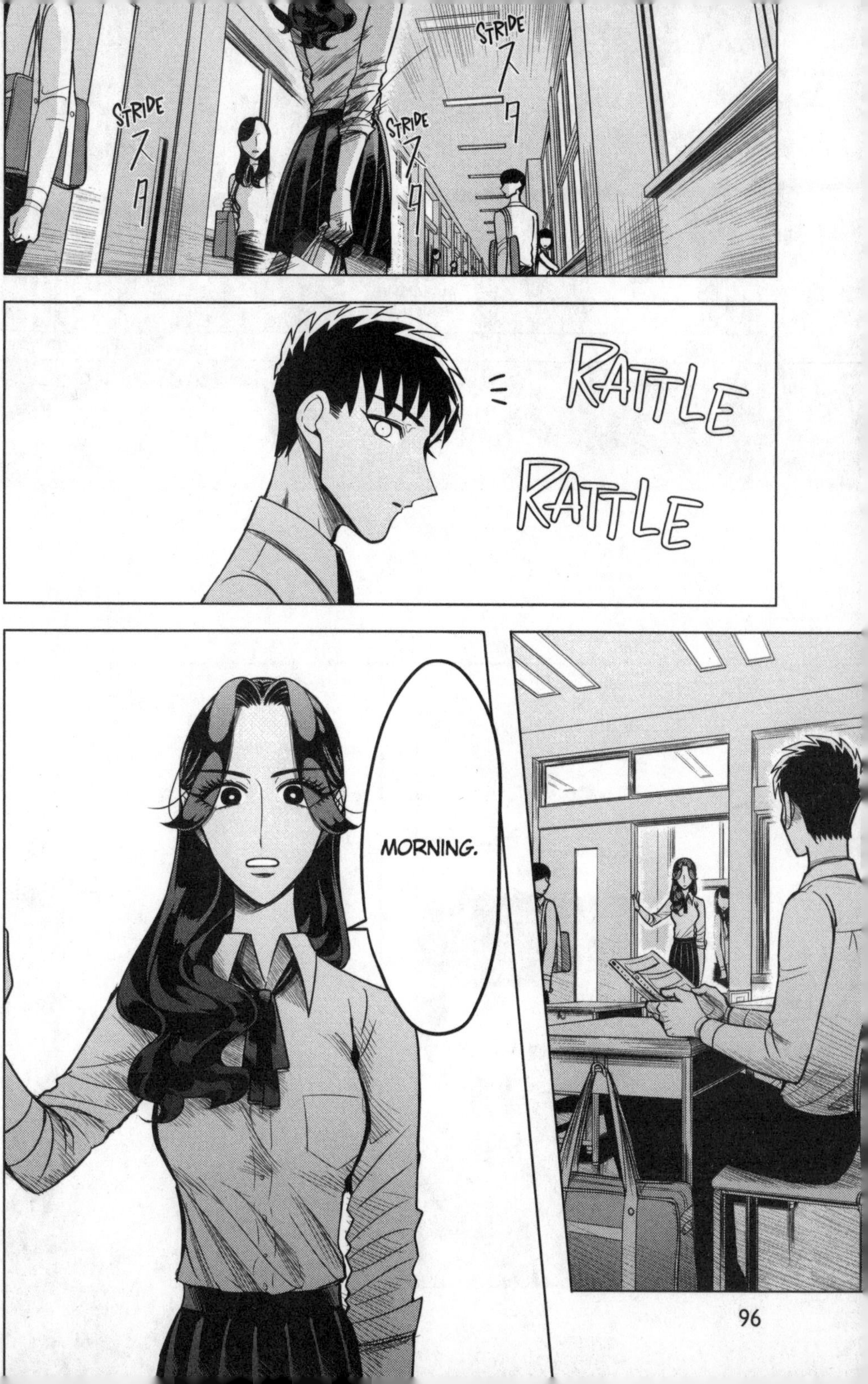
STRIDE
スタ
STRIDE
スタ
STRIDE
スタ
RATTLE
RATTLE
MORNING.

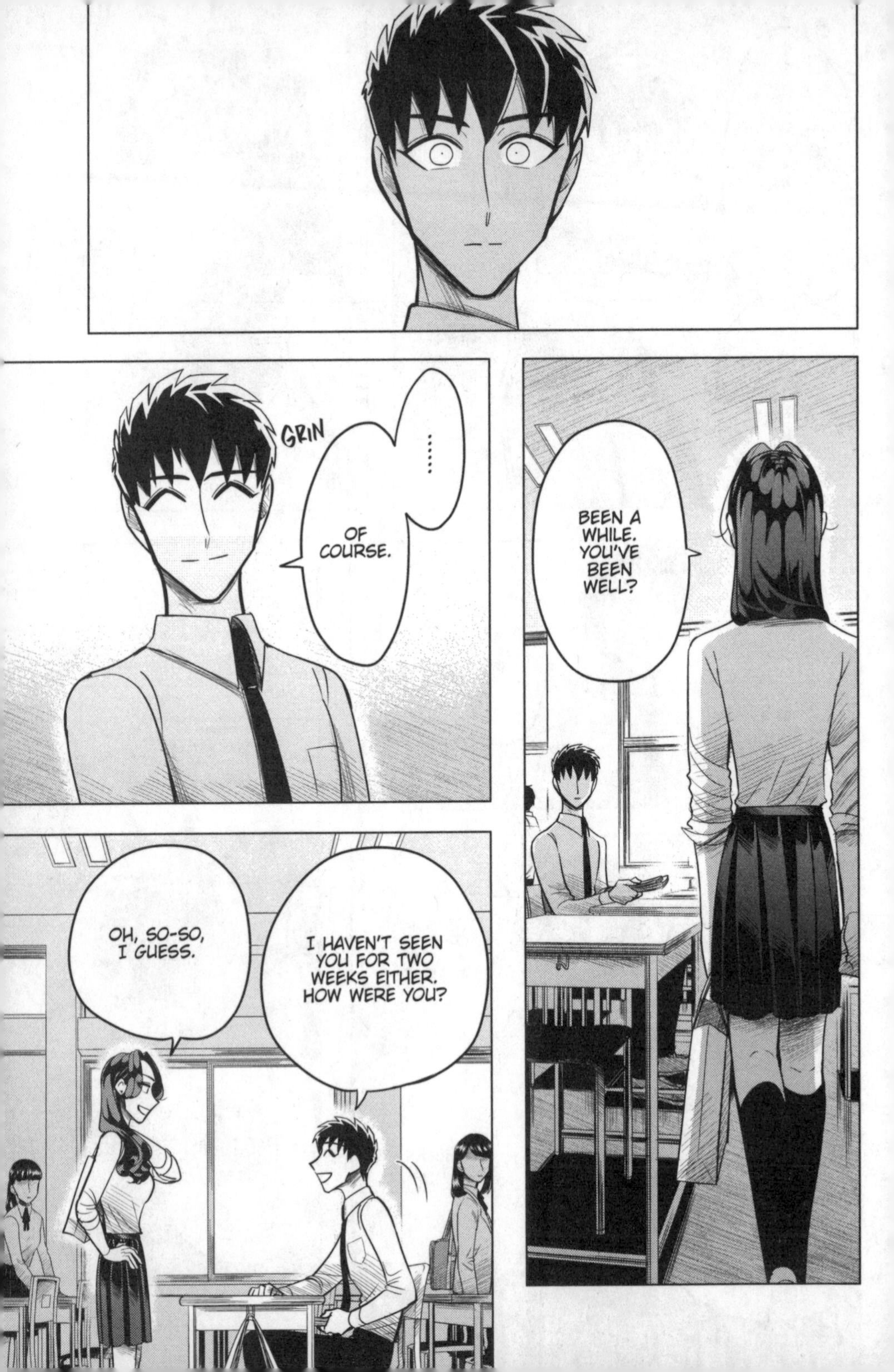
BEEN A WHILE. YOU'VE BEEN WELL?
...... OF COURSE.
GRIN
I HAVEN'T SEEN YOU FOR TWO WEEKS EITHER. HOW WERE YOU?
OH, SO-SO, I GUESS.

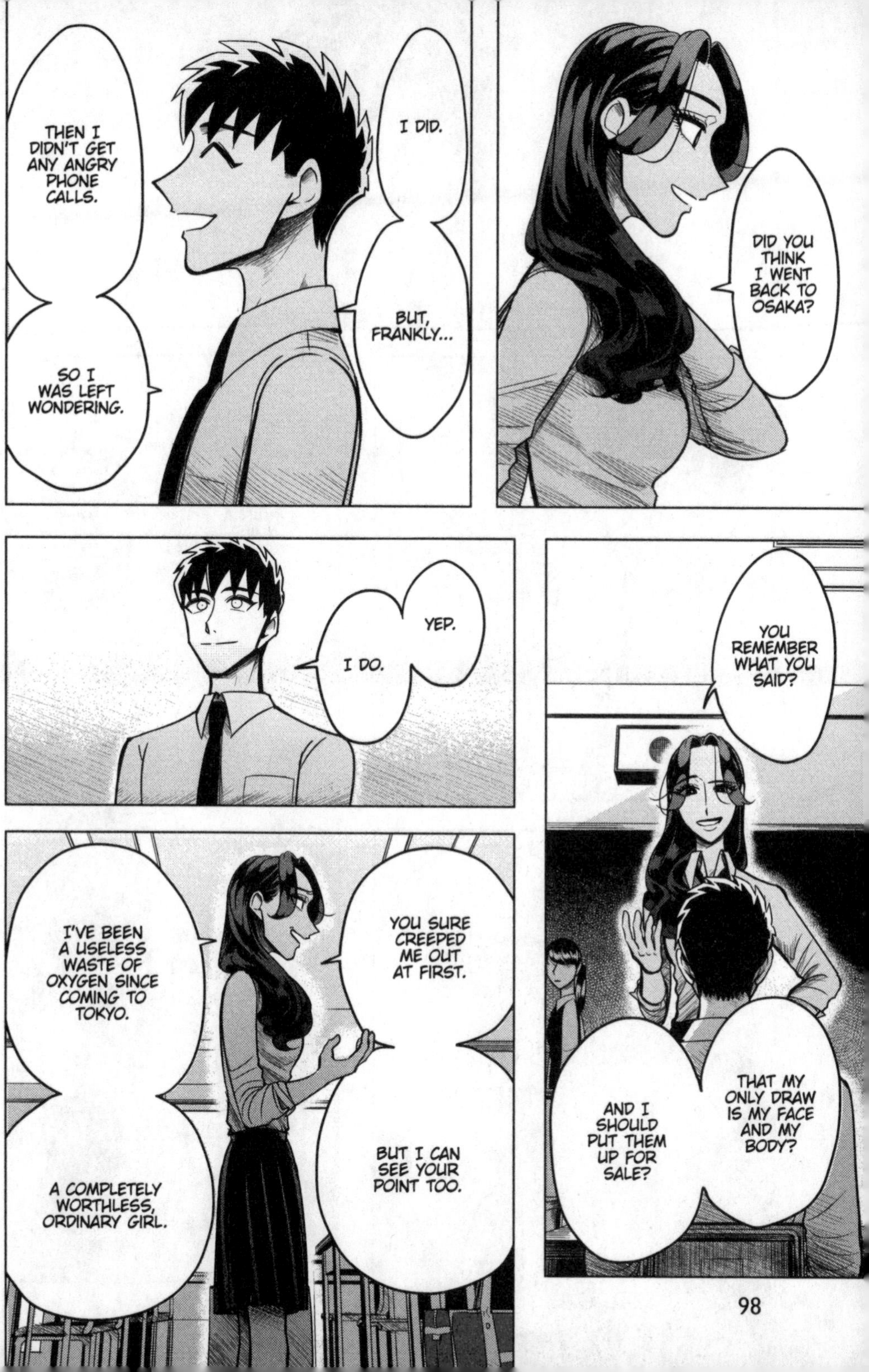
DID YOU THINK I WENT BACK TO OSAKA?
I DID.
BUT, FRANKLY...
THEN I DIDN'T GET ANY ANGRY PHONE CALLS.
SO I WAS LEFT WONDERING.
YOU REMEMBER WHAT YOU SAID?
THAT MY ONLY DRAW IS MY FACE AND MY BODY?
AND I SHOULD PUT THEM UP FOR SALE?
YEP.
I DO.
YOU SURE CREEPED ME OUT AT FIRST.
BUT I CAN SEE YOUR POINT TOO.
I'VE BEEN A USELESS WASTE OF OXYGEN SINCE COMING TO TOKYO.
A COMPLETELY WORTHLESS, ORDINARY GIRL.

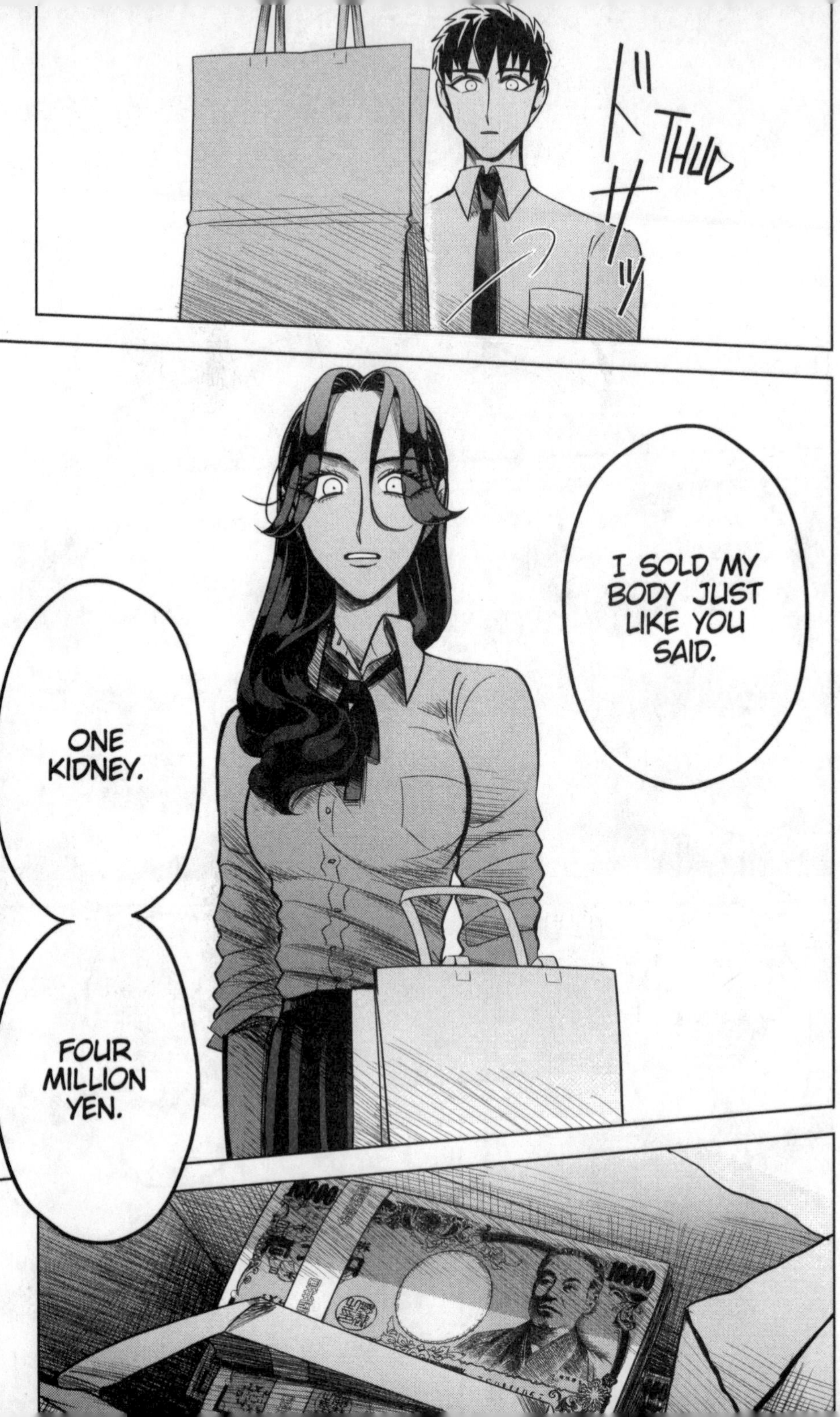
ドサッ
THUD
I SOLD MY BODY JUST LIKE YOU SAID.
ONE KIDNEY.
FOUR MILLION YEN.

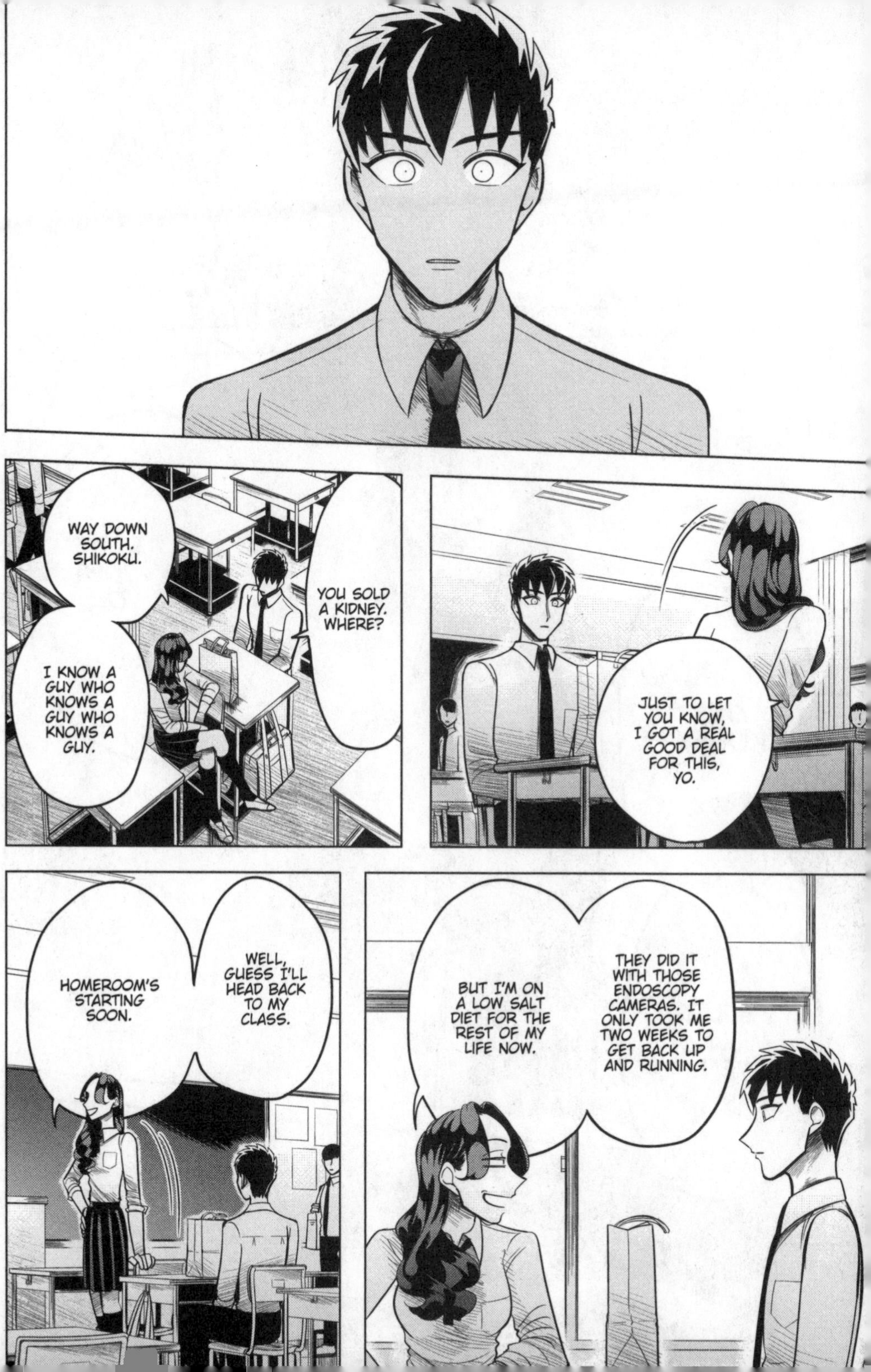
JUST TO LET YOU KNOW, I GOT A REAL GOOD DEAL FOR THIS, YO.
YOU SOLD A KIDNEY. WHERE?
WAY DOWN SOUTH. SHIKOKU.
I KNOW A GUY WHO KNOWS A GUY WHO KNOWS A GUY.
THEY DID IT WITH THOSE ENDOSCOPY CAMERAS. IT ONLY TOOK ME TWO WEEKS TO GET BACK UP AND RUNNING.
BUT I'M ON A LOW SALT DIET FOR THE REST OF MY LIFE NOW.
WELL, GUESS I'LL HEAD BACK TO MY CLASS.
HOMEROOM'S STARTING SOON.

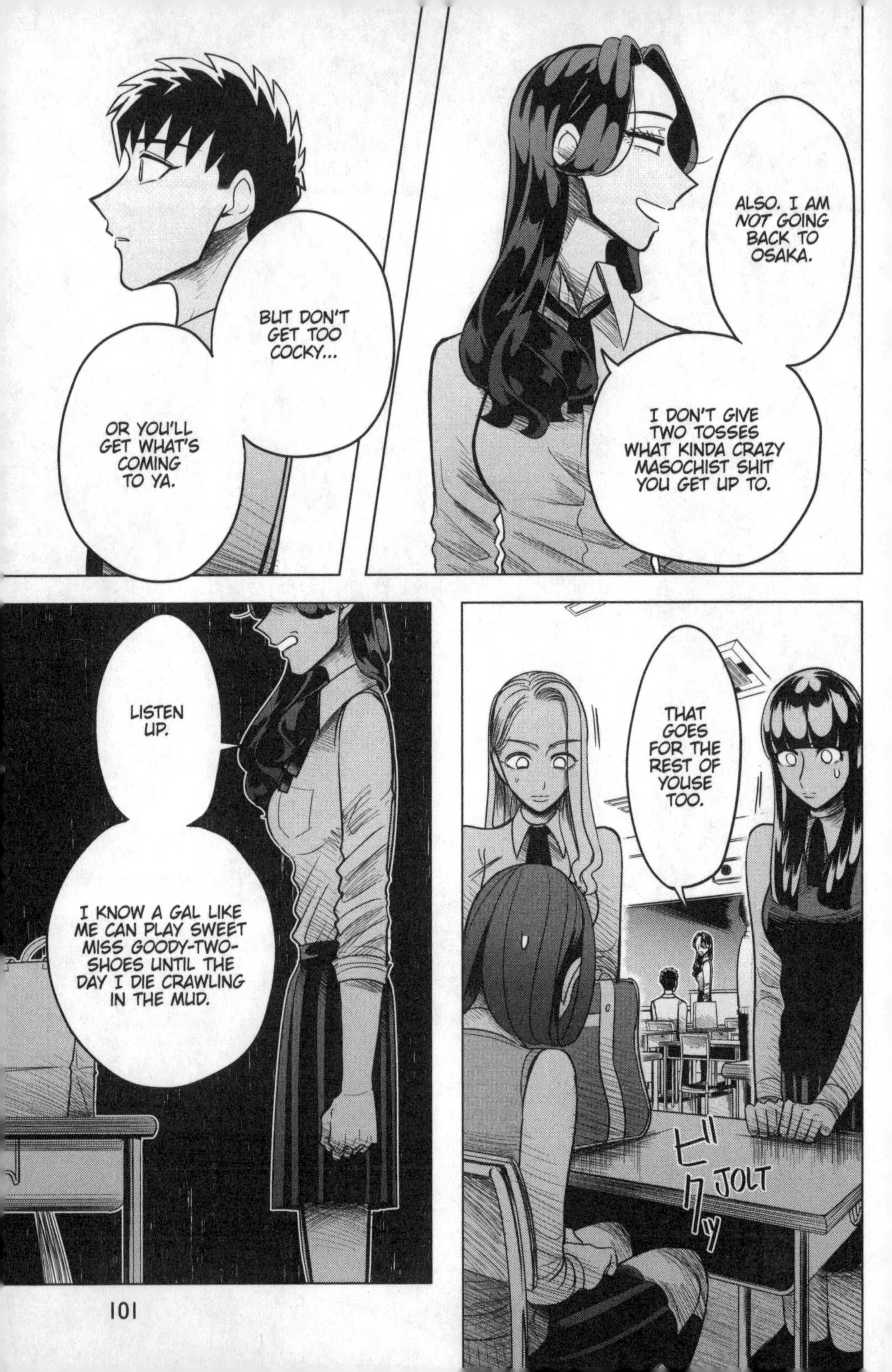
ALSO. I AM NOT GOING BACK TO OSAKA.
I DON'T GIVE TWO TOSSES WHAT KINDA CRAZY MASOCHIST SHIT YOU GET UP TO.
BUT DON'T GET TOO COCKY...
OR YOU'LL GET WHAT'S COMING TO YA.
THAT GOES FOR THE REST OF YOUSE TOO.
ビクッ
JOLT
LISTEN UP.
I KNOW A GAL LIKE ME CAN PLAY SWEET MISS GOODY-TWO-SHOES UNTIL THE DAY I DIE CRAWLING IN THE MUD.

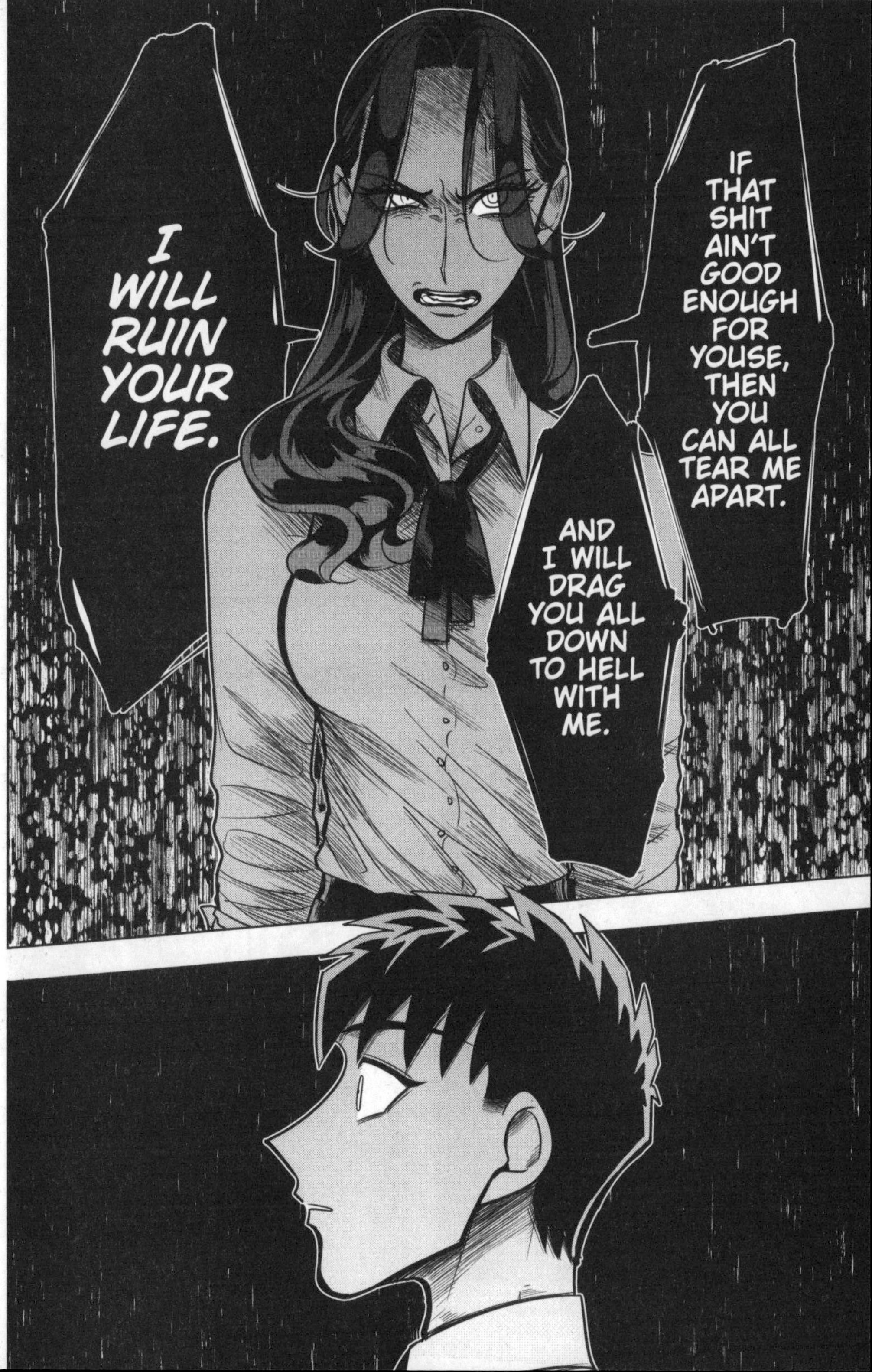
IF THAT SHIT AIN'T GOOD ENOUGH FOR YOUSE, THEN YOU CAN ALL TEAR ME APART.
AND I WILL DRAG YOU ALL DOWN TO HELL WITH ME.
I WILL RUIN YOUR LIFE.

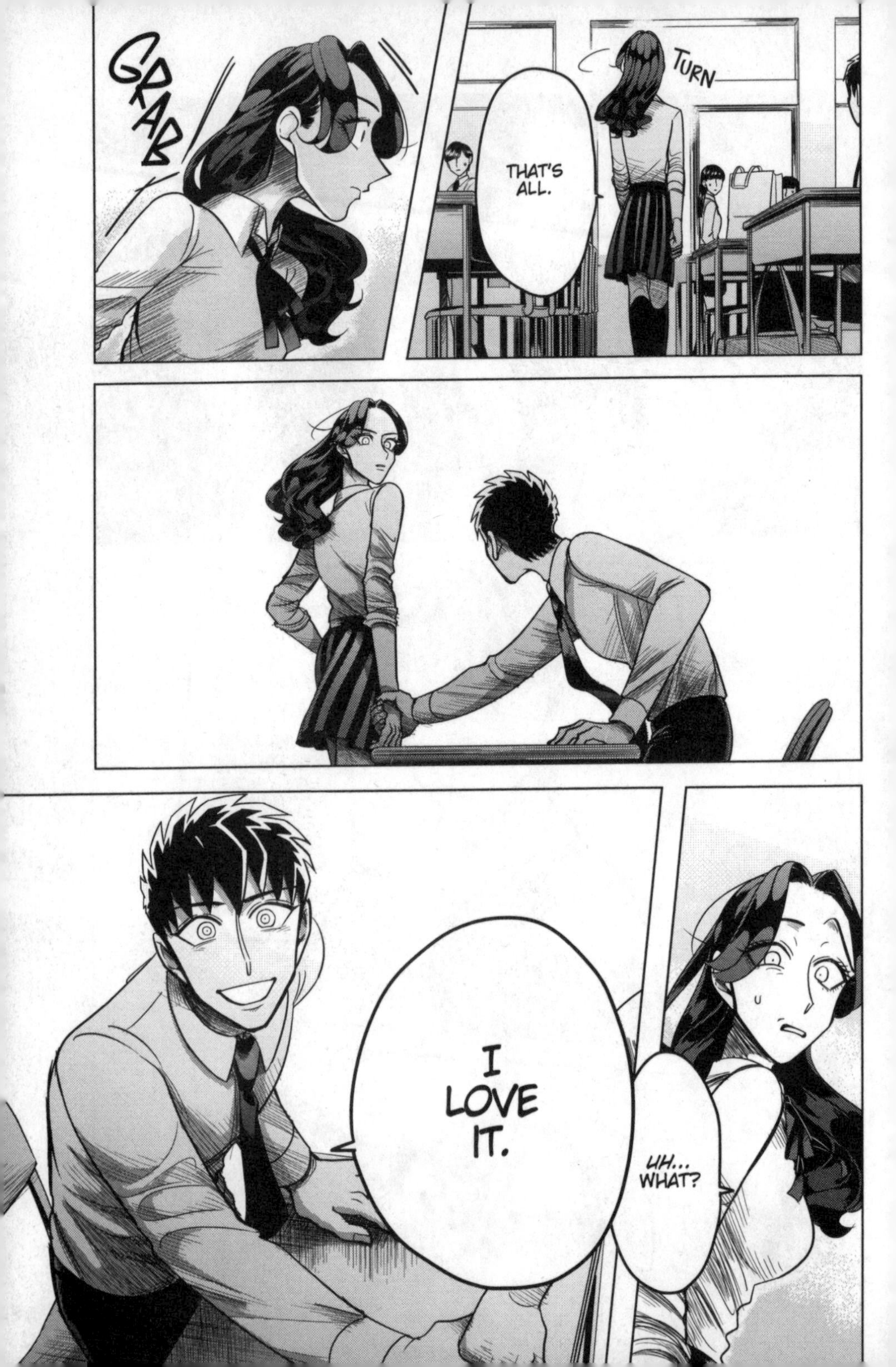
TURN
THAT'S ALL.
GRAB
UH... WHAT?
I LOVE IT.

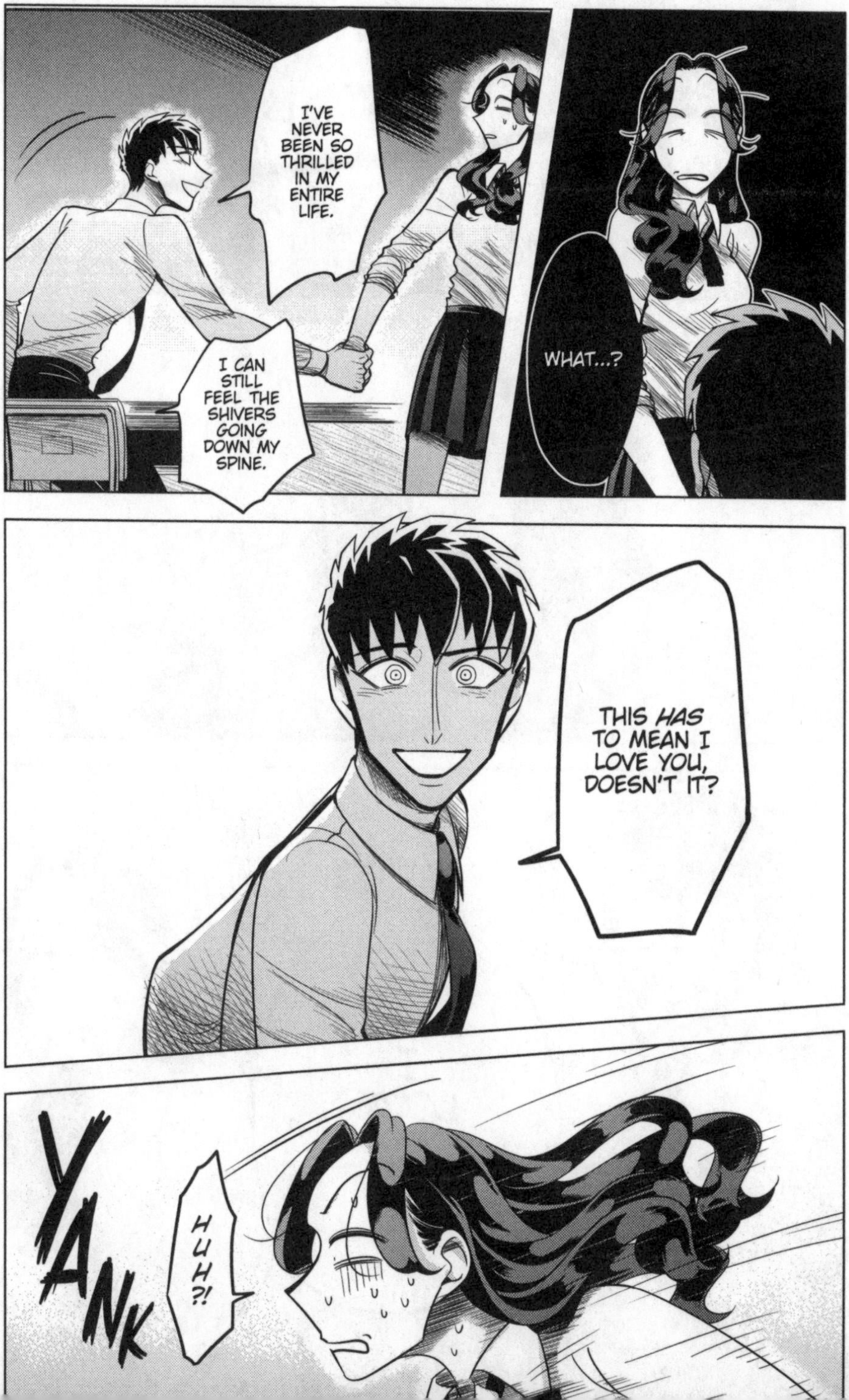
WHAT...?
I'VE NEVER BEEN SO THRILLED IN MY ENTIRE LIFE.
I CAN STILL FEEL THE SHIVERS GOING DOWN MY SPINE.
THIS *HAS* TO MEAN I LOVE YOU, DOESN'T IT?
HUH?!
YANK

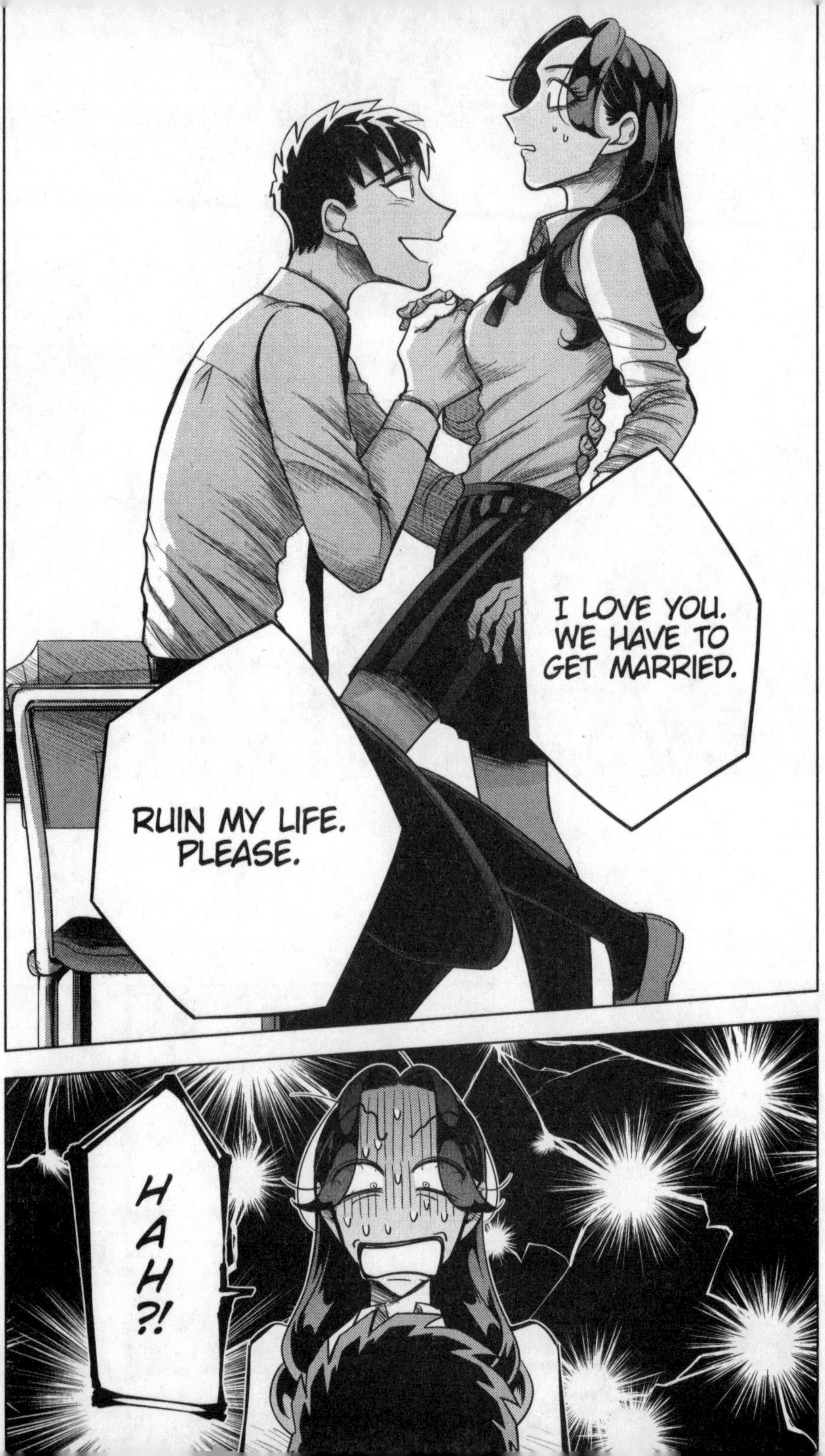
I LOVE YOU. WE HAVE TO GET MARRIED.
RUIN MY LIFE. PLEASE.
HAH?!

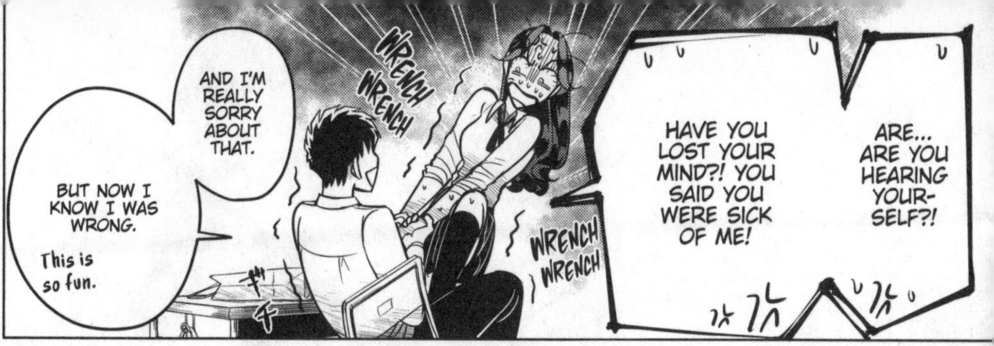
ARE... ARE YOU HEARING YOURSELF?!
HAVE YOU LOST YOUR MIND?! YOU SAID YOU WERE SICK OF ME!
WRENCH WRENCH
WRENCH WRENCH
AND I'M REALLY SORRY ABOUT THAT.
BUT NOW I KNOW I WAS WRONG.
This is so fun.
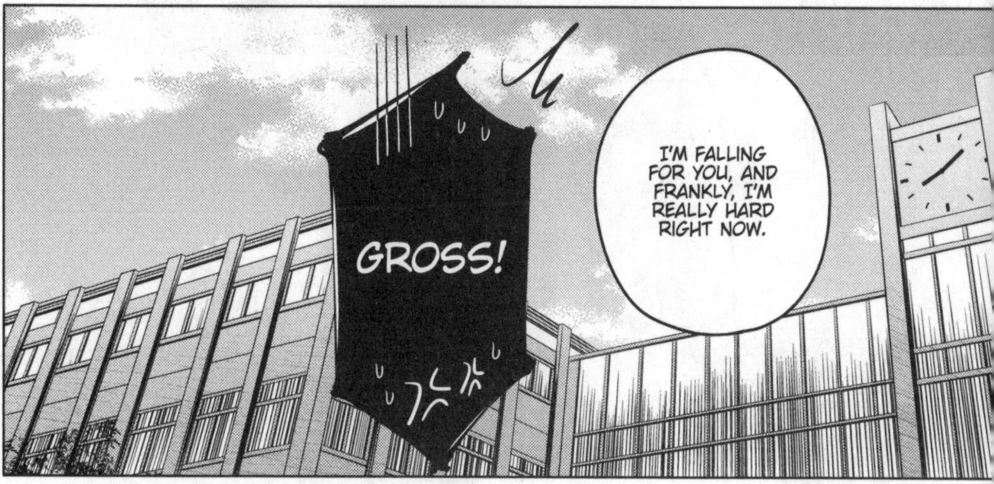
I'M FALLING FOR YOU, AND FRANKLY, I'M REALLY HARD RIGHT NOW.
GROSS!
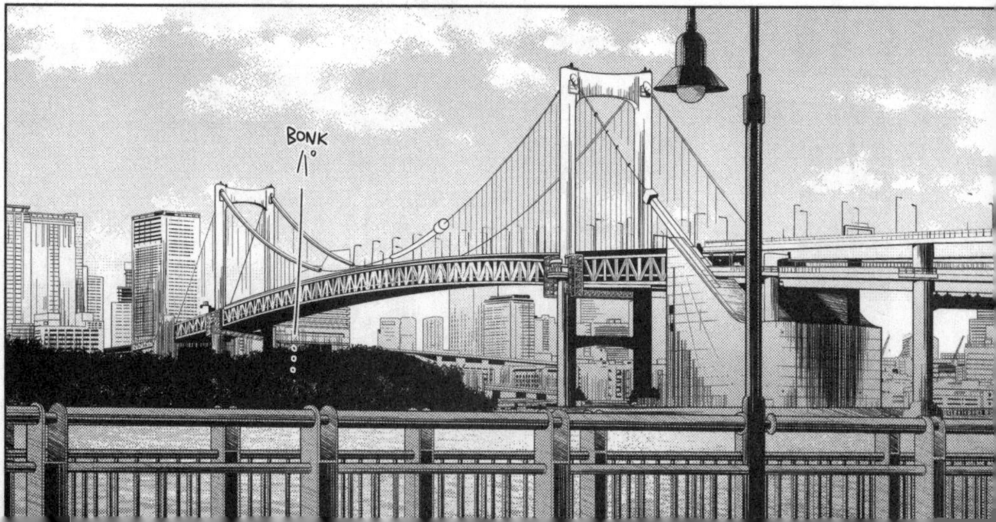
BONK

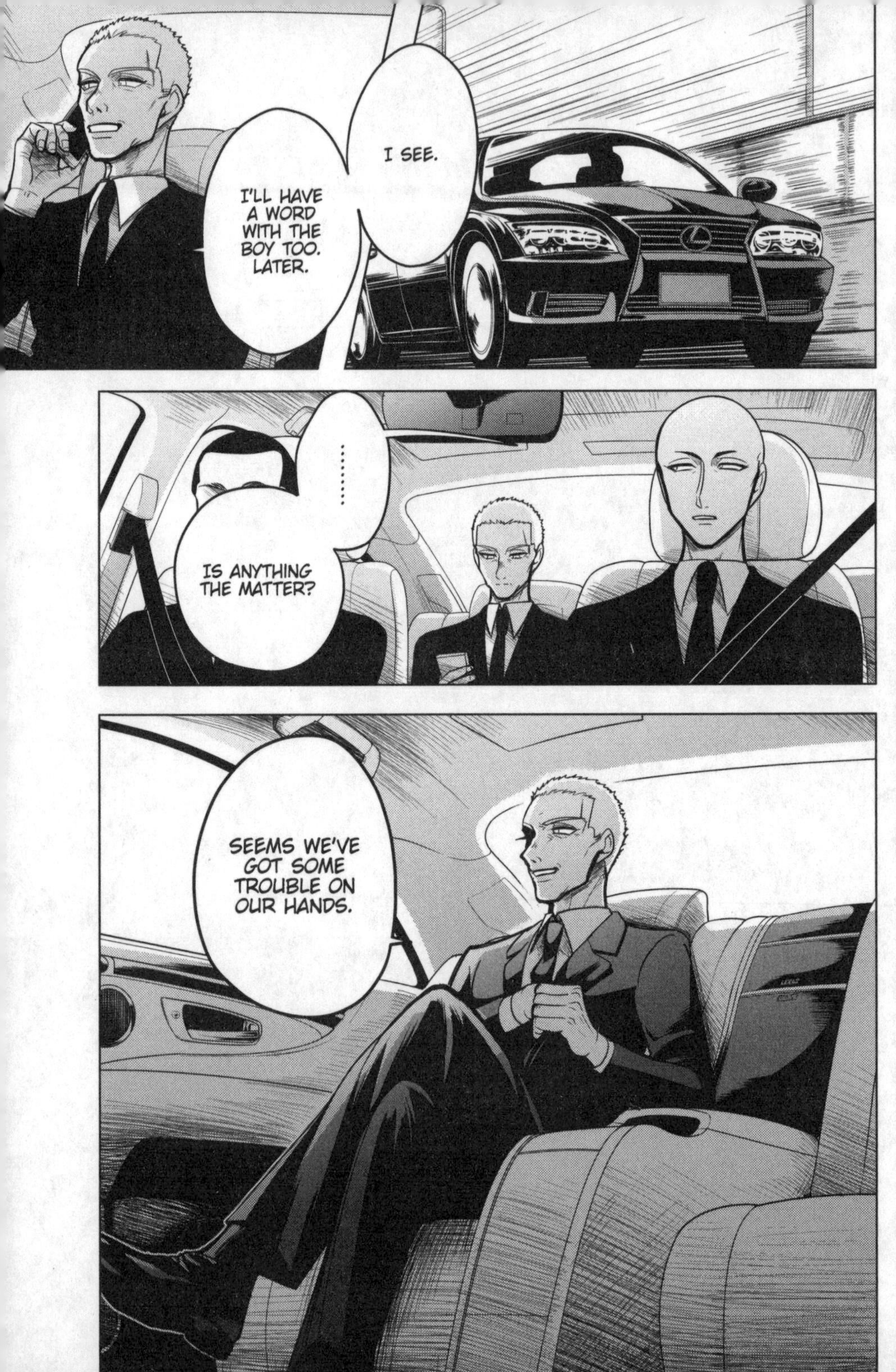
I SEE.
I'LL HAVE A WORD WITH THE BOY TOO. LATER.
......
IS ANYTHING THE MATTER?
SEEMS WE'VE GOT SOME TROUBLE ON OUR HANDS.

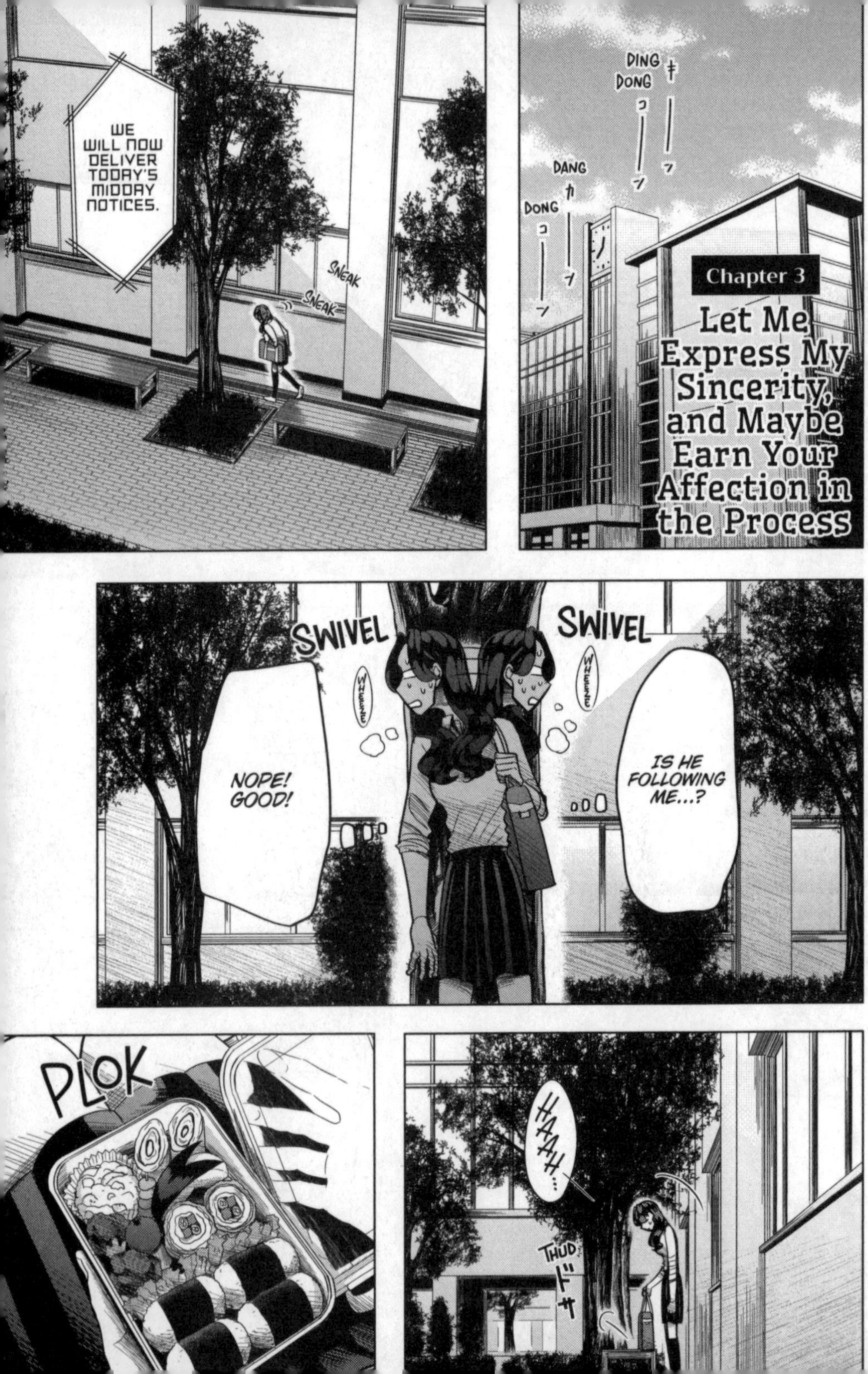
DING DONG
DANG DONG
Chapter 3
Let Me Express My Sincerity, and Maybe Earn Your Affection in the Process
WE WILL NOW DELIVER TODAY'S MIDDAY NOTICES.
SNEAK SNEAK
SWIVEL
WHEEZE
IS HE FOLLOWING ME...?
SWIVEL
WHEEZE
NOPE! GOOD!
HAAH...
THUD
PLOK

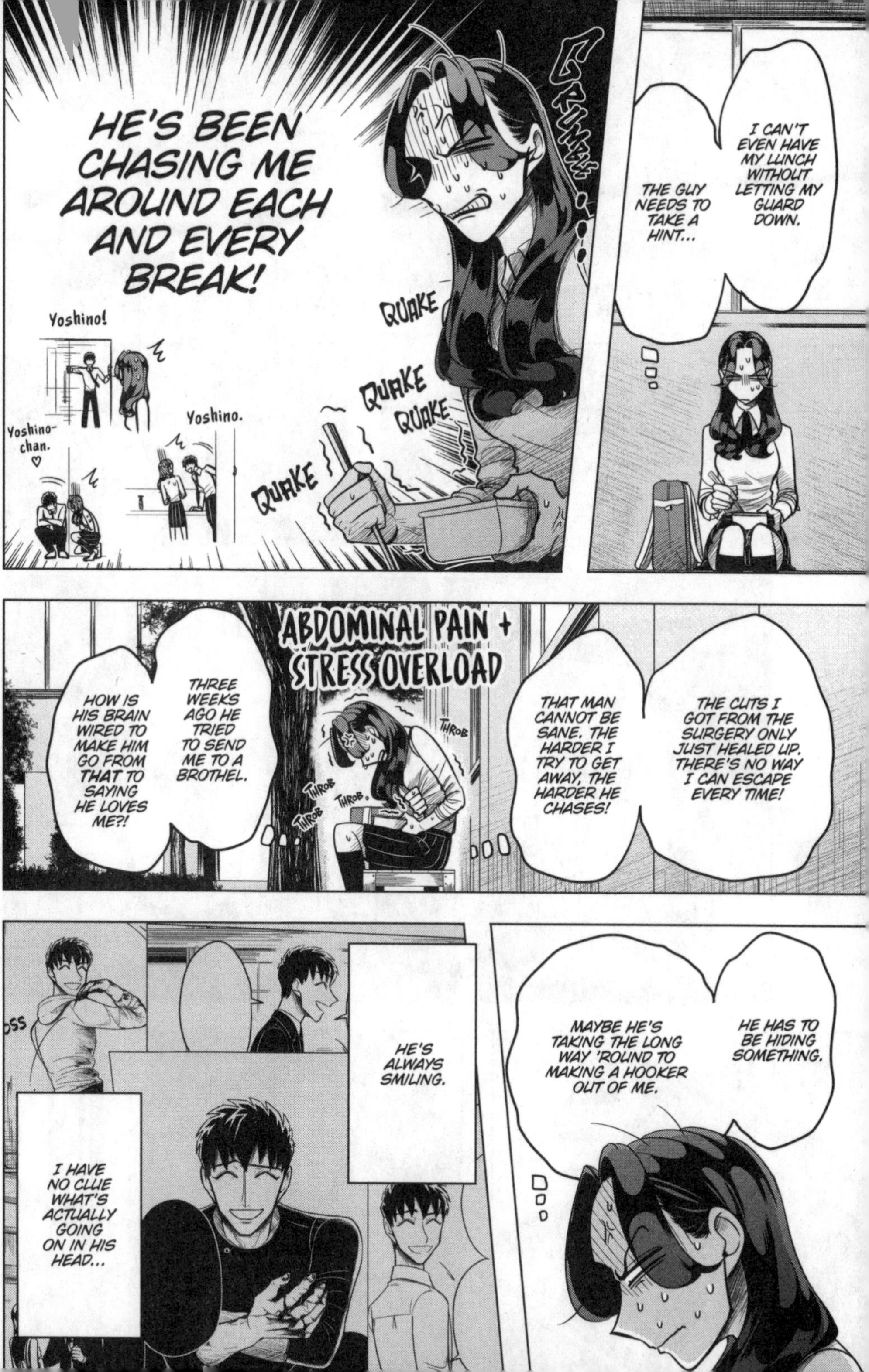
I CAN'T EVEN HAVE MY LUNCH WITHOUT LETTING MY GUARD DOWN.
THE GUY NEEDS TO TAKE A HINT...
GRUMBLE...
HE'S BEEN CHASING ME AROUND EACH AND EVERY BREAK!
QUAKE
QUAKE
QUAKE
QUAKE
Yoshino!
Yoshino.
Yoshino-chan. ♡
THE CUTS I GOT FROM THE SURGERY ONLY JUST HEALED UP. THERE'S NO WAY I CAN ESCAPE EVERY TIME!
THAT MAN CANNOT BE SANE. THE HARDER I TRY TO GET AWAY, THE HARDER HE CHASES!
ABDOMINAL PAIN + STRESS OVERLOAD
THROB
THROB.
THROB
THREE WEEKS AGO HE TRIED TO SEND ME TO A BROTHEL.
HOW IS HIS BRAIN WIRED TO MAKE HIM GO FROM THAT TO SAYING HE LOVES ME?!
HE HAS TO BE HIDING SOMETHING.
MAYBE HE'S TAKING THE LONG WAY 'ROUND TO MAKING A HOOKER OUT OF ME.
HE'S ALWAYS SMILING.
I HAVE NO CLUE WHAT'S ACTUALLY GOING ON IN HIS HEAD...

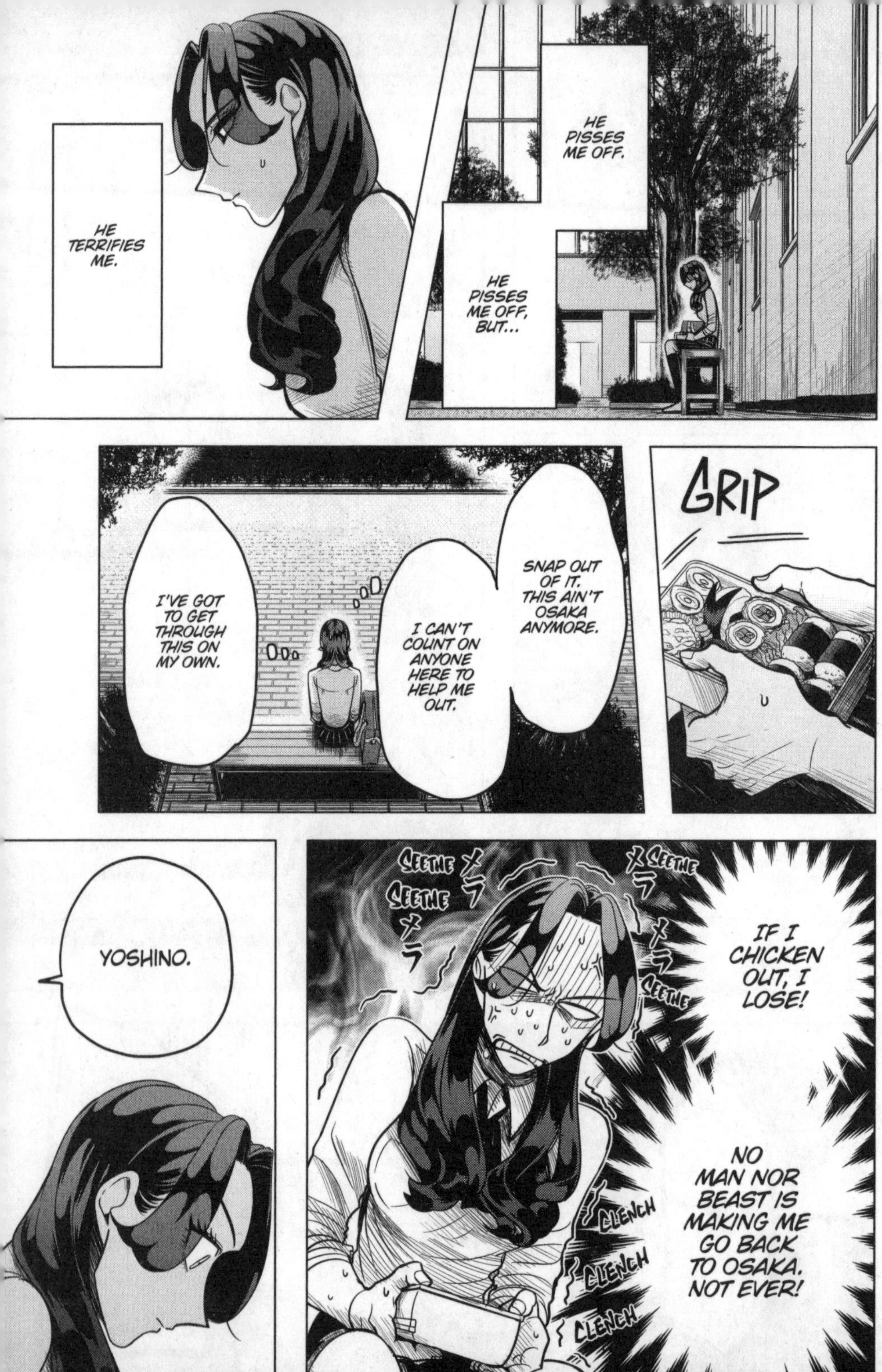
HE PISSES ME OFF.
HE PISSES ME OFF, BUT...
HE TERRIFIES ME.
GRIP
SNAP OUT OF IT. THIS AIN'T OSAKA ANYMORE.
I CAN'T COUNT ON ANYONE HERE TO HELP ME OUT.
I'VE GOT TO GET THROUGH THIS ON MY OWN.
SEETHE
SEETHE
SEETHE
SEETHE
IF I CHICKEN OUT, I LOSE!
NO MAN NOR BEAST IS MAKING ME GO BACK TO OSAKA. NOT EVER!
CLENCH
CLENCH
CLENCH
YOSHINO.

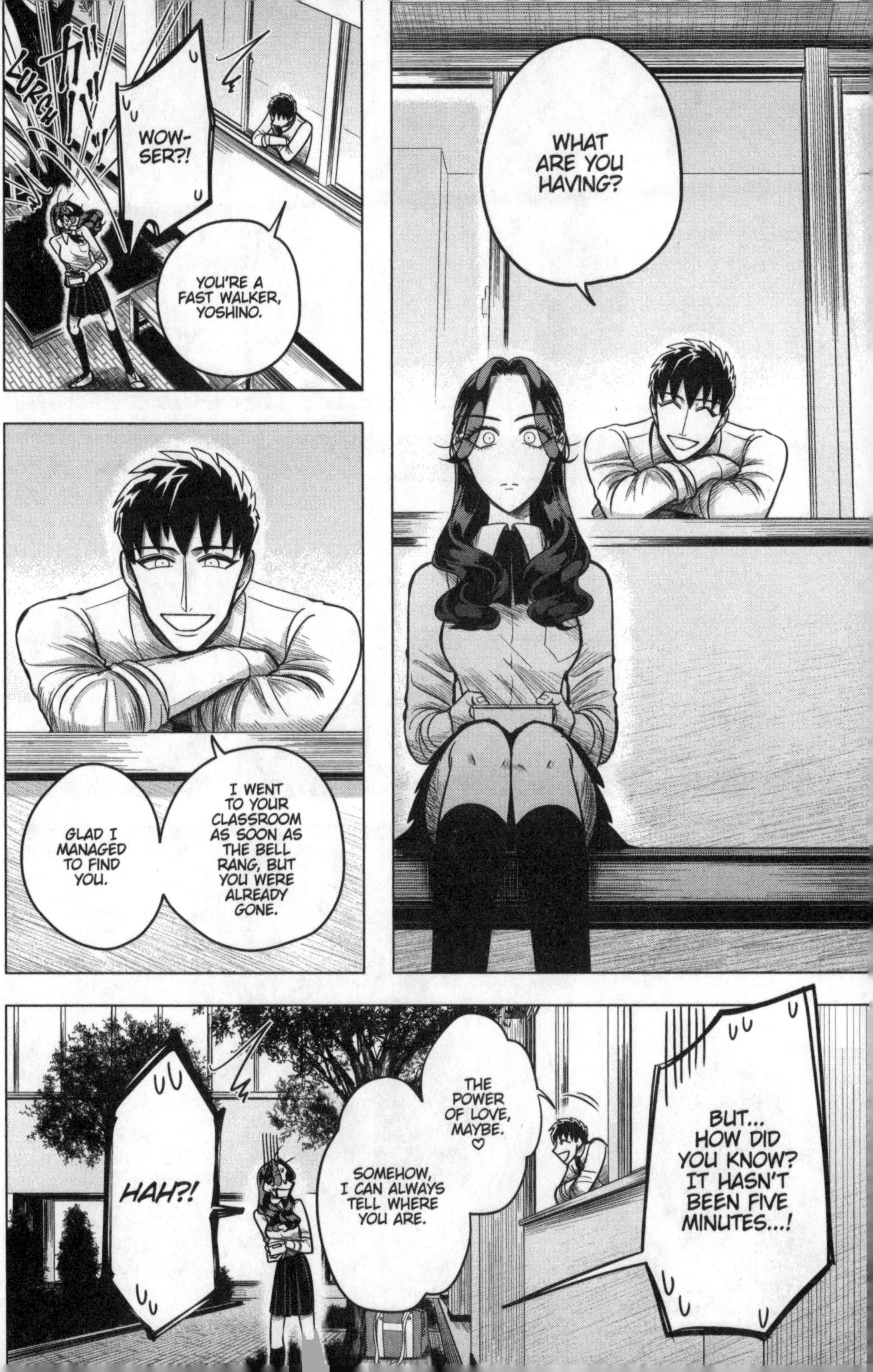
WHAT ARE YOU HAVING?
WOW-SER?!
LURCH
YOU'RE A FAST WALKER, YOSHINO.
I WENT TO YOUR CLASSROOM AS SOON AS THE BELL RANG, BUT YOU WERE ALREADY GONE.
GLAD I MANAGED TO FIND YOU.
BUT... HOW DID YOU KNOW? IT HASN'T BEEN FIVE MINUTES...!
THE POWER OF LOVE, MAYBE. ♡
SOMEHOW, I CAN ALWAYS TELL WHERE YOU ARE.
HAH?!

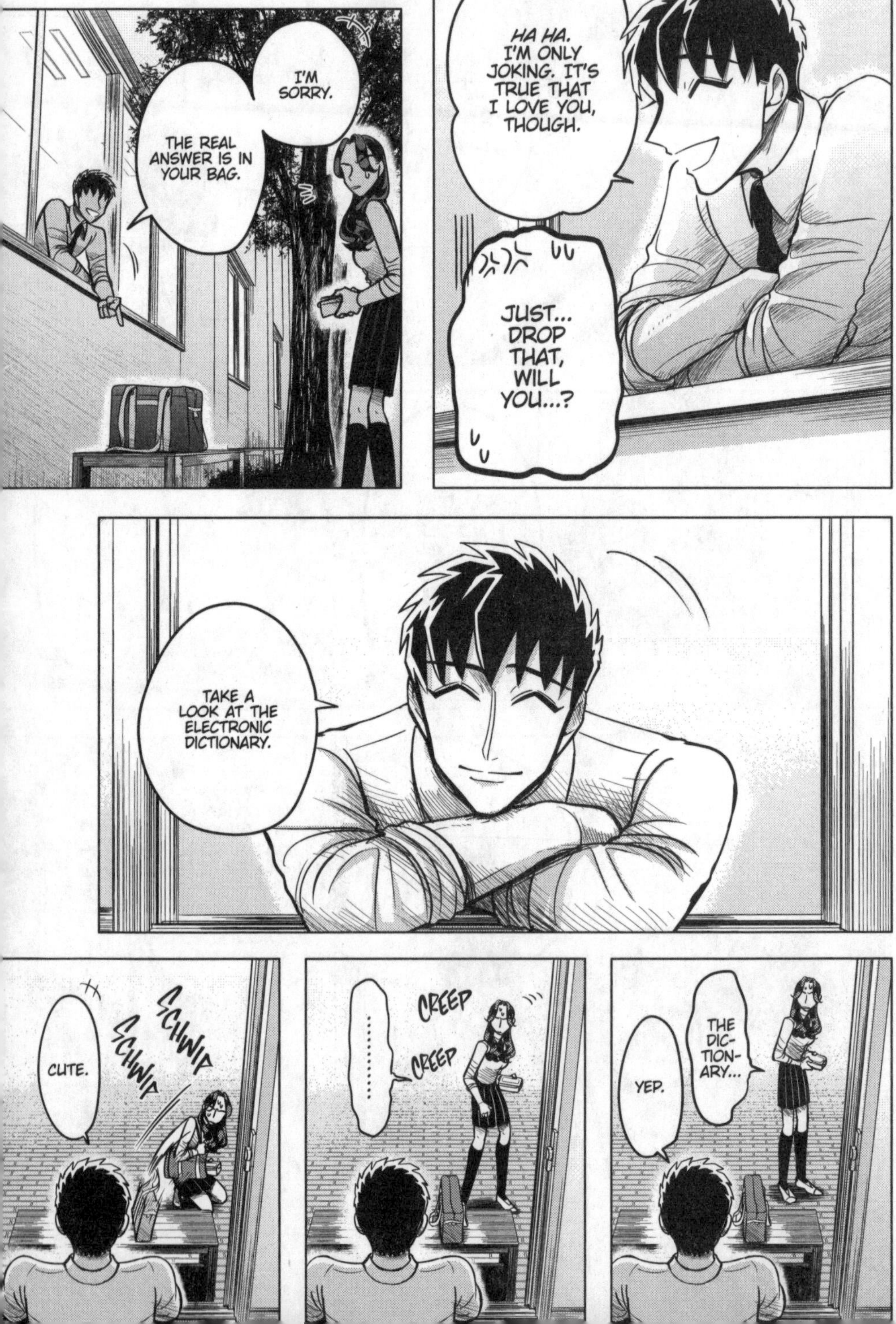
HA HA. I'M ONLY JOKING. IT'S TRUE THAT I LOVE YOU, THOUGH.
JUST... DROP THAT, WILL YOU...?
I'M SORRY.
THE REAL ANSWER IS IN YOUR BAG.
TAKE A LOOK AT THE ELECTRONIC DICTIONARY.
THE DIC-TION-ARY...
YEP.
CREEP
CREEP
......
SCHWIP
SCHWIP
CUTE.

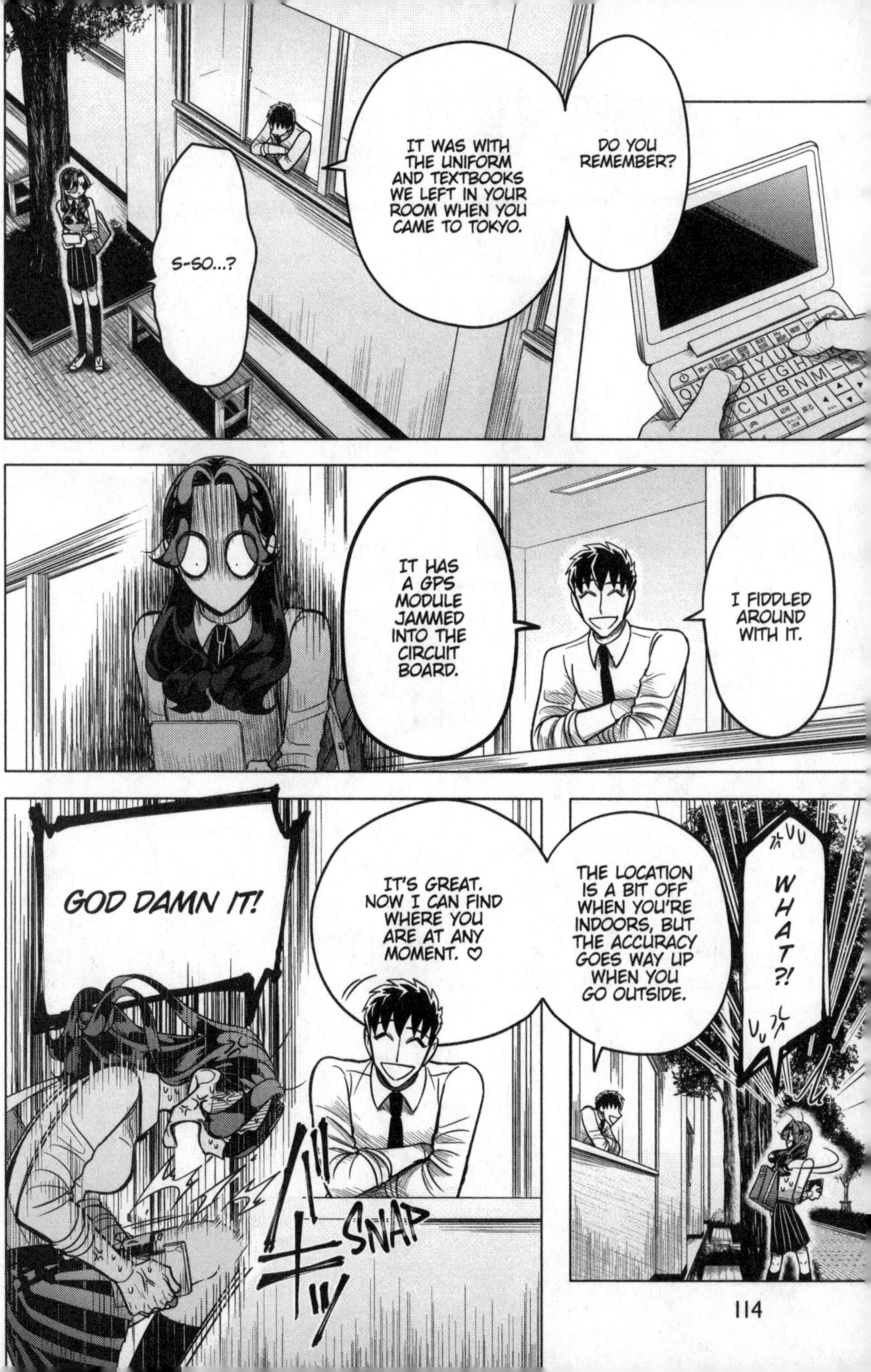
DO YOU REMEMBER?
IT WAS WITH THE UNIFORM AND TEXTBOOKS WE LEFT IN YOUR ROOM WHEN YOU CAME TO TOKYO.
S-SO...?
I FIDDLED AROUND WITH IT.
IT HAS A GPS MODULE JAMMED INTO THE CIRCUIT BOARD.
THE LOCATION IS A BIT OFF WHEN YOU'RE INDOORS, BUT THE ACCURACY GOES WAY UP WHEN YOU GO OUTSIDE.
IT'S GREAT. NOW I CAN FIND WHERE YOU ARE AT ANY MOMENT. ♡
WHAT?!
GOD DAMN IT!
SNAP

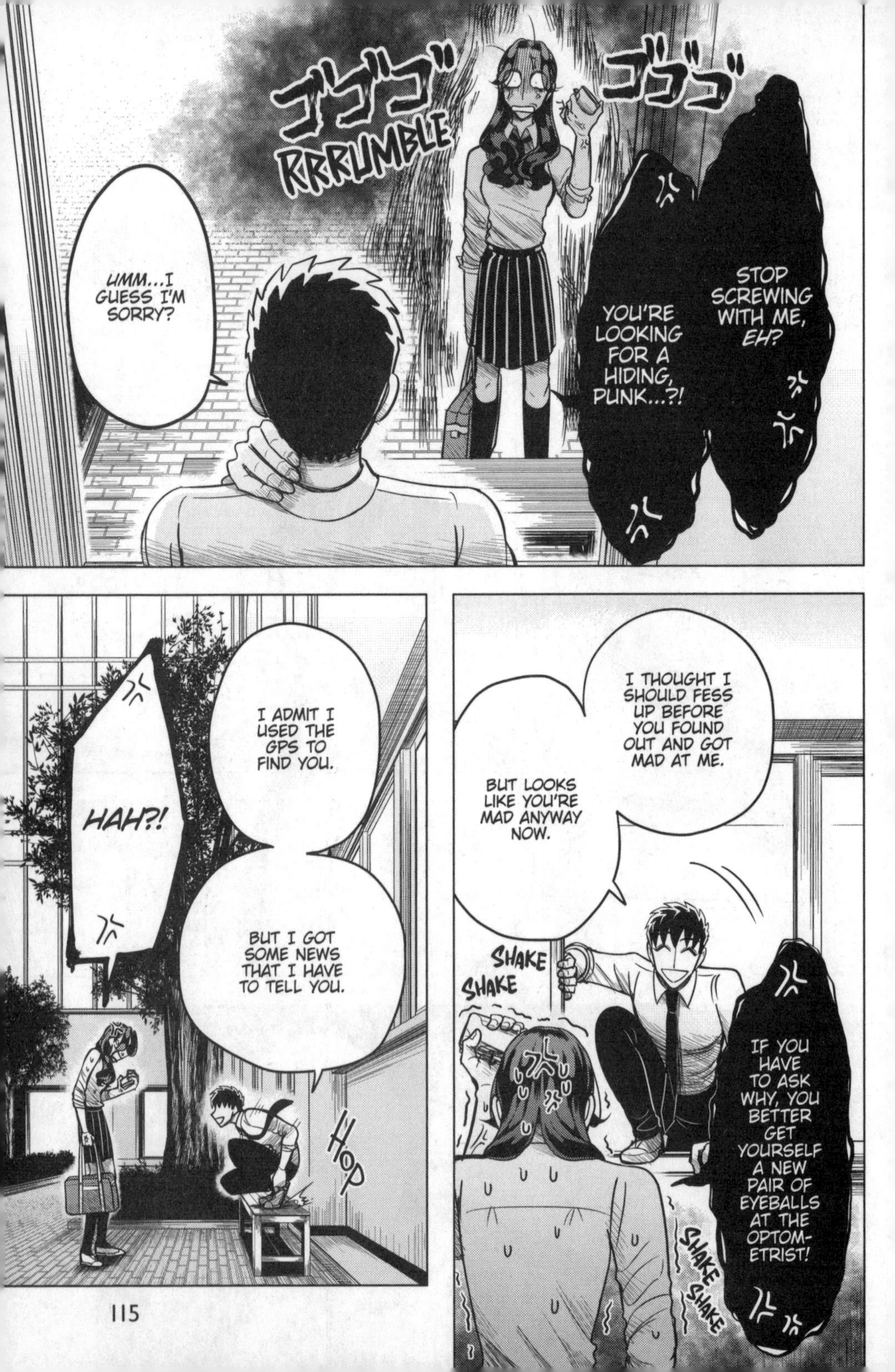
ゴゴゴ
RRRUMBLE
ゴゴゴ
STOP SCREWING WITH ME, EH?
YOU'RE LOOKING FOR A HIDING, PUNK...?!
UMM...I GUESS I'M SORRY?
I THOUGHT I SHOULD FESS UP BEFORE YOU FOUND OUT AND GOT MAD AT ME.
BUT LOOKS LIKE YOU'RE MAD ANYWAY NOW.
SHAKE SHAKE
IF YOU HAVE TO ASK WHY, YOU BETTER GET YOURSELF A NEW PAIR OF EYEBALLS AT THE OPTOM-ETRIST!
SHAKE SHAKE
I ADMIT I USED THE GPS TO FIND YOU.
BUT I GOT SOME NEWS THAT I HAVE TO TELL YOU.
HAH?!
HOP

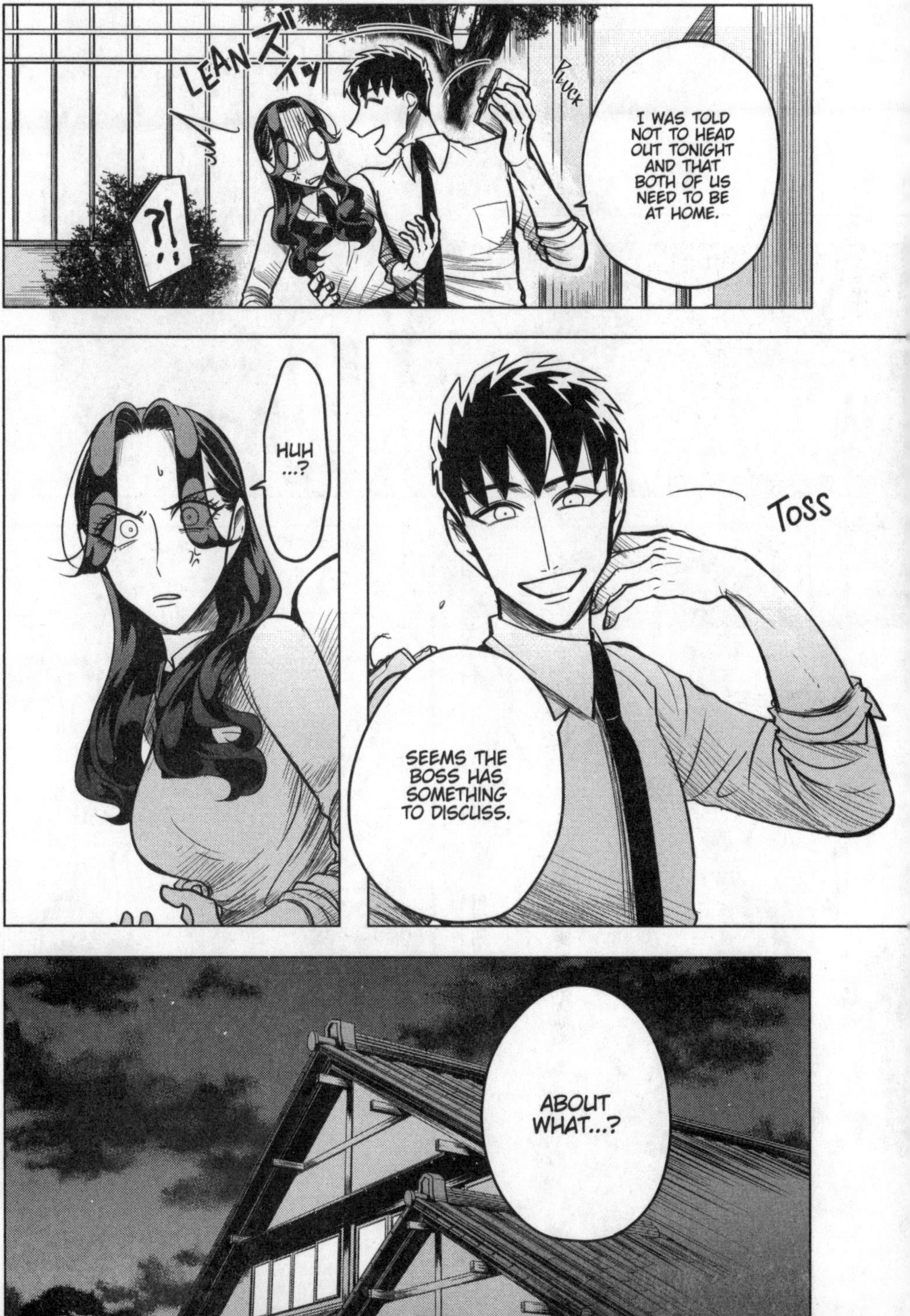
I WAS TOLD NOT TO HEAD OUT TONIGHT AND THAT BOTH OF US NEED TO BE AT HOME.
PLUCK
LEAN ズイッ
?!
TOSS
SEEMS THE BOSS HAS SOMETHING TO DISCUSS.
HUH ...?
ABOUT WHAT...?

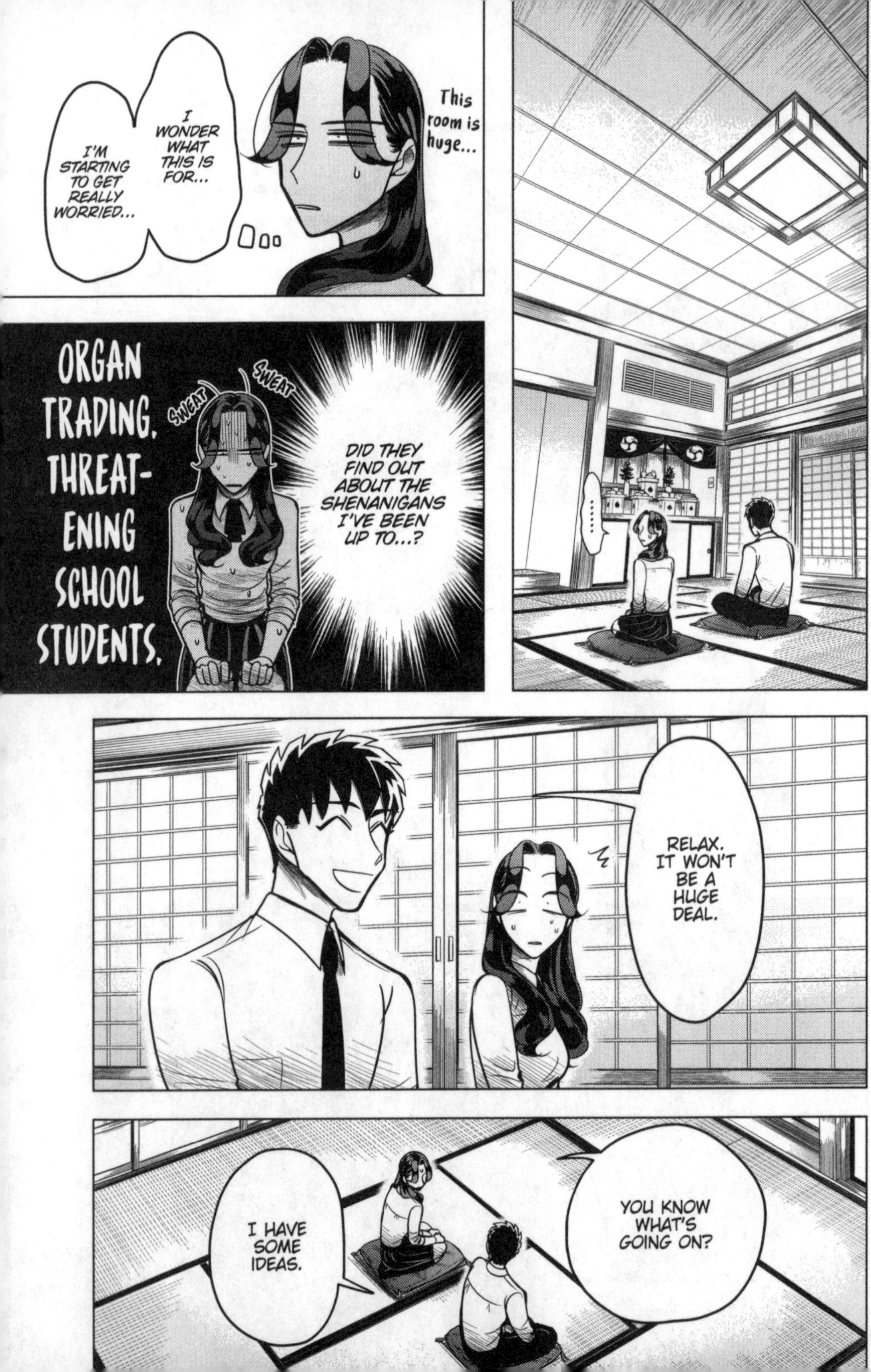
......
This room is huge...
I WONDER WHAT THIS IS FOR...
I'M STARTING TO GET REALLY WORRIED...
DID THEY FIND OUT ABOUT THE SHENANIGANS I'VE BEEN UP TO...?
SWEAT
SWEAT
ORGAN TRADING. THREAT-ENING SCHOOL STUDENTS.
RELAX. IT WON'T BE A HUGE DEAL.
YOU KNOW WHAT'S GOING ON?
I HAVE SOME IDEAS.

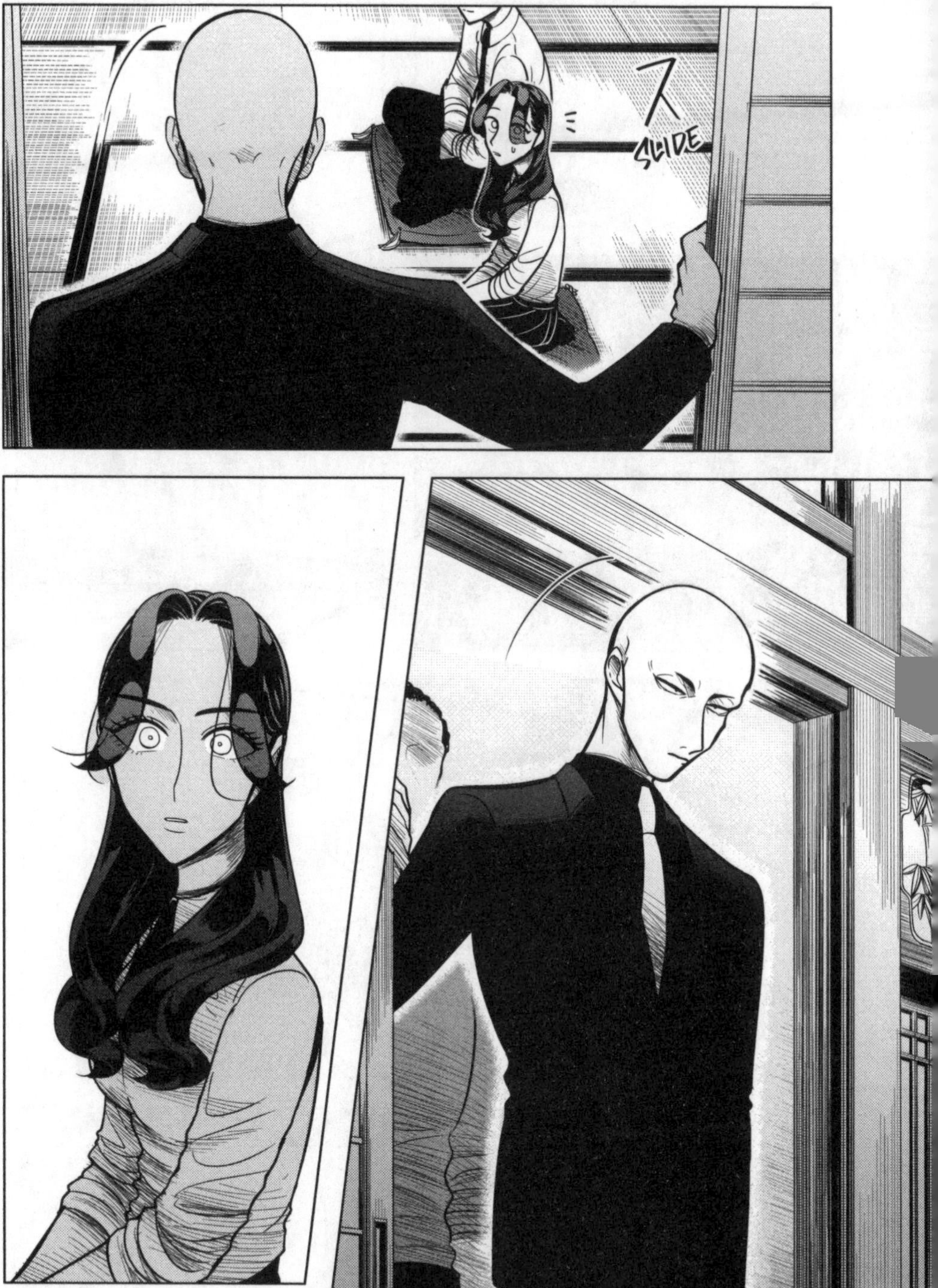
ス
SLIDE

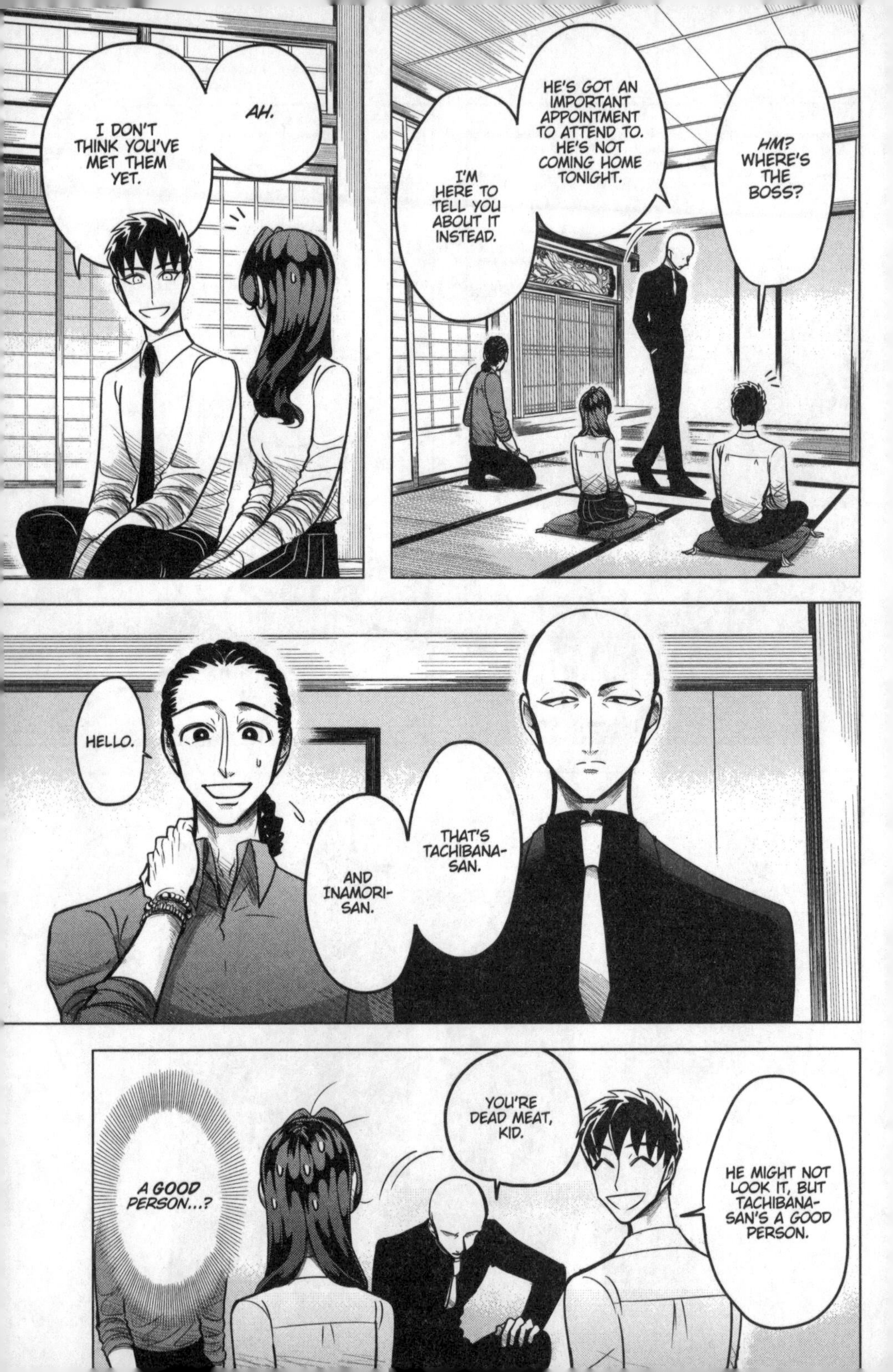
HM? WHERE'S THE BOSS?
HE'S GOT AN IMPORTANT APPOINTMENT TO ATTEND TO. HE'S NOT COMING HOME TONIGHT.
I'M HERE TO TELL YOU ABOUT IT INSTEAD.
AH.
I DON'T THINK YOU'VE MET THEM YET.
THAT'S TACHIBANA-SAN.
AND INAMORI-SAN.
HELLO.
HE MIGHT NOT LOOK IT, BUT TACHIBANA-SAN'S A GOOD PERSON.
YOU'RE DEAD MEAT, KID.
A GOOD PERSON...?

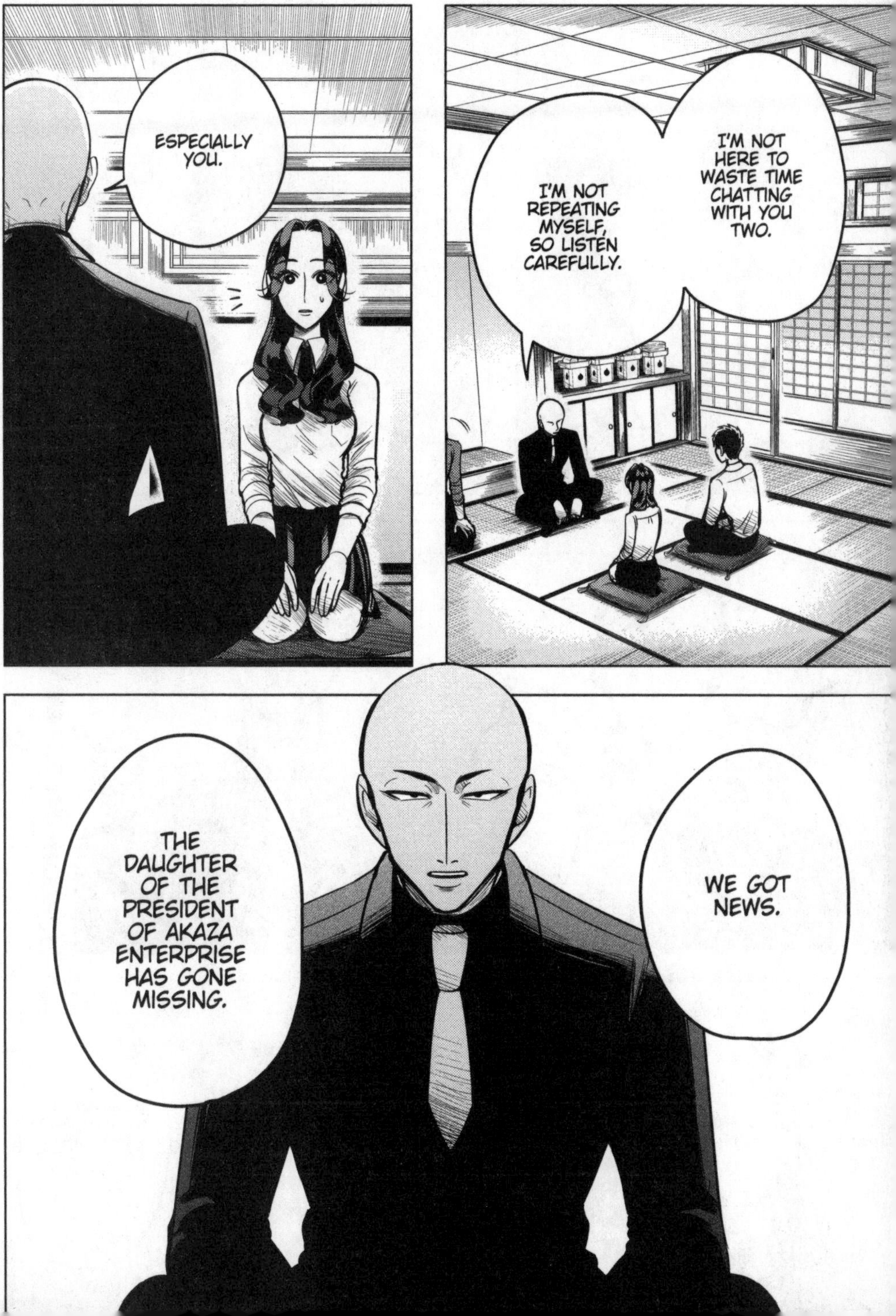
I'M NOT HERE TO WASTE TIME CHATTING WITH YOU TWO.
I'M NOT REPEATING MYSELF, SO LISTEN CAREFULLY.
ESPECIALLY YOU.
WE GOT NEWS.
THE DAUGHTER OF THE PRESIDENT OF AKAZA ENTERPRISE HAS GONE MISSING.

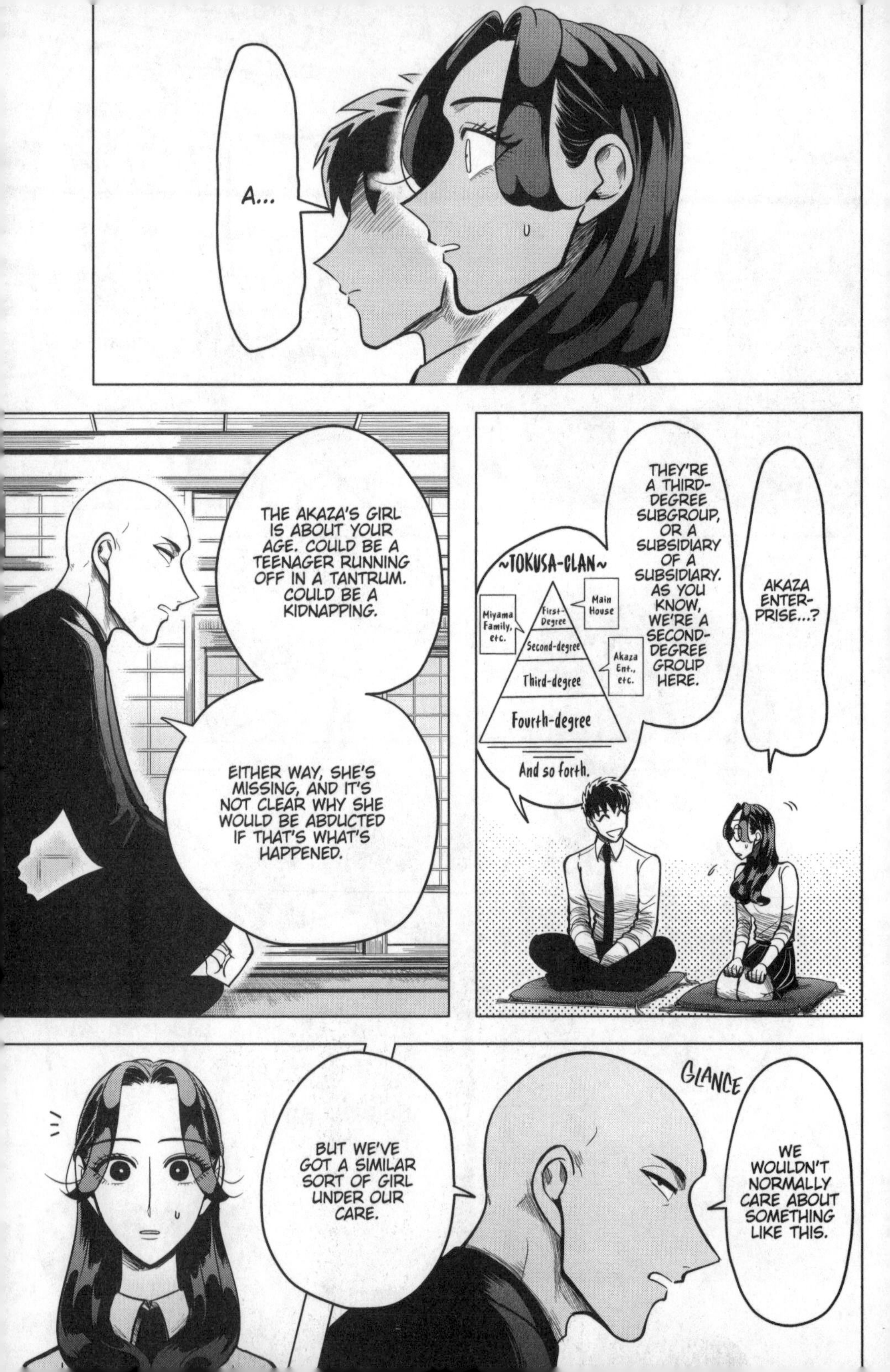
A...
AKAZA ENTER-PRISE...?
THEY'RE A THIRD-DEGREE SUBGROUP, OR A SUBSIDIARY OF A SUBSIDIARY. AS YOU KNOW, WE'RE A SECOND-DEGREE GROUP HERE.
~TOKUSA-CLAN~
Main House
Miyama Family, etc.
First-Degree
Second-degree
Akaza Ent., etc.
Third-degree
Fourth-degree
And so forth.
THE AKAZA'S GIRL IS ABOUT YOUR AGE. COULD BE A TEENAGER RUNNING OFF IN A TANTRUM. COULD BE A KIDNAPPING.
EITHER WAY, SHE'S MISSING, AND IT'S NOT CLEAR WHY SHE WOULD BE ABDUCTED IF THAT'S WHAT'S HAPPENED.
GLANCE
WE WOULDN'T NORMALLY CARE ABOUT SOMETHING LIKE THIS.
BUT WE'VE GOT A SIMILAR SORT OF GIRL UNDER OUR CARE.

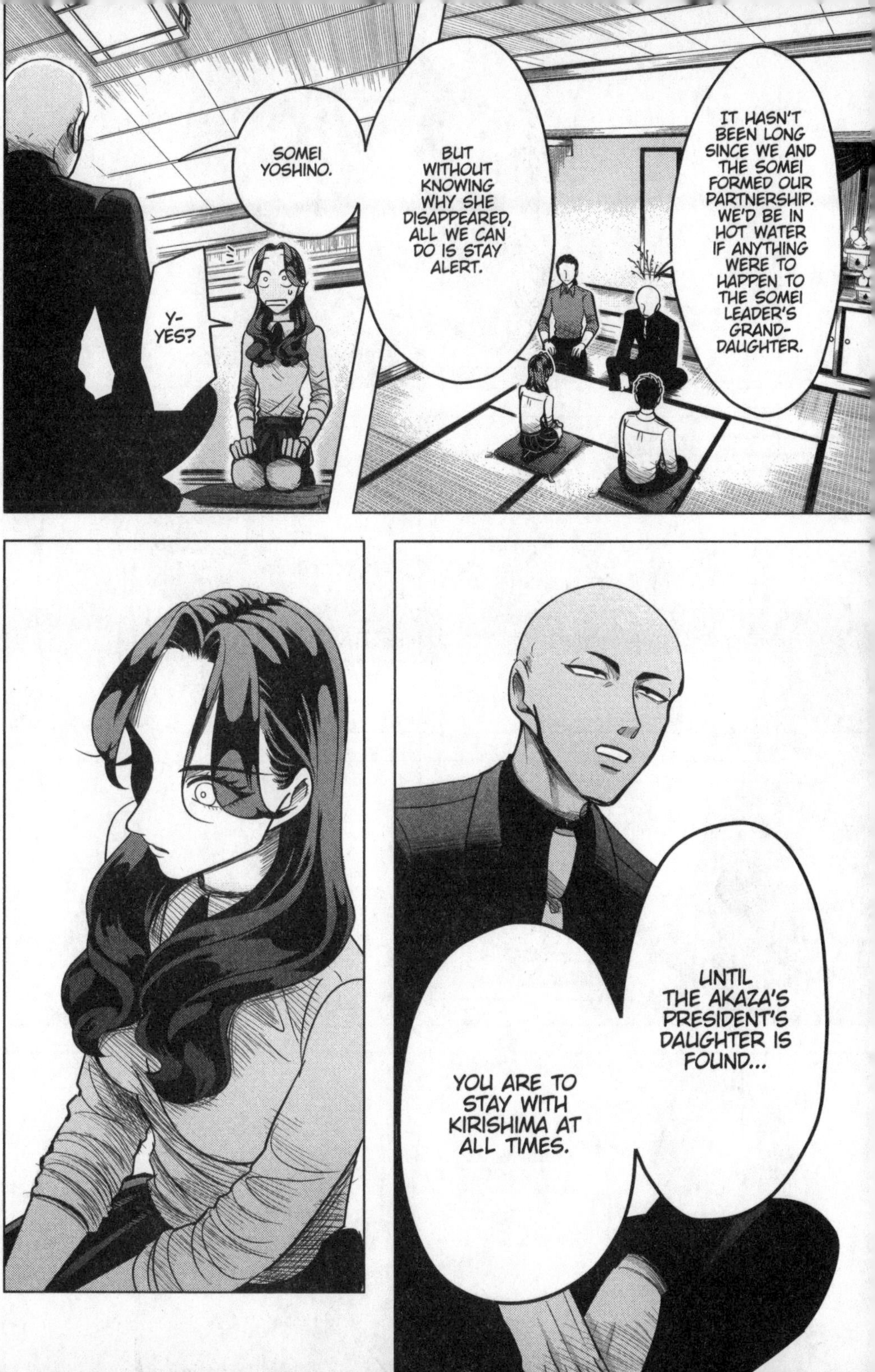
IT HASN'T BEEN LONG SINCE WE AND THE SOMEI FORMED OUR PARTNERSHIP. WE'D BE IN HOT WATER IF ANYTHING WERE TO HAPPEN TO THE SOMEI LEADER'S GRAND-DAUGHTER.
BUT WITHOUT KNOWING WHY SHE DISAPPEARED, ALL WE CAN DO IS STAY ALERT.
SOMEI YOSHINO.
Y-YES?
UNTIL THE AKAZA'S PRESIDENT'S DAUGHTER IS FOUND...
YOU ARE TO STAY WITH KIRISHIMA AT ALL TIMES.

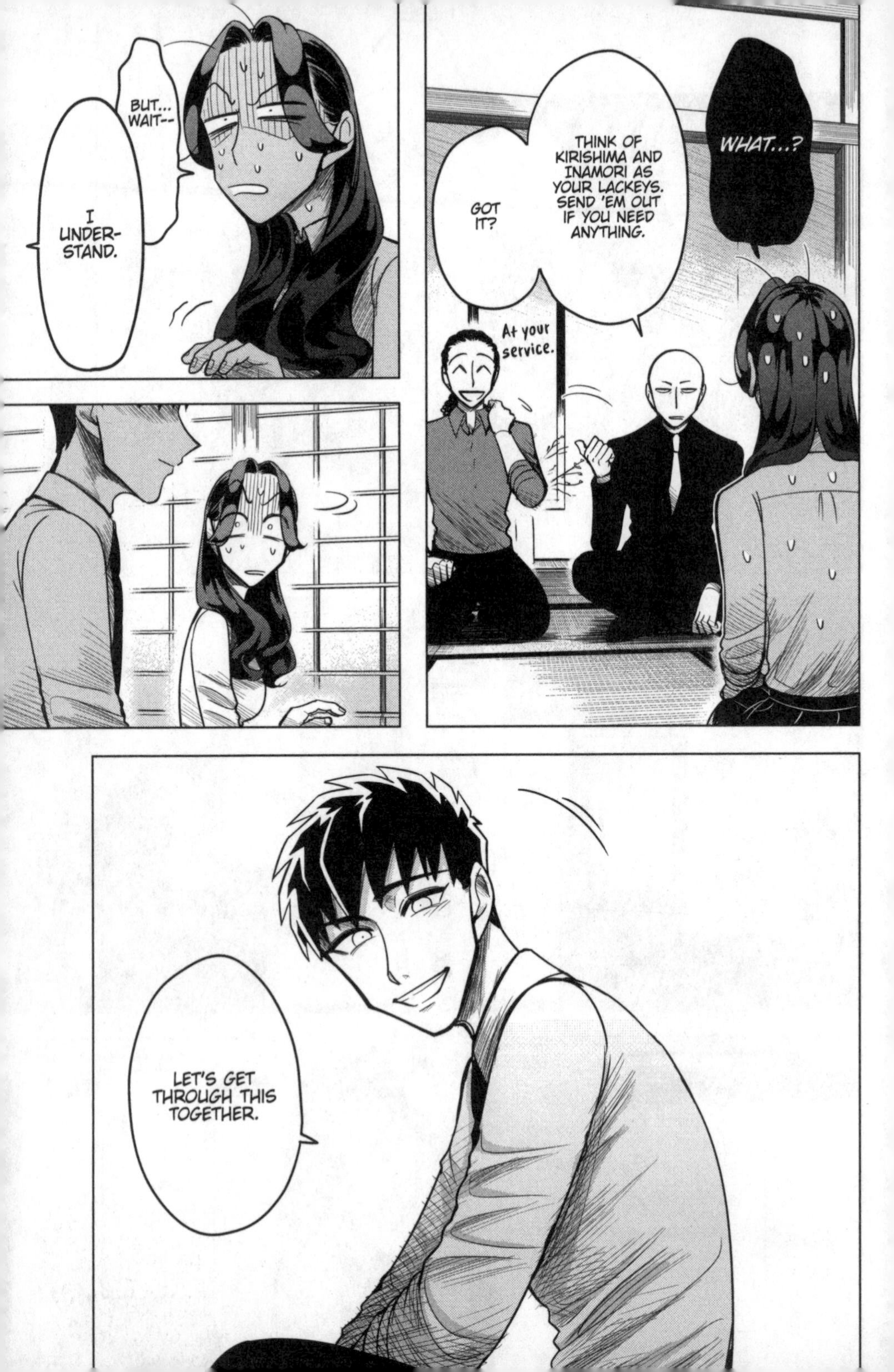
WHAT...?
THINK OF KIRISHIMA AND INAMORI AS YOUR LACKEYS. SEND 'EM OUT IF YOU NEED ANYTHING.
GOT IT?
At your service.
BUT... WAIT--
I UNDER-STAND.
LET'S GET THROUGH THIS TOGETHER.

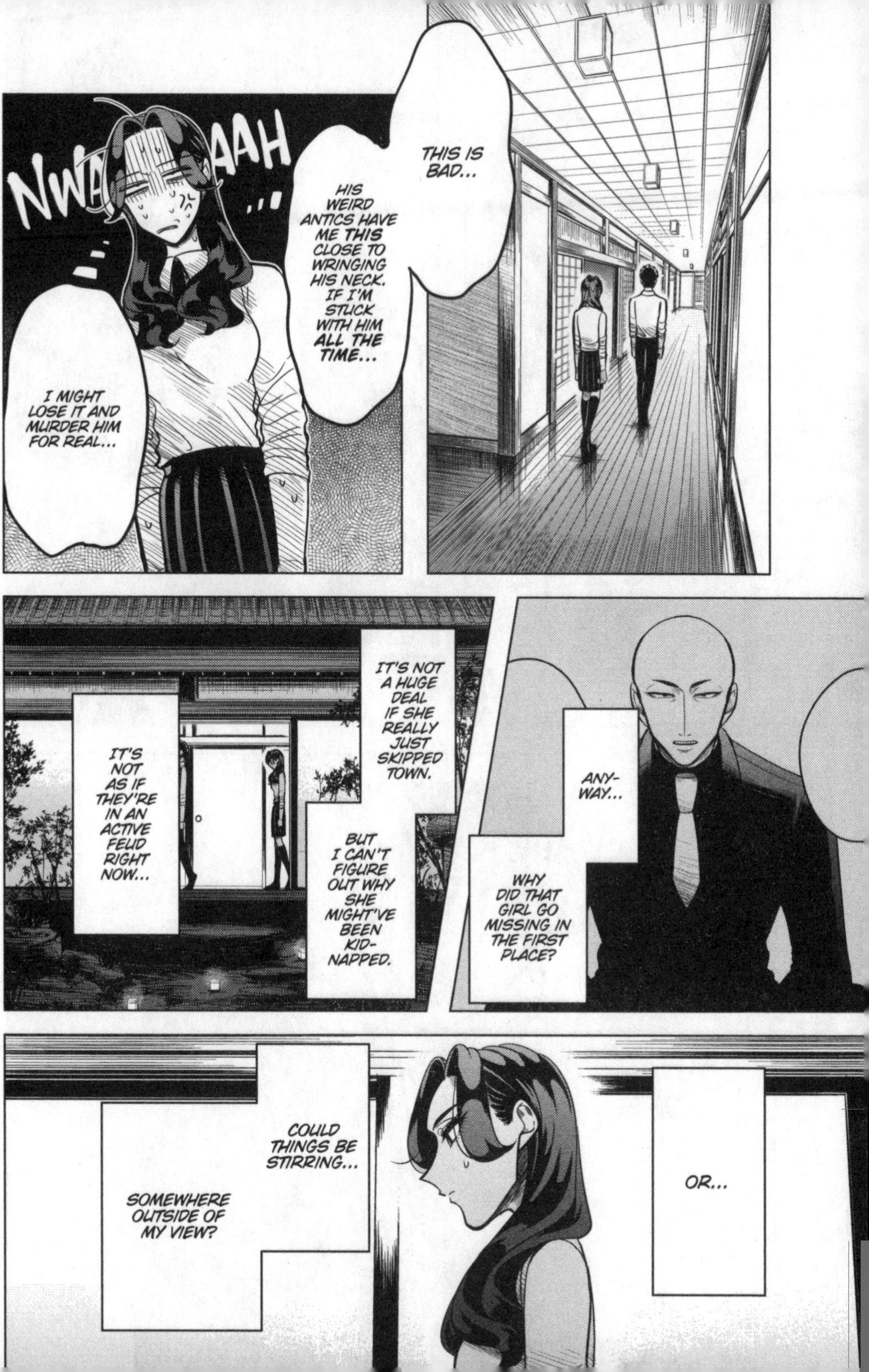
THIS IS BAD...
HIS WEIRD ANTICS HAVE ME THIS CLOSE TO WRINGING HIS NECK. IF I'M STUCK WITH HIM ALL THE TIME...
NWA AAH
I MIGHT LOSE IT AND MURDER HIM FOR REAL...
ANY-WAY...
WHY DID THAT GIRL GO MISSING IN THE FIRST PLACE?
IT'S NOT A HUGE DEAL IF SHE REALLY JUST SKIPPED TOWN.
BUT I CAN'T FIGURE OUT WHY SHE MIGHT'VE BEEN KID-NAPPED.
IT'S NOT AS IF THEY'RE IN AN ACTIVE FEUD RIGHT NOW...
OR...
COULD THINGS BE STIRRING...
SOMEWHERE OUTSIDE OF MY VIEW?

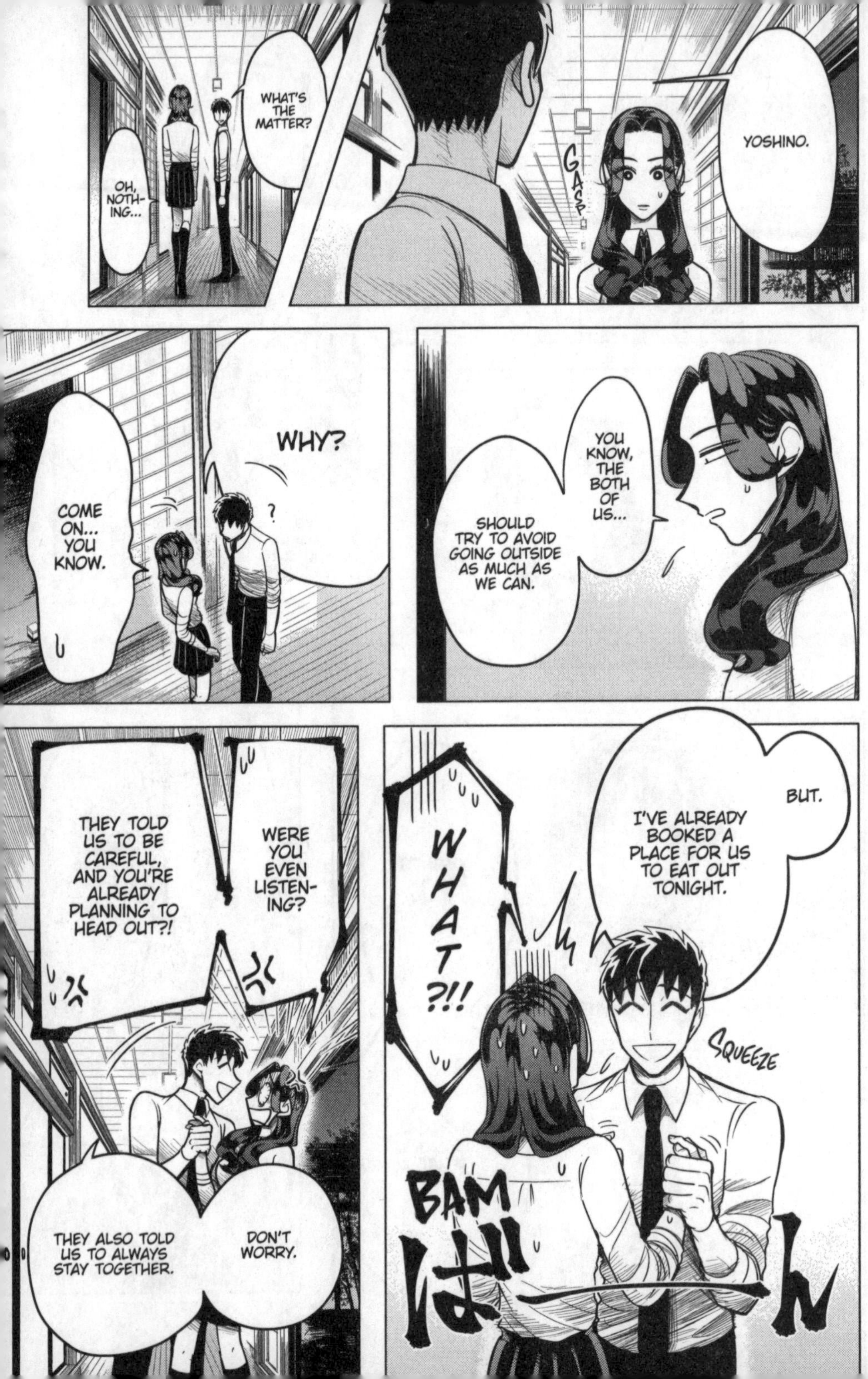
YOSHINO.
GASP
WHAT'S THE MATTER?
OH, NOTHING...
YOU KNOW, THE BOTH OF US...
SHOULD TRY TO AVOID GOING OUTSIDE AS MUCH AS WE CAN.
WHY?
COME ON... YOU KNOW.
BUT.
I'VE ALREADY BOOKED A PLACE FOR US TO EAT OUT TONIGHT.
WHAT?!!
SQUEEZE
BAM
WERE YOU EVEN LISTENING?
THEY TOLD US TO BE CAREFUL, AND YOU'RE ALREADY PLANNING TO HEAD OUT?!
DON'T WORRY.
THEY ALSO TOLD US TO ALWAYS STAY TOGETHER.

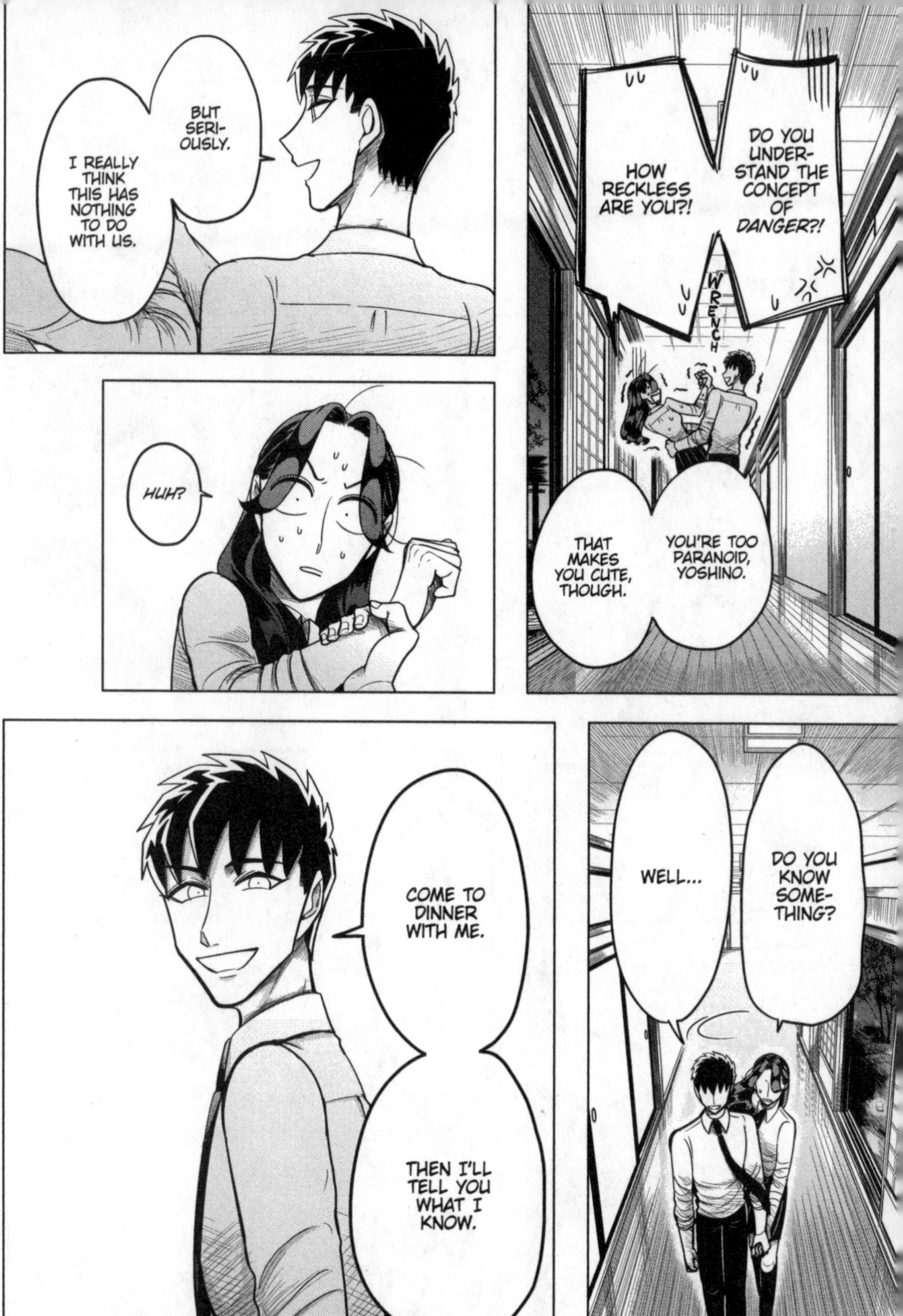
DO YOU UNDERSTAND THE CONCEPT OF *DANGER*?!
HOW RECKLESS ARE YOU?!
WRENCH
YOU'RE TOO PARANOID, YOSHINO.
THAT MAKES YOU CUTE, THOUGH.
BUT SERIOUSLY.
I REALLY THINK THIS HAS NOTHING TO DO WITH US.
*HUH?*
DO YOU KNOW SOMETHING?
WELL...
COME TO DINNER WITH ME.
THEN I'LL TELL YOU WHAT I KNOW.

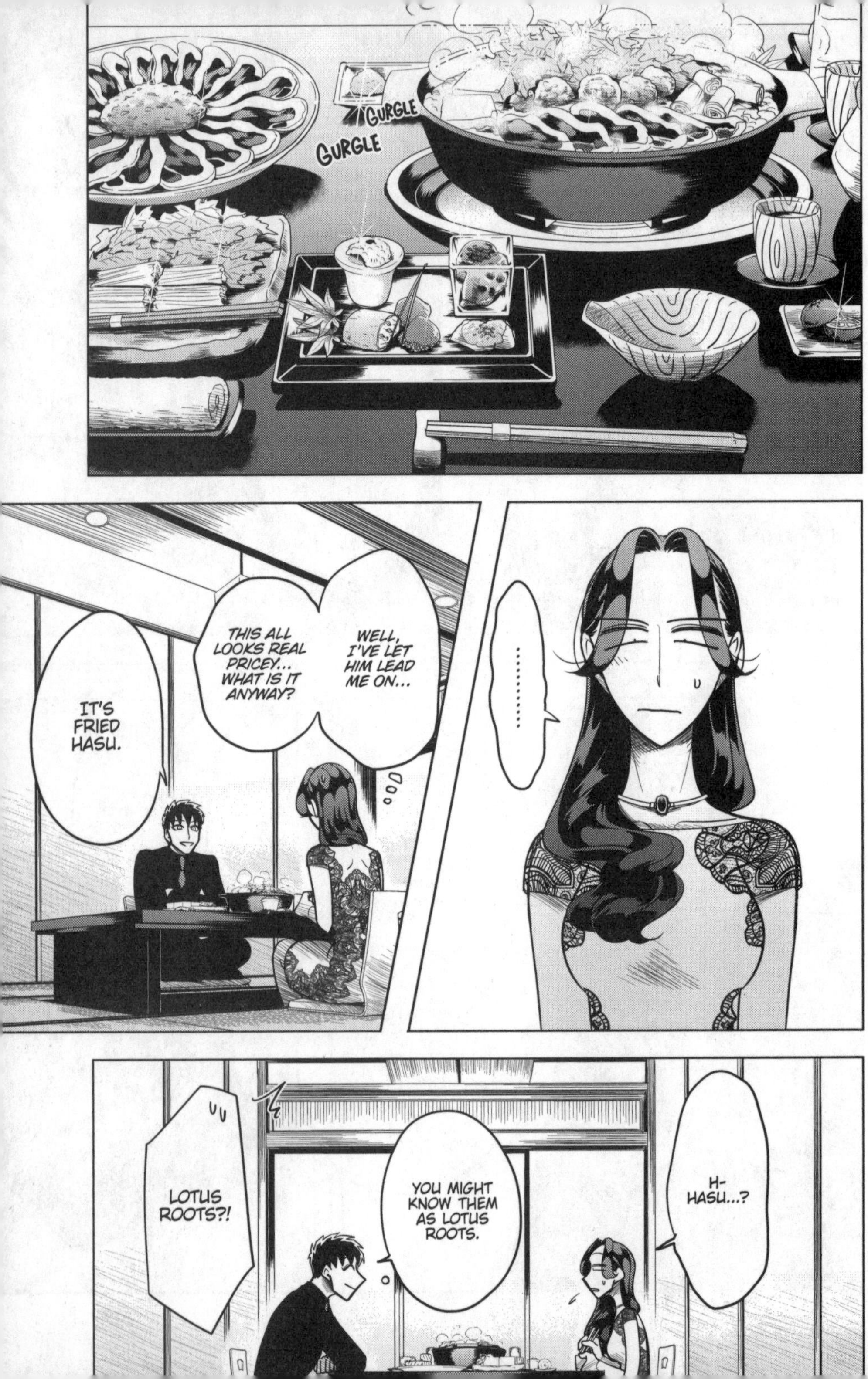
GURGLE
GURGLE
......
WELL, I'VE LET HIM LEAD ME ON...
THIS ALL LOOKS REAL PRICEY... WHAT IS IT ANYWAY?
IT'S FRIED HASU.
H-HASU...?
YOU MIGHT KNOW THEM AS LOTUS ROOTS.
LOTUS ROOTS?!

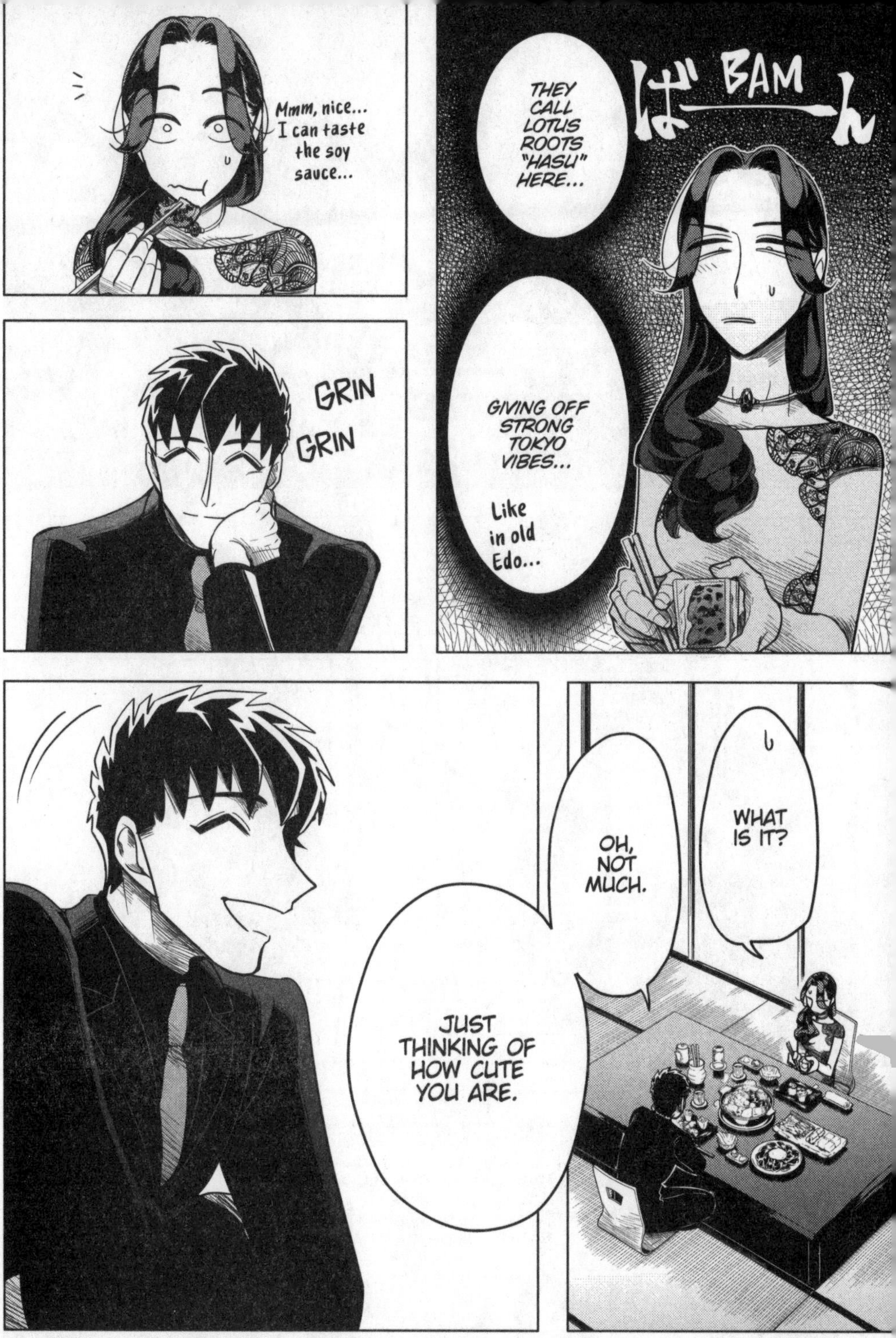

ばーん BAM
THEY CALL LOTUS ROOTS "HASU" HERE...
GIVING OFF STRONG TOKYO VIBES...
Like in old Edo...
Mmm, nice... I can taste the soy sauce...
GRIN
GRIN
WHAT IS IT?
OH, NOT MUCH.
JUST THINKING OF HOW CUTE YOU ARE.

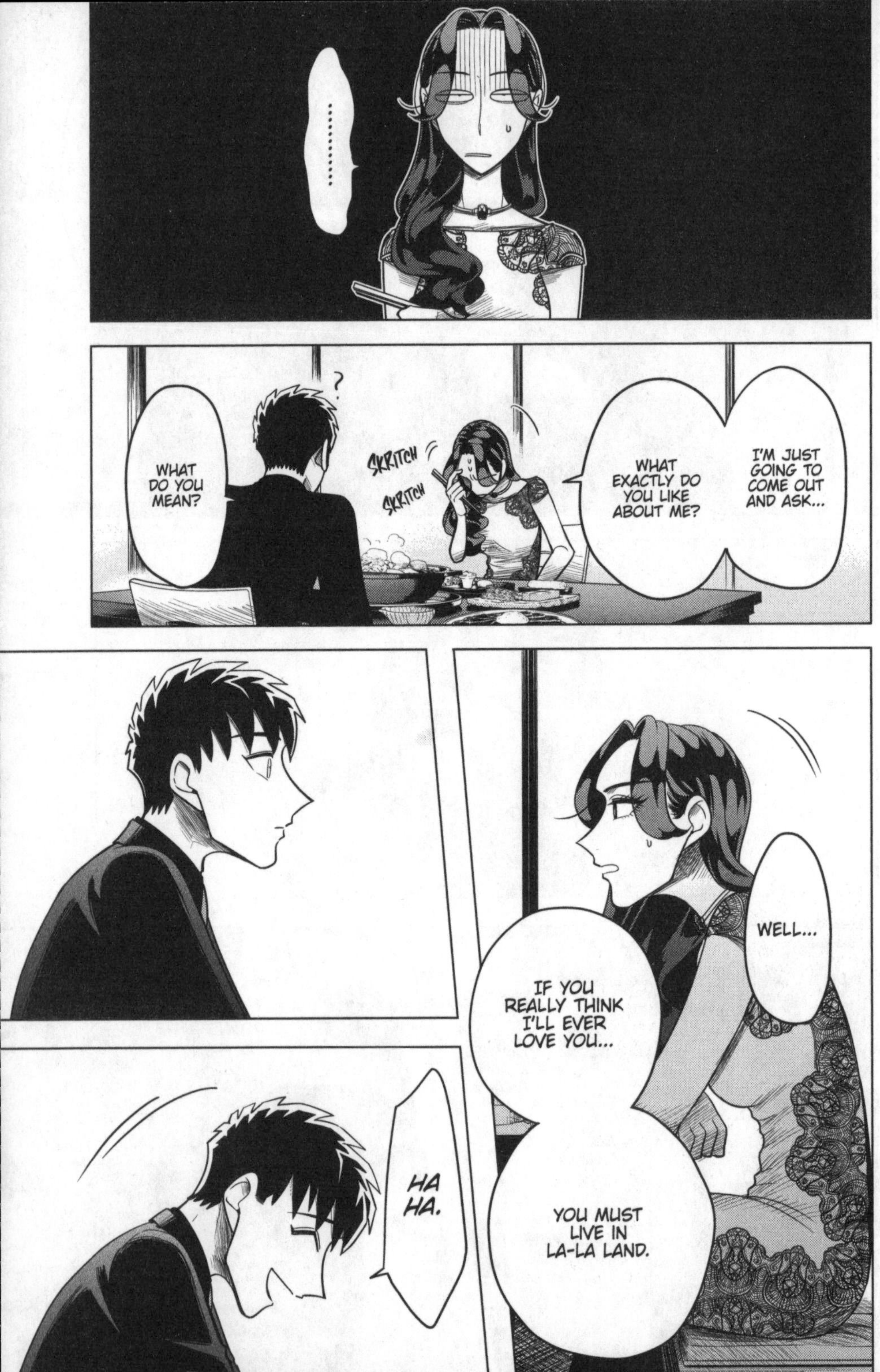

......
I'M JUST GOING TO COME OUT AND ASK...
WHAT EXACTLY DO YOU LIKE ABOUT ME?
SKRITCH
SKRITCH
?
WHAT DO YOU MEAN?
WELL...
IF YOU REALLY THINK I'LL EVER LOVE YOU...
YOU MUST LIVE IN LA-LA LAND.
HA HA.

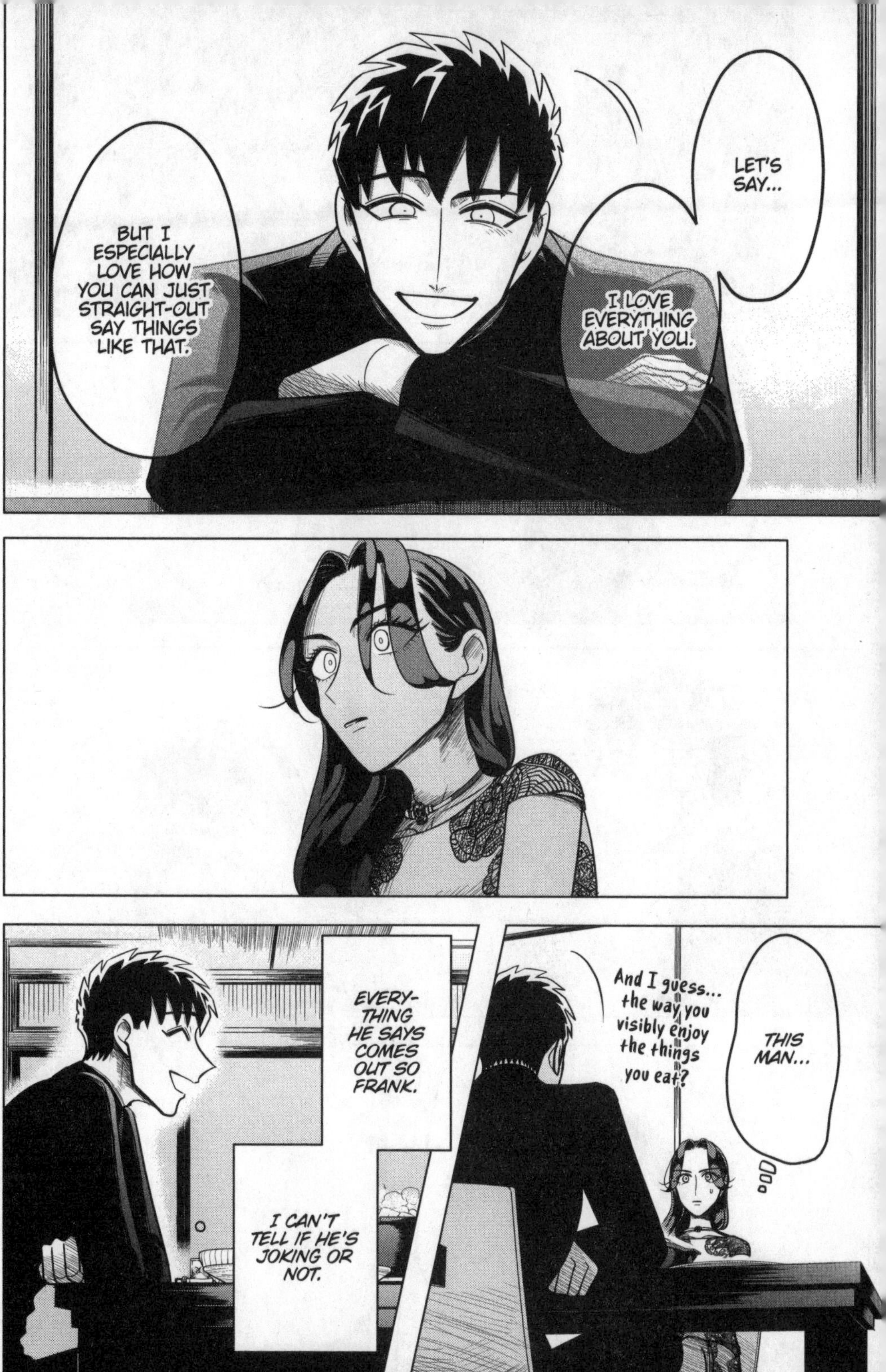
LET'S SAY...
I LOVE EVERYTHING ABOUT YOU.
BUT I ESPECIALLY LOVE HOW YOU CAN JUST STRAIGHT-OUT SAY THINGS LIKE THAT.
THIS MAN...
And I guess... the way you visibly enjoy the things you eat?
EVERY-THING HE SAYS COMES OUT SO FRANK.
I CAN'T TELL IF HE'S JOKING OR NOT.

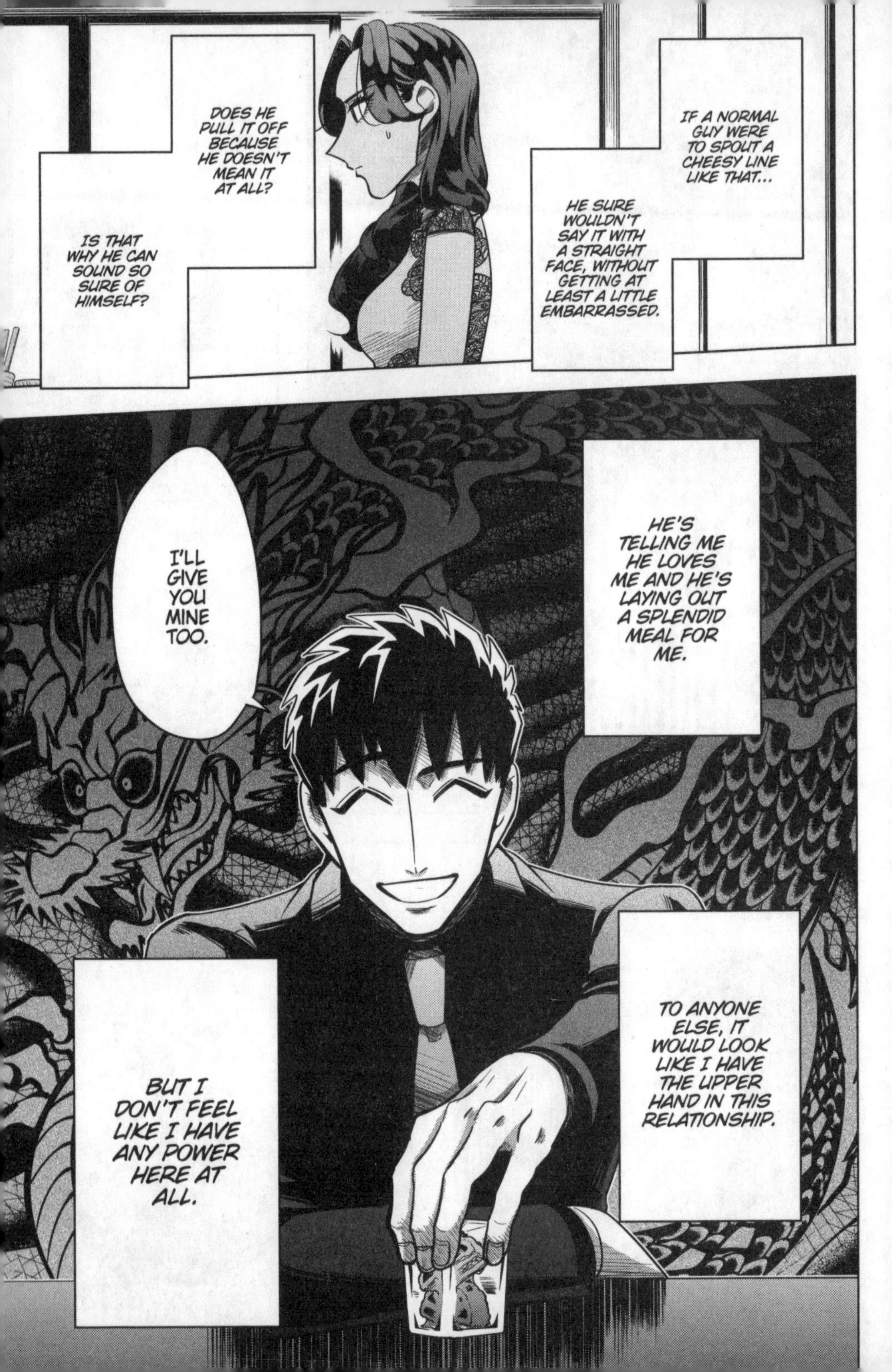
IF A NORMAL GUY WERE TO SPOUT A CHEESY LINE LIKE THAT...
HE SURE WOULDN'T SAY IT WITH A STRAIGHT FACE, WITHOUT GETTING AT LEAST A LITTLE EMBARRASSED.
DOES HE PULL IT OFF BECAUSE HE DOESN'T MEAN IT AT ALL?
IS THAT WHY HE CAN SOUND SO SURE OF HIMSELF?
HE'S TELLING ME HE LOVES ME AND HE'S LAYING OUT A SPLENDID MEAL FOR ME.
I'LL GIVE YOU MINE TOO.
TO ANYONE ELSE, IT WOULD LOOK LIKE I HAVE THE UPPER HAND IN THIS RELATIONSHIP.
BUT I DON'T FEEL LIKE I HAVE ANY POWER HERE AT ALL.

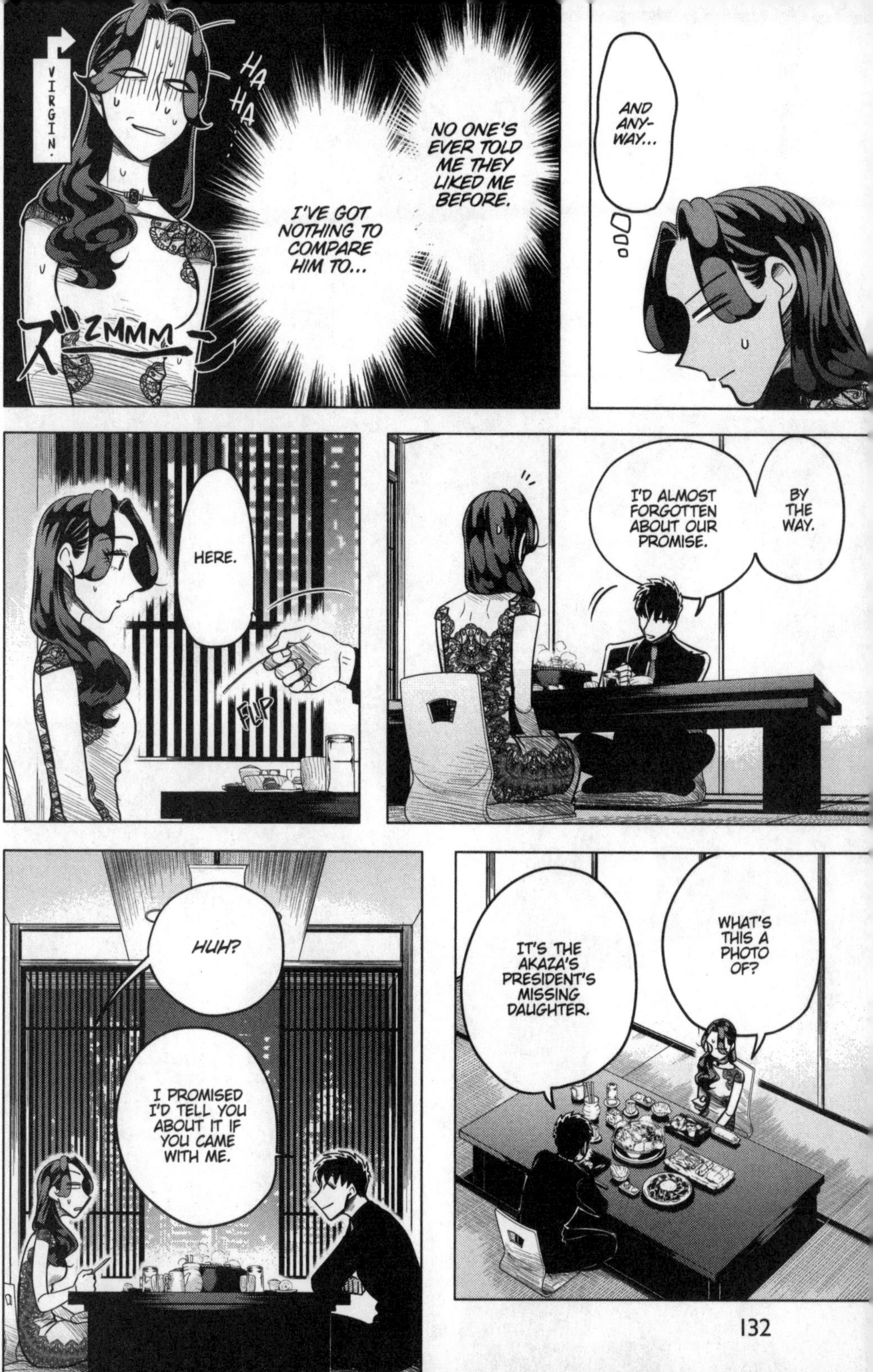
AND ANY-WAY...
NO ONE'S EVER TOLD ME THEY LIKED ME BEFORE.
I'VE GOT NOTHING TO COMPARE HIM TO...
HA HA...
VIRGIN.
ZMMM
BY THE WAY.
I'D ALMOST FORGOTTEN ABOUT OUR PROMISE.
HERE.
FLIP
WHAT'S THIS A PHOTO OF?
IT'S THE AKAZA'S PRESIDENT'S MISSING DAUGHTER.
HUH?
I PROMISED I'D TELL YOU ABOUT IT IF YOU CAME WITH ME.

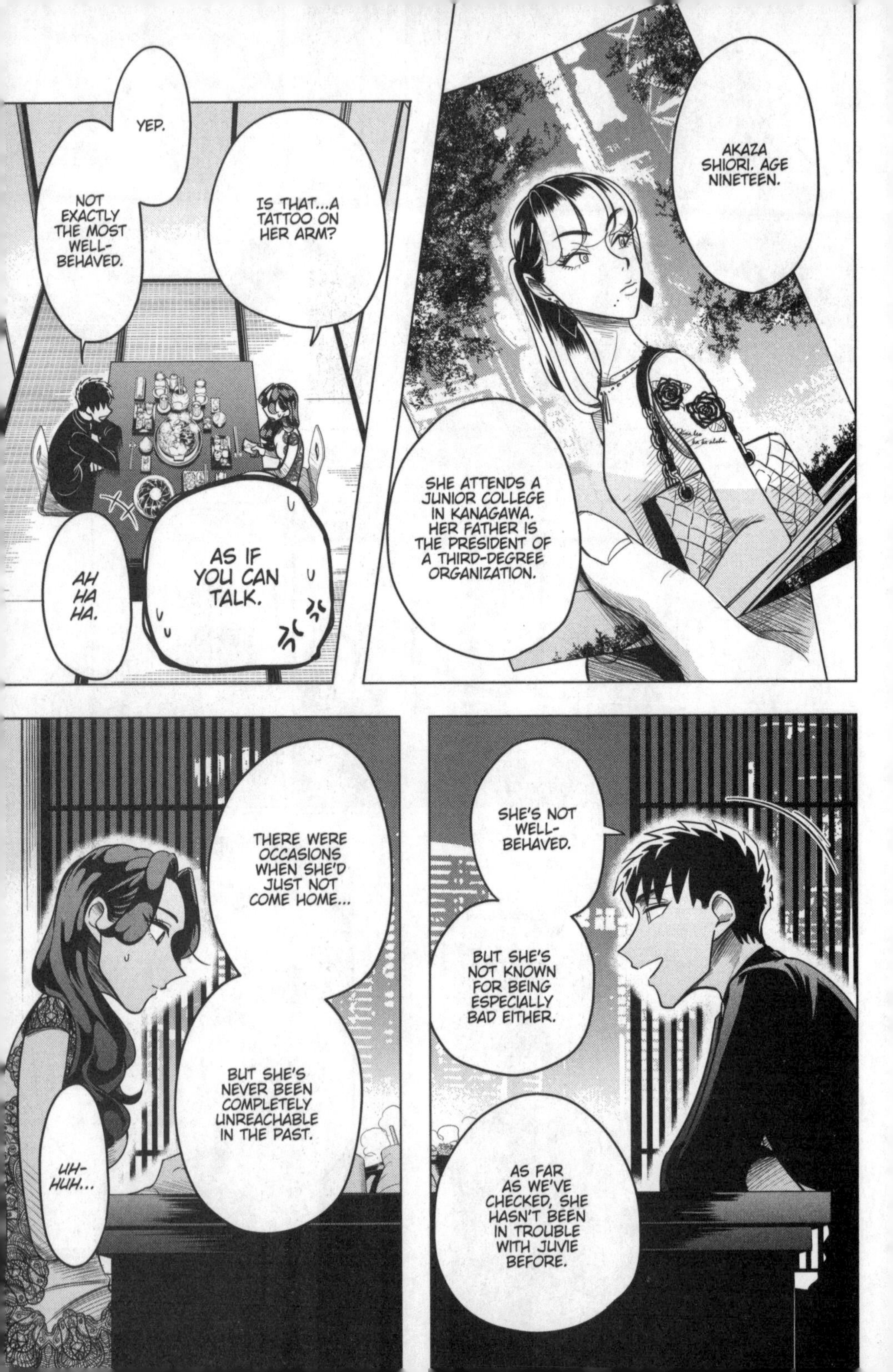
AKAZA SHIORI. AGE NINETEEN.
SHE ATTENDS A JUNIOR COLLEGE IN KANAGAWA. HER FATHER IS THE PRESIDENT OF A THIRD-DEGREE ORGANIZATION.
IS THAT...A TATTOO ON HER ARM?
YEP.
NOT EXACTLY THE MOST WELL-BEHAVED.
AS IF YOU CAN TALK.
AH HA HA.
SHE'S NOT WELL-BEHAVED.
BUT SHE'S NOT KNOWN FOR BEING ESPECIALLY BAD EITHER.
AS FAR AS WE'VE CHECKED, SHE HASN'T BEEN IN TROUBLE WITH JUVIE BEFORE.
THERE WERE OCCASIONS WHEN SHE'D JUST NOT COME HOME...
BUT SHE'S NEVER BEEN COMPLETELY UNREACHABLE IN THE PAST.
UH-HUH...

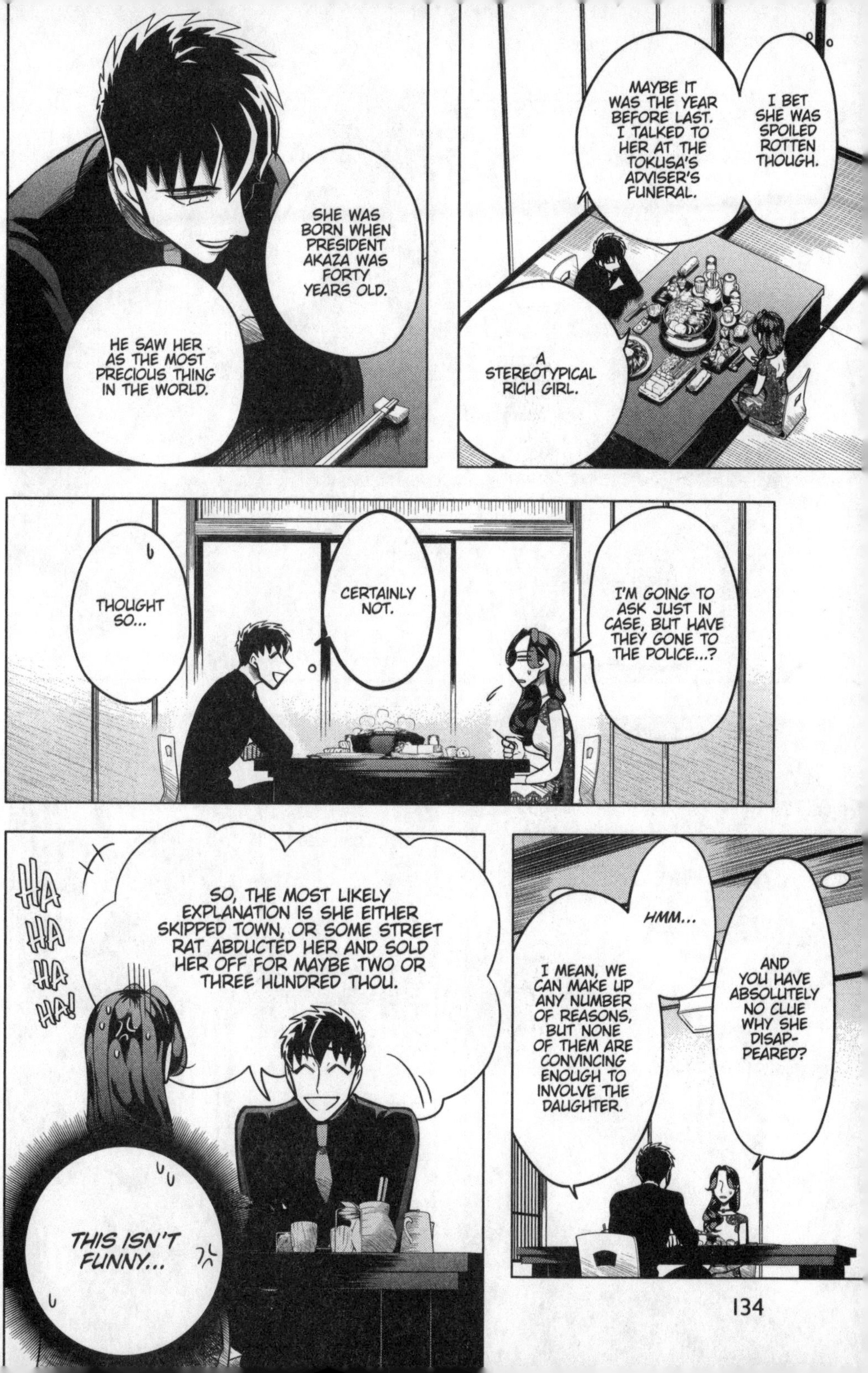
I BET SHE WAS SPOILED ROTTEN THOUGH.
MAYBE IT WAS THE YEAR BEFORE LAST. I TALKED TO HER AT THE TOKUSA'S ADVISER'S FUNERAL.
A STEREOTYPICAL RICH GIRL.
SHE WAS BORN WHEN PRESIDENT AKAZA WAS FORTY YEARS OLD.
HE SAW HER AS THE MOST PRECIOUS THING IN THE WORLD.
I'M GOING TO ASK JUST IN CASE, BUT HAVE THEY GONE TO THE POLICE...?
CERTAINLY NOT.
THOUGHT SO...
AND YOU HAVE ABSOLUTELY NO CLUE WHY SHE DISAP-PEARED?
HMM...
I MEAN, WE CAN MAKE UP ANY NUMBER OF REASONS, BUT NONE OF THEM ARE CONVINCING ENOUGH TO INVOLVE THE DAUGHTER.
SO, THE MOST LIKELY EXPLANATION IS SHE EITHER SKIPPED TOWN, OR SOME STREET RAT ABDUCTED HER AND SOLD HER OFF FOR MAYBE TWO OR THREE HUNDRED THOU.
HA HA HA HA!
THIS ISN'T FUNNY...

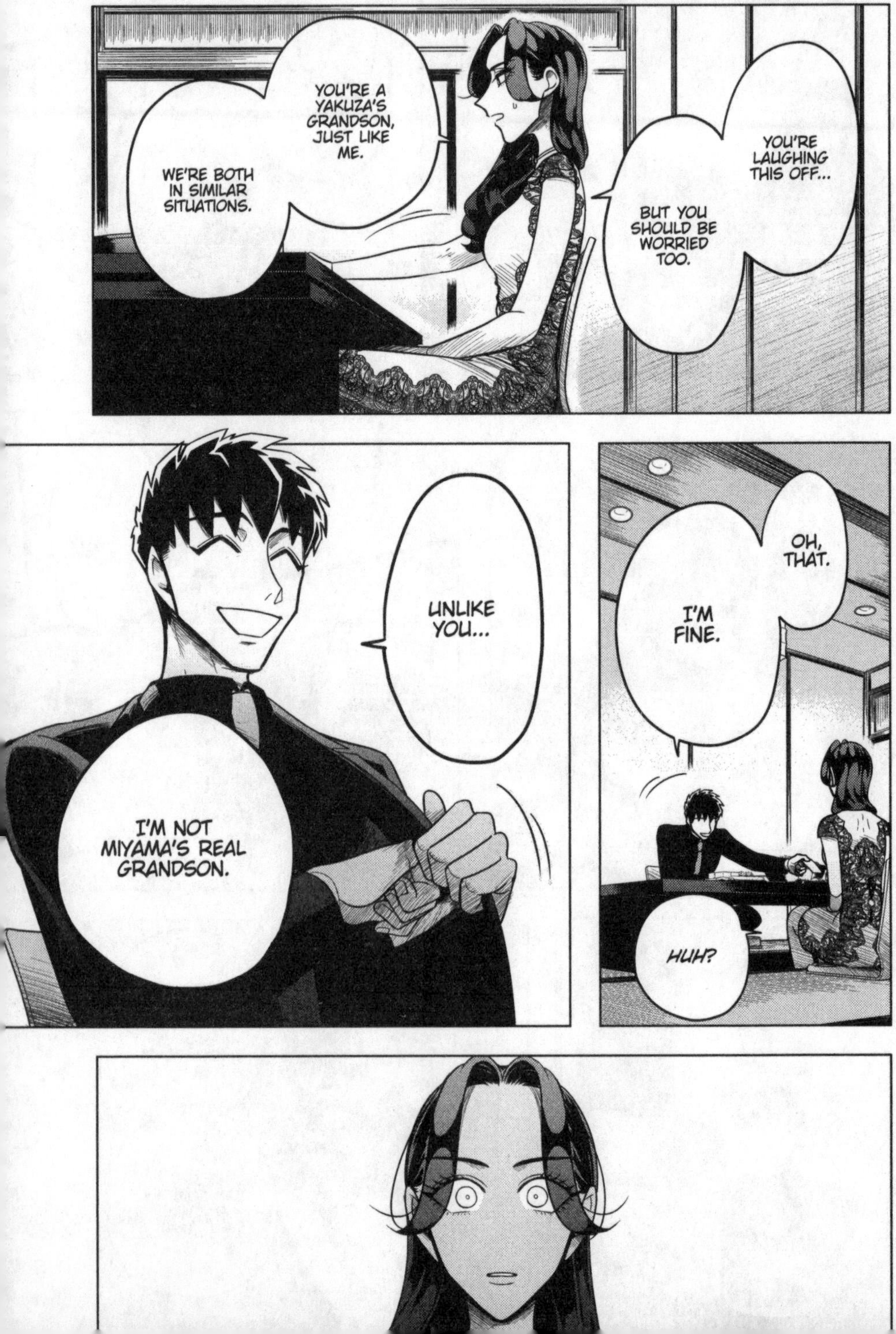
YOU'RE LAUGHING THIS OFF...
BUT YOU SHOULD BE WORRIED TOO.
YOU'RE A YAKUZA'S GRANDSON, JUST LIKE ME.
WE'RE BOTH IN SIMILAR SITUATIONS.
OH, THAT.
I'M FINE.
HUH?
UNLIKE YOU...
I'M NOT MIYAMA'S REAL GRANDSON.

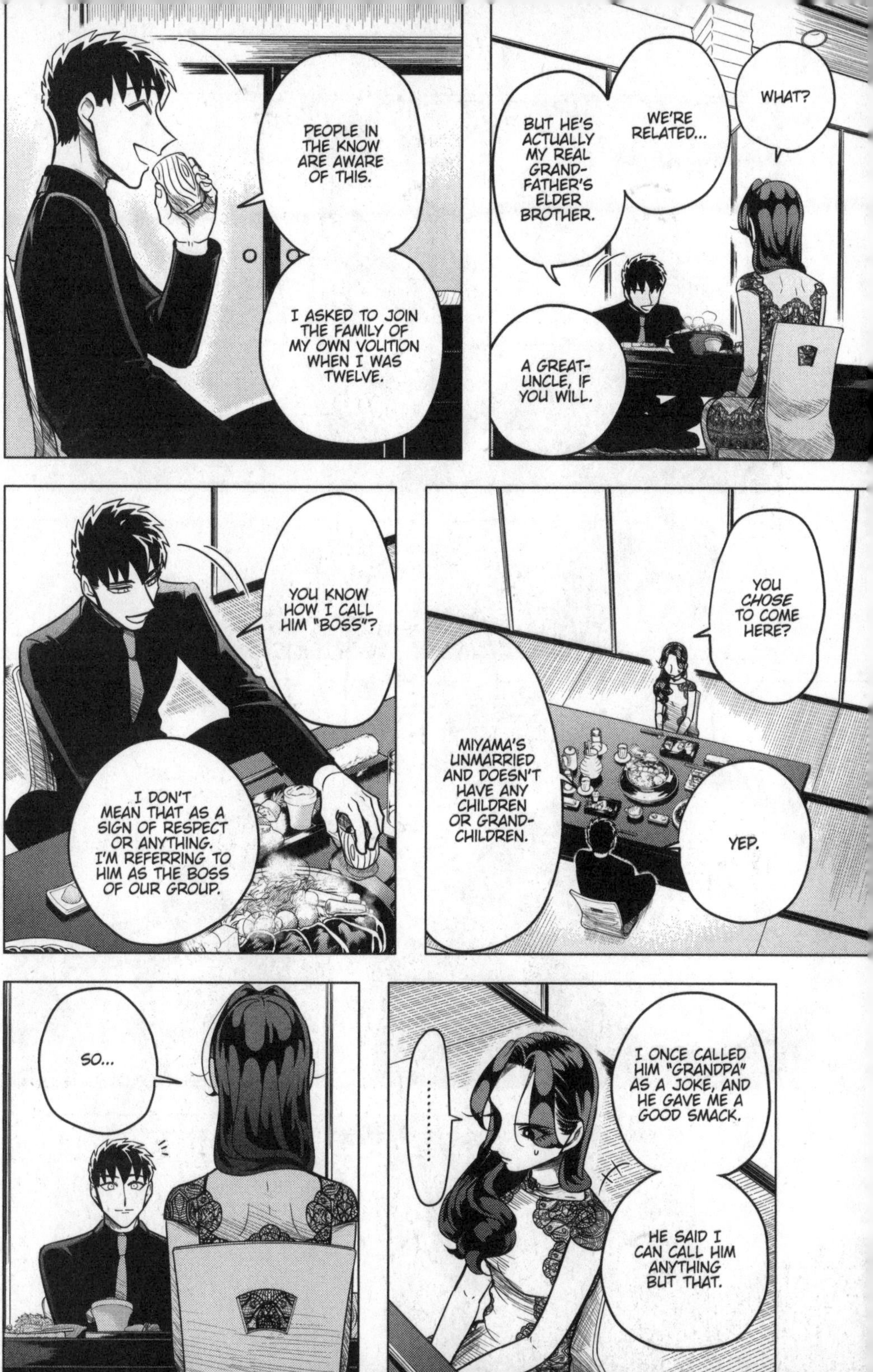
WHAT?
WE'RE RELATED...
BUT HE'S ACTUALLY MY REAL GRAND-FATHER'S ELDER BROTHER.
A GREAT-UNCLE, IF YOU WILL.
PEOPLE IN THE KNOW ARE AWARE OF THIS.
I ASKED TO JOIN THE FAMILY OF MY OWN VOLITION WHEN I WAS TWELVE.
YOU CHOSE TO COME HERE?
YEP.
MIYAMA'S UNMARRIED AND DOESN'T HAVE ANY CHILDREN OR GRAND-CHILDREN.
YOU KNOW HOW I CALL HIM "BOSS"?
I DON'T MEAN THAT AS A SIGN OF RESPECT OR ANYTHING. I'M REFERRING TO HIM AS THE BOSS OF OUR GROUP.
I ONCE CALLED HIM "GRANDPA" AS A JOKE, AND HE GAVE ME A GOOD SMACK.
HE SAID I CAN CALL HIM ANYTHING BUT THAT.
......
SO...

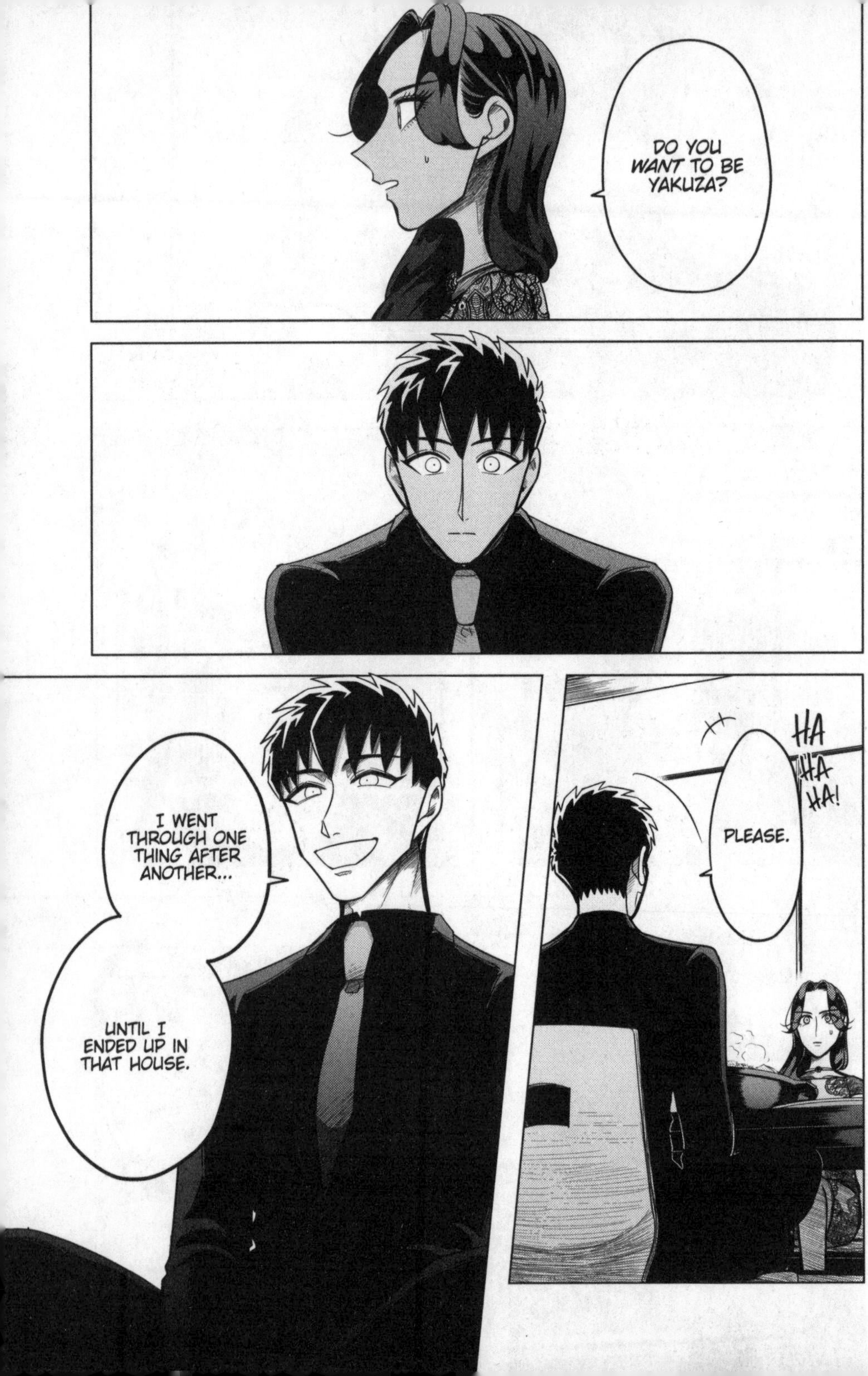
DO YOU WANT TO BE YAKUZA?
PLEASE.
HA HA HA!
I WENT THROUGH ONE THING AFTER ANOTHER...
UNTIL I ENDED UP IN THAT HOUSE.

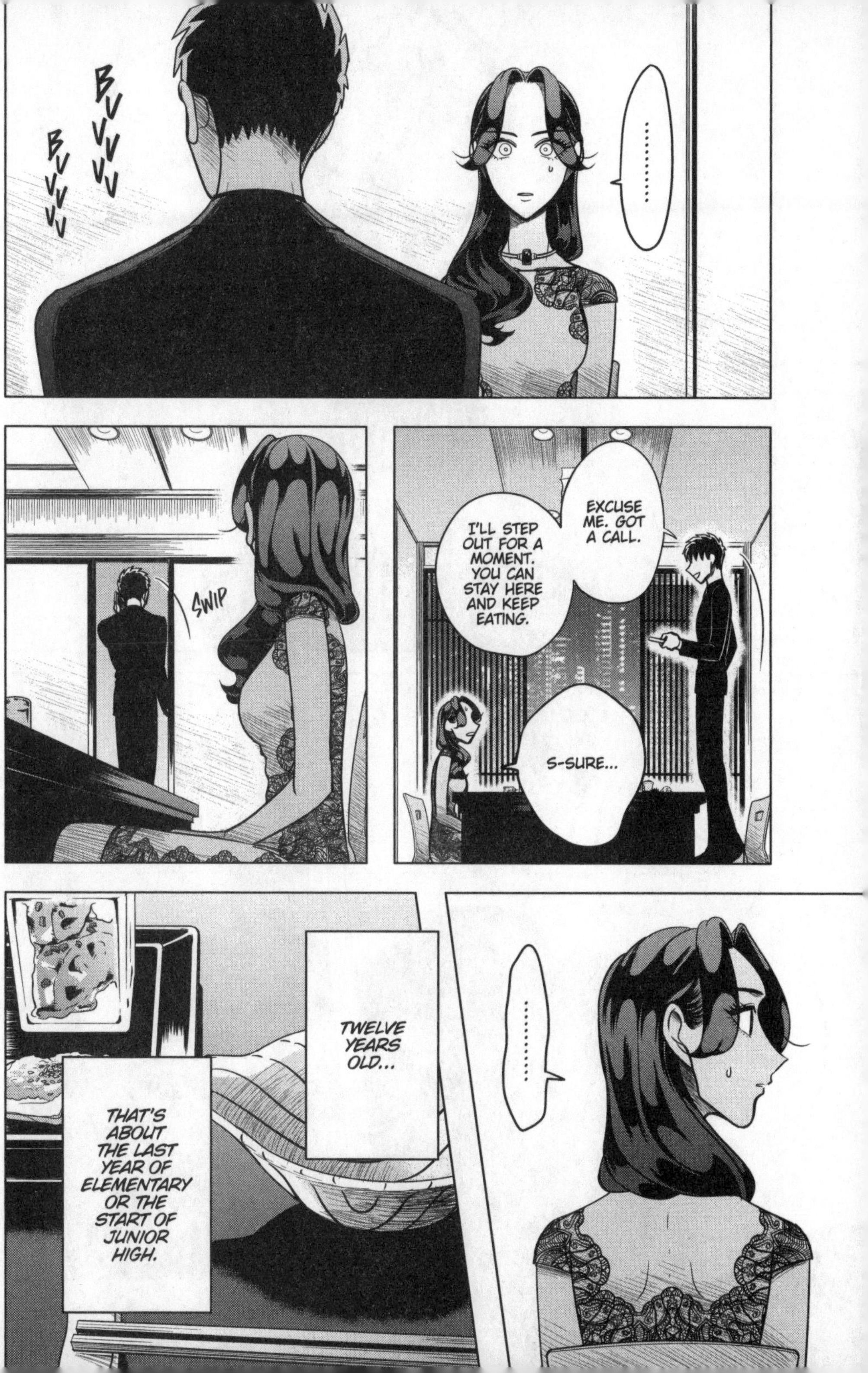
......
BVVVVVV
BVVVVVV
EXCUSE ME. GOT A CALL.
I'LL STEP OUT FOR A MOMENT. YOU CAN STAY HERE AND KEEP EATING.
S-SURE...
SWIP
......
TWELVE YEARS OLD...
THAT'S ABOUT THE LAST YEAR OF ELEMENTARY OR THE START OF JUNIOR HIGH.

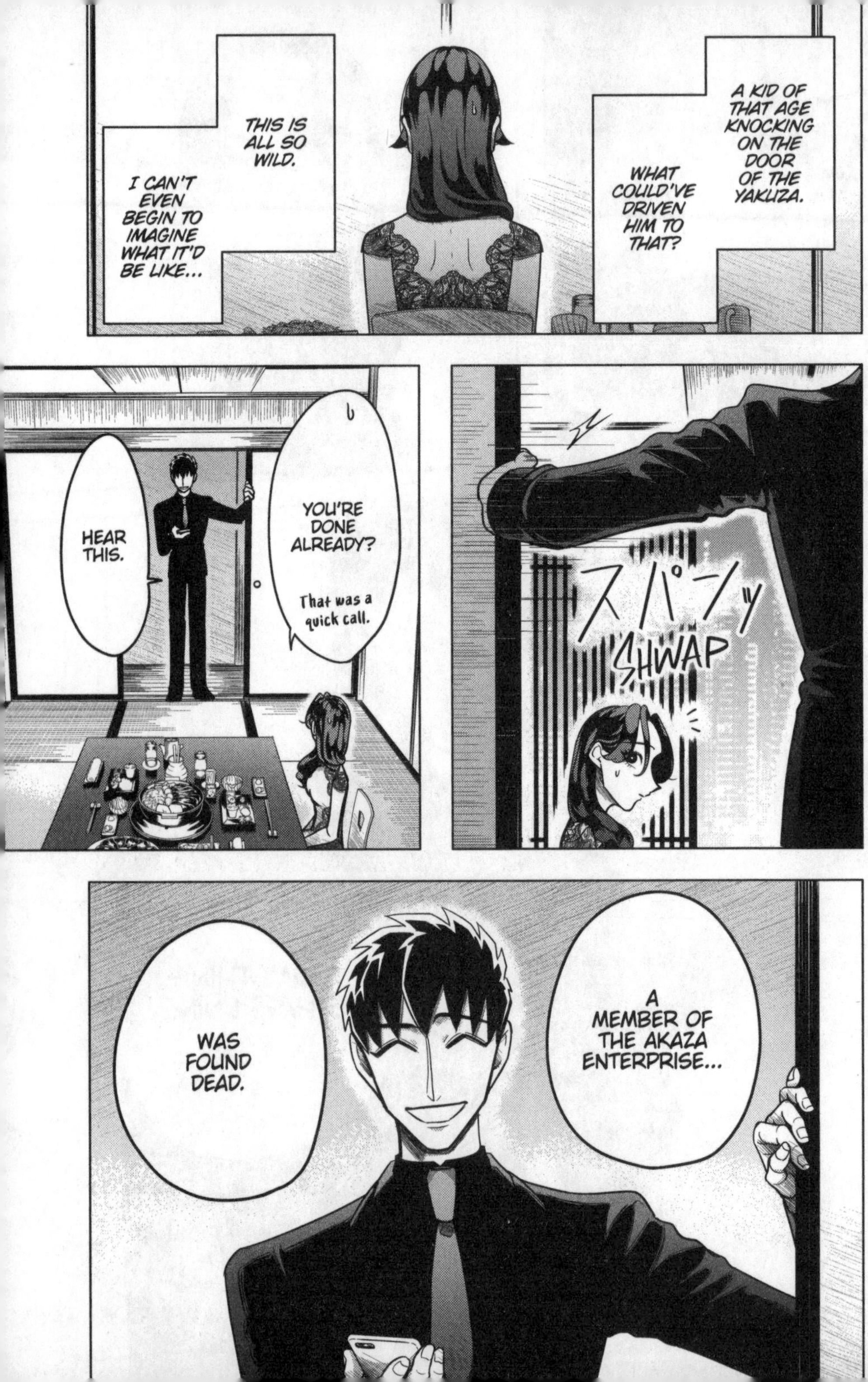
A KID OF THAT AGE KNOCKING ON THE DOOR OF THE YAKUZA.
WHAT COULD'VE DRIVEN HIM TO THAT?
THIS IS ALL SO WILD.
I CAN'T EVEN BEGIN TO IMAGINE WHAT IT'D BE LIKE…
スパンッ
SHWAP
YOU'RE DONE ALREADY?
That was a quick call.
HEAR THIS.
A MEMBER OF THE AKAZA ENTERPRISE…
WAS FOUND DEAD.

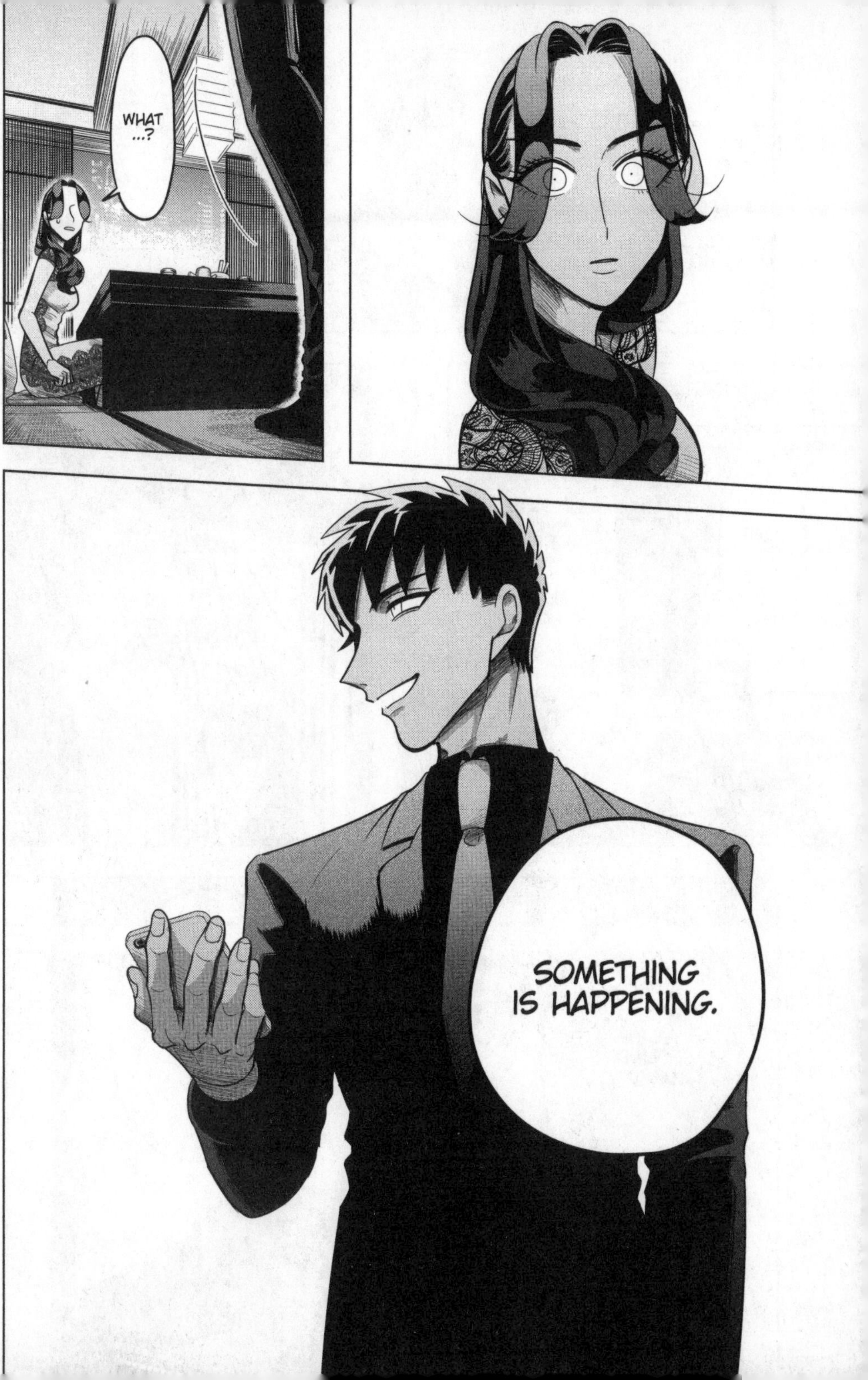
WHAT ...?
SOMETHING IS HAPPENING.

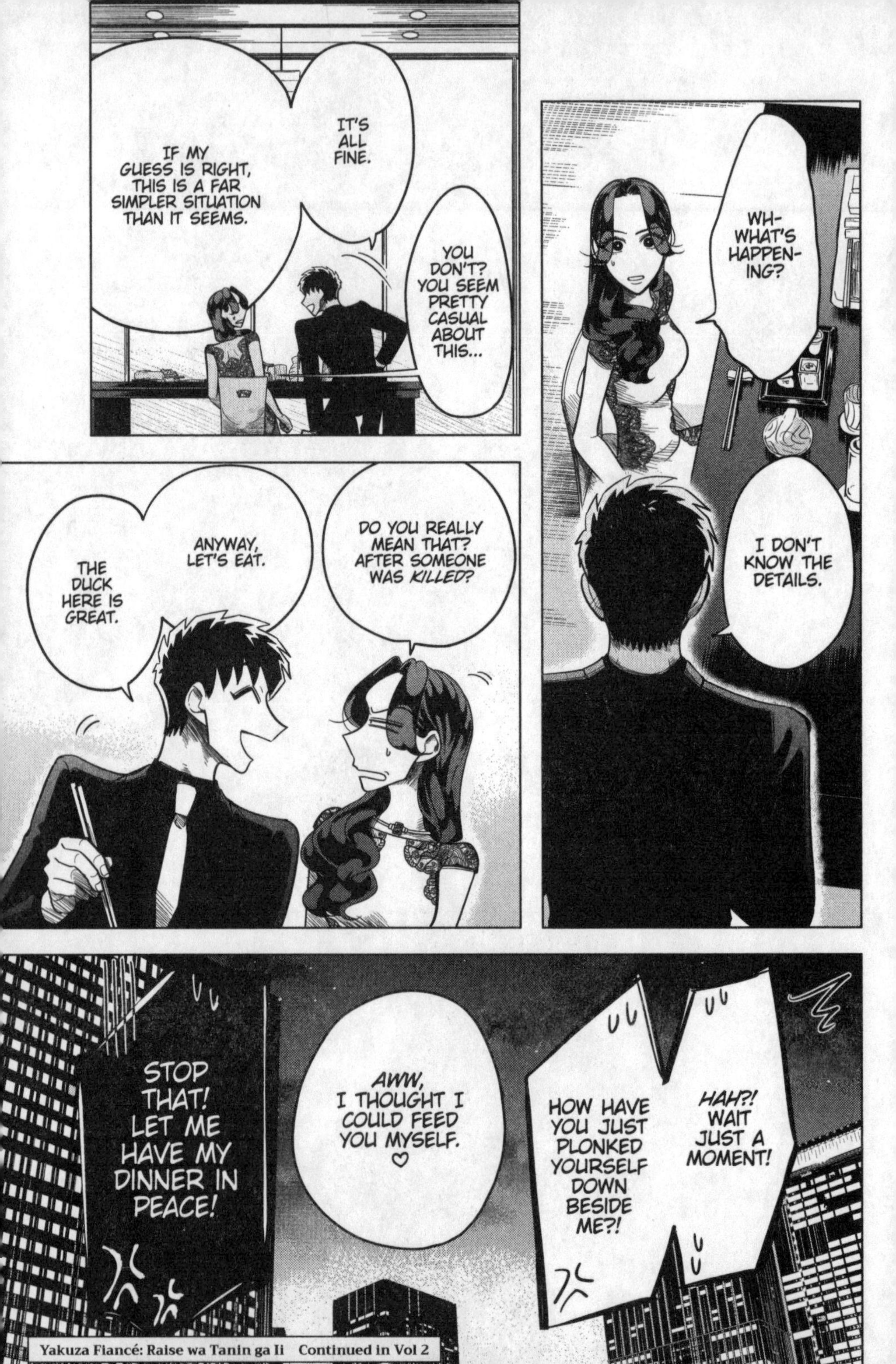
WH-WHAT'S HAPPENING?
I DON'T KNOW THE DETAILS.
YOU DON'T? YOU SEEM PRETTY CASUAL ABOUT THIS...
IT'S ALL FINE.
IF MY GUESS IS RIGHT, THIS IS A FAR SIMPLER SITUATION THAN IT SEEMS.
DO YOU REALLY MEAN THAT? AFTER SOMEONE WAS *KILLED*?
ANYWAY, LET'S EAT.
THE DUCK HERE IS GREAT.
*HAH?!* WAIT JUST A MOMENT!
HOW HAVE YOU JUST PLONKED YOURSELF DOWN BESIDE ME?!
*AWW,* I THOUGHT I COULD FEED YOU MYSELF. ♡
STOP THAT! LET ME HAVE MY DINNER IN PEACE!

Yakuza Fiancé: Raise wa Tanin ga Ii Continued in Vol 2

# Bonus 1

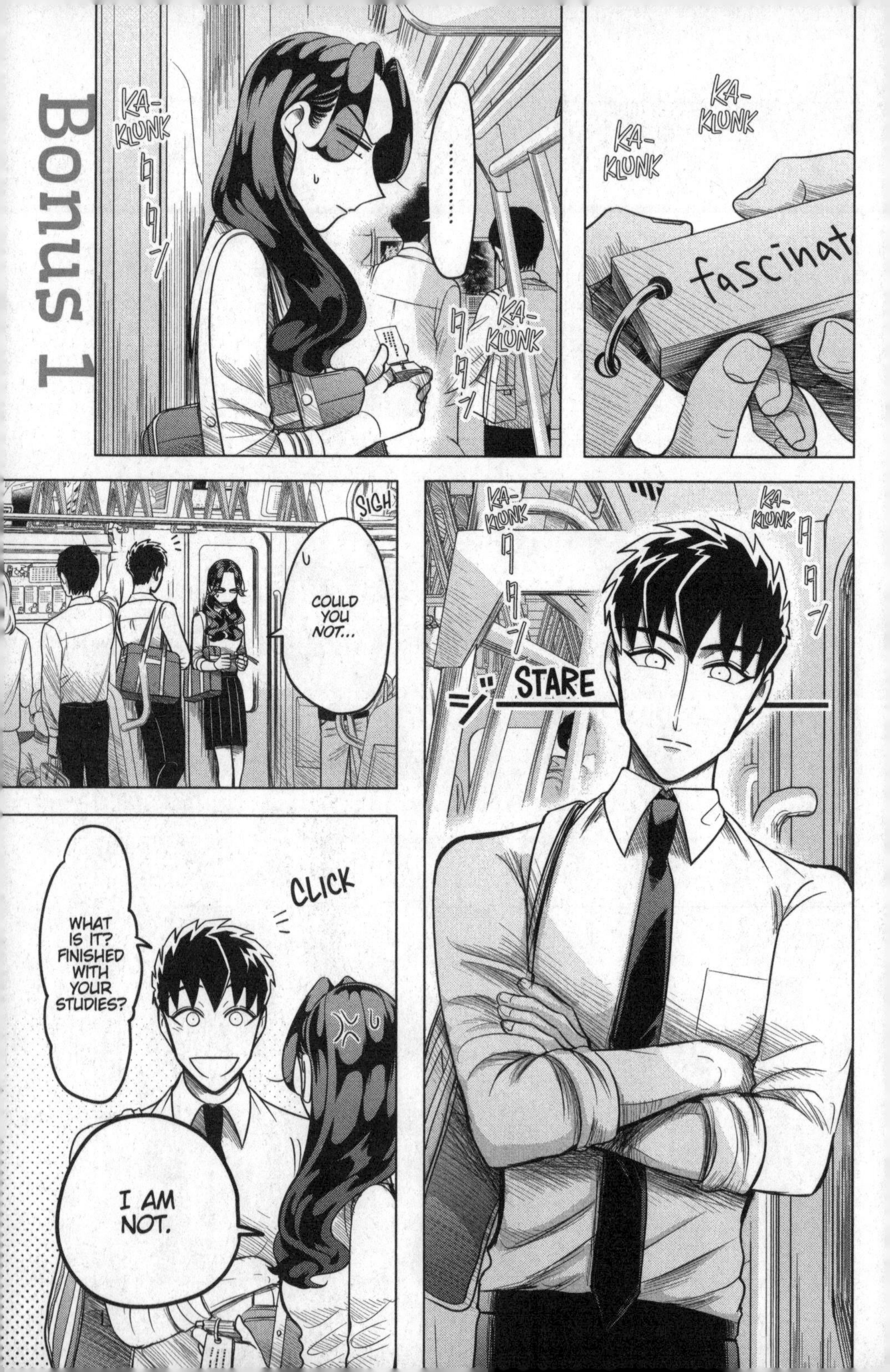
KA-KLUNK
KA-KLUNK
fascinate
KA-KLUNK タタン
......
KA-KLUNK タタン
KA-KLUNK タタン
KA-KLUNK タタン
STARE
SIGH
COULD YOU NOT...
CLICK
WHAT IS IT? FINISHED WITH YOUR STUDIES?
I AM NOT.

YOU'VE BEEN EYEBALLING ME THIS WHOLE TIME. CAN YOU STOP STARING AT ME LIKE THAT?
I'M NOT EVEN ALLOWED TO LOOK AT YOU?
I WAS STAYING QUIET BECAUSE YOU SEEMED SO BUSY.
YOUR STARING IS *REALLY* DISTRACTING. PLEASE, JUST LOOK SOMEWHERE ELSE.
HUUUH...
OKAY.
HAAH...
FLIP
......

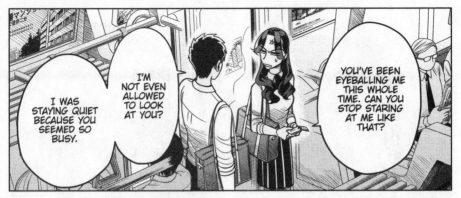

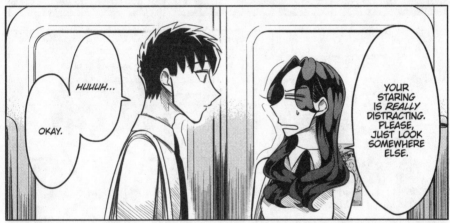

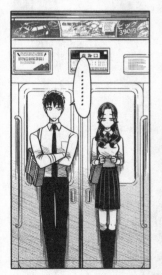

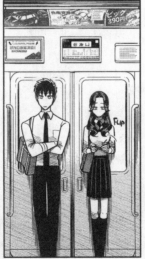

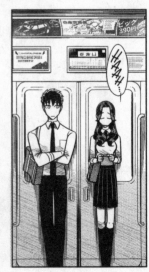

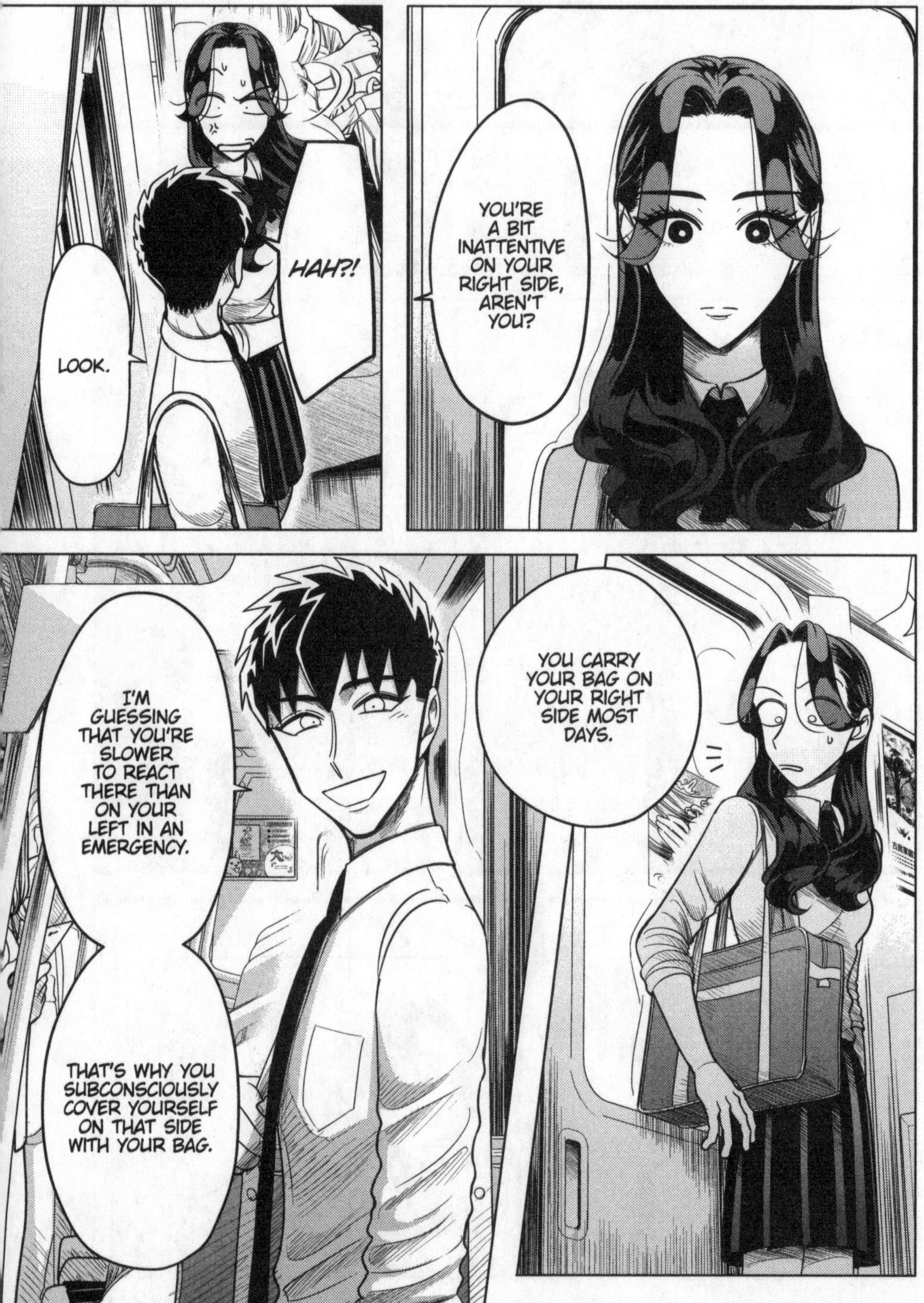
YOU'RE A BIT INATTENTIVE ON YOUR RIGHT SIDE, AREN'T YOU?
HAH?!
LOOK.
YOU CARRY YOUR BAG ON YOUR RIGHT SIDE MOST DAYS.
I'M GUESSING THAT YOU'RE SLOWER TO REACT THERE THAN ON YOUR LEFT IN AN EMERGENCY.
THAT'S WHY YOU SUBCONSCIOUSLY COVER YOURSELF ON THAT SIDE WITH YOUR BAG.

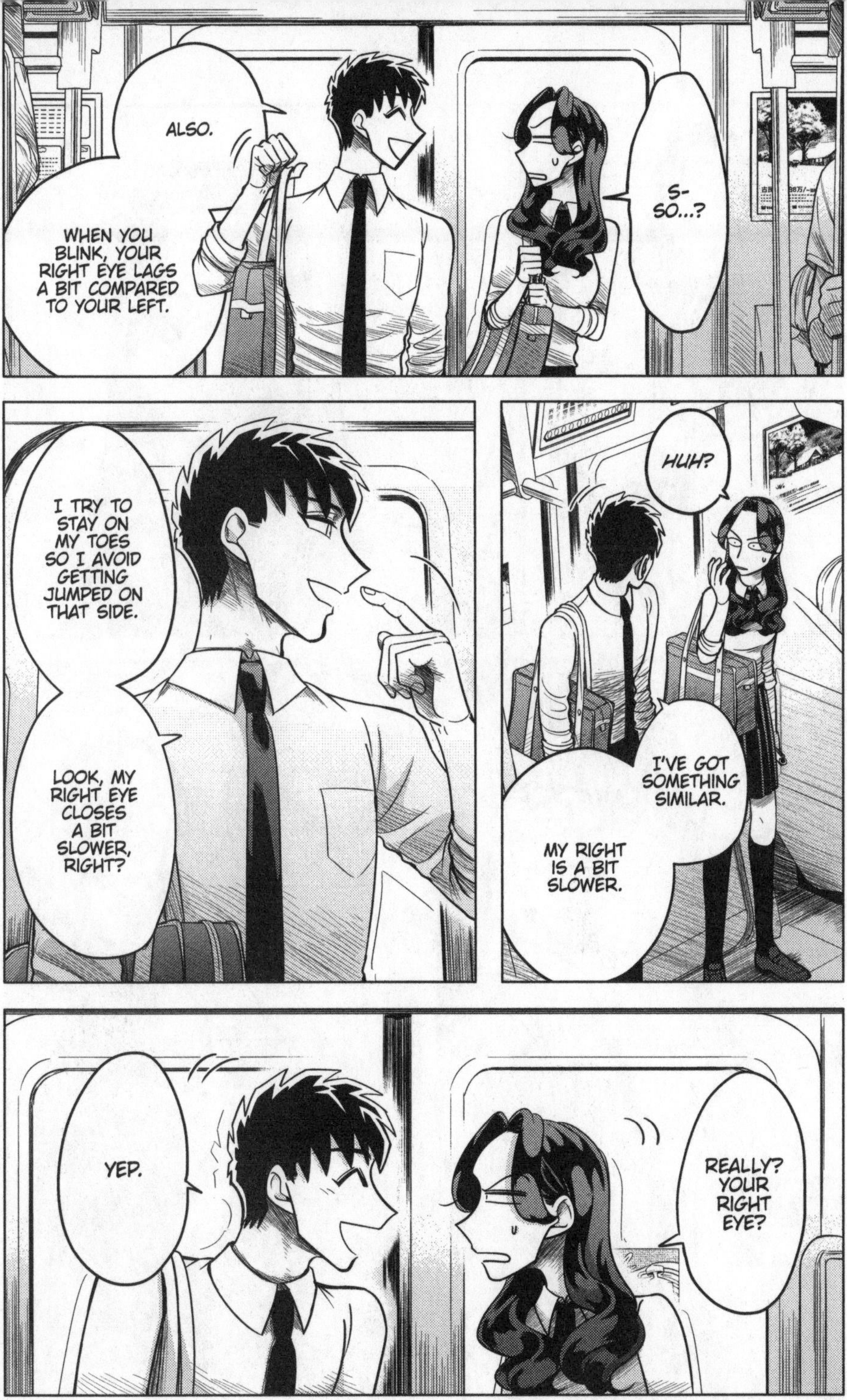
ALSO.
WHEN YOU BLINK, YOUR RIGHT EYE LAGS A BIT COMPARED TO YOUR LEFT.
S- SO...?
HUH?
I'VE GOT SOMETHING SIMILAR.
MY RIGHT IS A BIT SLOWER.
I TRY TO STAY ON MY TOES SO I AVOID GETTING JUMPED ON THAT SIDE.
LOOK, MY RIGHT EYE CLOSES A BIT SLOWER, RIGHT?
REALLY? YOUR RIGHT EYE?
YEP.

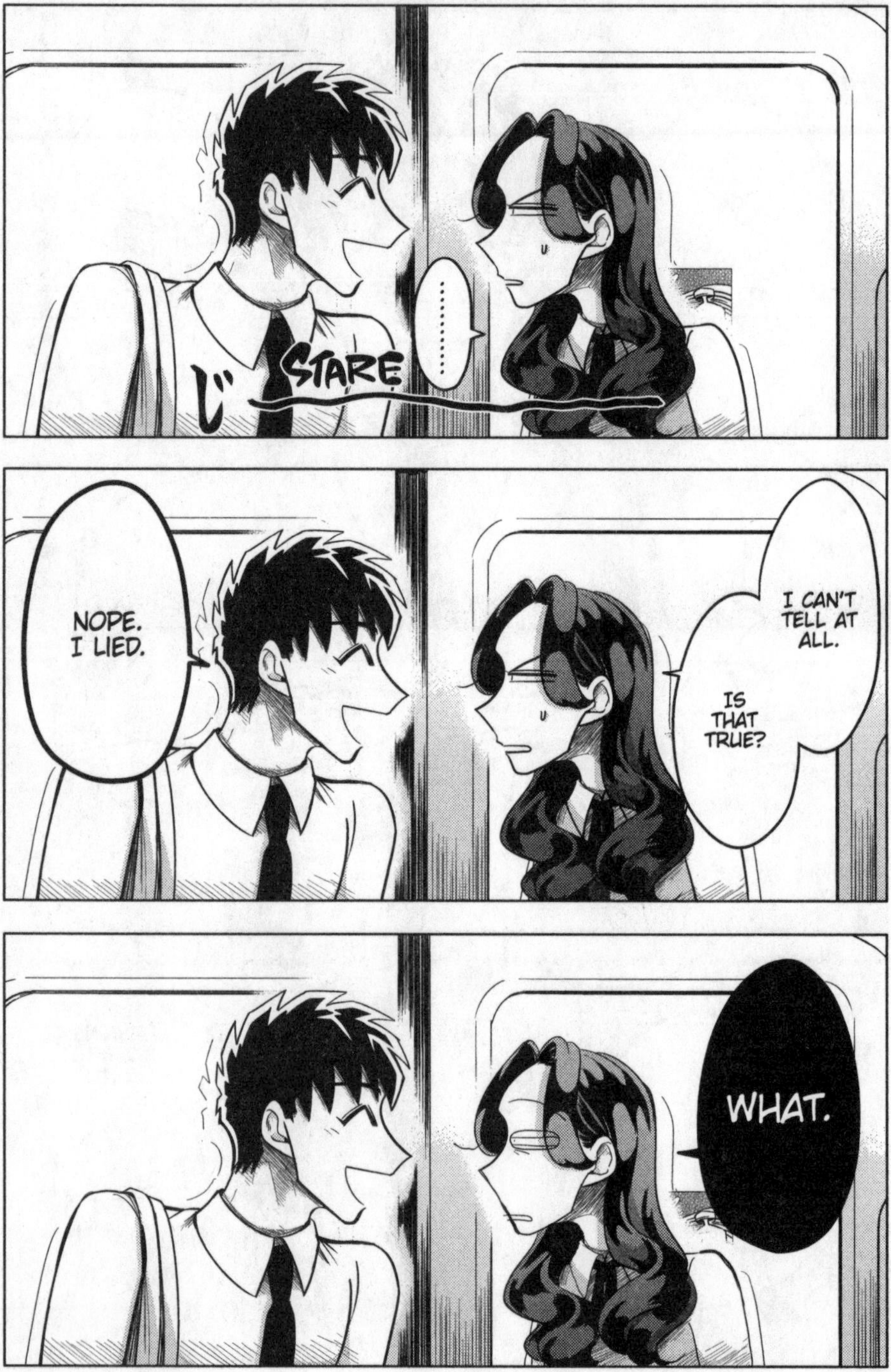
......
じ STARE
I CAN'T TELL AT ALL.
IS THAT TRUE?
NOPE. I LIED.
WHAT.

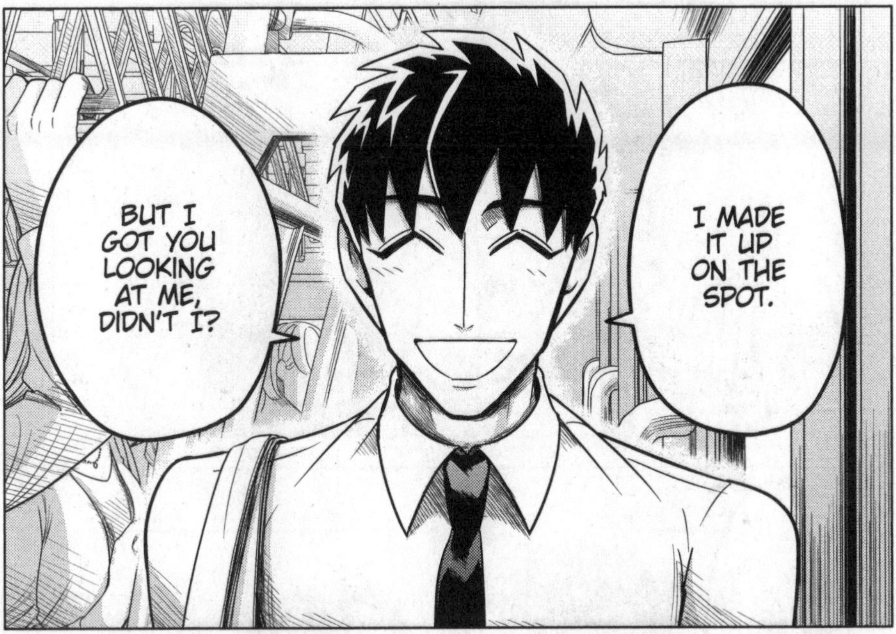
I MADE IT UP ON THE SPOT.
BUT I GOT YOU LOOKING AT ME, DIDN'T I?

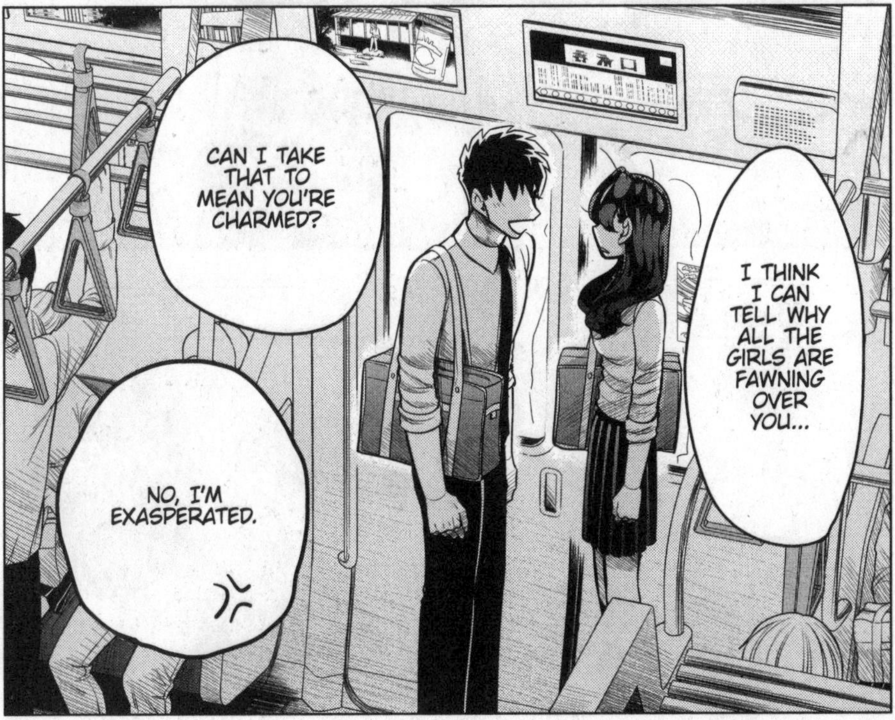
I THINK I CAN TELL WHY ALL THE GIRLS ARE FAWNING OVER YOU...
CAN I TAKE THAT TO MEAN YOU'RE CHARMED?
NO, I'M EXASPERATED.

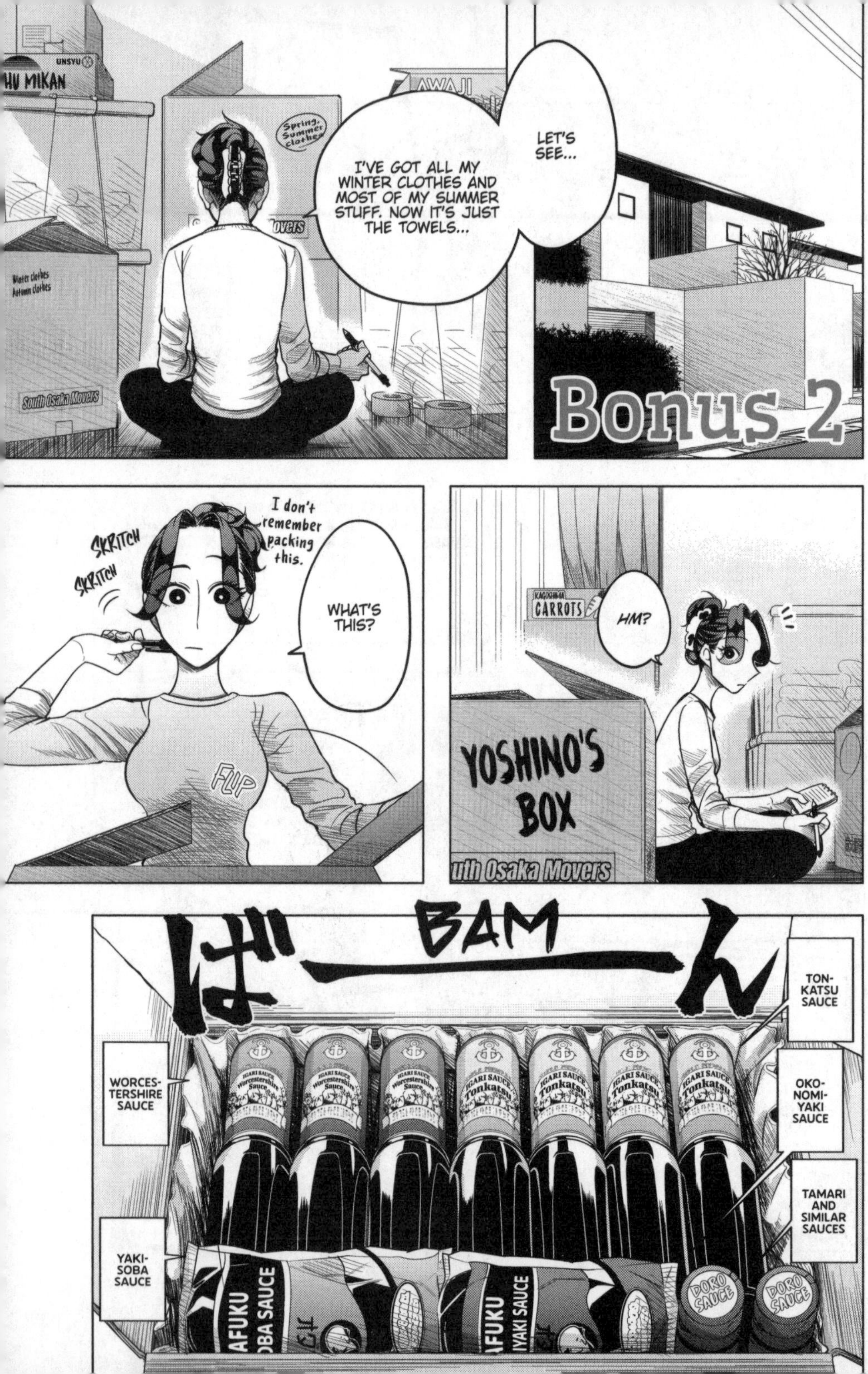
Bonus 2
AWAJI
LET'S SEE...
I'VE GOT ALL MY WINTER CLOTHES AND MOST OF MY SUMMER STUFF. NOW IT'S JUST THE TOWELS...
Spring, Summer clothes
Winter clothes Autumn clothes
South Osaka Movers
KAGOSHIMA CARROTS
HM?
YOSHINO'S BOX
South Osaka Movers
SKRITCH
SKRITCH
WHAT'S THIS?
I don't remember packing this.
FLIP
BAM
TON-KATSU SAUCE
OKO-NOMI-YAKI SAUCE
TAMARI AND SIMILAR SAUCES
WORCES-TERSHIRE SAUCE
YAKI-SOBA SAUCE
DORO SAUCE
DORO SAUCE

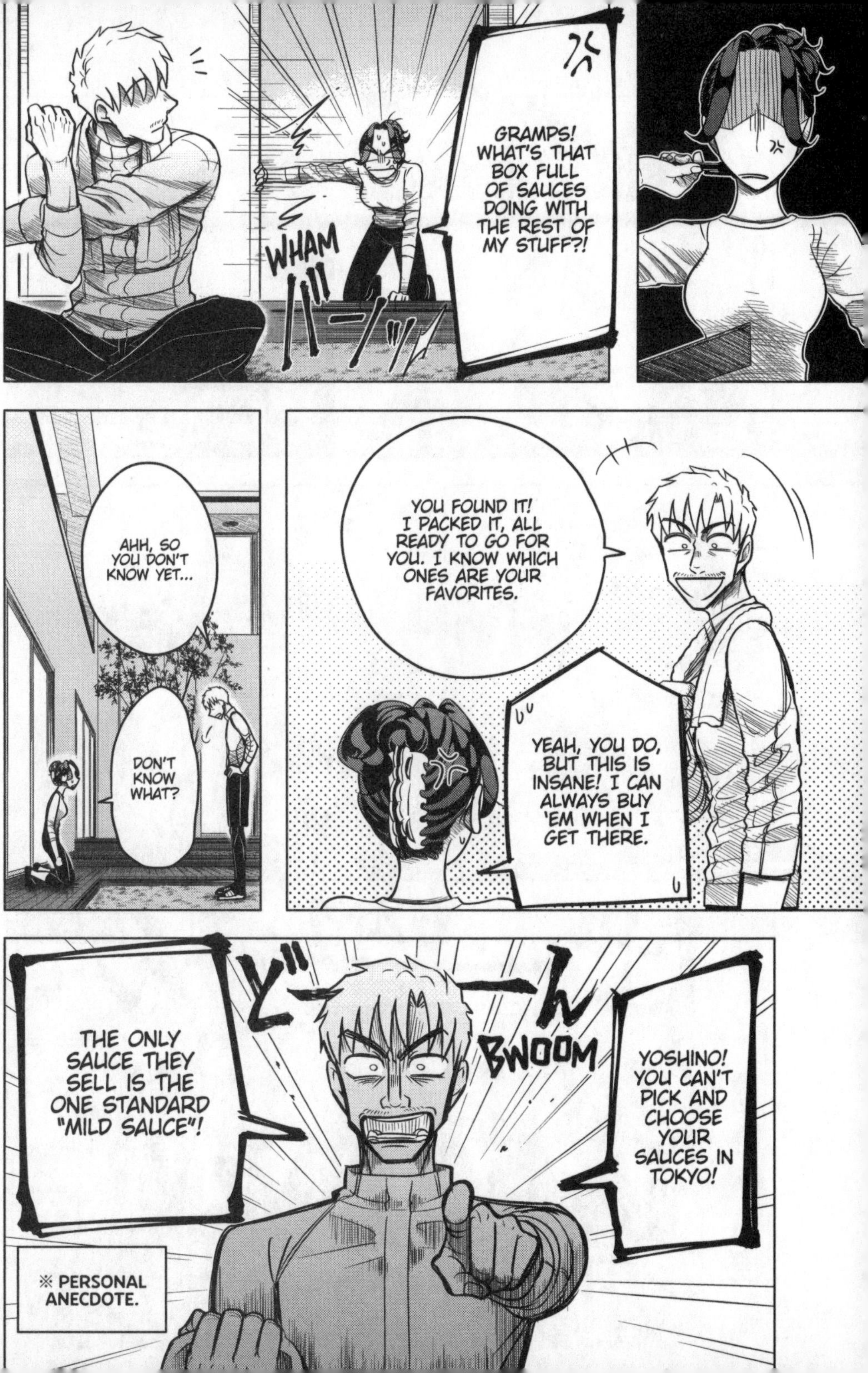
GRAMPS! WHAT'S THAT BOX FULL OF SAUCES DOING WITH THE REST OF MY STUFF?!
WHAM
YOU FOUND IT! I PACKED IT, ALL READY TO GO FOR YOU. I KNOW WHICH ONES ARE YOUR FAVORITES.
YEAH, YOU DO, BUT THIS IS INSANE! I CAN ALWAYS BUY 'EM WHEN I GET THERE.
AHH, SO YOU DON'T KNOW YET...
DON'T KNOW WHAT?
YOSHINO! YOU CAN'T PICK AND CHOOSE YOUR SAUCES IN TOKYO!
どーん
BWOOM
THE ONLY SAUCE THEY SELL IS THE ONE STANDARD "MILD SAUCE"!
※ PERSONAL ANECDOTE.

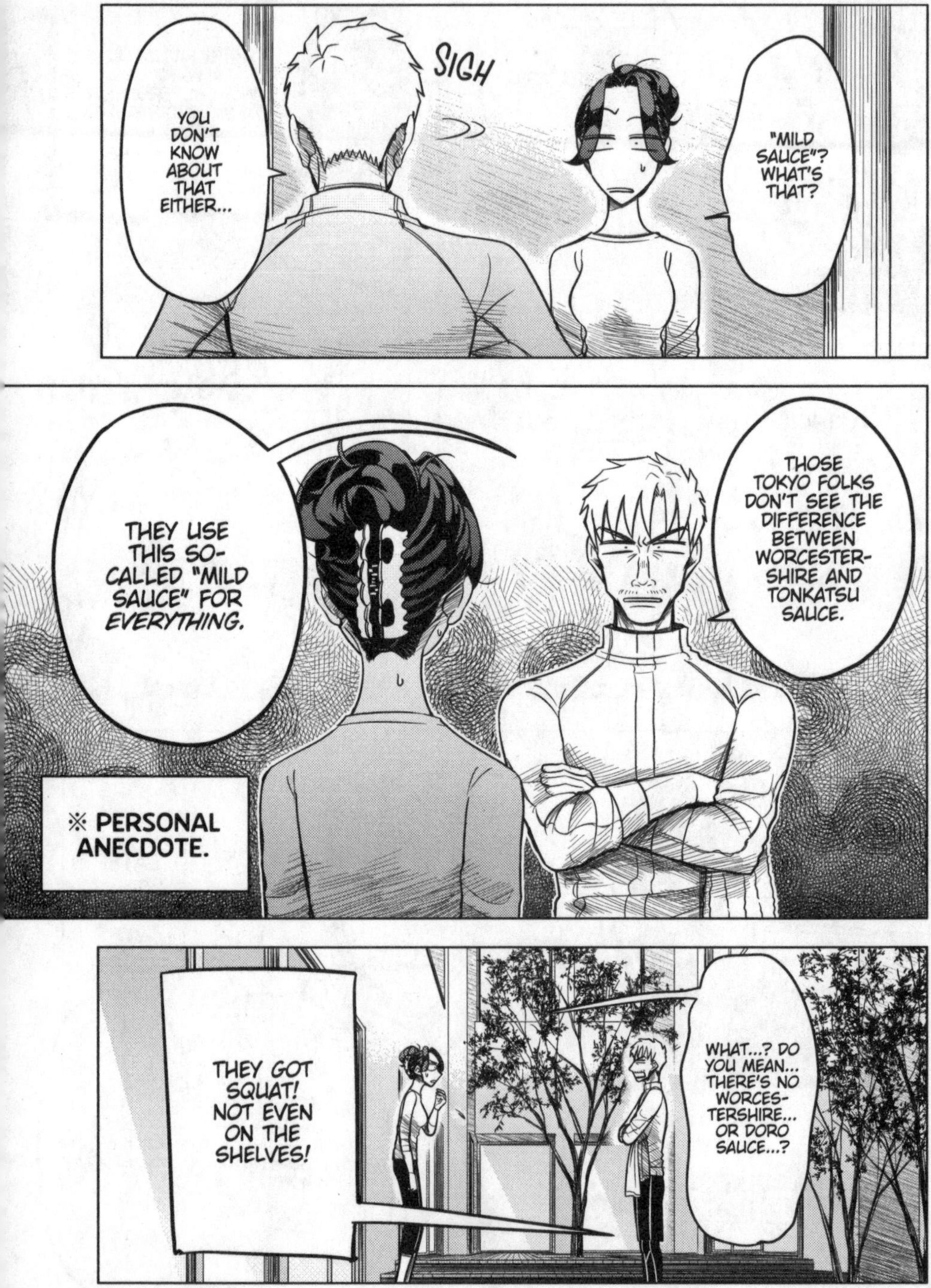
"MILD SAUCE"? WHAT'S THAT?
SIGH
YOU DON'T KNOW ABOUT THAT EITHER...
THOSE TOKYO FOLKS DON'T SEE THE DIFFERENCE BETWEEN WORCESTER-SHIRE AND TONKATSU SAUCE.
THEY USE THIS SO-CALLED "MILD SAUCE" FOR *EVERYTHING.*
※ PERSONAL ANECDOTE.
WHAT...? DO YOU MEAN... THERE'S NO WORCES-TERSHIRE... OR DORO SAUCE...?
THEY GOT SQUAT! NOT EVEN ON THE SHELVES!

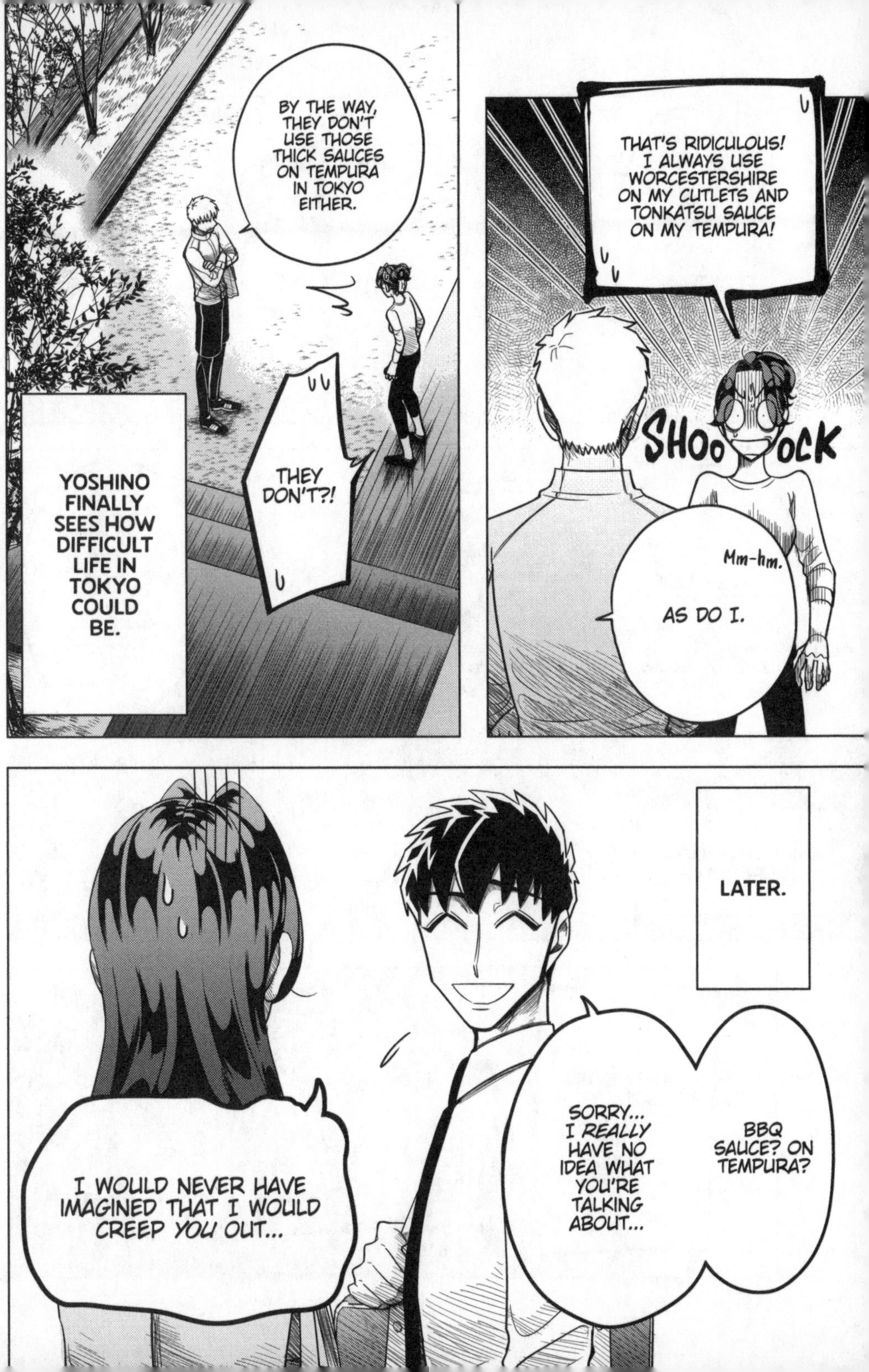
THAT'S RIDICULOUS! I ALWAYS USE WORCESTERSHIRE ON MY CUTLETS AND TONKATSU SAUCE ON MY TEMPURA!
SHOOOCK
Mm-hm.
AS DO I.
BY THE WAY, THEY DON'T USE THOSE THICK SAUCES ON TEMPURA IN TOKYO EITHER.
THEY DON'T?!
YOSHINO FINALLY SEES HOW DIFFICULT LIFE IN TOKYO COULD BE.
LATER.
BBQ SAUCE? ON TEMPURA?
SORRY... I *REALLY* HAVE NO IDEA WHAT YOU'RE TALKING ABOUT...
I WOULD NEVER HAVE IMAGINED THAT I WOULD CREEP *YOU* OUT...

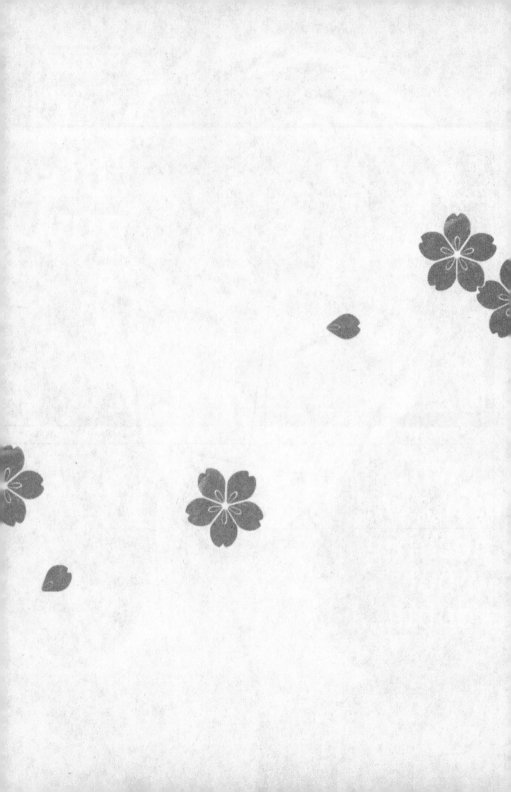

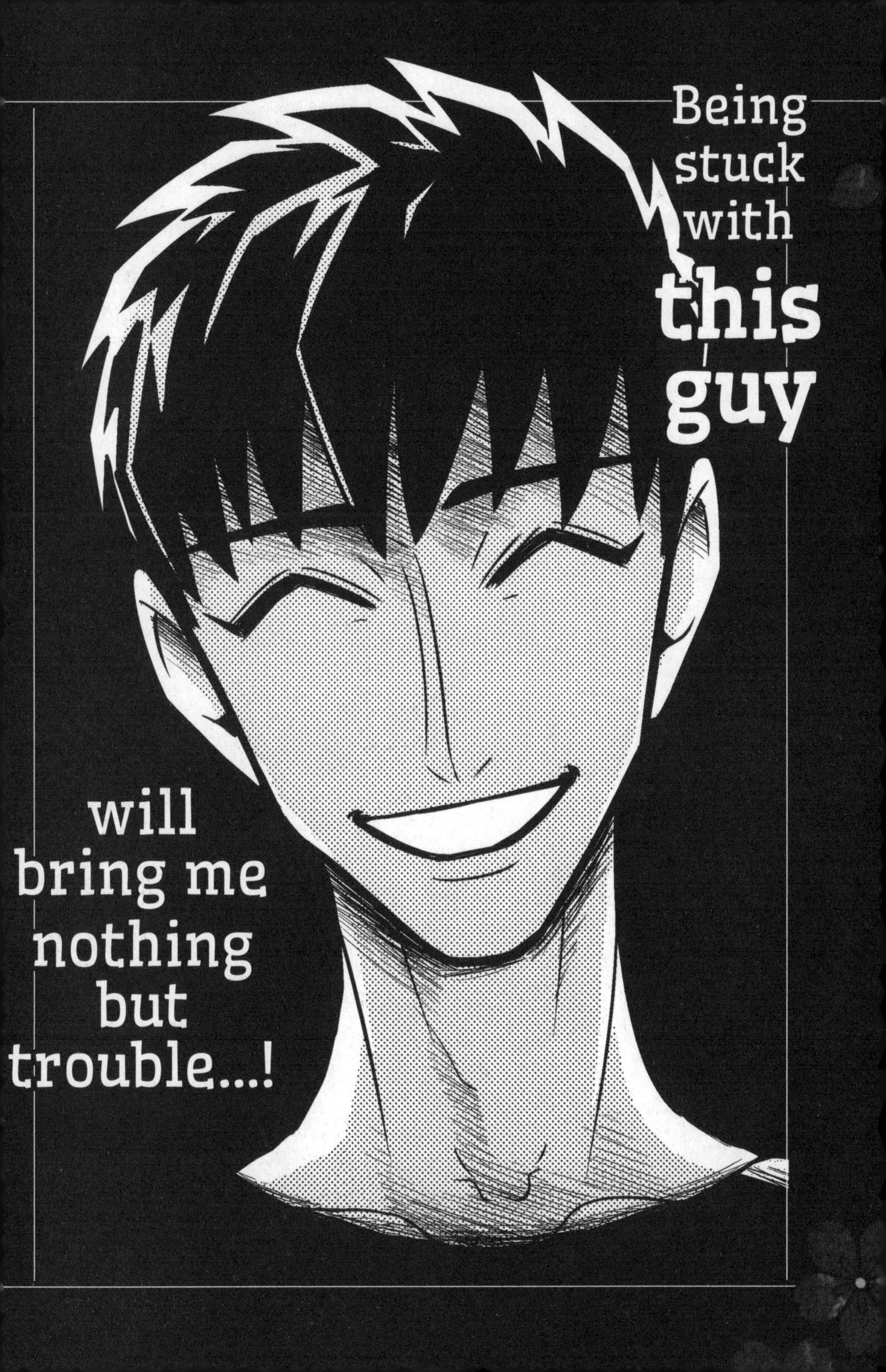
Being stuck with this guy
will bring me nothing but trouble...!

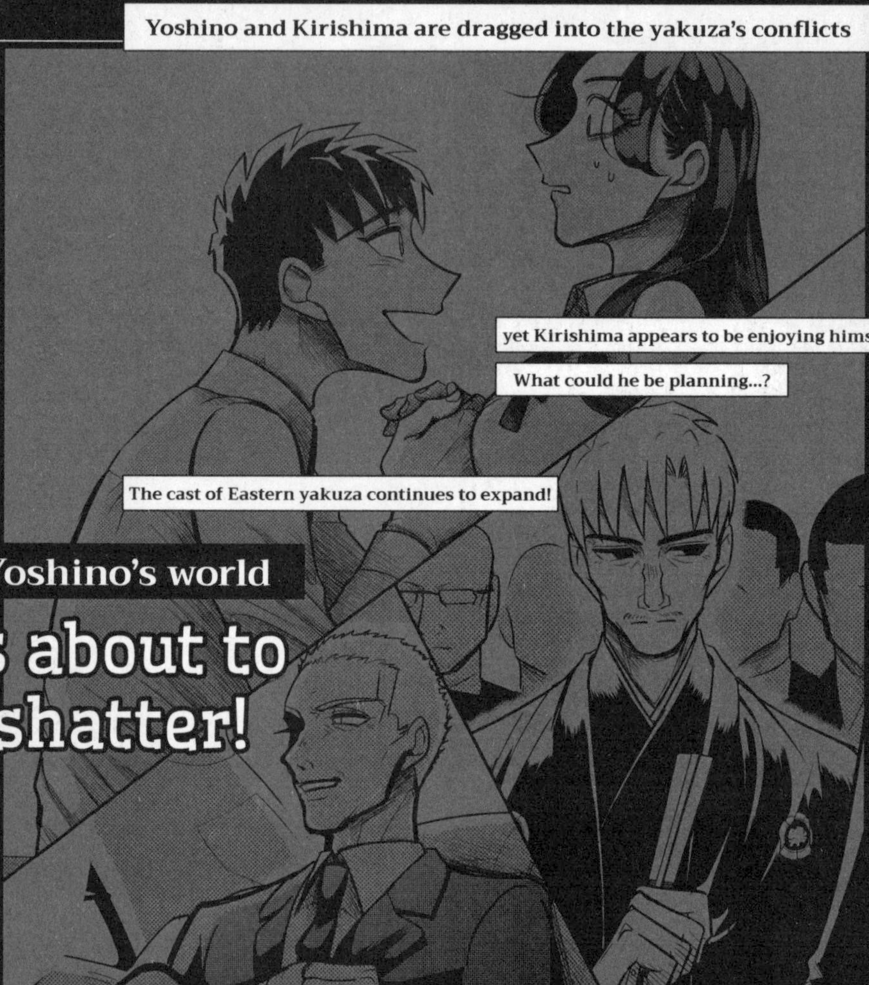
Yoshino and Kirishima are dragged into the yakuza's conflicts
yet Kirishima appears to be enjoying himself.
What could he be planning...?
The cast of Eastern yakuza continues to expand!
Yoshino's world
is about to shatter!

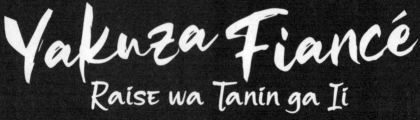

**Asuka Konishi**

Here's a quick one I jotted down. One of the reasons I started writing this story is that I love how campy the yakuza are in western media. Needless to say, real criminal organizations aren't like this, but I hope you enjoy the camp for what it is!

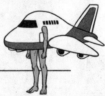

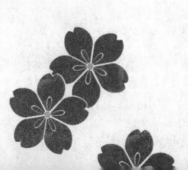

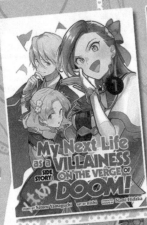
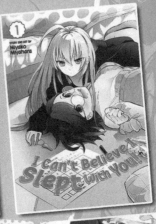
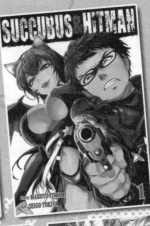
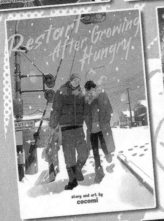
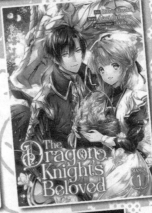
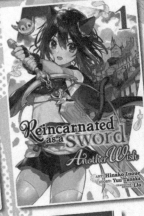
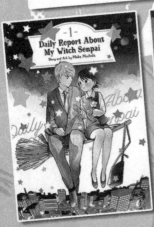
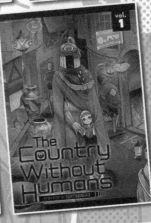
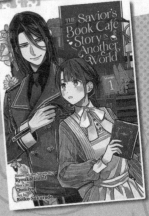

# SEVEN SEAS ENTERTAINM

W9-AKA-532

# Yakuza Fiancé

story and art by **ASUKA KONISHI**          **VOLUME ONE**

TRANSLATION
**M. Fulcrum**

ADAPTATION
**Sophia Tyrant**

LETTERING
**Arbash Mughal**

COVER DESIGN
**H. Qi**

COPY EDITOR
**B. Lillian Martin**

EDITOR
**Abby Lehrke**

PRODUCTION DESIGNER
**Christina McKenzie**

PRODUCTION MANAGER
**Lissa Pattillo**

PREPRESS TECHNICIAN
**Jules Valera**

EDITOR-IN-CHIEF
**Julie Davis**

ASSOCIATE PUBLISHER
**Adam Arnold**

PUBLISHER
**Jason DeAngelis**

Raisewa Taningaii VOL. 1
© 2017 Asuka Konishi. All rights reserved.
First published in Japan in 2017 by Kodansha Ltd., Tokyo.
Publication rights for this English edition arranged through Kodansha Ltd., Tokyo.

Seven Seas press and purchase enquiries can be sent to Marketing Manager Lianne Sentar at press@gomanga.com. Information regarding the distribution and purchase of digital editions is available from Digital Manager CK Russell at digital@gomanga.com.

Seven Seas and the Seven Seas logo are trademarks of Seven Seas Entertainment, Inc. All rights reserved.

ISBN: 978-1-68579-337-1
Printed in Canada
First Printing: November 2022
10 9 8 7 6 5 4 3 2 1

## ▨▨▨ READING DIRECTIONS ▨▨▨

This book reads from *right to left*, Japanese style. If this is your first time reading manga, you start reading from the top right panel on each page and take it from there. If you get lost, just follow the numbered diagram here. It may seem backwards at first, but you'll get the hang of it! Have fun!!

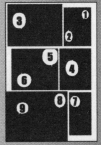